FERGUSON'S DEATH CHARGE AT KING'S MOUNTAIN.

FERGUSON'S DEATH CHARGE AT
KING'S MOUNTAIN.

Official Edition

THE NEW COMPLETE
HISTORY OF
THE UNITED STATES
OF AMERICA

By John Clark Ridpath, LL. D.

Author of Ridpath's History of the World

Volume VI

INCLUDING the traditions and speculations of the pre-Columbian voyagers; the discovery and settlement of the New Continent; its development under colonial government and the establishment and progress of the Republic.

APPOSITELY illustrated with original drawings, maps, portraits and notable documents, selected for their contemporaneity from the Royal Archives at Genoa, Madrid, Paris and London, by special permission of their governments, from the Department of State and the Library of Congress at Washington, and from private collections of rare Americana.

RIDPATH HISTORY COMPANY
WASHINGTON, D. C.

CONTENTS

PART VII.—THE REVOLUTION.

PAGE.

CHAPTER XLI. First Campaigns under Independence 2501

CHAPTER XLII. Saratogo and Philadelphia..... 2557

CHAPTER XLIII. Political and Military Machinery 2675

CHAPTER XLIV. French Alliance and English Groping 2711

CHAPTER XLV. The West and the Revolution 2763

CHAPTER XLVI. The British gain a Southern Foothold......... 2807

CHAPTER XLVII. The Navy and the Revolution 2859

CHAPTER XLVIII. The Bottom Reached............... 2901

Contents

Chapter   VII.   How Considerate Judy Joined
                   Congdon . . . .

Chapter   XVIII. The ... ...ception Prepared for ...

Chapter   XIII.   Bedtime and Arising Hour . . . .

Chapter   XIV.   Alfonso and ... .

Chapter   XV.   The Work and the Master . . . .

Chapter   XVI.   The ... ...tion ... ...

Chapter   XXVII. The Heart, ...

Chapter   XLIII. The ... ...ful . . . .

LIST OF ILLUSTRATIONS

VOLUME VI.

The Battle of Kings Mountain, ... *Frontispiece*

PAGE

Portrait of William Moultrie, ... 2506
Sullivan's Island and Fort Sullivan (Later, Fort Moultrie), ... 2506
Horatio Gates, ... 2522
Philip Schuyler, ... 2522
Sir Guy Carleton, ... 2522
Benedict Arnold, ... 2522
Robert Morris, ... 2544
Thaddeus Kosciuszko, ... 2554
Count Casimir Pulaski, ... 2554
General John Burgoyne, ... 2560
Lord George Germain, ... 2560
Benedict Arnold's Commission as Major-General, ... 2566
Barry St. Leger, ... 2586
Joseph Brant, ... 2586
Fort Stanwix and Battle of Oriskany, ... 2586
Plan of the Battle of Bennington, ... 2602
John Stark, ... 2602
The Battle of the Brandywine, ... 2616
Two Plans of the Battle of Germantown, ... 2630
Picture of the Chew House, ... 2630
Burgoyne's Encampment at Fraser's Funeral, ... 2654
Capture of Forts Clinton and Montgomery, ... 2654
Barracks of the Convention Army at Charlottesville, Va., ... 2654
Gates' Letter to Congress Announcing Burgoyne's Surrender, ... 2662
Continental and State Paper Money in the Revolution, ... 2684
Lafayette, ... 2704
Baron Steuben, ... 2704
Portion of Letter from Washington to Howe on Exchange of Prisoners, 2710
Carlisle's Memorandum of What England Would Have Left After the
    American Concessions, ... 2742
Congress' Counterblast to the Peace Commissioners' Manifesto, . . . 2746

	PAGE
Admiral Lord Howe,	2754
Count D'Estaing,	2754
Operations against Rhode Island in 1778,	2754
Daniel Boone,	2766
Cottage Built by Boone with His Own Hands (front view),	2766
Cottage Built by Boone with His Own Hands (rear view),	2766
Kentucky River Valley from Boone's Cottage,	2766
Simon Kenton,	2766
George Rogers Clark,	2778
The Mississippi, Illinois and Wabash Country in 1778,	2780
Magazine at Old Fort Chartres,	2780
The Savannah-Charleston Campaign,	2812
General Lachlan McIntosh,	2812
Henry Lee,	2836
Anthony Wayne,	2836
Stony Point,	2836
John Paul Jones,	2874
Commission to John Paul Jones for Service in Continental Navy,	2884
Captain John Barry,	2898
Captain Joshua Barney,	2898
Benjamin Lincoln,	2906
Charleston in 1780,	2906
Lord Rawdon,	2910
Tarleton,	2910
Sir Henry Clinton,	2918
Lord Cornwallis in Youth,	2918
Lord Cornwallis in Later Life,	2918
Francis Marion,	2924
William Richardson Davie,	2924
Thomas Sumter,	2924
John Kalb,	2942
Otho Williams,	2942
William Washington,	2942
Rochambeau,	2970
Major John André,	2976
The Odell House, Rochambeau's Headquarters at Dobbs' Ferry,	2980
The Beverley Robinson House, Opposite West Point, Arnold's Headquarters,	2980
Signatures of Presidents of Congress and Other Distinguished Revolutionary Leaders,	2988

CHAPTER XLI.

FIRST CAMPAIGNS UNDER INDEPENDENCE

The new republic and the mother country had each two great tasks before it: the one to maintain and the other to overthrow by arms the asserted independence; the one to frame a government for itself, the other if successful to reconstitute the old ones more stably.

1776 July

After independ- ence

Of the latter pair, the new government, though the debates began July 13, had to wait five years for installation: little loss, as it was an embodied paralysis, and the people were not ready for a good one until many years later. The British had two alternatives: to change their colonial policy, or merely to punish and disarm the patriots, with the end of establishing non-autonomous governments, based on the supremacy of the local loyalists and backed by permanent British garrisons. They chose the latter until too late, and succeeded as they deserved.

Govern- mental policies

The result of the military operations up to the next spring was roughly an epitome of the whole war: large British gains that did not profit them and small losses that ruined them, general success in the field and entire failure in the campaigns. The ministry had a massively simple plan of action, which would have effected its end had the

Military balance

1776

English strategic idea

The three campaigns

premises been correct. This was to invade the middle colonies and the Carolinas simultaneously with a strong force, relying on the more powerful loyalist element there to make it irresistible; also the borderers would be kept busy at home by the Indians,[1] and the Southern planters by threats of slave insurrection. Thus isolated, New England and Virginia, the two heads of the rebellion, could be crushed separately; Virginia indeed would be between hammer and anvil. In more detail:— One army was to seize the New York Bay and lower Hudson region, and thence overrun the space from New Jersey to Maryland, besides Quakerized

---

[1] This was a cardinal point of the King's and the ministerial plans. From New York and the Lakes south the Indians were to sweep the whole border, taking the colonies in the rear, while the British hireling army assailed them in front. This utilization of savages was one of the worst boomerangs of all English policy; yet the government clung to it tenaciously for forty years later, and prided themselves on it as astute statesmanship,—"using the means which God and nature had put into their hands." Aside from its atrocity, it was wholly futile. In no one instance did it exercise any influence on a Revolutionary campaign, except to ruin St. Leger's; while the horror and the fury of revenge it excited were worth armies to the patriots. It has been defended by saying that the Americans attempted to do the same. They did not. They made some few languid attempts to embody Indians in regular companies, to fight under civilized restraints; but from the very nature of the case, they could not let the savages loose against their own communities unrestrained. The English crime was not in engaging them to fight, which the Indians might fairly do in their own interest, and it hurt no more to be killed by an Indian than any one else: it was in engaging them to fight *as savages*, in burning and slaughter and torture among peaceful communities regardless of sex or age (George III. expressly specified the tribes to be so hounded on); or at best to fight along with white companies too few to restrain them from doing it, as it was certain they would. The English had no more right to set Indians on to do this than to do it themselves; and they are rightly punished by a brand of infamy for it. It should be said in justice that the English Liberals looked on it exactly as we have done, and denounced it without stint.

Rhode Island. This was in part the Howe plan, but solely as an element in a scheme of conciliation. A second from Canada, with the Tories and Indians, was to occupy the upper Hudson and Mohawk valleys. A third was to put South Carolina in loyal hands. Some 40,000 men were available for all, and fleets were to co-operate.

1776

Proposed British campaigns

It will be noted that the whole fabric—as of any permanent reconquest of America—rested on a great Tory class full of fighting zeal. Without this the armaments were absurd: in each case a small army corps could not hold down such a territory. The whole war on the British side was a groping around over the colonies for such a class, always a little farther on. Yet had it existed, the Revolution could not have begun, for zeal would have matched zeal in a deadlock or a civil war. Only on the New York and Carolina borders, full of lawless passions and social hatreds that assumed political disguises, did they find one sufficient to kindle a new set of Indian horrors and a civil war of measureless white ferocity.

Based on fighting Tory class

The facts

But for the time, the splendid American victory of Fort Moultrie and the even more splendid defeat of Lake Champlain prevented the Tories' and Indians' British allies from coming to them in Carolina and upper New York; and in the centre field, after a series of easy victories and captures, the demolition of a good share of the American army and the dissolution of most of the remainder, and the occupancy of the country almost to Philadelphia, two American victories over outposts

Results

1776–7

Result of campaigns

frightened the British back to the environs of Manhattan Island save for one near station. The seizure of lower Rhode Island had no military result, and merely locked up a strong corps out of use. After nearly a year's time, things remained about as they were; but it had become evident that the Americans could afford defeat and the British could not even afford victory, that the Tory help was a broken reed, and that with the stream of foreign supplies beginning to flow, the country could finally wear out the invaders.

Cause of British fumbling

Britain's energies, in fact, were crippled first by the fierce opposition of her own Liberals to the war and the half-heartedness of Liberal commanders, then by the gradual union of foreign powers against her; her national heart and her national strength were alike divided, and the hired armies sent over were never enough for an effective occupation or even invasion. The real occupation never extended beyond a few coast cities and districts; the first invasions ended in swift retreat, the second at Saratoga, the last at Yorktown.

Fort Moultrie

The great Southern victory, which gave the Union more than two years' security from assault on that side, had already been won at the Declaration, but was not yet known at Philadelphia. This was best: it was not needed as a spur, and was welcome as a justification and a weapon against the recalcitrants. Moore's Creek having made a North Carolina landing impossible or objectless, Clinton and Parker—who arrived in May, delayed by baffling winds—sailed to Charleston to make

South Carolina their base, arriving June 1. Lord
William Campbell assured them, despite his wet-
blanket reception, of a great loyal element only
waiting their presence; and a darker plot was on
foot. John Stuart, the British southern Indian
superintendent, and his resident deputy Cameron
connected with several Cherokee chiefs by marriage, had formulated a plan to exterminate the
Whig settlers from Georgia to Virginia at a blow,
confiscating their property and allotting it to new
and loyal colonists. To this end a grand Indian
rising and butchery was to co-operate with the
invasion from Charleston, the two joining hands
in the interior.

Of an easy naval capture of the low peninsula bathed in deep waters, none of them had a
thought of doubt. Little more had Lee, who had
discovered the plot by intercepted dispatches to
the southern royal governors, hurried thither from
Virginia, arrived June 4, took command of the
national and provincial forces, and wrote to Washington that the place was "utterly defenseless."

At the entrance of Charleston Harbor, there
curves in from the north one of the line of narrow sandy coast islands, four miles long, called
Sullivan's Island. On this, close to the southern
water-edge about six miles from the city, on a spit
between the bay and a rear cove, Colonel William Moultrie had begun "Fort Sullivan"; a connected row of open pens, sixteen feet wide and
ten high, built of dovetailed palmetto logs and
filled in with sand. He had but twenty-one guns

1776
June

Plot for
Indian
butchery

Lee at
Charles-
ton

Sulli-
van's
Island

1776
June

Defenses
of Char-
leston
Harbor

usable at a broadside, only thirty rounds of ammunition each, and 399 men fit for duty. A mile
west, across an arm of the bay, a small force occupied Haddrell's Point on the mainland, guarding
the roads thence to Charleston. South of the
channel were much stronger shore defenses.

British
fleet
waits

The British squadron spent a week in sounding
and buoying; then crossed the bar, and Clinton
sent ashore a proclamation warning the rebels
to lay down their arms, promising pardon. No
answer was returned. Close on three weeks more
the fleet lay a league off Sullivan's Island, waiting
favorable winds. Meantime the American troops
kept pouring in till Lee had over 6500, three-
fifths Continentals; and he used the precious
time energetically and judiciously in strengthening his defenses. He set 700 negroes at work in

Lee
fortifies
the city

the city throwing up new works, even across the
streets, had the warehouses near the wharves
pulled down not to obstruct the guns, the window-
leads cast into bullets, and fire-ships prepared.

Fort Sullivan even at the last was unfinished
in the rear, and thus quite untenable could the
British vessels reach the cove and enfilade the

Distrusts
Fort
Sullivan

gun platform. Lee called it a "slaughter-pen";
removed some of the troops and part of the 10,000
pounds of powder there; and would have ordered
it abandoned, but yielded to Edward Rutledge,
president of the Provincial Congress, who relied
on Moultrie's judgment. Lee was nearest right:
only accident prevented what he feared, though
American skill and bravery prevented the same

WILLIAM MOULTRIE.

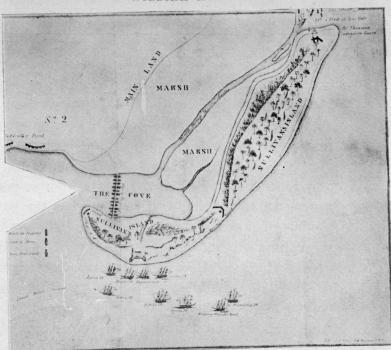

SULLIVAN'S ISLAND AND FORT SULLIVAN (LATER
FORT MOULTRIE).

(Haddrell's Point at West. Long Island at North.)

result without it. And having consented, he acted for once with professional honor, and more sense than the careless though indomitably brave Moultrie, to falsify his own predictions of disaster; urging on him simple rear defenses, which Moultrie would not put up, so that Lee had prepared to remove him on the very morning of the battle.

1776
June

Lee vs.
Moultrie

As great a danger was the British landing on Long Island next north of Sullivan's, to wade the breach, fordable at low tide, and storm the fort by its wholly open western flank. Clinton collected some 3000 men near the breach, and built redoubts. Lee stationed on the south side Colonel Thomson with about 780 riflemen; erecting also palmetto-log breastworks behind sand-dunes and screened by clumps of myrtle, and armed with two cannon. In fear lest Clinton instead should cross to the mainland and take that route to the city (an impossibility in fact from two miles of salt-marsh), Lee placed at Haddrell's Point a much stronger force and two batteries; designed also to protect Moultrie's retreat by water, and if possible rake the enfilading vessels.

Clinton
to
assault
from
Long
Island

Lee's
double
guard

On the 28th the combined movement was begun: Sir Peter Parker to batter the wooden fort in pieces; Clinton to rout the raw troops on the south bank, and capture them and the garrison entire in this island trap. But Clinton's men found the water, heaped up by eastern gales, over their heads, and several were shot while testing it; the flotilla of armed boats, to cover their advance by raking Thomson's redoubt, was itself

Clinton's
balk

1776
June 28

Fort
Moultrie:
Clinton's
fiasco

raked and riddled with grape-shot and rifle-balls at every approach to the shore; and Clinton, who had taken no soundings in advance and not thought of providing transport boats, remained helplessly out of the battle.

Meanwhile Parker's fleet of ten vessels advanced, headed by the flagship *Bristol,* on which Lord William Campbell was serving as a volunteer; and for many hours a furious storm of shot and shell poured against the face of the fort. One of the splendid stories of American heroism is that of Sergeant William Jasper of Savannah, who saw the flag fall outside, jumped through an embrasure and walked the whole length of the parapet to pick it up, climbed back and hoisted it on a sponge staff. But most of the cannon-balls sank harmlessly into the spongy palmetto, and the bombs burst in the sand; almost all the loss was due to those which passed through the embrasures, and only one gun was disabled.

On the other hand, the American artillery, as always, was terrible in accuracy and execution. The *Bristol* lost main- and mizzen-mast, and her hull was a wreck. Her cable-springs were shot through early in the action, and she swung with her stern close to the American fire; she was raked and shattered from stem to stern, her quarterdeck twice cleared of every soul but the admiral, himself slightly wounded (local tradition declared that the seat of his breeches was shaved off by a cannon-ball), and she alone lost 40 killed and 71 wounded, her captain and Campbell mortally.

The *Experiment,* next following, lost 23 killed and 76 wounded, her captain also desperately hurt and maimed. In all, 239 were killed and wounded on the fleet, besides Clinton's losses; in the fort 12 killed and 25 wounded.

Until half-past nine at night this duel raged. In mid-afternoon Moultrie's powder nearly gave out, and the British noted it and shouted their triumph; but Rutledge hurried over 500 pounds more and prevented a Bunker Hill, cautioning Moultrie, "Do not make too free with your cannon—cool and do mischief." But the fort owed its salvation to the fact that the three vessels sent to gain its rear ran aground. One had to be abandoned and burned, the others got away much damaged. Only one of the entire fleet remained fit for service, and it took nearly three weeks to refit the rest into seaworthy condition; the whole expedition then sailed for New York to assist in the campaign there, and Lee followed.

Fort Sullivan was renamed Fort Moultrie. Clinton and Parker each blamed the other for this bloody and humiliating failure; neither was willing to credit American heroism and artillery service. As to the border horrors genially contemplated by those whose scalps were safe, the Carolina and Virginia borderers held their lands by virtue of ability to quell these savageries: they inflicted such vengeance and ravage that the cowed and starving Cherokees, in January 1777, ceded to them a vast tract including much of East Tennessee.

1776
June 28

Fort
Moultrie:
British
losses

Narrow
escape
of fort

Campaign
abandoned

Indian
plot fails

1776
July-
Aug.

Great
British
superior-
ity

Over 24,000 superb regulars—including regiments from Florida and the West Indies, and the 11,000 German mercenaries who arrived July 12 with Admiral Lord Howe—were now massed against Washington's 18,000 raw troops, a fifth sick and as many more on detached duty. A general American defeat was certain: Washington's problem was to make it profit the British as little and delay their progress as much as possible.

Howe's
olive-
branch

First, however, Admiral Howe—who had only taken the command on condition of being made a peace commissioner with plenary powers—was to present an "olive-branch" sent over by North. It was a farce, in spite of the Howes' genuine good intentions; being merely a promise that all rebels—individuals or communities—who would yield and help put down the rebellion should be graciously pardoned, and Howe being instructed not to recognize the rebel governments or officers even for negotiation. This commission was sent in a general letter to the royal governors south of New England, to be circulated as widely as possible. As their address was mostly the British fleet, jail, or the other world, its actual circulation came from Congress, which published it in all the newspapers, to show the people Great Britain's

Ignomin-
ious
failure

intent to "disarm and amuse them," and "that the valor alone of their country is to save its liberties." It was a laughing-stock through the colonies: Governor Trumbull of Connecticut said we doubtless all needed pardon from God for our sins, but no American needed any from the King of Britain. Thus foiled, Howe sent it to "George Washington, Esq.," who of course, if only such, had no authority to conclude agreements for others; the messenger was told there was no such person in the army. Then Howe added "etc., etc.," after the "Esq.," and his envoy (August 19) said these "meant everything"; to which Washington replied that they "might mean anything," refused to receive the letter, and sent Lord Howe his compliments. As a last resort, the sincere Howe tried to get his old acquaintance Franklin to persuade Congress to send him a deputation acting as individuals. Franklin retorted with a sharpness which surprised and hurt Howe, but opened his eyes to the fact that the ministry had deceived him as to its actions and plans.

1776
July-
Aug.

Howe's
failure to
negotiate

This toying gave the Americans a breathing-time, badly needed. During it some British vessels moved up the Hudson, taking soundings and reconnoitring; the Americans harassed them from the banks, and built and armed galleys, which drove them back to the bay; Putnam placed obstructions in the North and East rivers, and tried fire-ships, both without success. But it was not till after the last hope of negotiation had failed that General Howe began upon his first military objective, the capture of New York from his base at Staten Island.

Skir-
mishes
on the
Hudson

Lee had planted various redoubts along the shores of Manhattan Island—of which Fort Washington on the northwest heights, with Fort Constitution (later renamed Fort Lee) on the Palisades

Man-
hattan
fortified

1776

**Fortifica-
tions
about
New York**

**Brooklyn
Heights**

**Howe's
plan of
invest-
ment**

opposite, supposably commanded the Hudson; thrown works across it below the present Canal Street, and barricaded many streets of the city, which then only reached to Chatham Street. On Governor's Island in the harbor was stationed Prescott and a body of Bunker Hill troops. But the commanding location was Brooklyn Heights, corresponding exactly to Dorchester Heights at Boston; Greene had worked for months fortifying it, but was taken sick and obliged to give up the command to Putnam, who held it with several thousand men. It was some five miles above the south shore of Long Island; about half-way between lay a range of thickly wooded hills curving north, to which the American lines were extended to guard the passes that pierced them.

Howe made the judicious choice, which with his overwhelming numbers was quite safe, of striking for the key. On August 22-5 he landed above 20,000 troops at Gravesend, had the district reconnoitred, and pushed Cornwallis up to Flatbush to see if the pass beyond was strongly held; finding it so, he left him there, while he developed a simple but most effective strategic plan. Two roads north to Brooklyn Ferry crossed the range in the centre just beyond Flatbush; that west through New Utrecht crossed near the bay and skirted Gowanus Cove just under the Heights; that to Jamaica ran east of it for some miles, then one branch turned west and crossed at Cypress Hills to Bedford. His plan was to have strong divisions make feints against the centre and west passes, while he made a long detour through the east with his main body and took them in the rear; the three would unite in an easy victory, and completely invest the works on the Heights. At the same time the fleet was to prevent reinforcement from New York by a feigned bombardment: why it was not used to cut off escape over East River will always be susceptible of two answers.

1776
Aug.

Howe's
plan to
invest
Brooklyn
Heights

This movement brought over Washington, who reinforced Putnam with several bodies of the best troops in the army, including two to become immortal—John Hastel's Delaware regiment, and William Smallwood's brigade of Marylanders, now under William Alexander of New Jersey ("Lord Stirling" on his own claim). Washington also, judging from Cornwallis' position that the main attack was to be on the centre pass, had it strongly fortified and Sullivan placed there with some 3000 men; the Gowanus-road pass and that at the western base on the bay were also fortified and given a small guard; the far Cypress Hills pass was not thought in danger, and was not occupied, though patrolled. In truth there were not troops enough even for the other two.

On the night of the 26th the fleet began cannonading, with the desired result. Grant and his Highlanders took the western road; Von Heister and the Hessians the centre; Howe with Clinton, Cornwallis, and Percy the east. A Tory guided Howe's march; the loyalist population prevented warning being given to the Americans; their patrol was captured; and the new army, four

1776
Aug. 27

times Sullivan's numbers, marched unsuspected through the unguarded pass and opened a tremendous fire on his rear, while Von Heister at the signal stopped skirmishing and charged furiously in front, even his division far outnumbering the Americans. Forced from the redoubt and the hill-woods to the plain by the Hessians' onslaught, driven back into them by Cornwallis' dragoons, in a short time a third of the Americans were forced to surrender; the rest broke through the enemy's line, or scattered far in the woods and tall grass and gained the Heights. Then Cornwallis advanced to the west passes, where Putnam had sent forward Stirling, the Maryland and Delaware men, and others, to reinforce the trifling guard, and Grant had held them in play for four hours. By one of the most magnificent efforts of heroism and self-sacrifice in history, part of the Marylanders, at last reduced to five companies, held Cornwallis' entire host at bay till their comrades escaped; the survivors, after several desperate charges, being mostly bayoneted while making their last stand in a cornfield. More than 250 of this superb regiment gave up their lives in this battle. Stirling, left without a man to command, surrendered.

Battle of Long Island

Heroic Marylanders

Thus ended about noon the Battle of Long Island. Almost the only real fighting had been at the west pass; and the Maryland heroes must have sold their lives mainly man for man, as the losses of the two sides in killed and wounded were about equal, some 400. The Americans lost also

Losses

1000 or so captured. Their entire force engaged was about 5000, and they were overwhelmingly outnumbered at every point in the field. No conduct could have won victory; but a better guard at Cypress Hills might have enabled more of Sullivan's forces to escape.

1775
Aug.
27–30

Battle of
Long
Island

The 7000 Americans in the works expected an immediate storm; but to their extreme surprise, Howe's treble force, most of them perfectly fresh, were called off for the day. Washington, seeing that the main British army was here and New York was not the immediate objective, brought over some 2000 reinforcements to resist attack; and his judgment was confirmed by the British beginning to throw up intrenchments the next day as for a siege. But on the 29th, movements in the fleet indicated that it was preparing to cut off his retreat, as it might have done sooner. There was but a day or so between escape and certain capture of nearly his whole army.

Washington's extrication of his forces from this trap was a military masterpiece; perhaps the Howes' allowing it was also—they did not want America left helpless. He ordered preparations for a night attack on the British camp, to mislead any spy or traitor in the fold. He gave a verbal order to Colonel Hughes to have every water-craft from Spuyten Duyvil to Hell Gate seized and at Brooklyn Ferry by eight in the evening, which was done, aided by a dense fog; and the Marblehead and Gloucester fishermen of Glover's Essex County regiment were given charge of

1776
Aug.-
Sept.

Skillful
American
escape
from
Long
Island

them. By seven in the morning the whole army had been safely transferred across the river, with all the stores, cattle and horses, carts, tools, and even the ammunition and artillery excepting a few heavy pieces. Not an article was left for the British except the bare works. Greene's opinion that this was the most masterly retreat in history was echoed in Europe.

British
army oc-
cupies it

The British forces immediately occupied and strengthened the works, and extended the lines to Hell Gate. Admiral Howe brought up most of the fleet and anchored it close to Governor's Island, within easy cannon-shot of the city, and sent other vessels into East River. This seems like carefully locking the stable-door after the steed was gone; it may be surmised that the Howes preferred to have the steed keep on the run. By the 3d of September the whole British force was transferred to Long Island, except about 4000 left on Staten Island.

Amer-
icans
still hold
New York

Prescott's force on Governor's Island was now useless and exposed to imminent capture, and Washington skillfully withdrew it. The city both he and Putnam considered untenable, and wished to evacuate; but they were overruled for political reasons, and Putnam was given some 5000 men to defend it. The bulk of the army was stationed at Harlem Heights; the surplus stores were sent across Harlem River in fear of sudden necessity. It was at this time that, needing information of the British positions, he reluctantly allowed a brilliant and promising young

Connecticut captain named Nathan Hale, a Yale graduate, to undertake the service; Hale was captured and hanged with disgraceful aggravations, but turned his fate into an inspiring martyrdom by his utterances from one of the noblest of souls.

1776
Sept.

Nathan
Hale

The Howes would not give up their hope of conciliation, which seemed more likely after the victory; and the captured Sullivan was at once sent to Philadelphia to ask again the same private embassy from Congress, Lord Howe pledging his word to attempt a repeal of the hated acts of Parliament. John Adams denounced Sullivan as a decoy, and the request was an absurdity to a sovereign legislature; but Congress finally agreed, as a token of regard for Lord Howe (who was not to blame for his instructions) and of their wish not to prejudice any hope of settlement, to send a committee which he might view as he chose. Franklin, John Adams, and Rutledge were appointed, and met Howe September 11, but of course without result: they could listen to no terms but as an independent nation. Howe, deeply grieved, issued a proclamation declaring that the government fully intended to revise the obnoxious laws and "instructions," and urging Americans to rely on this solemn promise rather than take the risks of a wrongful and hopeless war.

Howe
renews
efforts at
concilia-
tion

Meets
com-
mittee

Issues
new
procla-
mation

Since the war must go on, four battalions of loyalists were created, with Tryon (still governor) as major-general; and Sir William played the next move by ousting Washington from the city,

Fresh
hostil-
ities

September 15. As the fleet commanded both rivers, and he had already a strong camp on Harlem River, he could perfectly well have captured the whole island and the American army by landing his remaining forces there; but he did not wish it. First cutting off transport across the Hudson by ships at Bloomingdale, under cover of a fire from others at Blackwell's Island he landed an overwhelming force between Kip's Bay and Turtle Bay (near Thirty-fourth Street Ferry), where the Americans had breastworks. Both militia and Continentals were seized with a panic and fled, leaving Washington himself exposed to capture fifteen rods off. "Are these the troops with which I am to defend America?" he said bitterly, dashing his hat on the ground.

Putnam could not have escaped had British divisions at once been thrown across the island. But Howe held them where they were for a while, save a detachment down East River; and Putnam hurried his troops north along the Greenwich road. At Murray Hill the leisurely British advance overtook their rear, picked off fifteen men in a skirmish fire, and gathered up some 300 prisoners; but made no serious assault. Meanwhile Howe, with Clinton and other of his most prominent officers, instead of directing the attack, accepted an invitation to lunch at the fine mansion of the great merchant Robert Murray (father of the famous grammarian Lindley Murray), from its Quaker mistress; and spent a couple of hours very pleasantly, joking her on the spectacle of her flying countrymen, while most of these gained Harlem Heights, as she purposed.

The British took possession of the city. Washington stretched his lines across the island from Harlem Heights to Fort Washington; the latter under Putnam's charge, while Greene (recovered, and shortly made a major-general and commander of the troops in the Jerseys) commanded Fort Lee on the Jersey side. As King's Bridge across Spuyten Duyvil Creek, two miles in the rear, was in Washington's hands, he had a secure retreat. The next day (16th), the British drove in the centre outposts and tried to draw on a general engagement outside the works. Colonel Thomas Knowlton and his Connecticut rangers, aided by a Virginia reinforcement, waged a brilliant and obstinate fight in which Knowlton was slain; but Washington prudently withdrew his troops to the works. This Battle of Harlem Heights cost the Americans about 60 men and the British 300, and raised the spirits of the former. They also benefited while here by a general exchange of prisoners, getting back Stirling, Sullivan, and Morgan.

Howe lay quiet for nearly a month. He and his brother were constantly hoping that the colonies would recede and accept their offers; but aside from this, he might well think it the best even of military moves, for time seemed to be weakening his opponents as rapidly as would battles. The Continentals' one-year terms of enlistment were rapidly expiring, they very generally refused to re-enlist, and Washington faced

1776
Sept.-
Oct.

Bad state
of army

the imminent probability of having no army to
command. Meantime a large percentage of those
around New York were sick, there were no proper
hospitals, and the victims lay about in almost
every barn, stable, and shed, and even outdoors
under fences and bushes.

Patriots
and
Tories

Many privates and even officers disgraced and
damaged the cause by plundering citizens on pretense of their being Tories, despite Washington's
efforts to restrain it; insuring ample retaliation
later. But for now a special Conspiracy Committee
headed by Jay, with unlimited powers and an
armed force, terrorized the Tories into submission; filling jails and churches with prisoners,
sending many to work in an underground Connecticut copper mine, and confiscating their property. The Tories had their turn of revenge by
making thousands of patriot prisoners rot in the
vile prison-ships of the harbor, and raiding New
Jersey.

Howe ma-
nœuvres
Wash-
ington
off Man-
hattan

Howe finally decided that he must give Washington a friendly push off Manhattan Island, as
a reminder that war was going on. He accomplished it with his usual economy of bloodshed.
Two vessels went up the Hudson October 9,
between Forts Washington and Lee and over
Putnam's new obstructions, and cut off supplies
from the west. As a menace of doing likewise
from Connecticut, on the 12th he moved the bulk
of his army to the mainland of the Sound, drove
off the American regiments on guard, and established himself at New Rochelle. Washington then

withdrew most of his army from Manhattan and formed a new line on the heights west of the Bronx, finally concentrating in a fortified camp at White Plains; thus restoring his communications and outflanking Howe, who made no effort to prevent it, and lay quiet over a fortnight.

1776
Oct.

McDougall with 1600 men held Chatterton Hill on the right, across the Bronx and a marsh; this isolated outpost commanding the American right flank challenged Howe's professional pride, and on the 28th with Clinton and Von Heister he stormed it (the Battle of White Plains), losing 229 men against the Americans' three or four hundred including prisoners. He then leisurely began works in front of the American position; Washington thereupon withdrew five miles north to the rocky hills about North Castle, and Howe did not follow him. "All matters," wrote Washington, "are as quiet as if the enemy were one hundred miles from us."

Battle of
White
Plains

Meanwhile the danger from the north had passed away till spring, in the form so familiar all through the Revolution,—a British victory which daunted the victors from following it up. The abortive American invasion of Canada was to be retorted by a Canadian invasion of New York under Sir Guy Carleton, with a well-equipped regular army of 13,000. Against him was a dispirited raw force of not above 5000, riddled with small-pox and camp fever under which 2000 were on the sick list, death and desertion having already reduced it by half since spring.

Invasion
from
Canada

Wretched
American
force

During the summer, reinforcements increased it to some 8000, the main force at Ticonderoga and an outpost at Crown Point. Gates had been made its commander in the retreat from Canada; reaching New York, he wished to remain independent of Schuyler, commander of the northern department. On being refused, he began a campaign of vicious secret detraction of him, given all its power for harm by the existing New England hatred.[1] We shall have more of this feud, an evil one for the cause.

To reach this point, Carleton could only take the old path by Lake Champlain, a waterway cloven through the unbroken wilderness; this needed a fleet, and the time it took to collect one was our salvation. A hot race began in June for the naval control of the lake.

For America this service was undertaken by Arnold, to the immense relief of Schuyler and Gates, he being at once an ex-shipmaster and of almost superhuman energy. Additions to the

1776 Summer

Gates vs. Schuyler

Champlain route

Arnold and a fleet

---

[1] There were two main causes. One was the old quarrel of the Hampshire Grants (Vermont). Schuyler, as a leader in the New York Assembly, had fought New Hampshire hotly over their possession. His New England troops were sulky and half mutinous at serving under their greatest enemy, though he was of high ability and energy and the most unselfish patriotic zeal; Gates played on the feeling by espousing the New England side, and that interest obtained his appointment from Congress. The other was that New-Yorkers very generally—members of a system based on large semi-feudal landholding—were loftily contemptuous of the New England small farmers and the pushing swarm of fortune-seekers they sent out; a sentiment glaringly exhibited in Irving's caricature of the itinerant Yankee schoolmaster Ichabod Crane in the *Legend of Sleepy Hollow*, and in Paulding's work. Schuyler shared the feeling, and put it into his manners; and it did not endear him to New-Englanders.

HORATIO GATES.

PHILIP SCHUYLER.

SIR GUY CARLETON.

BENEDICT ARNOLD.

few vessels on hand must be built on the spot: yet all artisans, tools, nails, sailcloth, guns and ammunition, and other necessaries had to be obtained from the New England seaports, by depreciated Continental money, and transported far across roadless mountain and forest; and every timber new-felled. But in three months Arnold had sixteen small vessels afloat, armed with seventy guns; manned to be sure with "five hundred half-naked men, the refuse of the regiments," he said, and fresh-water sailors, and even so a hundred short of a full complement. But his refuse fought and died like brave men, as did the English "scum": few human souls are beyond inspiration by others.

1776
Summer-
Fall

Arnold
builds
fleet

Its
manning

Carleton, however, had the English treasury and the admiralty stores to draw on, besides those on hand at Quebec and on the St. Lawrence; vessels, timber, and ship-yards, and contractors for all needed. A three-masted ship with thirty guns, and two large schooners, were navigated from England to the rapids above Montreal, taken in pieces and carried overland to St. John's, reframed and launched on the Sorel; twenty gunboats and a floating battery were dragged over the rapids and up it, with over 200 transports. The war-vessels and the weight of broadside in their ninety-three guns were each more than double Arnold's; and they were manned by over 700 picked seamen and gunners, finely officered.

Arnold's only possibility was that of American commanders generally in the Revolution—

1776
Oct. 11–13
to make the British victory so costly as to be equivalent to a defeat, in loss and delay and the heartening of the people. South of Plattsburg, not far from the scene of McDonough's victory in 1814, lies Valcour Island a mile from the western shore, the intervening channel shoaling north. Arnold stretched his little fleet across this channel to the south, so that he could only be assailed in front and not flanked, and awaited Carleton; who came up October 11 and joined battle. It was the first between American and British fleets, and a presage of future glories of seamanship, gunnery, resolute daring, and defiance of death. For seven hours Arnold and the heroic rabble fired with his spirit held their position, at first taking the offensive, under a cannonade that killed or wounded a sixth of their number and left four vessels practically wrecks, —one sank shortly after, and the flag-schooner had run aground and been lost; while bodies of Indians blazed away at them from both mainland and island forests. But they had destroyed three British vessels, and Carleton at nightfall had to leave full victory till the morning, posting his fleet across the channel to prevent escape.

In the hazy darkness, however, Arnold extricated them all with marvelous skill, and had a night's start with a north wind for escape. But leaks compelled a halt; two sinking gondolas took more time transferring their guns; the wind shifted dead ahead, and the crews had to take up kedging and rowing: and on the morning of the

Arnold's
skillful
escape

13th the British overtook them once more and opened fire. One already disabled galley soon struck; but Arnold, with a still worse crippled one, and a few gondolas, faced the whole British fleet to let the rest escape. For four hours three British vessels mounting forty-one guns poured their concentrated fire on this shattered six-gun galley and its one-gun mates, till it was a splintered ruin strewn with dead and wounded—a star of American valor and British marksmanship, for American gunners would have sunk the whole in ten minutes; and still Arnold would neither fly nor surrender. Surrounded at last by seven, he managed to slip his remnants through, run them into a creek and burn them, taking off his men. With these and the escaped crews he skillfully evaded an Indian ambuscade and reached Ticonderoga.

1776
Oct.

Arnold's
self-sacri-
ficing
heroism

Carleton took possession of Crown Point; his army coming up, he sent advance parties to Ticonderoga. It looked too strong to storm—the lesson of Bunker Hill was never lost, and he had just had a new one of stubborn American courage; the season was too late to begin a siege; he held the lake securely for operations in the spring; and despite the disgust of his chief officers— Burgoyne, Phillips, and Riedesel—he went back to Canada and put his troops in winter quarters. Upper New York was saved; Schuyler sent eleven regiments under Gates to reinforce Washington; and to him we turn once more.

Carleton
with-
draws
till
spring

Howe, as Washington remarked with natural bewilderment,—not comprehending that his foe's military movements were subordinate to a large political end of which the Americans were beneficiaries,—"must undertake something on account of his reputation." The most obvious was to force an evacuation of Fort Washington, with Harlem Heights and the Americans' last hold on Manhattan Island. He therefore moved to Dobbs' Ferry on the east bank, threatening at once the fort and New Jersey. To guard the latter, Washington sent Putnam with 5000 men to Hackensack. He rightly believed the fort and its companion Fort Lee to be worse than useless,—no defense of the Hudson, and only locking up thousands of men for capture when invested by land and water,—and prepared to abandon them; while for a real command of the Hudson against a descent from Canada, he sent Heath with 3000 men to occupy Peekskill, at the entrance of the Highlands, shortly changed to West Point and Canopus Creek. Howe, not doubting that the forts would be evacuated as at Brooklyn Heights on the first menace, placed Percy before Harlem Heights, moved Knyphausen's Hessians down over King's Bridge within cannon-shot of the fort, and shortly followed from Dobbs' Ferry with his whole force.

But Greene, perhaps deceived by Bunker Hill, was convinced that the forts could be held, and Congress and popular clamor determined they should be held; and Washington yielded. Howe had no alternative but to take what his antagonists forced on him. A deserter (as was first discovered in 1876) gave him full plans and descriptions. The fort was of no strength: a poor open earthwork without even water inside, only the Hudson 300 feet below; and so small that when the outposts were driven in the garrison could not manœuvre, but were a helpless solid mark. On November 15 Howe sent a summons to surrender, which was defied, and Greene reinforced the garrison under Colonel Magaw to 2800 men. The next day the British overwhelmed the American outliers with 15,000 men attacking from four directions at once. The Americans were pushed off the Heights and into the fort only after a stubborn defense, which cost the British some 400 men and the Americans 150; but once in, instead of a Bunker Hill, they were compelled to an immediate surrender. A fifth of the effective American army was lost at a blow, with 161 cannon, vast quantities of small arms, ammunition, and other stores,—lamentably the tents and blankets needed for the coming winter.

Cornwallis was now given a free hand to recover "East Jersey," by advancing to Brunswick (New Brunswick) only. On the night of the 19th he crossed the river with 6000 men and his artillery, and moved on Fort Lee with such celerity that Greene had barely time to hurry the garrison across the Hackensack to the main army, abandoning the artillery and stores. Washington, already here, had not over 4000 men, and miserably below the British in every respect: undisciplined, discouraged, ill-fed, half-shod, ragged, blanketless, and shelterless. He had expected 5000

1776
Nov.

Capture
of Fort
Wash-
ington

Corn-
wallis
invades
New
Jersey

more to meet him in a Maryland "Flying Camp" and militia from other colonies; but less than half that came, and the former on the point of disbanding. He had expected New Jersey to rise against the invaders and swell his ranks; but that State, in the gripe of tough old ravagers, naturally shrank from a seemingly useless martyrdom.

New Jersey cowed

Cornwallis pursued so hotly that Washington, liable to be trapped between the Hackensack and Passaic, retreated across the latter on the 21st, reaching Newark the 23d; Cornwallis did not come up till the 28th, when the Americans retired to Brunswick; on December 1 they left it again, their rear-guard sharply assailed there by the British. All through this retreat, the American rear pulling down the bridges were within sight and range of the British pioneer corps sent to rebuild them.

Cornwallis drives Washington before him

Cornwallis' goal reached, he stopped; and the Howes issued a new proclamation, November 30, offering pardon and protection to all who would submit within sixty days. Hosts of citizens in the occupied or menaced regions, including many important civil and military patriot leaders, deeming the cause lost and themselves and their property at the mercy of hireling hordes bred to ravage, hastened to come in. For the next ten days two or three hundred a day took the oaths: among them Samuel Tucker, president of the New Jersey convention that had sanctioned the Declaration, chairman of its Committee of Safety, judge of its supreme court; the chief officers of

Fresh Howe proclamation

Immense effect

the Monmouth battalion; Joseph Galloway and the Allens of Philadelphia, delegates to Congress; even Dickinson wavered. In the middle colonies, 2703 Jerseymen and 1282 New-Yorkers, with many Pennsylvanians, formally submitted within the time.

Washington—who on November 30 lost the "Flying Camp" and others, nearly half his force, by expiration of terms—had hastened forward to Princeton; left Stirling and Adam Stephen there with 1200 men to check the enemy's advance; and gone on to Trenton, to secure the extra baggage and stores behind the Delaware. Effecting this December 2-6, he turned back toward Princeton with 1200 more to make a stand; but meantime Howe had reinforced Cornwallis and advanced once more. Washington met his Princeton corps in full retreat and retraced his march to Trenton, renewing his orders to Lee, and writing Heath to send him one of the two brigades at the Hudson, not needed till spring; collected every boat on the river for seventy miles, and on the 8th crossed it with his artillery and stores. Here he halted, posted his troops to guard the fords and the Philadelphia roads, and sent Putnam to fortify that city. Howe's force came to Princeton shortly after the Americans evacuated it, rested there seventeen hours, and spent seven more traversing the twelve miles to Trenton, reaching the river as the last Americans crossed it.

Cornwallis favored hunting up boats and moving on to capture the "rebel capital"; but

1776
Dec.

British
lines
along the
Delaware

The
Bruns-
wick
magazine

Winter
plans

Congress
leaves
Phila-
delphia

Howe was exultant over the superb success of his darling plan, saw the country coming to his feet and the American army melting away without need of such strenuousness, and said the river would soon freeze enough to cross. He placed the Germans along it, on the north at Pennington;[1] in the centre at Trenton under Colonel Rall, a brave jolly hard-drinking officer with little discipline, but reputed for storming Chatterton Hill; and south at Bordentown and Burlington, below the great bend of the river, under Donop. In rear, guarding his chief magazine at Brunswick, were the Highlanders under Grant, who was made commander of New Jersey; communication with the Delaware lines was maintained by a post at Princeton, with New York by those at the Hackensack and Elizabethtown. He then returned to New York, and the army went into winter quarters; but it was understood that as soon as the river ice would bear artillery, Donop should cross and cut off Washington's communications with Philadelphia, which would be at once occupied. Numbers of citizens took fright, sent their families out of the city, and hid their loose valuables. On the 12th, at Putnam's advice, in alarm over the effect of the proclamation and the British approach, Congress had removed to Baltimore (where it reassembled on the 20th). First, however, it clothed Washington with dictatorial power

---

[1] So says Washington; but as this post—some miles back from the river and eight north of Trenton—is never heard of again, in all the turmoil raging around it, the detachment was probably soon drawn in.

as to the war till further orders; and voted to raise a regiment of cavalry, of which the army had only one or two companies.

So completely was Howe's mind at rest, that some days previous he had detached 6000 men in transports, with Clinton in command seconded by Percy and Prescott, to occupy Newport, Rhode Island; on the 8th, eleven war-ships co-operating, they landed. The small American garrison evacuated the place without resistance; and the second city in New England, with a harbor affording an ideal station for raiding its southern coast and protecting New York, passed into British hands, as well as the entire island of Aquidneck. Commodore Esek Hopkins, with some Continental cruisers and several privateers, fled up the bay and were blockaded at Providence. Within the sixty days' limit, 851 Rhode-Islanders submitted under the Howe proclamation. These winnings were dearly paid for, however, by keeping a fourth of the central army out of the field for the next three years.

But why had Washington, with 11,000 availables under his orders,—aside from Heath's 3000 on the Hudson, to be diminished only in the last necessity,—been forced to flee almost to Philadelphia without striking a blow in defense, with a few regiments dwindling fast through physical misery, expired terms, and outright desertion, till scarce 3000 crossed the Delaware? Because Lee, whom he had left with 7000 men at North Castle to follow him when ordered, was playing merely for his own hand. He was determined *not* **to** help Washington out of a scrape, and *to* use that scrape to gain himself at least an independent command, if possible Washington's place; **in** either event some dazzling victory which his vanity assured him, and the power of making terms of peace. Ward's resignation had left him senior major-general. He, not Moultrie, had the halo of the splendid achievement at Charleston, and it shone for the country in contrast with Washington's months of unbroken disaster; and men could not but connect it with the one being a veteran of military science in Old World armies from Poland to Portugal, the other a native militiaman. Washington's name as yet carried no glamour outside of Virginia.

Lee secretly exchanged letters in detraction of him far and wide with influential persons—including Adjutant-General Reed and Dr. Rush, powerful in the politics of the capital, and the executives of Massachusetts and Rhode Island;

broadly insinuating the urgent need of supplanting him by Lee's self, and defying Congress for the country's salvation. Confident of backing, though ordered to join his chief at once on the fall of Fort Washington, and daily with growing insistence thereafter, he never did so during all the dire necessity of that miserable flight across New Jersey. His troops would have enabled Washington to exact from Cornwallis a bloody price for a slow advance; keep the country from discouragement, thousands from accepting the

Howe offer, other thousands from withholding money or supplies, soldiers from deserting or refusing to re-enlist. If any one act could have ruined American liberty, Lee's selfish insubordination would have done it.

He neglected the orders wholly as long as he dared; then made excuses of lacking means to cross in time; and only moved November 30, crossing the Hudson December 2-3. Even then he hung back; declared himself "detached to make an important diversion"; ordered Heath to send 2000 of his men instead, which Heath refused and Washington indignantly disallowed; intercepted St. Clair at Haverstraw on the 4th with four of Schuyler's regiments, and joined them to his own command. Two of them, however, were Jerseymen whose terms were just expiring, and disbanded to a man on reaching their State. Lee's force was now reduced by expiry and desertion to some 4000, ready to mutiny over entering a winter campaign without shoes, blankets, or the barest needs of life.

Moving slowly southwest along the east flank of the New Jersey Highlands, almost openly proclaiming his purpose of an independent campaign, and on the 10th ordering Heath to send him three other northern regiments just arrived, on the 12th with his forces he reached Vealtown, eighteen miles from the enemy; left Sullivan in command, rode three miles ahead with a slight guard and quartered at a tavern. A local loyalist noted the glittering prize within grasp, galloped madly

1776

Lee's
capture

Wash-
ington's
dispo-
sitions

to inform the British, and a party of dragoons bagged it. They would have been less triumphant had they known the valuable service they were rendering the patriots, but those also guilelessly fancied it a crowning misfortune.[1]

Washington under his new powers at once recruited three battalions of artillery, by increasing their pay twenty-five per cent.; and some 1800 Philadelphia militia under Colonels John Cadwalader and Joseph Reed joined him, who were stationed at Bristol to guard against Donop's crossing. On the other hand, the clamor of New York about endangering the Hudson, and an alarm that Howe's Newport fleet was threatening New London and probably planning an invasion of Connecticut, forced him to halt Heath's brigade and the northern regiments at Morristown Heights, where also some 800 militia had collected; and on the 20th he sent Maxwell to command them and keep the British anxious. But

---

[1] Lee was taken to Princeton, and proffered his oath of submission under Howe's manifesto; Howe refused it to a "deserter," sent him to confinement in New York, and wrote to Germain for orders concerning him. Lee wrote abjectly to Washington for help, which was sent—a threat to Howe that six captive German officers should answer for Lee's life; and to Congress for a deputation to hear a mysterious confidence of his,—in fact the old scheme of arranging a compromise,—which was not sent. Thereupon Lee turned traitor outright, and furnished Howe—from conscientious motives, he said—with plans for conquering the colonies which misled him to their salvation. Germain ordered Lee shipped to England for trial; but the firmness of Washington, who was far above petty grudges and only wished to recover a valuable officer for his country, finally forced an exchange in 1778 for General Prescott, unluckily enough. One English nobleman understood the situation correctly, and wrote to Germain that the capture was regrettable, and Lee "the worst present the Americans could receive."

on the same day Sullivan with the remnant of Lee's force, some 3000, and Gates with the other four northern regiments, about 1200, joined him. Both bodies, however, were largely a set of broken-down tatterdemalions, fitter for hospital than camp. Not long afterward came in a body of country militia, raised by Mifflin after a tour of great exertion.

For months Washington had been protesting energetically against the utterly inefficient, wasteful, and precarious system of enlisting troops for short terms, and making drafts of militia. There had been some 47,000 Continentals and 27,000 militia in the field during the year; yet rarely more than five or six thousand of both could be got together for any one operation. Even so, the commander never knew how many he could count on, and the ground was cut from under his feet. Then too the militia would not endure discipline, though as Washington said, an effective army must be "a perfect despotism"; and they infected the regulars with insubordination. As to the Continentals, their terms were forever expiring at the most fatal minute; and at best, their year was up and they left just as they were beginning to learn their duty.

The people rightly dreaded and abhorred a standing army, and had revolted largely because they would not have one quartered on them; and were unwilling to enlist for years together. Yet both dislikes must be overcome for the time, if they were to obtain what they revolted for. A

1776
Autumn

committee of Congress had visited Washington at Harlem Heights, and finally drawn up a plan partly after his ideas: a consolidated army of 66,000 men in battalions [1] of 750; enlisted in quotas by the States, armed and clothed and their battalion and company officers appointed by them, though paid and supplied at general charge. The

New army system

Canadian regiment organized at Montreal in November 1775 was to be kept up, recruited anywhere and managed at Congress's discretion; it was termed "Congress's Own." Enlistments were to be for the war, $20 bounty to each and 100 acres of land at the end, officers more land up to 500 for colonels. "For the war" was so indeterminate and daunting, however, that enlistments were scarce, and a three-years' term without land bounty was shortly allowed. National manufactories of arms and stores were established at Springfield, Massachusetts, and Carlisle, Pennsylvania.

It was hard to gain general consent to this scheme even on paper; and paper it mostly

Only paper

remained. With the thronging disasters and dying hopes of the cause, the offers were not enough, and the States began a competition in heavy extra bounties, while their own counties and

Ill-judged bounties

towns bid over them; a self-defeating policy, as possible recruits were inclined to wait and stand

---

[1] Instead of regiments; this to abolish the rank of "Colonel," which embarrassed the exchange of prisoners with the English—their colonels being great titular dignitaries who had nothing to do with the troops, while the lieutenant-colonel was the actual regimental commander.

out. Congress in turn offered $8 to each person obtaining a recruit.

On December 26 Congress extended Washington's dictatorship to six months: he might remove all officers below brigadier, fill all vacancies, impress supplies (on payment), and arrest for civil trial all persons disaffected or refusing to take Continental paper money. It validated his artillery contract, and on his urgent petitions increased the paper cavalry to 3000, voted an engineer corps, and authorized him to recruit *and officer* sixteen more battalions of infantry.[1] On this very day he had given a dazzling proof what glories he could win with any decent armament.

He had now nominally about 8900 Continentals besides the local militia, but actually not over 5700 such as they were; and even this petty force was on the verge of dissolution, and the American cause with it. The terms of Sullivan's and Gates' Eastern regiments would expire with the year, leaving perhaps 1500 national troops, with such short-term militia as might come and go; and with all heart and hope gone out of them, homesick, disgusted with their State officials' appointing and dismissing their officers for all reasons but merit, added to their hungry and shivering misery day and night, there was no re-enlisting the former. "These are the times that try men's souls,"

---

[1] The value of this, with his power of filling vacancies, was in partially undoing the serious mischief caused by the States insisting on their share of the army patronage, as they do now of civil patronage; which drove some of the best generals from the service, and contributed to Arnold's treason. He could bring in and retain good officers.

1776
Dec.

Thomas Paine had written on the 19th, in the first number of *The Crisis;* and it was only the greater souls that endured the trial. Washington saw that the one last hope of the cause was to shortly strike some brilliant blow and rehearten the fainting ones; and for a week he had had such a one in mind as soon as Lee's army reinforced him.

Last chance for liberty

The plan was based on the obvious fact that the German regulars cantoned along the Delaware were scattered loosely, not posted for co-operation; the presumptive one that they never dreamed of the wretched little American army striking back, and were careless as to guards; and when a time at last could be set, the probable one that all who were able would get drunk Christmas night. Washington would cross over with his army and break the lines by a night surprise, weaken them by a heavy loss, force them to fall back on New York, and call New Jersey to arms. Its patriot militia this time would surely flock to him under the new hope; and he knew that the outrages of marauding German troopers, veteran in having conquered districts at their mercy as well as in fighting, were turning even loyalty into deadly hate and vengefulness.[1] Washington with his

Plan for breaking British lines

Hope from hatred of Hessians

---

[1] We have already said that the American riff-raff were about as bad; but the ostensible patriots who called themselves "Skinners," and the ostensible Tories who called themselves "Cowboys," marauding in New York and New Jersey through the war, balanced each other in creating disgust for their respective causes. The old professionals of European free-quarters were the more thorough, the more dangerous to make defense against, and furnished a single object for hatred to fix on; hatred the more rancorous that their foreign speech placed them alike beyond appeal or common sympathies. They were

main body was to cross nine miles above Trenton, and before daybreak descend upon Rall. General James Ewing with a body of Pennsylvania militia was to cross a mile below Trenton, seize the bridge over Assanpink Creek, its southern boundary, and cut off retreat or reinforcements. Cadwalader and Reed in one place, Putnam in another, were to cross and assail Donop in front; Griffin, who was in his rear at Mount Holly with a few hundred men, was to join battle simultaneously; the whole attacking in as many places and creating as much confusion as might be, to crush the corps if possible, at all events spread a general alarm, and prevent reinforcing Rall. Gates, who had received a furlough as not well and anxious to lay some useful plans before Congress, was asked to save quarrels over rank at Bristol by taking command for the two or three days needed; but declined. He believed the scheme would

1776
Dec.

Plan of
the
Trenton
surprise

Gates
refuses
share

---

regarded, in fact, as the next thing to Indians. Hence they hurt the British cause far more than "patriot" atrocities did the American; and the offenses of British-born troops were lumped in as part of their charge. All the Howes' conciliation did not advantage their side a tenth as much as the "Hessians" harmed it. Miscellaneous plunder of friend and foe, wanton arson, sometimes violation, murder at will or suspicion, let loose among a hitherto free quiet unmolested people, were simple madness as methods of restoring loyalty. Even if there were but few cases of the worst of these things, that was enough to do the work of many in establishing a reign of terror. Yet the British officers, after a few weak efforts, left the troopers unrestrained at least from plunder—"it kept them from desertion," and "part of the Germans' understanding in hiring out was liberty to make their fortunes." The officers were of course authorized, like Washington on his side, to take from Tory or patriot all that the army needed, for pay: but they stretched it into a license to the soldiery for looting without pay, which made the Howes' "protection" a farce and the oath of loyalty useless forswearing; and Donop instructed his men to hang to the nearest tree every member of any band who fired on them.

1776
Dec. 25-6

British
loss at
Trenton

the 600 Hessian light-horse and infantry there fled to Bordentown and Donop's lines, but Rall's fleeing regiment was intercepted and captured. The British centre outpost was annihilated. The Americans had lost two killed, the British 18 with 78 wounded; but about 1000 were made prisoners, with six fine brass field-pieces, 1200 stand of arms, and quantities of ammunition and other stores— including warm clothing in which the ragged Continentals endued themselves.

Their
fright
and
panic

Washington at once recrossed the river with his spoil; he could have remained had he known the tremendous effect his smashing blow had produced, far exceeding his expectations. The size of his army was magnified by his enemies' terror to 5000, 10,000, even 15,000; the Germans were panic-stricken, and dared not remain with their scattered divisions so exposed. Donop's corps had been disposed of as effectively as if Cadwalader had succeeded, and with more surety and no loss, by a stratagem of Hannibalian skill. Griffin notified Cadwalader that he would achieve the essential aim by decoying Donop too far away to be of any service either in helping Rall or preventing

Griffin's
valuable
ruse

Cadwalader's crossing. He made a feint of attack about noon of the 25th, drew out nearly all Donop's force, slowly withdrew skirmishing till he had led them to Mount Holly, a day's march, then slipped away and left them to return at leisure.

Cadwalader on the 26th learned of the victory at Trenton, and spent till noon the next day in a new and successful effort to cross; then he learned that Washington had recrossed, and that he was himself at Donop's mercy. But he soon found that the Hessians, instead of pursuing the Americans, were fleeing from them in consternation. Donop, returning from his chase after Griffin, had heard the news of Trenton, and with his whole force had decamped in wild disorder from Burlington to Bordentown; gathered in the 1000 troops there including the Assanpink fugitives, but left all his stores and his sick and wounded, and started northward for Brunswick. He marched all night in his haste to escape, and sent one division to reinforce the battalion at Princeton and have redoubts thrown up at once. All lower New Jersey was abandoned.

Reed on learning this wrote forthwith to Washington urging him to return, cut off Donop before he gained Brunswick, and also the detachment at Princeton. Washington joyfully crossed a third time. The hardships of that dreadful night had disabled half his troops, including Stirling; many could not move till shoes, stockings, and breeches were furnished; but the victory had released the militia from guarding the Delaware, and some 3600 soon joined him, giving him towards 5000 men across the river. He occupied the heights about Trenton; wrote to McDougall and Maxwell at Morristown to gather and hold together all the militia possible until he could join them with regulars, harass the enemy if feasible, cut off convoys, etc.; and to Heath, on the point of receiving heavy New England reinforcements, to leave a small guard at

*1776
Dec.
26–31*

*Flight of
Hessians
after
Trenton*

*Washington
returns
to
Trenton*

**1776–7
Dec.–Jan.**

the Highlands, in no danger at this season, and march south by Hackensack till further orders.

With new hope from this splendid victory, implored by their officers, and promised the Pennsylvania militia bounty of $10 for six weeks' service ("extravagant," admitted Washington, "but what could be done?"), over half the Eastern troops agreed to stay for that time; but there was no public money left, and he, Stark, and other officers had to pledge their private fortunes for the pay, over $20,000. Even so, money for regular pay and for indispensable equipments and munitions was lacking; the bulk of new recruits brought no arms, and were useless save for the army stores. Washington appealed to Robert Morris, a great Philadelphia business man and patriot, who raised a loan of $50,000 on his own credit early New Year's morning and sent it on; only one of many like services he did for years, which absolutely saved the American cause from perishing.

Troops agree to stay a while

Robert Morris raises money

Howe meanwhile had been luxuriating at New York in a grand Christmas celebration of his being made K. C. B., and basking in a glory reflected also from Europe as having completely stamped out the war in a single season. Cornwallis had actually sent his luggage aboard ship to embark for England; but at this astounding blow,—5000 veteran regulars swept from the Delaware, and a fifth of them captured, at a single onslaught of "a ragged and undisciplined militia," and half the province to reconquer,—he was hurried to the front again. He collected at Princeton with its

Cornwallis to the front again

ROBERT MORRIS.

new earthworks the entire army not needed for garrison or guards, some 8000, while Howe with 1000 more prepared to follow; and on January 2 left three regiments and some cavalry there, and set out for Trenton. It was a slow and weary march over thawing muddy roads, while step by step his progress was stubbornly fought and delayed: by skirmishers at Maidenhead that made him leave a brigade behind to guard communications; by Hand's Virginia riflemen at Five Mile Run; by troops that lined the woods for a two-hours' march of torment at Shabbakonk Creek, three miles from Trenton; by 600 musketeers and a detachment of Greene's with two cannon a mile from the village. It was near sundown when his main body, somewhat over 5000, reached it.

Washington had withdrawn his army to the south bank of the Assanpink, with forty cannon planted to sweep the bridge we already know. Without delay, Cornwallis formed his men in solid column and attempted to carry it. Under the storm of missiles that mowed them down, they recoiled in disorder; again and again they advanced, only to be decimated, halt, and fall back. For so short a conflict their losses were terrible: "the Assanpink was nearly filled with dead bodies," says one. This second battle of Trenton had much greater importance than is given it in histories; it was a striking American victory, every repulse of the British greeted with shouts of exultation, and greatly encouraged the troops. How Cornwallis viewed it is shown by his action. Vastly

1777
Jan. 2

Cornwallis'
march to
Trenton

Repulsed
from Assanpink
bridge

Unrecognized
victory

1777
Jan. 2–3

Corn-
wallis
plans
"bag-
ging"
Wash-
ington

overrating the size of Washington's force, he sent
in hot haste for the Maidenhead brigade and two
of the three Princeton regiments, and camped well
out of range for the night; rejecting one officer's
advice to ford the stream at once and bring on a
general action, and another's to attack the camp
that night for fear the army might escape. "Let
the men rest," he said, "and we will bag the fox
in the morning." His plan was to force a passage
above the American position with part of his army,
inclose theirs between his two divisions, the creek,
and the Delaware, and compel a surrender.

Washington knew the odds against him, and
dared not risk them with his small raw army,
brave men and good officers and good gunners as
he had. He had a far better plan. Concentrating
Who
plans
counter-
stroke
the British forces against him must have stripped
their main interior posts, Princeton and Brunswick, of all but a moderate guard easily overwhelmed by his own force. Capturing them, especially the great Brunswick magazine, would not
only be a superb prize, but leave the British not
a foot of ground in the Jerseys west of Newark,
compelling them to begin the campaign again from
New York; while from the very strong central
position of Morristown Heights, his aim from the
first, he would make any fresh movement across
New Jersey most perilous. As to Gates' bogy
of their moving on Philadelphia, they were not
likely to do it with him in their rear and leave
New York for him to attack. The problem was
to slip away unnoticed.

A road led along the creek and swung around its head to Princeton, passing east of the British lines; he sent a scouting party to make sure it was unguarded. The roads were deep in the mire of several days' thaw, and artillery could hardly be moved over them; but at nightfall a cold north-wester sprang up and speedily froze them solid. The baggage was sent off to Burlington. To deceive the enemy, the camp-fires were kept blazing through the night, guards were noisily changed, and bodies of men were set throwing up intrenchments close to the creek, with plenty of talking. These parties joined the main body in the morning.

Washington started for Princeton about midnight, destroying the bridges as he went; reached its southeast outskirts near sunrise; moved around to the right over a by-road to gain unnoticed the college, in and about which the regiments were quartered, and sent Mercer with some 350 men to break down the Trenton-road bridge over Stony Brook. The two regiments ordered down by Cornwallis had started, and the first under Mawhood was already over the brook; noting in his rear the little American body, he recrossed, picked up part of the rear regiment, and joined battle. Each had two cannon; but the British had bayonets, the Americans almost none. After a short fierce engagement, Mawhood charged bayonet, and the Continentals fled. The chief officers, loth to share the flight and trying to rally them, suffered a dreadful loss of lives ill to spare—the noble Scotch general Hugh Mercer pierced with many

1777
Jan. 2–3

Washington slips away

Reaches Princeton

Rout of American detachment

1777
Jan. 3
bayonets, Haslet of the Delawares, Fleming of the Virginians, Neil at his battery.

But Washington at the sound had hurried to the scene with his forces, intercepting the rest of the second regiment. Mawhood charged the militia in front, they wavered, but Washington by reckless exposure steadied them; fresh troops outflanked the British, and they broke and fled up the brook, chased for miles toward Trenton and many captured. The intercepted companies, after a gallant fight, retreated with the unsummoned regiment to the college; but on artillery being trained upon it, the whole decamped across the fields toward Brunswick, numbers being cut off and taken. The British in an hour's conflict had lost some 200 killed and wounded and 230 prisoners; the Americans about 35.

Of all Washington's military movements, Princeton is supreme: the sagacity with which he guessed the chance, the skill, daring, swiftness, and success with which he marched unperceived around the British force and struck its rearguard into ruin, are incomparable. This blow wiped out the western guard of the crowning prize, the Brunswick magazine eighteen miles off. But the Americans, awake all night and some of them for two (having joined Washington by a night march), worn out, and largely barefoot, were simply incapable of that hard day's march with a battle at the end; and by the time they had rested enough to start again, Cornwallis was close upon them. Rising that morning to execute his grand

Victory
at Prince-
ton

Wash-
ington's
master-
piece

Could not
be fol-
lowed up

movement, to his amazement he found only a silent deserted camp; soon the sound of cannon toward Princeton told him where they had gone, and he saw instantly for what. In alarm for Brunswick, he started north with his whole force at once; and after a tedious march over the bottomless roads and the bridgeless streams swollen with wintry thaw, he reached Princeton just as Washington had left it. There was no object in reoccupying Princeton with the Delaware line abandoned, and with full force he hastened on to Brunswick.

1777
Jan. 3

Corn-
wallis'
fruitless
chase
after
Wash-
ington

Washington went on through Somerset and Pluckemin to Morristown; writing again to Heath on the 5th to move down toward New York, as a feint to make Howe deplete the Jerseys of troops. But on that very day, in pursuance of the former order, George Clinton and the New York brigade swooped on the British force at Hackensack, which only saved itself by precipitate flight, abandoning its baggage; Newark was given up. The same day the New Jersey militia routed an equal body of Hessians at Springfield, killing and wounding nine and taking 39 prisoners. Maxwell shortly surprised Elizabethtown and took 100 prisoners and valuable stores. Of all their New Jersey conquest clear to the Delaware, the British now held only Paulus Hook (Jersey City) and South Amboy on the bay, and Brunswick isolated but too strongly held to attack; and King's Bridge marked their limit up the Hudson.

New
Jersey
outposts
recon-
quered

British
almost
wholly
expelled

Washington established his headquarters at Morristown, and ordered Putnam's force up from

1777

**Rousing
the
Jerseys**

**Already
done by
Hessians**

**Who
begin
deserting**

**Tories
forced to
leave**

Philadelphia to occupy Princeton, planting cantonments between; on his left he extended them to
Heath at Peekskill. Recruiting took on fresh life
with the fresh hope. Now too Washington could
hope to arouse the Jerseymen; and he sent around
influential men to stir them to action. "If what
they have suffered does not arouse their resentment," he said, "they must not possess the feelings of humanity." But they scarcely needed the
hint. Now was seen the deadly blow the Hessians
had dealt, not at America but Great Britain: the
British had themselves almost destroyed the one
element that made holding down the province
possible. Patriots and old loyalists rose together,
formed military bands, and patrolled the country,
hanging marauders and savagely resisting the
bands impressing supplies; growing bolder, they
formed larger bodies, assailed straggling detachments of regulars, and cut off convoys. The
Brunswick guard were sometimes actually hungry.
The Germans began deserting, which was perfectly safe, as the British had no machinery to
discover or reclaim them; and Congress assisted
the process by a German proclamation offering
every deserter a land bounty—a document folded
into the wrappers of tobacco plugs.

Washington on the 25th ordered all persons
who had taken British protections to take an oath
of allegiance to the United States or retire within
the British lines; in the latter case their property
was confiscated, and they revenged themselves by
fitting out privateers and ravaging coast property.

A New Jersey delegate objected that there was no United States until a confederation was formed, and each State required allegiance to itself; but constitutional forms were very elastic just then.

What Howe had done before from political policy, he now did from military policy and genuine fear of his foe: he forbore to push the campaign. Washington was too strongly posted for a winter expedition among the hills; and he had shown that he was among the foremost generals of the world. Making all allowances for the essentially precarious British situation,—maintaining scattered out-stations against a mobile army with the whole Union for a field of supply and retreat, —Washington's achievement was a work of first-rate military genius. With the last dissolving scraps of a thoroughly beaten, discouraged, and wretchedly unprovided army, half naked in the dead of winter, within a fortnight he had crushed out two strong outposts and forced the abandonment of two more; won three victories; captured over 1500 British soldiers; recovered from the British practically all New Jersey, just overrun; and turned the scale of his country's destiny at the very crisis, by thus keeping the army from disbanding and the great half-hearted class from submitting. And he had done this by sheer force of those qualities that make up the great captain, not the mere guerrilla leader: strategic conception, tactical skill, an almost reckless adventurousness and dash with the most careful preparation and the wariest caution, tremendous energy and iron

1777

resolution; and above all a great, patient, steadfast, glowingly patriotic soul.

Too many of his countrymen were blind to this, but not all. "Washington is the greatest man on earth," wrote Robert Morris; and Hooper of North Carolina echoed it, saying truly "how often America has been rescued from ruin by the mere strength of his genius, conduct, and courage, encountering every obstacle that want of money, arms, and ammunition could throw in his way." Nor was the realization that a great new soldier had arisen confined to this country: it resounded through Europe, and was of infinite service to us. The King and his ministry were savage at the irreparable mischief. "All our hopes were blasted by the unhappy affair at Trenton," said Germain; and he characteristically wrote to the Howes that when the sixty days were over, they must not let the "undeserving" escape punishment. They asked in return if they were to withhold pardon even at the cost of prolonging the war. The Liberals—steadily and powerfully though vainly fighting the American cause in Parliament—were jubilant. "The American Fabius," military critics called Washington: absurdly enough, for Fabius did not outmanœuvre Hannibal, exterminate his outposts, and force him to fall back to the coast, all in a few days. Washington was as fierce a fighter as Condé when he had anything to fight with.

But its greatest effect was in France, where statesmen were burning with desire for revenge

Washington honored in America

In Europe

English Tory wrath

Liberal exultation

on England for the loss of Canada; and where the
reaction against a pampered aristocracy devouring
and degrading the people, and a church suppress-
ing free thought, had filled society with an enthusiastic movement for humanity and for freedom.
Now Louis XVI. was new to the throne and
was not without sympathy for his brother King.
His ministers, however, were eager to support
a promising chance of depriving England of
her colonies, though they would not risk open war
with her till the Americans showed themselves
efficient allies; and they forced the King's hand.
Especially Vergennes the wily foreign secretary,
of penetrating judgment and marvelous executive
ability,—of whom, when minister to Turkey, Louis
had said that if directed to send on the Sultan's
head, he would reply that it was a delicate and
difficult matter, but the head would arrive,—was
watching affairs with unsleeping vigilance.

Arthur Lee, Virginia's agent in London, soon
after the outbreak sounded the French ambassador
there. Vergennes welcomed the venture, and employed the famous Beaumarchais, creator of "Fi-
garo," to make arrangements; but Lee lacked
authority, and negotiations at arms' length were
too slow. The next spring Congress sent over as
authorized agent Silas Deane, a Connecticut ex-
merchant, who arrived in May. Beaumarchais
came to terms with him: an imaginary Hortales
& Co. were to ship, via the West Indies, arms from
the King's arsenals and other war-stores valued at
a million livres ($186,000), on pledge of Congress'

1775–6

French
sym-
pathy
with
America

Ver-
gennes

Arranges
loan

Beau-
marchais
and
Deane

1776

remitting tobacco and other articles in payment. Of the first three vessels so dispatched, two were captured by the British; the other helped equip the new regiments.

Another function of Deane's was less successful. Trained artillerists and engineers being scarce, he was to engage a few foreign ones; but he was beset by offers from sources whose influence he disliked to alienate, and sent over some fifty with assurances of rank and command which roused wild wrath among the American officers. The nomination of one, Du Coudray, as major-general commanding the artillery, made Greene, Sullivan, and Knox threaten to resign in a body if it were confirmed. Yet most of them were men of large real ability: among them a noble self-exiled Pole, Thaddeus Kosciuszko, afterwards his country's greatest hero, who was now made engineer for the northern department.

Deane's foreign officers

Du Coudray

Kosci- uszko

There were still more soaring ambitions, legitimately following from the same causes that gave Lee and Gates their worship even in America. The Duc de Broglie wanted to be civil and military dictator and savior of the country; but the price he asked was much too high, and we had too many would-be saviors who were apt to turn out mere traitors. But among the private adventurers were men of real nobility of character, anxious to help a brave people fighting for their liberty—and fighting an unloved country. Foremost among these was a boy of nineteen, Gilbert Motier, Marquis de Lafayette, heir of one of the greatest French houses.

Broglie

Lafayette

COUNT CASIMER PULASKI.

THADDEUS KOSCIUSZKO.

He fitted out and stored a ship at his own cost; left his luxurious existence and his beloved young wife; and despite the King's prohibition and a short imprisonment, sailed for America April 26 to offer his sword and purse to Washington, serving as a private without pay in the cause of freedom. With him came John Kalb, a German soldier of fortune in French service, but of the highest professional honor and excellent abilities; and eleven other French officers. Another disinterested recruit was Count Casimir Pulaski, an exiled Polish nobleman.

Just after the Declaration, Congress had voted secret negotiations for treaties of alliance and commerce with European countries; they proved mostly abortive. Deane was made a commissioner for the French treaty, to be joined by Lee; and in October Franklin was added. He reached Nantes December 7 on the *Reprisal,* first American warship to enter European waters, which captured two British prizes on the way; the British Tories thought and hoped he was fleeing his country, but others knew better. Stormont the British ambassador demanded of France the return of the prizes. Vergennes replied that England could not expect France to bear the burden of her wars; and to a complaint about the French volunteers for America, that Frenchmen liked adventure. Franklin, the typical republican philosopher and statesman, a picturesque and venerable figure of antique simplicity, yet of charming manners and converse and rich stores of thought, was received with an

1776–7

Lafayette

Kalb

Pulaski

European treaties sought

Stormont and Vergennes

Franklin

the British a mile of the sixty from the lake to Albany, except as won by fighting; it gave no one the command of the lake against a superior fleet. It was one of those ugly obstacles ruinous to leave and fruitless to take. Even so, it must be garrisoned and communications kept open by a line of detachments; which would weaken Burgoyne's moderate corps too much for effective use, though a trifle to the united army, first victorious. Sixty miles was no distance in Europe, over plenty of good roads, through countries rich with every supply: here for part of the way there was but one wretched road through unbroken swampy forest, the rest few and poor, the country almost empty of supplies and easily rendered wholly so. But this was not known; and had it been, surely English troops would find no difficulty in that short march. Burgoyne, despite the Boston proof that a collection of militia companies could paralyze a regular army, still despised the provincial forces to be overcome; and the dream of loyalists rising and flocking to him converted every deficit to an overplus. That skirting New England's flank involved the risk of attack by that flank was forgotten for the same reasons, and because the need of sending out flying corps was not foreboded.

Dullness and self-indulgence completed the disaster earned by ignorance, prejudice, visions, and ambitions. If the chances for accomplishing anything were imperiled by making three second-rate forces out of one invincible force, they would

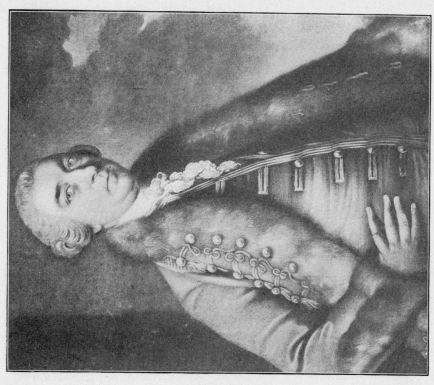

LORD GEORGE GERMAIN.

(From the Emmet Collection. New York Public Library.)

GENERAL JOHN BURGOYNE.

almost certainly be ruined by any of the three dropping out; and Germain should have seen that inflexible orders must be given to all. Such were given to Burgoyne for the Canada pair; but Howe, relied on as father of the plan, was left to his discretion. Even when he wrote that he had another in mind, Germain only "trusted" it would not interfere with this; finally dictated a positive order, but would not postpone departure for the country half an hour to have it copied and sign it; and on his return, incredible as it seems, forgot the whole business—which shows that he had been merely countersigning other men's ideas, but does him no more credit. George III. would have remained in town the whole summer first, and would not have forgotten the fate of his armies.

The American cause too was deeply affected by personal issues. One skein of them lifted an incapable officer into power of bringing on a dreadful disaster, helped to incense a very great one into treason, and later threatened to displace our greatest and most indispensable one.

The feud of New England against Schuyler, partly from interest and partly from manners, has been noted; it aided in making him the scapegoat of the public irritation over the Canada failure,—laid to his slackness in supporting the armies there,—and was secretly envenomed by Gates for reasons before given. A regular set was made upon him, by direct charge and insinuation, so persistent and virulent that at last he resigned all his public trusts and demanded a court of

1777

Germain's orders to Howe

Lazy dullness

Gates, Arnold, Washington

The Schuyler feud

1777

inquiry. Congress, by a handsome official letter of Hancock's, refused to accept the resignation, and he withdrew it.

Gates

Gates was much disappointed. He was not without abilities, though not eminent either for courage, energy, decision, or military judgment; nor without good feeling when his advancement was not involved. But he was inordinately conceited, small-souled, and purely self-seeking; considered any appointment below the highest grade an affront; and throughout made underhand war on Schuyler, Washington, Arnold, Morgan, Greene, and every other officer who stood in his way. He was now bent on gaining Schuyler's place, acting independently of Washington, and being really his superior and conducting the war. He refused as before mentioned to share the Trenton surprise, and spent the next two months besieging members of Congress: championing the New England side as to Vermont,[1] asserting that he had commanded at Ticonderoga and prevented Carleton joining Howe, and disparaging Schuyler, a member but absent. The latter played into his hands by a tart letter to Congress complaining of

Present purposes

Action

---

[1] This controversy is persistently misunderstood and misstated. The Green Mountain Boys were not fighting over a question of jurisdiction, but of property. New York insisted on ousting the Vermont settlers or making them buy their properties over again: the settlers—predominantly from Connecticut, also from Massachusetts and New Hampshire—believed it was because the governing ring, having taken for themselves all the best available lands of that colony, wished to utilize those of the New Hampshire Grants in rewarding their henchmen. This, not abstract New-Englandism, was why the New York surveyors were driven out and marked with the "beech seal." Gates is entitled to the credit of being on the right side, but not probably to that of a disinterested passion for justice.

its action. The majority, perhaps not sorry for an excuse,—for New England's enmity prejudiced the public service by withholding both help and obedience, and its members formed much of Congress' vital energy,—took offense, demanded an apology, and without consulting Washington sent Gates in February to command at Ticonderoga: the most important post in America, he styled it.

Gates at once showed his hand in full. He left a plan for the disposition of all the American armies in the coming campaign; made requisitions for troops direct to Congress, "the common parent of all the American armies," instead of Washington, and was backed by it; wrote braggingly to Congress that Ticonderoga might be accounted secure—which merely meant confidence in their honoring his requisitions, but confirmed them in a mischievous delusion;[1] and proposed to give Schuyler a minor appointment. Schuyler in April found the position intolerable; resumed his seat in Congress; and with difficulty regained his headship May 22, on his pledge that Ticonderoga should be held. Gates was still to retain his active command there. As it turned out, Schuyler's worst enemy could not have wished him worse or Gates better; but Gates was furious with disappointment at the bursting of his bubble. He reported to Schuyler June 4, but five days later

1777
Feb.-June

Gates supersedes Schuyler

Is puffed to bursting

Schuyler reinstated

Gates' rage

---

[1] On May 30 he wrote to Washington for Congress that the numbers were "shamefully deficient," and notified the Massachusetts government that "not a moment was to be lost" in hurrying up more men; but this was taken as "business" to get all he could, and the impression of his confidence remained.

got leave of absence and flew to Congress again; where he made such a scene that he had to be ejected, but his "influence" prevented its harming him. June 5, Schuyler sent Arthur St. Clair to take his place.

Arnold had been much worse treated than Schuyler, as having tangibly earned more. He **Arnold** was senior brigadier, and on his record was far the most brilliant general in the army next to Washington, and certainly the most famous; surpassing even him in being a naval hero as well. The wilderness march, the storm of Quebec, the battle of Lake Champlain, formed a then unique body of achievements. On February 19 Congress appointed Stirling, Mifflin, St. Clair, Stephen, and Lincoln major-generals over his head; good offi- **Passed over** cers, but all five, on the facts then or now, far from making up an Arnold. Washington was astounded and incredulous; the newspapers said Arnold had had a prior appointment, and he thought it must be this or a technical blunder. He begged Arnold to wait till he investigated, before acting hastily. Arnold was cut to the heart and proposed to resign at once.

The explanation was the old one of the States demanding their share of the "patronage": offi- **Alleged reason** cers were henceforth to be assigned to the States according to the number of troops they furnished; Connecticut had two major-generals already (Putnam and Spencer), and the others would allow her no more. This was doubtless a real and powerful reason (Lincoln had been raised from the militia over the heads of all the regular brigadiers, to please Massachusetts); but it might not have ruled against such glorious deeds, had there not been others or excuses. One was a charge that he had misappropriated goods under guise of impressment at Montreal. This was in fact pure revenge from an officer whom he had accused of looting British officers' baggage, and who was refused a committee of inquiry by every official who looked into it, and by a Congressional committee. The Board of War later denounced his charges against Arnold as "cruel and groundless aspersions"; but while pending, they were a grateful pretext for the feud already begun by the Ticonderoga quarrels, wherein also this officer was a chief. It was further deepened by Arnold's warm and open championship of Schuyler, which in addition drew the lightning of Gates' rancor upon him, as Washington's esteem did Gates' jealousy; and not helped by the proud unconciliatory temper which so often goes with a vehement generous spirit and consciousness of large abilities and lofty aims. Schuyler was of the same breed.

Arnold accepted the official reason with the self-restraint and magnanimity he showed so often afterward, and withdrew his resignation for his country's sake. The same day he was thus passed over, Stark was so too in the list of new brigadiers (as insubordinate), and at once left the service.

Howe, waiting for reinforcements and then for developments hereafter noted, employed himself meantime in clearing his neighborhood. On

Marginal notes:

1777

Reasons for Arnold's treatment

Unjust charges

Further reasons

Arnold remains, Stark resigns

1777
March-
April

Howe's
minor
move-
ments

March 23 he sacked the magazines at Peekskill, the lowest American post on the Hudson. On April 13 Cornwallis surprised and cut up Lincoln near Brunswick. On April 23 Howe sent Tryon with 2000 men to destroy a large magazine at Danbury, near the western border of Connecticut.

Tryon, going by the Sound and overland from between Fairfield and Norwalk, on the 26th and that night burnt not only the stores but the town, after the amiable habit of royal ex-governors. By

Tryon's
retreat
from
Danbury

this time Silliman from Fairfield with 500 militia was upon his track; soon joined by Wooster and Arnold (visiting his family in New Haven) with 100 or so ex-Continentals picked up on the road. The troops divided: Wooster to assail Tryon's rear, in doing which the old hero was mortally wounded but his men took forty prisoners; Arnold and Silliman to cut off Tryon's retreat through Ridgefield, gaining more recruits as they went. With a quarter of the British force, Arnold

Arnold
fights
him at
Ridge-
field

blocked their march for some time along a barri-caded ledge-road, till outflanked, his horse killed under him by nine bullets at once, and he escaping capture or death by marvelous readiness and bravery. Their next day's march—in which Tryon burnt the houses and village-clusters on his way—was like another Lexington retreat; and was again barred by Arnold at the Saugatuck

At the
Sauga-
tuck

bridge. They evaded him by fording the stream, driving off a troop of militia; but with three cannon on their flank, the Americans forced them to a halt and a sharp combat, completely broke

In CONGRESS.

The DELEGATES of the UNITED STATES of *New-Hampshire, Massachusetts-Bay, Rhode-Island, Connecticut, New-York, New-Jersey, Pennsylvania, Delaware, Maryland, Virginia, North-Carolina, South-Carolina, and Georgia,* TO

Benedict Arnold Esquire

WE, reposing especial Trust and Confidence in your Patriotism, Valour, Conduct and Fidelity, DO, by these Presents, constitute and appoint you to be — — — —

Major General

in the Army of the United States, raised for the Defence of American Liberty, and for repelling every hostile Invasion thereof. You are therefore carefully and diligently to discharge the Duty of *Major General* by doing and performing all manner of Things thereunto belonging. And we do strictly charge and require all Officers and Soldiers under your Command, to be obedient to your Orders as *Major General.* And you are to observe and follow such Orders and Directions from Time to Time, as you shall receive from this or a future Congress of the United States, or Committee of Congress, for that Purpose appointed, or Commander in Chief for the Time being of the Army of the United States, or any other your superior Officer, according to the Rules and Discipline of War, in Pursuance of the Trust reposed in you. This Commission to continue in Force until revoked by this or a future Congress.

DATED at *Philadelphia May 2d 1777*

By Order of the CONGRESS,

John Hancock

PRESIDENT.

ATTEST. *Cha. Thomson secy*

BENEDICT ARNOLD'S COMMISSION AS MAJOR-
GENERAL.

them, and would probably have captured the whole flying rout had not a body of marines landed from the fleet. Arnold had a second horse shot under him and his collar shot through. The British lost about 300 in the expedition, the Americans 100.[1]

1777
April-
July

Tryon's
rout

The country rang with Arnold's exploits, and Congress was fairly shamed into some amends. They appointed him a major-general, presented him a caparisoned horse, and hurried up the dragging Montreal investigation to a swift decision that the charges were sheer malice. Still they would not restore him his seniority of rank. Washington asked him to take command at Peekskill; he declined in order to ask Congress to do him justice, and to audit his claims, he having sacrificed much of his own fortune and strained his credit in supplying the Canadian army's necessities. Congress was inexorable on the first, but referred the second to a committee, which did not report.

Arnold
and
Congress

Arnold in June was made commander of the force at Philadelphia to ward off an expected attack of Howe, which did not come. On July 10, his patience worn out with injustice, he sent in his resignation to Congress; but the same day it received a letter from Washington announcing Burgoyne's advance, from Ticonderoga toward the Hudson, and asking in strong terms to have Arnold sent on to lead and animate the militia.

Sends in
resig-
nation

---

[1] A month later Return Jonathan Meigs played a very brilliant return game for this; destroying a large British magazine at Sag Harbor, with a dozen or more merchant vessels at the wharf, and capturing the entire garrison of ninety men.

1777

Arnold's fine spirit

Arnold was sensitive to Washington's high esteem, burning with patriotic zeal, and eager for warfare; he not only suspended his resignation, but with rare generosity offered to serve under his juniors, trusting to the future to gain his rights.

Ticonderoga at once overrated and neglected

The Americans overestimated Ticonderoga's importance as much as the British, but universally believed the rumored movement against it a feint: Schuyler thought, to mask a New England campaign in concert with a New York force up from the coast;[1] Washington and Congress, to divert troops from the defense of Philadelphia. Burgoyne's probable force was also persistently underrated: Washington was sure it could not be over 5000. Hence, though public opinion was hysterically determined on the retention of the post, all effort was directed to other quarters, themselves needing more of everything than they could have; and it was left half naked. It had two or three miles of lines, besides Mount Independence south across the lake narrows; and the fall before, every competent officer there had

Great force needed

estimated ten or twelve thousand men as the minimum for holding it. On June 12 St. Clair found it manned by 2200 or so, several hundred being militia constantly dropping out; miserably ill equipped and supplied, and too short of pro-

Not furnished

visions to allow the calling in of reinforcements; at best not enough to man half the works, so that

---

[1] Germain really had told the Howes that the King wished all the New England ports occupied *or destroyed*, but they declined to take the hint.

in a siege all must be on duty day and night, and soon worn out if not earlier overpowered.

1777
June

In a word, the place was a mere trap if invested; the persistent American hope was a frontal assault, but the British had learned common-sense. Abandoning the north side and concentrating on Mount Independence would increase the fighting chance but not the food; even so, Schuyler and St. Clair dared not do it till forced, in fear of censure and reverse orders from the Board of War, which had laid out new works to hold the former. Schuyler hurried up some provisions and other supplies, mechanics to strengthen the works, and militia to make good the withdrawals; but on the 20th, a council of war headed by him voted to evacuate altogether if supplies could not be greatly augmented. He had been so galled with sneers as white-livered that he did not report these facts to Washington or Congress, who were led to believe that the garrison equaled Burgoyne's force and was competent to hold out.[1]

Embar-
rass-
ments at
Ticonde-
roga

The key to the whole situation was Sugar Loaf Hill 1400 yards south across the Lake George outlet, 600 feet high and absolutely commanding both forts and the lake around; and Gates' adjutant John Trumbull the fall before had urged its sole occupation, abandoning the others. A few hundred men with moderate supplies, both to be had,

Com-
manded
by Sugar
Loaf Hill

---

[1] It is fair to remember that till Burgoyne's very arrival, even the commanders on the spot believed that Ticonderoga was not his objective, and they would not have to justify their statements. The scouts sent out to gain information as to his march were slain by the Indians or could learn nothing.

**1777
June**

in place of 10,000 and huge stores not to be, could hold it and detain a considerable hostile force [1] till a relieving army came up; and the enemy's

**Sugar
Loaf Hill**

seizing it would make the others untenable. Gates scouted the idea—the hill was too steep to haul artillery up, and too far off to be dangerous; though Trumbull, Arnold, and Wayne disproved both. Trumbull laid the plan also before Schuyler and the Board of War, but both accepted

**Relocating
Ticonderoga disfavored**

Gates' judgment as an expert professional and paid no attention to it. St. Clair could not have adopted it without their permission; and to occupy all three posts with his handful of men would only be consigning the other two to destruction.

Burgoyne, leaving some 3750 regulars with the chagrined and recriminatory Carleton, set out from St. John's on June 15 with about 7500 troops

**Burgoyne's
force**

(including 148 Canadian militia), three of the best generals in Europe,—the Highlander Simon Fraser heading the British regulars, William Phillips the artillery, and Baron Riedesel the 3116 Germans, three-fourths Brunswickers,—and lesser officers of distinction; a superb artillery train of 142 guns; and an interminable supply train swollen by the officers' vast extra baggage, their wives coming with them as on a picnic. To one of these, the brave, generous, and accomplished

**Madame
Riedesel**

Madame Riedesel, we owe a charmingly vivid account of many personal details of the campaign.

---

[1] Of course if the 10,000 could be had, it would be better to occupy this and the old lines too, as detaining the whole of any British invading army instead of a corps. But even the latter would cripple it. In any event this spot was foremost and vital.

On the way some 400 Canadian Indians— Iroquois, Ottawas, Algonquins, and Abenakis— joined, and shortly began to bring in a harvest of miscellaneous scalps. This troubled Burgoyne, who was a humane man and had flattered himself with restraining them to civilized methods. At the falls of the Bouquet near the west shore of the lake, where he remained a week assembling the forces, on the 21st he held a "congress" of them and made a high-flown speech; including an injunction under penalty not to kill non-combatants or scalp any but the dead, with the lure of a reward for living prisoners. They sardonically agreed. At Crown Point he halted three days to establish magazines and let the rear come up, leaving 200 men for a guard. Thence he issued a grandiose proclamation to the Americans, menacing the "hardened enemies of Great Britain" with the extreme of Indian vengeance if they held out.[1] About 100 Tories came in during the month, in place of the thousands he had counted on.

On the 1st of July his forces encamped before the twin American posts, connected by a bridge and having the channel barred by a boom and a colossal chain; by the 4th Ticonderoga was wholly cut off, and Mount Independence all but the neck

1777
June-
July

Burgoyne's
Indians
begin
slaughter

He has
them
promise
humanity

Threatens Americans
with
their
inhumanity

Invests
Ticonderoga

---

[1] He was constantly exploiting this threat to terrorize the patriots, and deeply outraged when charged with meaning it or helping to carry it out. British border commanders were always between the devil of ministerial orders, and the deep sea of the suicidal Indian ferocity, rapacity, and instability. They also valued the real Indian services as scouts and guides, till they proved dearly bought.

picked up on the road,—about 1000 nominal
effectives, but many too sick for service,—halted
for the night at Hubbardton six miles back; contrary to St. Clair's orders, but probably from
inability to march all night. About five the next
morning, Fraser—who had saved his men's legs
by sailing up East Bay, and been guided to the
camp by a local Tory—was upon them. Hale's
regiment, many of them invalids, broke and ran
almost at once with their sick colonel; cut off
on the Castleton road by an equal detachment
sent around by Fraser, they surrendered. The
others not only held their own against this much
superior British force, but inflicted such tremendous loss—161, near a fifth—that Fraser was
falling back, when Riedesel came up and overwhelmed the Americans (two of St. Clair's militia

regiments camped within a couple of miles defying his orders to reinforce them). The Germans
lost 22 men, but Francis was killed and the patriots routed, some 200 being taken prisoners.

Most of the militia went home; a couple of
hundred and of Continentals straggled to Rutland

ten or twelve miles east, whither St. Clair had proceeded on hearing of the fall of Skenesborough.
Warner was sent to Manchester twenty-two miles
north of Bennington to enlist a fresh force. But
the British feared to provoke any more such

battles away from their main body, and on the
12th St. Clair managed with 1500 men to reach
Fort Edward on the Hudson, where the whole
northern army was now gathered. Schuyler was

doing all that incessant labor and energy could
do to raise the country and provide men, arms,
munitions, and food; but that was a work of time,
and the first numbered barely 4500, dreadfully
lacking in all the rest.

An uproar of disappointment, fear, and rage
greeted this abandonment of the "key" of the
north "without a blow," and post after post with
it, though in fact some hard blows had been given.
The country had been steeped in the idea that
the loss of this key would leave the house open
and defenseless. It had been kept in a fools'-
paradise partly by hopes it left to execute themselves; in part by optimistic assurances, based
on men and supplies hoped for and an attack
hoped against, from commanders afraid of being
accused of panic and displaced if they harped on
the cold truth. And it was right in feeling that we
must make the British earn their way by inches
in stubborn fighting; but not at the cost of losing the whole army, as to which the commander
must judge. Washington had suffered from that
impatient ignorance. In its wrath, Congress
(whose Board of War was supreme culprit in
retaining the works at an untenable spot) ordered
all the northern generals recalled and court-martialed; but Washington induced saner counsels,
though sharing the sentiment with more balance.[1]

*1777
July*

*Public
rage over
Ticonde-
roga*

*Action of
Congress*

---

[1] He insisted, however, that St. Clair ought to retire and ask for a
court of inquiry. He was misled by the unhandsome conduct of
Schuyler (perhaps the sole occasion with that high-minded gentleman),
who was nervously afraid of a fresh onslaught, hastened to deny having ever suggested the evacuation, and wrote to the New York Council

1777
July

Bur-
goyne's
army
depleted

And ob-
structed

There was some further loss in store, and
more fright and anger; but in fact the fatal process of attrition had begun for the British. Burgoyne asked Carleton to garrison Ticonderoga
with some of his reserves; Carleton refused as
commanding only *in Canada*,[1] and Burgoyne had
to "drain the life-blood of his army" for a garrison (910). While he halted three weeks at Skenesborough to regather his army and supplies,
Schuyler heaped obstacles on the path to Fort
Edward and drove off all the stock. The navigation of Wood Creek was blocked up; every defile
on the road from Fort Anne was turned into a
chevaux-de-frise of felled trees with interlocked
branches; the forty or fifty bridges and the log
causeways over the huge swamps, one of them two
miles long, were all broken down or up; the creek
channels were choked with stumps and stones,

---

that St. Clair had 5000 men in the fort. Schuyler wronged his better
nature for nothing: a few weeks later he lost the command in spite
of it. St. Clair like a man took on himself the sole responsibility,
echoed Schuyler's disclaimer emphatically in every quarter as if
Schuyler's reputation were the dearest thing in the world to him, and
never once cited the council of war of June 20. At the same time he
firmly declared that he had done only the right thing; and the court
next year could but coincide. We have shown that the primary causes
of the disaster were no one's fault,—incredulity of attack till too late
to furnish help in time, and misconception of the help needed (partly
from the commanders' politic cheerfulness); the secondary but equally
vital, Gates' indolent conceit of his own judgment which led to keeping the works in a place at the enemy's mercy. It is one of the usual
ironies, that the one man personally to blame was not only unblamed,
but glorified and made supreme for having been sure to prevent it if
present; and the scapegoats were the ones who had saved the northern
army from going with the fort.

[1] He was left in command of his province, Burgoyne being commander-in-chief of the expeditionary army as soon as it crossed the
border.

and the waters thus overflowed upon the clayey paths.

1777
July

Seemingly this ought to have given the British hard fighting as well as slow marching and fatigue work: Arnold having now joined Schuyler and been placed in command of the half of his force next the enemy, it was certainly not possible or it would have been done, but we can only guess at the reason. Nervous terror of the Indians who filled the forest, among troops unused to fighting them, was pretty certainly the chief one: mere prowling bands created a panic more than once, and Schuyler begged Washington for a reinforcement of Indian-fighters as a prime necessity. At any rate, he evacuated Fort Edward and fell south a short distance to Moses' Kill before Burgoyne started from Skenesborough (23d), neither the British sappers remaking the road nor the troops on the march being resisted by other foes than the still terrible mosquitoes.

Dread of
Indians

Hasty
American
retreat

Fort Edward was another of those colonial posts within artillery range of higher ground, quite good against Indians for whom they were built, but not against civilized forces with siege guns: the public naturally wondered why the fact was never found out till the enemy came too near for change. We have seen why: with the chief one, lazy conceit of a trusted expert; the others had never been expected to come in play, and money and time were needed for more exigent things than fortifying new sites on chances. But there was a renewed outcry of indignation and

Fort
Edward

Why
colonial
forts
were
retained

dismay:[1] Congress lost all patience, recalled St. Clair and Schuyler and asked Washington to choose Schuyler's successor, but privately making it plain that it must be Gates. Washington declined the invidious task, and Congress on the 4th appointed Gates: it had practically no choice,[2] but the action was fertile in mischief without compensations. His real qualities added nothing to the army's strength; his imagined ones earlier might have encouraged soldiers and people, but when he reached his post the whole danger was over,—St. Leger's force dispersed, Burgoyne crippled by a tremendous blow from New England and seeing ruin either in advance or retreat.

Schuyler fell back from Moses' Kill to Fort Miller, then to Stillwater, twenty miles above Albany; writing hopelessly of the prospect of finding a defensible spot or keeping Burgoyne

Margin notes:

1777
July 30–
Aug.

Gates to
succeed
Schuyler

Too late
for use

Schuyler
contin-
ues to
fall back

---

[1] Neither one so senselessly unreasonable, on the facts then before the public, as is currently assumed. They had not Burgoyne's surrender to assure them of ultimately foiling his expedition, as we have; and their censure was as much for letting the enemy reach Fort Edward unscathed as for not standing a siege in Fort Edward. Indeed, but for the facts above, it would still be almost incredible that not a moment's stand was made in these pathless swampy forests, across these ruined causeways, and behind these tree screens easily turned into log ramparts, by one of the most daring fighters that ever lived, with a matchless power of making men fight and die under him. Schuyler was held responsible as commander, but we cannot ignore Arnold's presence leading the van.

[2] Lee was in captivity, Arnold not acceptable to the New England political leaders, and no one else had a large enough national reputation to make the public easy in mind. We constantly do injustice to both Congress and its constituents in forgetting that they were not prophets, and could only appraise officers on the knowledge they had, not on what we know and they did not. As to Washington, he had taken Gates' measure, but could not refuse to appoint him without affronting indispensable support.

from reaching Albany, and despondently of his troops. Few were coming in and many were deserting. Half the Massachusetts men insisted on going home for the harvest, and the rest were to follow in three weeks—he candidly acknowledged later that unwillingness to serve under him was a principal motive; and he and the New York civil authorities poured appeals on Washington for Continentals in their place. Washington had already sent Arnold, a corps in himself, Lincoln, a great Massachusetts favorite, and a brigade from Peekskill; he now sent north from his own army, needing all its strength for Howe, another brigade and Morgan's superb battalion of 500 riflemen,—the latter to fight the dreaded Indians in their own style.

But Burgoyne was not advancing: only after a fortnight (August 13) did he move his headquarters to Fort Miller a few miles south. He was facing for the first time the realities of his campaign, and the just retribution—which ought to have been foreseen—of the Indian alliance. The country was not loyal, save in small numbers and still less stomach for fight. To make it less so, the savages spread far in front and on his flanks, murdering indiscriminately not only age and sex, but patriot or Tory. Whether or no the Bouquet River conferees kept within bounds, a still unrulier body came in at Skenesborough: a mixed band of Western Indians, including the ferocious Wyandots and more of the fierce Ottawas. The whole were under command of two famous

1777
Aug.

Massa-
chusetts
troops
will not
stay

Wash-
ington
rein-
forces
Schuyler

Bur-
goyne
stalled

Largely
by Indian
outrages

1777
July-
Aug.

New
bands
worse
than old

partisan leaders, the Canadian La Corne de St.
Luc, and the half-breed Charles de Langlade who
had led the Indians at Braddock's destruction; the
pair were emphatic that the Indians must have
their own license or they would not stay, and
scorned Burgoyne ever afterward as slow-witted
for lack of cordiality and aid toward them. New
or old, plenty of them cared more for blood,
Indian glory, and finery, than gain: took scalps
where they could find them, the more greedily if

Indian
ravage

the victims had handsome clothes, and the British
commanders were reluctantly forced to turn a
blind eye.[1]

Jenny
McCrea's
murder

One special incident carried a burning realization of the Indian horrors far and wide, and
brought to a head the revengeful bitterness over
them, greatly spurring on the New England rising
against Burgoyne.[2] It is part of the just Nemesis
of wrong that it was less atrocious than other
deeds they were committing every day; but the
charm of the victim made it spread like wildfire,
and it became the theme of all Northern firesides,

---

[1]When an Indian band slaughtered an entire loyalist family, just
before Jenny McCrea's murder, Fraser told complainants that "this
was a conquered country and we must wink at these things." Com-
pare the license given to the Hessians (note, pages 2538–9). The methods brought their own retribution: using the implements of "God and
nature" in defiance of the laws of God consolidated American hatred
by the laws of nature.

[2]But we must not follow the absurd exaggeration of the histories,
in the cause of romance: Bennington would have been fought and
Burgoyne overwhelmed had the tragedy never happened. The Americans would not have let their country be conquered supinely but for
the chance of an Indian murder; nor even let Bennington be sacked
any more than Concord. It merely made Bennington perhaps a more
crushing victory and hastened the end.

needing no embellishment to make it a type of pity and horror.

1777
July
23-26

At Fort Edward lived a loyalist Scotch widow, Mrs. McNeil, claiming kinship with Fraser; and not far away the Scotch patriot John McCrea, whose beautiful sister Jane was betrothed to the loyalist David Jones of the same place. Jones became a lieutenant under Fraser; McCrea a colonel under Arnold, and on the retreat proposed to take his sister along. As this would separate the lovers indefinitely, and from McCrea's hatred of Tories perhaps forever, Jones persuaded her to make Mrs. McNeil an ostensible farewell visit, then slip away to the British lines a few miles off and have the chaplain marry them. Her brother sent a bateau with an escort of soldiers to bring her and the family effects down the river on the 26th; instead she gave her friend the slip and started Burgoyneward. Just then the escort and a few of the small American garrison left at the fort to repress Indian raids, scouting in the same direction, were attacked and several killed by a Winnebago band; who, pursuing the rest, espied her wedding bravery as she saw the chase and fled back in terror, followed her, broke in, and carried off both women. The fugitive soldiers aroused the remaining garrison, and a party gave chase. The women became separated. Mrs. McNeil, her captors richer by her clothes and the reward, was shown at the camp a scalp brought in by the Winnebago chief, Le Loup, which she knew to be Jenny's from the superb lustrous raven hair that had

Marginal notes:

Jenny McCrea and her family

She starts off to be married

Abducted

Scalp brought in

1777

Jenny
McCrea:
facts of
her death

Results

reached the floor. He declared that the pursuing soldiers' bullets had killed her; which was plausible, as her death lost him the reward, and she was found pierced with three bullets and not tomahawked. But Burgoyne, horrified and with no faith in Indians, at once investigated, and found that Jones had sent an Indian party under the half-breed Duluth to act as invisible guardians; that Duluth had claimed her custody from Le Loup, and the latter, furious at losing both clothes and reward, had shot her—apparently while she had seized the opportunity to attempt escaping, which accounts for the three shots. Burgoyne would have hanged Le Loup, but dared not; and the name of Jenny McCrea became a battlecry throughout the North.[1]

---

[1] This summary, drawn from a careful analysis of the varied and clashing evidence, more closely reconciles all the best accredited facts, on the whole, than any other yet given. It will be seen that the popular story, usually sneered at as a "legend" or "myth," is in essentials the exact truth; in fact, it follows Burgoyne's own account in answering a letter of accusation from Gates, except for two variations, both for intelligible reasons. He makes Jones send after her for her safety, not marriage, as being a less selfish motive; and makes the quarrel as between two Indian escorts, to suppress the abduction by his Indian allies. The one irreconcilable contradiction is that Jones is said to have denied sending after her; if so, it was to disclaim agency in bringing about her death,—which wrecked his life thereafter,— since Burgoyne's story learned from himself leaves no doubt of it. For obvious reasons, both he and Duluth were anxious to conceal the facts.

There are various minor contradictions which will never be harmonized, because they rest on stories of "old residents," each anxious to stand in the foreground as witnesses and father some novel point. Mrs. McNeil herself, the chief source of information, told stories for many years constantly growing more divergent from the earlier ones; and she was an inventive braggart by nature. Her Indian murderer was a Wyandot chief, "The Panther," not the Winnebago "Wolf." The point is of no consequence. More material is the fact that two

A more immediate result of the whole Indian business was, that to Burgoyne's naïve surprise the terrified inhabitants fled the district, taking their live stock and food stores with them; it grew hard to find daily rations, and a large quantity of provisions he had swept up from around Lake George lay at Fort George, because he could not find draft cattle to bring them the eighteen miles to Fort Edward. After a fortnight's time there were only four days' rations ahead; he had not oxen or horses to draw the 42 cannon he had retained of his 142, and could not mount his 500 German dragoons, 1500 horses ordered in Canada

1777
July-
Aug.

Bur-
goyne's
army in
straits

---

medical witnesses testify to have found Jane's skull smashed in, on removing her body many years later; but as those who buried her testify to the reverse, they must have preference. Another "old resident" *saw* her tomahawked and scalped, the Indians probably inviting him to be present at the ceremony. Still another heard shots and saw her fall from her horse on the hill over which the Indians were pursued, the quarrel over custody apparently taking place in full flight and without checking it. The accidental shooting is of course out of court: Burgoyne would have been delighted to rebut accusations with it. The one vital circumstance after all is that she was murdered, with many other innocent non-combatants, through the British letting loose ungovernable savages on civilized districts.

Burgoyne was told by St. Luc that all his Indians would leave him if he punished the murderer, and he dared not risk reporting the cause to the ministry. He asserted later that after this he enforced so much more severe restrictions on them, refusing to let them go on expeditions without a British officer in company, that in a day or two they all left him. Then how did they come to be vigorously bringing in scalps a week later, and where did the hundred at Bennington come from? Quite likely he did try to tighten the screws; and their individual desertions, tired of the service and of him and his complaints and coldness and grudgingness, may have been quickened by it. But in the main it is the romance of an honorable and kindly man ashamed of his unclean hands. His own reports, and his and St. Luc's recriminations later, are decisive that the Indians did not desert heavily till after Bennington, and these restrictions are not mentioned even as a contributory cause.

having for some reason been driven by land along the lake border and never arrived.

Meantime the other expeditions were even less in train to reach Albany. Howe was not trying, but unknown to Burgoyne was off to take the middle colonies in the rear from Maryland; and St. Leger [1] was stalled in the valley a hundred miles away.

St. Leger's white force was about 300 British and German regulars, 300 Tories (Johnson's "Royal Greens" [2] and another corps), and some 75 Canadian militia; with fourteen small pieces of artillery. Its farcical pettiness for such an expedition, with the inevitable frittering away by maintaining communications and by sickness and casualty, shows on its face that it was meant only for a nucleus: Indians and Tories were to complete it—indeed, Indian terrorism and Tory good-will were to obviate all necessity for serious fighting. The gross over-valuation of both elements is characteristic of Burgoyne's entire campaign of dreams.

Tryon County (everything in this region from the Johnson estates around the present Johnstown west) was taken as sure in advance, through the immense Johnson influence. Plausible as this

Marginal notes: Howe and St. Leger / St. Leger's force / Indian-Tory dream

---

[1] He was an Englishman of Huguenot blood, now forty; a veteran of the French and Indian War; major of brigade, but brigadier-general for this expedition only.

[2] His *Orderly Book*, edited by William L. Stone, shows that this force was not officially so called. The author would here acknowledge Mr. Stone's kind and important service on several points of this campaign.

seemed, it was mad nonsense. That influence acted mainly on those already ejected with it, and the new owners of their farms would be patriots to a man, fighting to the death against being dispossessed in turn; and aside from this, raising the Indians against the settlements must force them as wholes to stand together. Alien mercenaries, savages, and refugees burning with vengeance for their lost homes and coming to resume them, were a precious medley for retaining even such loyalty as had existed. The very fact that loyalism meant Indian riot had killed it for the mass of whites, and caused the expulsion of the element that would ally itself with such devildom. The British government could not have white affection and anti-white savagery both at once: it made its choice and had its reward.

In this case it was especially dazzled by the prospect of securing the alliance of the powerful Iroquois confederacy, the Six Nations. It did gain a heavy majority and the most warlike,—the Mohawks on the east, the Senecas and Cayugas on the west, and the real help of the central tribe, the Onondagas, though they remained officially neutral; but the prize was a Dead Sea apple. The Oneidas and Tuscaroras, however, swayed by the missionary Samuel Kirkland, took the American side, gave it valuable help as informants and scouts, and later some of their chiefs were commissioned as officers; but they were never let loose on butchering raids against the Tory families. For the first time since its formation, the league

1777
July–
Aug.

Mohawk
Valley
politics

Sense-
less
Indian
policy of
England

Politics
of the Six
Nations

Confed-
eracy
divided

**1777
July–
Aug.**

**Six
Nations
doomed**

was rent asunder and its members fighting against each other: a presage of the coming ruin of all alike. Indeed, they had no future whichever side won: civilization was rolling against their borders and must soon overflow them.

St. Leger was so confident of an easy task that he detached nearly 50 of his small force on special duties. Accompanied by Johnson, and his brother-in-law Major Stephen Watts commanding the Greens (grandson of Cadwallader Colden and nephew of James De Lancey), he landed at Oswego in July, with about 650 white men and 250 Indians. He was soon joined by Colonel John Butler and his son Walter with 70 to 75 Tory rangers; the brilliant and influential Mohawk chief Thayenda-negea [1] or Joseph Brant—the greatest man of his tribe, Guy Johnson's secretary—brought in 300 of his tribesmen; and Butler induced the chief Seneca and Cayuga leaders to hold a council there. They were very reluctant to stake their lands on a death-grapple with the colonies; but Brant's eloquence and force of character, aided by bribes and promises of colonial plunder, overcame their scruples, and 250 to 300 of their warriors joined. Brant was now the real head of the confederacy.

Late in July, St. Leger with about 1500 of his motley crew moved forward from Oswego. The

**St.
Leger's
mongrel
force**

**Senecas
and
Cayugas
won over**

---

[1] Thä-(or tä-)yen-da-nau'-ga. He was now thirty-five; from his early promise had been given a civilized education by Sir William Johnson, served the British in the French and Indian War and Pontiac's War, and had been flattered by the court to win his good-will. Trained in the feelings of the whites, he used his influence to restrain his immediate commands from the atrocities that alienated it.

BARRY ST. LEGER.

JOSEPH BRANT.

FORT STANWIX AND BATTLE OF ORISKANY.

patriots had repaired old Fort Stanwix, renamed
Fort Schuyler, within the present Rome; near the
western bank of the upper Mohawk, commanding
the "carry" between that and a stream leading
to Oneida Lake and Oswego—the chief trade route
between the Hudson and the Lakes. The stream,
through forest and swamp, had been so obstructed
that it took the bulk of St. Leger's force many
days to bring up their stores; but an advance party
reached the fort August 2. The garrison of 750
men, commanded by Colonel Peter Gansevoort
with Colonel Marinus Willett second, was very
scant of artillery ammunition, but had other stores
for six weeks.

Neither St. Leger nor his superiors had expected anything more than the usual ruinous ill-
manned Indian-fort; and he was disconcerted at
finding so strong a work, demanding a regular
siege for which he had no heavy artillery, and
with a garrison greatly outmatching his troops
at hand. But he put on a bold front and summoned
it to surrender, with the offer to take the garrison
into British service, the usual promises (not kept)
of protecting the district and paying for requisitions if it yielded, and the usual threats (always
kept) of otherwise letting loose the Indians on it.
This being ignored, the cannon were grouped in
small batteries and set up a bombardment *in ter-
rorem,* trenches were begun, and the Indians encircled the fort in howling chorus all the night.
The white troops were too few to maintain close
co-operation: the camp of the regulars was on the

1777
July-
Aug.

Fort
Stanwix

Attempt
to
frighten
it into
sur-
render

Partially
invested

north, that of the Tories south with the Indians just beyond.

Until the danger was at their own door, the Tryon County people like others were hard to call from private affairs that needed them; but now they awoke. In the van was the large element of German blood, descended from refugees of the religious wars or persecutions, without British ties or affections and generally patriots of the one motherland they knew; though they had their Tories also. Their leading representative, General Nicholas Harkheimer or Herkimer, the brave old commander of the county militia, in a short time had about 700 men at hand, and marched to relieve the fort, whose capture would let this flood of uncurbed savagery down on the valley. On the 5th they camped near Oriskany, eight miles away; and Herkimer in the evening sent four messengers thither, proposing that in the morning Gansevoort should fire signal cannon, and then make a diversion to hold the enemy in play till he came up.

Indian scouts had reported his advance; and St. Leger sent Johnson and Brant with a Tory and Indian force to intercept it. These selected an ambush that evening, two and a half miles west of Oriskany: the woods lining the narrow road (which ran along the upland swells just south of the wide marshy flats that margin the Mohawk) at the top of its ascent from a swampy depression which it crossed by a log causeway. By morning this spot was occupied by about 50 Greens holding the front, with 30 of Butler's rangers and

400 Indians on the sides, to fire at a signal and close in on the rear. As the morning waned and no guns were heard from the fort, Herkimer's men grew impatient, begged to go forward, and on his refusal, began to twit him as a coward and perhaps a Tory; at last he gave way, and they started on in disorderly exultation.

Just as the front regiments, some two-thirds of the whole, had climbed the ascent about ten o'clock, the Indians in turn grew too impatient to wait the signal, and began to rain bullets among them; the white troops did likewise; and from either side a file of yelling savages ran down around the rear, cutting off the baggage and ammunition wagons and the rear regiment. The latter fled in panic, followed by part of the Indians and worse slaughtered than if they had stood. The van suffered awful carnage from the hidden rifles, and the knives and tomahawks of the screeching fiends who leapt out to dispatch the wounded; but nerved by desperation, braced themselves for the fight and scattered to cover. A volley killed Herkimer's horse and shattered his leg; he had himself propped in his saddle against a beech-tree, and gave orders as before. Whenever a patriot fired, Indians would rush upon him and tomahawk him before he could reload; then behind their trees the militia fought in couples, one reserving fire for this rush, and punishing it till the savages grew wary. Gradually the ambushers crept closer, stalking the patriots from the side or behind; the latter formed circles

1777
Aug. 6

Patriots
begin to
make
stand

among the trees [1] to prevent it. Thenceforward,
though from their dreadful losses now heavily outnumbered, hope dawned for them, as the foe could
gain few shots except at even hazard, which the
very object of the ambush was to avoid; and only
scattering discharges were heard.

At length a thunder-storm broke—a godsend
to the patriots, whose only powder was in their
belts. For over an hour the mongrel allies drew
off to closer coverts to keep theirs dry; while

Unex-
pected
fortune

Herkimer chose for his men a spot so defensible
that it seems strange the enemy should have left
it for them—the north end of their field, a steep
knoll sloping to the flats beyond and the gullies
on its sides, easily assailable only from the south.
Here all his men formed in one great circle. As
the sky cleared the allies approached once more;
but now the patriots had the vantage in turn,
and the enemy began to shrink back. Just then

British
rein-
forced

Watts came on the scene with a fresh detachment of the Greens, sent from camp on news from
the Indian runners of the check sustained. He
evidently had fighting blood in him, and for the
first time there seems to have been something like a
real battle, in which he was desperately wounded.[2]

---

[1] Not small trees filled in between with underbrush, as usual now,
but mostly great trunks well apart with clear spaces. With the cutting away of these, the small-fry has grown up.

[2] Local tradition tells how, as old neighbors faced each other, one
side rancorous with revenge and the other with hate for the allies of
Indian massacre, patriots would jump from cover, and with yells and
curses both fought with steel and musket-butt, or grappled at hair or
throat and fell with their knives each in the other's heart. The account
of losses shows that this must be almost pure myth: there may have
been one or two cases, or what is more likely, incidents of other contests

Not long afterward the boom of cannon from the fort came to their ears.   The crafty Butler at once turned it to account for a well-nigh fatal ruse, disguising a body of Greens by homespun over-garments and sending them from the west to the patriot lines as reinforcements; but a keen eye detected the uniforms and several were shot down.   At last the Indians, in sudden dismay at their unwonted losses, set up a wail and fled toward the fort, and the Tories hastened after them.   The couple of hundred or so of the patriots left alive and sound from the six-hours' struggle were in no case to follow: they were glad to escape and carry their wounded back to Oriskany, leaving the beleaguered fort to its fate.

This did not appear a gloomy one at the moment.   The messengers had found all approaches beset with Indians, and only reached the fort by a wide detour through a supposedly impassable and so unguarded swamp, towards eleven o'clock.   The garrison had noticed parties stealing away from the southern camps, and heard the firing to the east.   Gansevoort and Willett saw that Herkimer must have come forward and been assailed by a large force, which must pretty well have stripped

1777 Aug. 6

Oriskany: Butler's ruse

End of battle

Herkimer's message delayed

---

may have been transferred to this.   The fact is, that more than any other Revolutionary contest this battle has come to belong to mythland: from its nature as a pell-mell of irregulars and savages, mostly out of each other's sight in the forest, the products of tangled memory and picturesque decoration could rarely be contradicted, and have attained appalling luxuriance.   Reckless popular historians have contributed to fix them or still wilder distortions in the popular mind; and local pride has helped in exaggerating the patriots' victory, which was only the fortunate escape of part of them from death.

1777
Aug. 6

the camps. A sortie would not only prevent further reinforcements, but probably overwhelm the
remainder; and Willett was ordered to make it
with 250 men and a cannon. Completing his
preparations just before the thunder-storm, he was
obliged to wait till it was over, and as we know,
most of the remaining Tory camp guard had

Oris-
kany:
Willett's
sortie

gone; then a swift charge drove the rest of the
Tories into the river and the few Indians into the
woods, leaving several dead. The whole camp
stores were carted to the fort in three journeys of
seven loaded wagons. St. Leger sent a company
to cut off Willett's party, and led another to harass
them from over the river; but Willett drove off
both and regained the fort without losing a man.

The spoils included all Johnson's papers,—
plans of campaign, maps, orderly books, and letters,—full of valuable information; all the Ind-

Spoils

ians' blankets and garments (they having stripped
themselves nearly naked for the fight),—of less
value in themselves than as adding to the owners'
ill-feeling against St. Leger; and five colors which
Gansevoort derisively hoisted over the fort, sur-
mounted by the first American stars and stripes
as adopted by Congress June 14—made on the
spot out of white regulation shirts, a captured
blue cloak, and the red petticoat of a soldier's

First
American
flag

wife. But if the garrison had known that less
than 150 white troops were left around the fort
altogether,[1] they could easily have dispersed them

---

[1] We have to depend on St. Leger's figures, but they seem justified
by coincident facts. He says he had only 250 (white) men around the

all, captured the batteries, and ended the campaign then and there.

In its ultimate consequences, the ambush fight was an American victory of the first importance. It caused the desertion of St. Leger's Indians and the consequent abandonment of his campaign, which Arnold might or might not have compelled; and assured Burgoyne's destruction, which even after Bennington would at least have been much more difficult if the northern army had had to make head also against St. Leger pushing down the valley, at the head of a grand Iroquois rising spurred by success. But its immediate result was a decisive defeat for the patriots: they failed to affect the siege of the fort in any way, and the survivors seem mostly to have gone home. More than half their number had been killed, wounded, or captured—fully 400 of the 700; half of them slain outright—a disproportion natural with men forming targets at close range or struck down with the tomahawk, and with the Indians killing all the wounded they could reach. A number died later; among them the noble Herkimer, from the unskillful amputation of his leg.

The whites of the other side had only six killed and four wounded; but so heavy a loss (from their

---

fort, and all the Indians at hand went to the ambuscade (a few must have remained or come in during the day); the rest, some 400 whites and 400 Indians, were off on fatigue work or guarding communications. The garrison did not know this; but the trivial resistance met by Willett during his long holding of the camp should have made it clear that very few troops were in the vicinity. Even if, as is probable, St. Leger was able to call in some near detachment, he was still greatly outnumbered.

1777
Aug. 6-13

Indian
losses

Indian
venge-
fulness

St. Leger
tries
threats
again

standpoint) fell on the Indians,—33 dead including several important chiefs and trusted warriors,
with 29 wounded,—that they were mad with grief
and rage. They had been assured that they would
only have to look on while their white allies crushed
the patriots, and share the plunder; and they
had borne the brunt of the fray. They partially
consoled themselves by murdering their white
prisoners; suspecting collusion between the hostile
white parties in getting Indians killed off, they
murdered some Tories as well, brooded and grew
sulkier day by day.

St. Leger tried to frighten the garrison into
surrender by pretending to have destroyed Herkimer's force, and again threatening Indian massacre to themselves and the countryside if they
held out; Gansevoort defied him, and Willett
scathed the British officer who brought the message, for such devilish language from civilized
Englishmen. But the fatigue parties having come
in, and some fresh Tories to make good the losses;
St. Leger made the investment more effective
and advanced the parallels closer. Meantime
Johnson, Butler, and Colonel Claus (the Tory
commandant of St. Leger's Indians) signed a proclamation of promise and threat to the inhabitants
of the valley, and Walter Butler undertook a secret
mission to distribute and reinforce it.[1]

---

[1] He was captured and condemned to death as a spy; but unfortunately let off with imprisonment on account of influential old-time
friendships with prominent patriots. Carelessly guarded, he escaped
from Albany, and burning with hatred, became one of the most terrible
scourges of the borders, outdoing the Indians in inhuman ferocity.

The garrison did not know what had become of Herkimer; provisions were scant: and Willett and a lieutenant, by a notable feat of daring and labor,—floating over the river with a log and crawling on hands and knees through the swamps, —made their way on August 12 to Schuyler's headquarters at Stillwater to ask for help. Schuyler, anxiously watching this new danger from the west, had already sent part of a Massachusetts brigade up the valley; he now called a council of war to consider sending a larger force. His officers were so hotly averse to weakening the petty army in face of Burgoyne, that one of them loudly whispered the vilest insinuation of his motives; in flaming wrath he assumed the whole responsibility, and called for a general to head a volunteer party. Arnold instantly responded, and before the next noon 800 more of the same brigade and others had enlisted under his inspiring leadership.

Marching up the valley and picking up the previous detachment, he reached Fort Dayton on the 20th with 946 Continentals; about 100 militia had joined, more were coming in, and the Oneidas were expected to join; but a council of war the next day estimated St. Leger's force at 1700, and voted to ask Gates for a heavy reinforcement and await it before advancing.[1] Arnold, however,

1777
Aug. 7–21

Messengers get to Schuyler

Who orders relief party sent

Arnold sets out

---

[1] As Willett was with them, they must have known the greater part of the force to be Indians; and Arnold's ten or eleven hundred plus the garrison outnumbered the whole, and was nearly treble the white force. Evidently there was the same terror of the Indians, among troops not rendered cool or contemptuous by familiarity like the borderers, which had prevented hindering Burgoyne's march.

1777
Aug. 6-21

Siege of
Fort
Stanwix

knew that every day was precious; in fact the garrison, hearing no news of relief, the trenches within 150 yards and supplies giving out, were contemplating surrender to avoid butchery, though Gansevoort declared he would cut his way out in the night first. Arnold resolved to march on despite the council; and was already hurrying toward the fort with part of his men, to relieve it or die, when he received a message from Gansevoort that the siege was raised and the enemy fled.

Raised

St.
Leger's
Indians
wish to
quit

The Indians, in St. Leger's simple and expressive phrase, "became more formidable than the foe we had to expect." They felt revengeful over their bereavements, poor and wrathful at the sacking of their camp, disappointed in their hope of plunder, tired of a long dull siege in place of adventure, and suspicious of treachery; and determined to quit. But they preferred to have St. Leger save them from open breach of the agreement by abandoning the enterprise himself, and set themselves to frighten him into doing it. Arnold's advance supplied the opportunity: they kept bringing in more and more disquieting accounts, and his army grew to portentous size.[1]

Try to
scare him

[1] The accepted version of these false rumors, embodied in all histories, is as follows:—Butler had taken with him to help distribute his proclamation a half-witted Dutch boy of the Valley,—full however of crazy cunning,—named Jan Joost (hon yōst) Schuyler or Cuyler, who had run away from home and joined the Greens; the boy was condemned to death with his employer. His mother begged so hard for his life that Arnold at last granted it on condition of his trying to create a panic in St. Leger's forces; guaranteeing her zeal in urging it on him by holding another son as hostage, and sending a friendly Oneida Indian with him to watch him and aid. His condemnation was known to the British; and to confirm his having escaped on the way to the

At last they threatened to leave, and some two hundred did. St. Leger begged them at least to help him retreat by night in orderly fashion with his stores; but they got at his liquor and began a drunken pandemonium. In mortal terror, their white allies fled for the boats on Oneïda Lake, leaving everything behind,—tents standing, artillery, ammunition, baggage, provisions, and even St. Leger's writing-case with his private papers, —and many throwing away their guns for swifter flight.

By noon of the 22d the whole army was dispersed, with the exultant garrison on its heels. The Indians, to indemnify themselves for the lost plunder and scalps by taking such as lay to hand, had gone ahead and gutted the boats, and followed on the track of the fugitives almost to Oswego, murdering all stragglers and laying night ambushes. Many of the troops found the rendezvous

1777
Aug. 21
et seq.

Indian
alliance
kills at
the
breech

St.
Leger's
army
dispersed

---

gallows, his coat was shot full of holes. Arnold knew also that those stricken by the "Great Spirit" were looked on with awe and entire trust by the Indians. On the 21st Jan Joost came running breathlessly into the Indian camp, told his tale, said that Arnold's army was close at hand and advancing, and pointed to the leaves on the trees for its numbers. Taken to St. Leger, he told him that Arnold would be there in a day with 2000 men. Just then the Indian, with two or three other Oneidas he had picked up, came in from another quarter, all with the same or a worse account, and that Burgoyne's army was cut to pieces. Thereupon the Indians fled, and the whites could only do likewise.

This racy and dramatic story was taken down from local tradition in 1796 by Dr. Belknap; but neither Arnold, Willett, nor St. Leger alludes to such an incident. Every historical student knows that such tradition is the most worthless of evidence, and that its capacities of invention and especially of *substitution* are infinite. And after all, the plain prose is the more satisfying, as poetic justice: the Indian alliance simply wrought its own destruction by its intrinsic nature, and recoiled on the heads of its makers.

too late or never; and the half-starved, half-naked, half-armed men who re-embarked for Canada were a sad wreck of the original force. Two of the four British companies were sent from thence to reinforce Burgoyne. Arnold, after issuing a proclamation to counteract Butler's, returned with his army and rejoined Schuyler, who had withdrawn his diminished lines to Half-Moon, the islands in the Hudson at the junction of the Mohawk.

Thus Burgoyne's auxiliary campaign was at an end, the whole northern army free to concentrate against him, and the west country to swell that army with its militia. This crushing news fell upon him over a week after he had sustained a ruinous disaster from the east country, losing at a blow a seventh of his own army and all hopes of Tory reinforcements and fresh supplies alike.

We have seen his needs and difficulties: chief among them, lack of provision by lack of transport from his depots to his army. Now, the principal depots of the supplies gathered throughout New England for Schuyler's army were at and around Bennington, twenty-four miles southeast in the Green Mountains: flour, grain, cattle, salt, potash, lead, etc. Still more to his purpose, the district was noted for horses, the transport of the supplies employed a great number of carts (besides those in use by the farmers but impressible), and he was told that quantities of both were at Bennington under a small militia guard. A swift stroke might sweep all these into his net, and would cripple the patriot forces collecting thereabout; while a march through the heart of the New Hampshire Grants, with a menace that Burgoyne was on the move toward Boston, would overawe and paralyze New England. Again the Tory will-o'-the-wisp lured him to ruin. Some dozens more had joined at Skenesborough, including Skene, who assured him that the people of the Grants were loyalists five to one; and the little regiment of some 200 already formed, Peters' "American Volunteers," could be sent as a skeleton to incorporate them into. In fact, some did take British protections, and even join that army; but the Vermont Council of Safety confiscated their property. This body had been formed as a provisional government early in July; the Grants on January 17 having declared themselves independent, and in June asked admission into the Union as the State of Vermont. Congress sharply refused it June 30, on the angry protest of New York, and the British hoped this would cool the patriot section toward the cause.

For this expedition, of which rapid movement was of the very essence, Burgoyne sent 420 heavily accoutred German dragoons, slow and clumsy, 100 of Fraser's British riflemen, 100 Canadian rangers, the loyalist regiment and Skene,[1] and

1777
July-
Aug.

Hopes
from Ben-
nington
expe-
dition

Encour-
agements

---

[1] This is half as much again as the force given by Burgoyne in his report; but the captured of Baum's command alone were a hundred more than their grand total, 150 must have been killed, thirty had been left to guard the magazine they captured, and we know that a great many escaped. As Burgoyne's superiors could not check his figures, he could and often did report, like other officers, what would best serve his purpose at the time. The work entitled *Saratoga*, ostensibly by a German officer of Baum's command named Glich, and often

1777
July-
Aug.

150 Indians, with two cannon; the whole under a brave and skillful officer, Lieutenant-Colonel Frederick Baum. The Indians were to "scour the country" from Otter Creek to the Connecticut.

Plans of Benning- ton raid

The whole force was to descend the latter from Rockingham to Brattleboro and return to Albany, feigning the Boston design; make prisoners of all the patriot civil and military officers, enforce requisitions on all the towns and take hostages, and bring back at least 1300 horses! This for some 800 white men. The rising of Tories was to accomplish everything. Baum's final orders were much modified, but to the same general end.

Lincoln had been sent by Schuyler to take command at Manchester—where Warner had the remnant of his Continentals, about 140—and beat

Langdon finances Vermont defense

up for recruits. Meantime Vermont had appealed to New Hampshire; and the Speaker of that Assembly, the wealthy merchant John Langdon, pledged his fortune to fit out an expedition,—saying that if victorious he might be reimbursed, if liberty was lost it was worthless to him. Stark's great ability and magnetic leadership were of the first moment; and he agreed to leave his retirement

Stark given roving com- mission

and take command, on condition that he should be subject only to the State and independent of Congress. The Assembly acceded, put half the militia under him for service on the western border, and gave him a commission authorizing him to act with the forces of any State or the

cited as an authority on this battle is a fiction written by a clergyman. There was no such officer.

United States, or independently, at will. His name in a few weeks drew some 1200 men to his standard; 200 were left to guard the Connecticut, 100 sent scouting on Otter Creek, with the rest he arrived at Manchester August 7. Lincoln by Schuyler's orders directed him to join the army on the Hudson with them. Stark hesitated: the proposed raid—broached by Riedesel July 29, and at once reported to the Americans by their secret sympathizers—made it highly inadvisable to strip Vermont of defenders just then. He did not absolutely refuse, however; but told Lincoln that if he went he would obey no orders but Schuyler's own, for he would not be commanded by former subordinates or other juniors promoted over his head. Lincoln wrote this to Schuyler, who sent Stark a courteous entreaty to waive his claims for the country's sake, and forwarded Lincoln's letter to Congress. That body on August 19 censured the New Hampshire Assembly for granting such a commission, as destructive of military subordination and most dangerous in this crisis; and requested them to make all their officers obey orders alike where the United States had to pay expenses. Their principle was quite correct, but so was Stark's final decision not to go, amply justified before the resolution was passed.[1]

1777
July-
Aug.

Stark a
free-
lance

Question
of
joining
Schuyler

Congress
censures
New
Hamp-
shire

---

[1] This case is persistently misstated in the histories. They assert that Stark refused to obey Schuyler's orders on the ground of his independent commission; and often add that he was censured by Congress. Neither is true. He intended to join and obey Schuyler, and was on his way when the imminent danger in front and the requests of the Vermont Council of Safety held him back; in fact he joined Gates later.

1777

Baum
advances
toward
Ben-
nington

Stark
bars his
path

Both
wait

By the 13th Baum's stroke was so obvious and near that the Vermont Council of Safety ordered the State forces to concentrate at once at Bennington. Stark (with Warner but not his troops) camped with about 900 men six miles north, just east of a great loop of the little Walloomsac River. By the road along and over this the invaders must approach. The same day Baum set out, and arrived at Cambridge twelve miles west; on the way his Indians cut up an American party. Stark was informed, and supposing it a mere incursion of Indians, sent 200 men the next morning to drive them off. Soon learning that a large force with artillery was behind them heading for Bennington, he sent urgent messengers thither for its militia, and to Manchester after Warner's regiment and the scouts; and advanced across both arms of the loop. Not far on he met his detachment retreating, Baum a half-mile in its rear; and formed a line of battle. Baum was startled at this unexpected army, and sparred to avoid an engagement; Stark drew back east of both arms and encamped to await his reinforcements; Baum took post on a huge heavily wooded hill west of the west arm, some 400 feet high and at least 1500 climb, and a low knoll a little south of it the other side of the stream among cleared lands, and sent back to Burgoyne for reinforcements. As if celerity were of no service, the 641 additional troops dispatched to his aid, with two more cannon, were chiefly heavy Germans as before; commanded by Lieutenant-Colonel H. C. Breymann.

JOHN STARK.

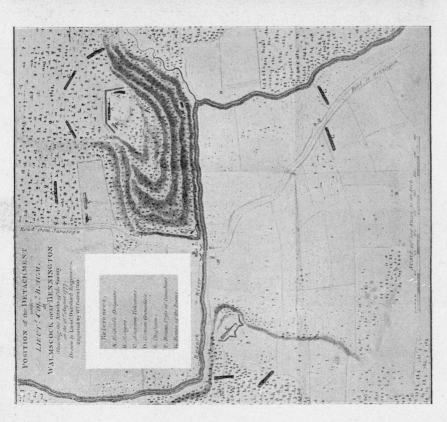

PLAN OF THE BATTLE OF BENNINGTON.

The morning of the 15th brought a furious all-day storm of wind and rain. Baum set to work fortifying: the loyalists and some Germans (all under a British officer, Francis Pfister) held the knoll, Canadians and grenadiers a few log houses on both sides of the river bridge near by, other Germans breastworks just west, German chasseurs the southeast slopes of the west hill, the other troops the redoubt upon it, while the Indians surrounded the latter in the woods. The hill was fairly accessible to the north alone, and here were the heaviest intrenchments. Both sides filled the forest all about them with skirmishers. The British riflemen's priming was soon useless, and they drew back to the shelter of the log houses; the Americans managed to keep their powder dry enough to pick off thirty of the fatigue workers, besides two Indians.

The 16th was clear and sultry. Symonds' Berkshire Continental regiment had come in during the night; Stark had now 1500 men (though Warner's and the scouts were still absent), but without artillery or bayonets, against an enemy with both and in part the flower of European soldiery. It must be surrounded and surprised.[1] One body was sent north and another south to

1777
Aug.
15-16

Baum's
fortifi-
cations

Skir-
mishing

Stark's
tactics

---

[1] According to tradition, Stark first jumped on a rail fence, and steadying himself by the post, shouted: "Now, my men, yonder are the Hessians. They were bought for seven pounds tenpence a man. Are you worth more? Prove it. Tonight those works are ours, or Molly Stark sleeps a widow!" Other narrators give shorter and other versions, but always the same ending, which must represent authentic memory. Doubt has been cast on it because his wife's name was Elizabeth; but his grandchildren assert that he regularly called her

make long detours and flank the fort, a third to hide in a cornfield near the knoll; while Stark with the rest crossed the east arm and bewildered the enemy, drawing out a harmless cannonade, by marching around a hillock in plain sight. The flanking parties, instead of keeping in solid bodies whom Baum's outliers would have given a slow and bloody advance to near the fort, straggled around in small harmless-looking groups, whose shirt-sleeved farm garb convinced him they were the expected Tories coming in; some professed ones had come during the march, but seem to have been patriot decoys, who turned and fired upon the British and deserted to their countrymen when the time came. Baum, despite the alarmed remonstrances of his officers, would not molest the new-comers, but had his pickets yield them up strong points of vantage among the trees on the hill-face.

About three o'clock all were in position, and suddenly a crashing volley burst from three sides on all the west-hill defenders at once; the patriot columns closed swiftly around the redoubt, while Stark with his division waded the stream and charged right up the steep eastern slope. The outlying troops were speedily driven in on the intrenchments, and the inmates rising over their parapets to fire were answered by swift

---

"Molly" as a pet name, and the story rings genuine. The "fighting parson" Allen, with the Berkshire regiment, complained that the men had been called out so often on false alarms they were reluctant to come; Stark replied, "If the Lord will send us sunshine and I don't give you fighting enough, I'll never call you out again!"

volleys from practiced marksmen. In Stark's words, the noise of the muskets ever reloaded with lightning celerity was like "one continued clap of thunder." The Indians almost at the first fire fled through a gap, their grand chief and others slain and still others captured. At the signal the body in the cornfield rushed silently out and up the eastern hillock, and girdled the works with fire. After one to two hours of duel, the ammunition wagon in the western redoubt blew up;[1] and with a mighty cheer the Americans poured over the walls at every angle. The British riflemen leaped the parapets and mostly escaped. The Germans fought like heroes; but after a fierce combat where sabre, pike, and bayonet contended with clubbed musket when loading was impossible, and Baum was mortally wounded, the outnumbered remnant swarmed over also and scattered in flight—chiefly down the southern slope toward the road they had come, followed and mostly captured by the militia. At the explosion of the caisson, the party around the eastern redoubt had swept forward in a wave and scaled it; the defenders, after a brief contest in which Pfister was mortally wounded, in turn jumped the walls and fled, but the greater part were captured, including 157 of the Tories. The Canadians and chasseurs were quickly cut off and most of them taken.

1777
Aug. 16

Bennington:

First victory

Baum fatally wounded

His force annihilated

---

[1] Burgoyne says this accident occurred to Breymann's relief corps, not in the redoubt; and the accounts of some participants in the attack make no mention of it, an odd omission if so dramatic an occurrence took place. But the weight of evidence is in favor of the text; and memories are treacherous.

1777
Aug. 16

Benning-
ton:

Brey-
mann
arrives

As part of the pursuing Americans neared a
mill and magazine a mile and a half west, captured by Baum in his advance, they were suddenly confronted by a fresh battalion of Germans.
Breymann was coming up, having taken thirty-
two hours to march twenty-two miles; the horrible
road, mired with fourteen hours' rain, was partly
accountable, but the heavy clothes and trappings
more. The patriot force was largely dispersed
hunting down fugitives, roping up and guarding
prisoners, or gathering in Baum's stores, and
too tired and stiff to feel like rousing for a fresh
combat which meant more weary marching; even
Stark was loth to move. But at this juncture
Warner's regulars and the scouts came upon the
field, and hastened forward to give battle: they
had marched all night in the rain, and spent the
forenoon drying and cleaning their guns at Bennington. Though pushed back at first for nearly
a mile toward the hill, the new troops formed a
nucleus for the others to rally around; and Breymann after a succession of charges and repulses,
his cannon captured and recaptured, was in turn
forced back over his road through a vast ambush,
companies constantly hastening around to his flank

Second
fight

and rear. Making a last stand in a field near the
mill, just as darkness settled down his decimated
and hopeless remnant gave up and fled, leaving
wounded, baggage, and artillery behind; it was too
dark for general pursuit, but many were overtaken
and captured as they struggled through the mud
or the woods. Of about 1450 white men in both

divisions, 934 [1] had been lost: 207 found dead on the field, about 700 prisoners including the wounded, a few unaccounted for. The Americans had lost about 30 killed and 40 wounded (Stark to Gates); and the spoils included 1000 stand of arms with the precious bayonets, four wagon-loads of ammunition and eight of other supplies.

1777
Aug. 16
et seq.

Second
victory

The country went wild at this splendid victory, the annihilation of over a thousand European veterans by a few hundred more of American farmers. Stark was given his brigadiership instead of being disciplined. A week after the battle, and just as St. Leger's force had taken to flight,—in a word, when the tide had decisively turned and Burgoyne was in the toils, largely owing to Schuyler's action,—Gates came up and took over the command. Schuyler acted like a patriot and a gentleman: he offered his aid to Gates in any fashion or capacity desired. Gates acted according to *his* nature, snubbed and ignored him. He was safe, reaping the harvest others had sown and brought to ripeness; later, he reaped what his own incapacity had sown.

Rejoicings over Bennington

Schuyler and Gates

For some weeks there was a lull, while Burgoyne waited vainly for Howe, and tried to plan what to do with his diminished and ill-supplied

Burgoyne in the toils

---

[1] This is Burgoyne's report, and is so closely in accord with the patriot tally of dead and captured that it is probably correct. But his roll after the capitulation sets down the losses at Bennington as 1220, which cannot be harmonized with anything. Still more curiously, that roll gives six cannon lost in this battle, and the patriots captured only four: what became of the other two? Our own opinion is, that the battle was used as a profit-and-loss account to force a balance in the latter list.

army. Most of his remaining Indians had left him after Bennington, sick of losses, restrictions, and refusal of share in the army's scanty supplies. His lines were from Fort Edward south to the Batten Kill; the Americans three weeks later moving north from Half-Moon to Stillwater. Howe must now claim our attention.

1777
March-
April

Charles Lee, still in British custody, proved a Trojan horse to them; not intentionally, but in pursuance of his old game to have the glory of ending the war, stimulated by anxiety to save himself from being hanged. Debarred from hope of effecting the former through a great American victory, he now sought to effect both at once by being the agent of a great British one. On March 29 he had put in Howe's hands an elaborate written scheme on whose success he "staked his life." It was based on the usual exaggeration of the *militancy* of loyalism, this time including nearly the whole population of Maryland and Pennsylvania. Lee advised sending a few thousand men around by the Chesapeake Bay to occupy Alexandria and Annapolis, at once cutting off Virginia help from Philadelphia and causing Maryland to rise solidly for the King; while the bulk of Howe's army was to resume the New Jersey campaign and capture Philadelphia, New England being kept from aiding Washington by the dread of Carleton. Then a proclamation of amnesty would bring over the "central colonies" in less than two months. Conquest of the northern provinces answered no purpose, they not being "the seat of government,

"Mr.
Lee's
plan"

To
capture
Phila-
delphia
and raise
border
Tories

strength, nor politics"; while capturing the "rebel capital" would paralyze the rebel government. Of course this was mere wiseacre profundity: the country had no centre; Philadelphia was a convenience, not a necessity.

Howe was evidently impressed with the political ideas, which fell in with his own. They came too just as Germain had tartly refused the 15,000 men he asked for as necessary to finish the war that year; and four days later he replied that in that case the Canada expedition could receive little help from him, and he had other plans—evidently Lee's. As to the strategic portion, however, he preferred an undiminished army to deal with Washington. A quick campaign would leave him time enough for the Hudson co-operation, and perhaps make it unnecessary. Collecting 18,000 men at Brunswick, with boats enough to prevent another delay at the Delaware, he began a fresh advance through New Jersey June 13. Washington, guessing the British objective, had moved from Morristown to the Middlebrook heights, ten miles from Brunswick and twelve from Princeton, to flank their line of march. He had only ten brigades, about 8000 men; but he called in part of the Hudson guard, and the New Jersey militia turned out. To lure him into open ground, Howe evacuated Brunswick and fell back to Amboy. Washington moved after him with Stirling's van in the lowlands, the main force at Quibbletown; Howe made a sudden dart north to envelop the left flank, and Stirling had some

Howe im-
pressed

Howe
plans
fresh
Jersey
campaign

Feint
against
Wash-
ington

Fails

Clinton's
raid
on New
Jersey

caused the arrest of eleven rich and influential Philadelphia Friends. Clinton retorted by an invasion of New Jersey, which recalled part of its militia and weakened Washington's force at the Brandywine shortly after.

Fleet
still a
mystery

Again the fleet was seen standing south: this must mean a fresh attack on Charleston, which could not be reached overland in time to aid its defense, and Washington planned a campaign to drive Clinton from New York. But the next day it was reported going up the Chesapeake, and on August 25 Howe landed his troops at Head of Elk

Howe's
remark-
able
voyage

(now Elkton), Maryland, forty-five miles southwest of Philadelphia. To this day his journey remains the most extraordinary in military annals. The reason for his not attempting to reach Philadelphia by the Delaware was doubtless in part what he declared, the forts and obstructions guarding it, which cost much time and loss later; but near its unguarded mouth he was thirteen miles from Head of Elk overland, and he had spent nearly four weeks in going thither by water, 400 miles around, with baffling winds. The political aim of securing the border States certainly predominated.

Disap-
pointed in
loyalists

Washington hurried down two divisions to save the stores and live-stock at Head of Elk, which was done; and the Maryland and Delaware militia took the field. Howe found no welcome, but a country of armed enemies or annoyed indifferents. His proclamation fell flat: Luther Martin issued one against it, and here as elsewhere the patriot class were the fighting class. His baggage and stores being landed, and horses and other transport material got together, Howe began his march on Philadelphia September 3, with about 15,000 effectives besides an engineer corps. Washington had heartened Congress and the patriots and cowed the Tories by marching his army through the city; and collected at Wilmington, twenty-seven miles south on Brandywine Creek, about the same number, though very largely raw militia. But there was much sickness, and the usual melting away by time-expiry and desertion; Clinton's raid drew back part of the Jerseymen to defend their own State; and when detachments had been made to guard supply depots, not above 11,000 were left.

1777
Sept. 3
et seq.

Washington's
army at
Wilmington

The country on Howe's route was level, generally open, and decently settled, not like Burgoyne's wilderness; his road was easy, his supplies not hard either to obtain or transport. The population was largely of loyalist or neutral Quakers and Germans: no Lexington rising was to be feared. In this regard Lee had put him on the right track, though overstating the case; he had struck the weakest joint in the nation's armor. The real objection was that the prize was of no great consequence, while the sacrifice of Burgoyne entailed the death-blow to the British cause.

Howe's
easy
task

Poor
policy

Howe's direct road to Philadelphia lay through Wilmington and along the Delaware; but the deep unfordable lower courses of several streams confronted him, and Washington had

Choice
of roads

taken position along Christiana Creek, with his right toward the Brandywine. Howe made a feint against the American centre, and threw his left far north. Washington divined that Howe meant to turn his right by crossing the Brandywine, and catch him as at the Assanpink, between the creek and the Delaware and the British army, this time perhaps with the fleet to assist; and there would be no such escape as before, while Philadelphia would be uncovered. He therefore moved north himself to Chadd's Ford on the Brandywine, where the main road from the Bay crossed to reach the Lancaster-Philadelphia road some miles east; and took post along the creek for several miles above and below, covering or watching the fords and the roads which led from them to the same great highway.

The Brandywine, formed by the junction of two forks five miles above Chadd's Ford, is here a placid stream about a hundred feet wide, running south by east through a broad swampy valley, and sometimes skirting hills on one side or the other. One of these hills, quite steep, abuts it on the east from just below Chadd's Ford to near Pyles' Ford two miles below, the lowest on the creek; along its slopes, as the most defensible position, were stationed Armstrong's Pennsylvania militia to guard Pyles' ford. The centre at Chadd's Ford was composed of Maxwell on the heights a mile west as an advance guard, Greene's division (Muhlenberg's and Weedon's brigades) on the east, Wayne's division and Proctor's

Marginal notes:

1777 Sept. 3 et seq.

Howe's manœuvres

Washington at the Brandywine

Topography

Position of forces

artillery on heights just north. The left, under Sullivan with Stephen and Stirling, lay across Brinton's Ford over a mile north, with a strong outpost at Jones' Ford two miles still north, and scouting parties further on even to the fords at the forks.

Forcing this position in front might be impossible and must be at terrible cost; and Howe repeated the tactics of his Battle of Long Island. Knyphausen was ordered to hold the Americans in play till the bulk of the army gained their rear; and about nine in the morning of September 11, amid a dense autumn fog which made it impossible for parties to see each other at any distance, an advance column of his Hessians moved on Chadd's Ford from the camp five miles west of the Brandywine, and drove Maxwell back to the edge of the stream. Their extended front, and the difficulty of distinguishing the color of uniforms in the fog, led Washington to believe them the main British body. He reinforced Maxwell, who drove back the Hessian detachment on the main body; Knyphausen sent another to take Maxwell in flank, and the latter drew back across the creek; Knyphausen brought his guns to the heights and began an artillery duel with Proctor, and set men at work intrenching. Several American bodies crossed and assailed the British parties, soon reinforced by Maxwell who drove the Hessians from the heights; Knyphausen sent forward a large force which again forced Maxwell across, and maintained a languid artillery play.

1777
Sept. 11

Brandy-
wine:
Howe's
flank
march

Meantime Howe and Cornwallis with almost 10,000 men, the flower of the army, had started at daybreak and were marching seventeen miles around, to ford the forks and come south on the American rear. Officers of the scouts discovered the northward march of heavy British bodies, and advised Sullivan by the middle of the forenoon, and again later; by half-past eleven Washington was notified. He had already suspected some ruse from the absence of all attacks on his right, and instantly resolved to make Howe smart for dividing in presence of the enemy; to place his whole army between the two sections, driving off if not breaking the nearer and supposably main one, at worst holding it at bay with a moderate force, throw the remainder on the flanking party and destroy it. Inferring from the report that the latter body, "from all accounts 5000 men," was still beyond the river, he ordered Sullivan to cross and hold it in check till the first movement was completed; while he with the main body crossed at Chadd's Ford and attacked the British centre in front, and Greene crossed above and took it in the rear.

Wash-
ington
resolves
to punish
it

About this time the chief of scouts at the forks reported that no enemy had appeared there, and a special scout confirmed it; Sullivan notified Washington, and withheld obedience to his orders as founded on mistaken information. Washington concluded that the march had been a feint to toll Sullivan's forces northward, and that the party was returning to join the centre body and

Mis-
leading
reports

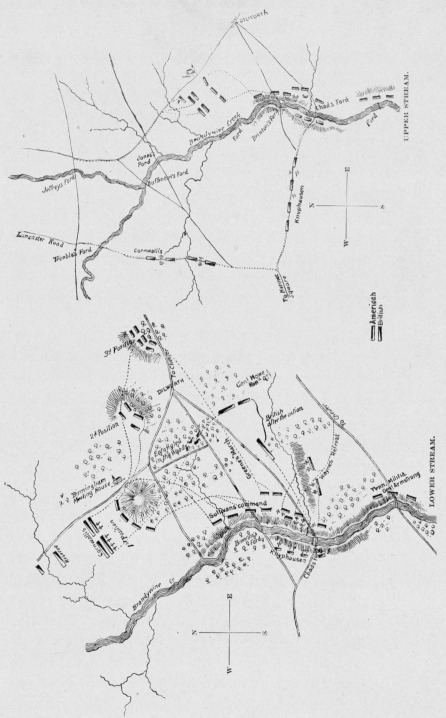

UPPER STREAM.

Wistworth

Brandywine Creek
Ford

Brinton's Road

Chad's Ford

Ford

Jones's Ford

Buffinton's Ford

Jeffreys Ford

Knyphausen

Lancaster Road

Trimble's Ford

Cornwallis

To Kennel Square

American
British

THE BATTLE OF THE BRANDYWINE.

LOWER STREAM.

3d Position

DILWORTH TO CHESTER

Gen'l Howe's
Head Q'rs

2d Position

British
after the action

To Chester

Entangled
in the Woods

Green's March

Wayne's Retreat

Birmingham
Meeting House

Penn. Militia
Gen'l Armstrong

Sullivan's command

Cornwallis

Reserve

Brenton's
Ford

Knyphausen

Chads road

Brandywine Cr.

force Chadd's Ford; recalled Greene, and sent scouts to look further. At a quarter past one they found the main British army occupying Osborne's Hill, northwest of Birmingham Meeting-House (where roads from the north united and turned northeast to join the Lancaster highway), directly in the rear of Sullivan and not two miles away; the fog had made the huge hazardous circuit a perfect success.

1777
Sept. 11

Brandy-
wine:
Success
of Howe's
flank
march

Sullivan at once sent the news to Washington, swung his divisions around at right angles to the creek, and hastened them to a hill southwest of the meeting-house, covering the roads both to Chadd's Ford and Philadelphia; the front extended to the "Street Road" up from Jones' Ford to the Lancaster highway. The new French major-general Deborre held the right, Stirling and Stephen the centre, Sullivan the left, both flanks guarded by thick woods. There was a half-mile gap between centre and left, however, which might enable the British to flank both; Sullivan was advised of the danger and started to close it up. But the movement was made in face of Cornwallis, the most vigilant and energetic of commanders, whose troops had been resting for an hour after their long hot march. Before Sullivan's were in place and order,[1] the overwhelming

[1] This is based on Sullivan's reports and later averments. Henry A. Muhlenberg, in the life of his grandfather John Peter (of Greene's division in this battle), says that Sullivan quarreled with Deborre as to which should occupy the extreme right, traditionally esteemed the post of honor; and that Sullivan in turn marched his brigade around to come in on Deborre's right, whence his not being ready for action

British columns at about three o'clock had swept down Osborne's Hill, driven back the vanguard at the Street Road, and were moving in irresistible mass straight against the entire American front.

They overlapped Deborre's right flank on the Dilworthtown road; and after a short resistance, under a furious bayonet charge his brigade broke and fled through the woods, their commander wounded in bravely trying to rally them.[1] This let the entire flood down on Stirling's right flank; shortly afterward his left also was uncovered by the rout of Sullivan's brigade, which scattered in small bodies toward Chadd's Ford. The British right wing, pressing on, lost its direction in the woods and headed for the latter place. The rest, seven or eight times Stirling's numbers, now closed in from three sides on his brigade of 800 men. The fight of these against such hopeless odds was magnificent. Thomas Marshall's Virginia regiment, for one, isolated in a wood, was flanked on both sides and lost half its officers and a third of its men before it gave way. Sullivan who had two aides killed, Stirling, Conway, Lafayette who was wounded, Duplessis and De

1777
Sept. 11

Brandy-
wine:
British
rout
wings of
American
rear

Centre
holds out

in time. We find no other authority for this; but being probably derived from General Muhlenberg, it cannot be wholly scouted. Yet it can hardly be reconciled with Sullivan's position on the left when he was attacked, while his own story is in harmony with it. The dispute may have been real, but not have gone so far as Muhlenberg thought.

[1] After the battle he was recalled and ordered before a court of inquiry by Congress; whereupon he threw up his commission and returned to France, declaring that it was outrageous to hold him responsible because Americans would not fight.

Fleury, Pulaski, and others, approved themselves heroes, encouraging, posting, and rallying the men. But under a terrible artillery slaughter personally conducted by Cornwallis, musketry fire and charges with the bayonet, one after another of the battalions broke off by the right and hurried in disorder through the woods; pursued by the British to near Dilworthtown, and a party who tried to make a fresh stand again routed.

The American army was in the jaws of destruction: its right wing broken to pieces, Howe in the rear of the rest, Knyphausen in its front. At the sound of the battle raging northward, the latter ceased feints and massed his men for a determined effort to force a passage, just as Greene had received an order from Washington to hurry north to rescue the right and keep the Philadelphia road open. Wayne and Maxwell were left at Chadd's Ford, and for two or three hours with 2500 men they held the whole German corps of more than double their number at bay, unable to force a passage against American marksmen and a continuous artillery fire. Greene with Weedon's and Muhlenberg's brigades started on a run, and in less than fifty minutes had traversed four miles and were deployed in line of battle; as they met the routed battalions they opened ranks to let them through, and again closing up, checked the pursuing enemy by destructive volleys. Washington had now come up. Muhlenberg was stationed across the Dilworthtown road, Weedon on his left in a narrow defile

1777
Sept. 11

Brandy-
wine:
British
break
American
rear

Knyp-
hausen
assaults
in front

Long
in vain

Greene
checks
British
advance

1777
Sept. 11

flanked by forest. A bloody conflict ensued:
again and again fierce British charges were driven
back with the bayonet. Edward Stevens' Virginia and Walter Stewart's Pennsylvania regiments won conspicuous laurels. Weedon was
overpowered and retreated to Muhlenberg's rear,
and the whole force was outflanked; but it gave
ground slowly, and prevented serious further
pursuit.

Brandy-
wine:
Howe's
pursuit
checked

Now Cornwallis' right emerged from the
woods and came down on the flank of Wayne;
this weakened his defense at the ford and let
Knyphausen across. Seeing that the battle above
was lost and his own force in the gravest peril,
he skillfully withdrew his main forces, covered
by a mask of skirmishers whom he then called in,
and the whole gained the rear of Greene, followed
by Armstrong's militia from the hill and Pyles'
Ford. Two British battalions were heavily cut
up by Maxwell's sharpshooters in trying to occupy
a hamlet on a hill near Dilworthtown. Howe had
not cavalry to pursue,—a lack which over and
over saved the Americans from destruction. At
Chester (not the present city on the Delaware,
but the crossing of Chester Creek higher up) the
deep stream was spanned by a bridge; behind it
the broken American battalions were protected
and reorganized. They had lost perhaps 800
killed and wounded and 400 prisoners; the British reported a loss of 584 in all, but they often
understated their losses, and from later evidence
Howe probably did so here.

Wayne
over-
powered,
retreats

Safe
American
retreat

Brandywine is one of the most creditable of American battles, and still astonishing after all explanations. Heavily outnumbered by troops far superior in discipline and equipment, taken by surprise, assailed at once in flank and rear, half the force broken up,—Washington's army instead of being annihilated, as by every military rule and probability it should have been, inflicted probably two-thirds as great a loss as it suffered, and was in perfectly good order and morale the next day. A study of the details shows that the credit is to be shared evenly between its magnificent officering —no finer body of leaders existed in the world, for skill, dash, and daring, from Washington down—and the marksmanship and heroism of the better part of the soldiers.

As a precaution in case of such defeat, the public stores and hospitals and much private property had already been removed from Philadelphia. Congress now adjourned to Lancaster, and thence later to York; first summoning the militia of Pennsylvania and adjoining States to immediate service, clothing Washington with dictatorial powers as the year before,—including later that of hanging any one within thirty miles of a British force who furnished them supplies, guidance, or information,—and ordering Putnam on the Hudson to send 1500 men to his relief. Washington had Hamilton make requisitions of clothing, shoes, and blankets on the city before it should pass into the enemy's hands. Among private circles there was general panic; hundreds abandoned

Marginal notes:

1777
Sept. 11
et seq.

Brandy-
wine:
remark-
able
American
feat

Congress
leaves
Phila-
delphia

Which is
first
requi-
sitioned

everything and fled to remote places, and even the mountains.

But Howe knew that his victory had opened no clear passage to the city, and that Washington's army, really but little weakened, must still be disposed of first. He intended if possible to manœuvre it out of the way. He spent the two following days at Dilworthtown making arrangements for his sick and wounded; sending out detachments to seize Chester and Concord, and especially Wilmington, where they would have more civilized comforts and be in touch with the fleet. The latter party by a sudden onslaught seized the governor of Delaware, John McKinley, in his bed, and captured a shallop lying in the river with the public records and a mass of plate and jewels.

Washington retreated leisurely across the Schuylkill to Germantown, a few miles north of Philadelphia; and so little had the splendidly redeemed defeat disheartened his army, that after a single day he was able to lead them back toward the British for another stand. Armstrong and the Pennsylvania militia were left to intrench along the Schuylkill and remove all the boats to its eastern side; Washington moved on the Lancaster road to gain West Chester, a few miles north of the late battlefield, and attempt flanking Howe's left. Howe learned of the movement through Tory spies; and at Warren's Tavern twenty-three miles from Philadelphia, Washington's advance (Wayne) found itself confronted by Howe's

(Donop and his Hessians). A violent rain prevented joining battle, and lasted all night; the Americans, without blankets or tents, had their cartridges drenched beyond use, and Washington could only withdraw his forces from certain destruction by a day's and night's march through deep mud, to Warwick on Yellow Creek, half-way to the important magazine of Reading.

Wayne was left behind with 1500 men and four guns to form a junction with General Smallwood and Colonel Gist, who were advancing with 1800 of the Maryland militia, to harass the British rear and cut off their supplies. He encamped in a thick wood, and his scouts found Howe's army united and waiting for dry weather to advance, apparently unconscious of a foe's proximity; and he sent urgently to Washington to take advantage of the opportunity for a surprise. But Howe was kept informed of every step, and was only waiting for night (of the 20th) to execute a surprise of his own. Then Sir Charles Grey with Tory guides led a force of British and Hessians to near the Paoli tavern east of Malvern, turned into the woods, silently slew the American pickets, and shortly after midnight struck Wayne's left flank just as Wayne, alarmed by reports of patrols being missed, was deploying his men in the light of his own camp-fires. Hidden in the darkness and with the Americans in glaring view, Grey's men rushed on them with the bayonet and "stuck them like so many pigs, one after another," in the words of a Hessian sergeant. The Americans fired

1777
Sept.
16–20

Warren's
Tavern:
battle
prevented by
rain

Wayne
to beat
up Howe

Himself
beaten up

Butchery

several volleys almost at random, but in a few minutes were broken up and scattered in flight; 53 were killed—many, it was said, while begging for quarter [1]—and about 100 wounded, and 70 to 80 captured. Wayne with some cavalry and infantry held back the assailants and brought off most of his force, but lost two cannon and large quantities of small-arms and stores. Smallwood a mile in the rear undertook vainly to reinforce him.

Disaster at Paoli

The next day Howe began a rapid march up the west bank of the Schuylkill toward Reading. Washington kept abreast of him on the east side, and both armies encamped where Pottstown now stands. In the night Howe made a swift and silent countermarch for some distance to a lower ford, crossed at daylight, and being thus between Washington and Philadelphia, marched toward it unhindered; for Washington had no object in bloodshed which could not hope to prevent the occupation. Howe's main body camped at Germantown; but Cornwallis, with a large force and a number of distinguished officers, made a formal entry into Philadelphia on the 26th. The Quakers and Tories greeted the glittering cavalcade of

Howe gains Philadelphia by manœuvre

Final entry

---

[1] Grey was called the "no-flint general": his regular orders were to use the bayonet without firing, for which purpose he had the flints taken from the guns—and it was said also to give no quarter. This may be exaggerated, but there is no reason why one commander should have been selected for this opprobrium rather than another without some ground. This affair was so firmly believed by the Americans to have been accompanied by butchery after surrender, that it was always known as the "Massacre of Paoli"; and Grey's name was held in an abhorrence confirmed by the massacre of an entire regiment at Tappan the next year, by his corps. He was either exceptionally merciless or very unlucky.

brilliant uniforms, dashing horsemen, long columns of grenadiers and long trains of artillery, with demonstrations of extravagant joy. They were somewhat disillusioned when they found that they were looked on as a conquered community, that loyalists as being provincials were despised about as much as patriots, and that the winter's occupation by the British cost them more in requisitions and forced levies than years of Continental possession would do. Four British regiments with Cornwallis were quartered in the city. Batteries were planted to defend it; and two American frigates which tried to silence them ran aground and were captured.

John Adams, then head of the Board of War, was furious at Washington for not holding the fords, and prayed for "one great soul," "one leading mind." Samuel Adams and Mifflin shared the feeling. The public was despondent. Washington was not: affairs were not nearly so bad as the fall before, and Philadelphia was a city like another; news of Bennington and St. Leger's flight had reached him, and he saw that Burgoyne was doomed if Howe could be kept from joining him. He wrote to Putnam for 2500 men, and to Gates to send back Morgan's riflemen if he could spare them. Gates could not, truly enough; and his own work just then was the more important. But Washington, encamped between Perkiomen and Skippack creeks, fourteen miles from Germantown, received accessions of Putnam's men and Maryland and Pennsylvania militia, and waited

1777
Sept. 26
et seq.

Philadelphia loyalists' Dead Sea apple

Washington and his critics

He is reinforced

an opportunity of striking some such blow as at Trenton.

It came through the works with which the Americans had guarded and still held the river, despite the British holding of the capital. These were two sets of sunken obstructions in the channel, consisting of heavy wooden frameworks and projecting beams with iron points; and redoubts opposite to rake vessels attempting to pass them. One was just below the mouth of the Schuylkill seven miles from the city, guarded by Fort Mifflin on a mud island off the mouth and Fort Mercer at Red Bank on the Jersey side—the latter a strong work with heavy artillery. The second was three or four miles farther down, covered by a large unfinished redoubt at Billingsport in New Jersey. Behind these were vessels of war and floating batteries. They made Howe's hold on the city very precarious: he could receive no supplies by water, and at any time Washington might succeed in cutting them off by land, as they came up from Chester where they were debarked below the fortifications.

Lord Howe's fleet, reversing the singular voyage that brought it to the Chesapeake, appeared off Newcastle, Delaware, about the first of October, to attempt clearing the river. This could be done only by holding the Jersey side, and Sir William on the 2d crossed a body of troops from Chester to assist in the operations. About the same time he sent another body to escort a provision train up from Chester; and Washington, informed of the facts by secret service, determined to fall on his weakened army at Germantown by surprise. There was further hope in the constant desertions of the "Hessians," who were tempted by the comfort and prosperity of their German brethren away from a comfortless and inglorious service, and lured by the land bounties already mentioned as offered by Congress for enlistments, the larger ones of which seemed like owning a German barony. Hundreds took the bait and risked being shot if recaptured; they were usually assigned to remote garrison duty for protection, and none ever suffered the penalty.

Germantown, a couple of miles east of the Schuylkill, was practically but a single street two miles long, of stone houses amid orchards and gardens; the road continued south to Philadelphia, and north to Skippack where Washington lay. Just north it ascended the mild slopes of the swell called Mount Airy for about a mile; descended, and again rose to Chestnut Hill a couple of miles north. Their western flank was skirted by the little Wissahickon Creek, entering the Schuylkill southwest of the village centre. This was around the market-house, at the cross-roads formed by School-House Lane running west to the Schuylkill, and east continuing on northerly as the Lime-Kiln Road; to which ran a street from near the northern end of the village, at the massive stone house of Chief Justice Benjamin Chew (then a prisoner in Fredericksburg for refusing to give a parole). Another cross-road

1777
Oct.

Hessian
desertions

Germantown

Chew's
house

ran from the Schuylkill between Mount Airy and
Chestnut Hill to the Lime-Kiln Road. These
cross-roads started on the west from the Monatawny Road, which skirted the Schuylkill to
Philadelphia; and east of the Lime-Kiln Road ran
the Old York Road, which joined the Germantown
street two miles below the centre at the Rising
Sun Tavern, near which Howe had his headquarters. The British main body lay at right
angles to the main street, facing north; the left
wing was Knyphausen's Hessians, with outposts
of chasseurs to the mouth of the Wissahickon,
commanded by Sir Charles Grey; the right wing
under Grant was flanked by a wood, with an outpost of Queen's Rangers under Lieutenant-Colonel
Simcoe; a mile in advance, in a field near the
Chew house, was Colonel Musgrave with a regiment; and on Mount Airy a battalion of light
infantry.

Washington's plan was to assail the force on
every side, drive it back against the Schuylkill,
and capture it thus surrounded. To this end, the
main attack was to be on the right, by the Lime-
Kiln Road and the market-house; and this was
committed to Greene with about two-thirds of the
army—his own and Stephen's divisions flanked
by McDougall's brigade. Sullivan and Wayne,
flanked by Conway's brigade, and accompanied
by Washington in person, were to move straight
down the Chestnut Hill Road and assail Knyphausen; closely followed by Stirling with Nash's
North-Carolinians and Maxwell's Virginians as

a reserve. The left and rear were to be enveloped by Armstrong's Pennsylvania militia, via the Monatawny Road and School-House Lane; the right rear by Smallwood's and Forman's Maryland and New Jersey militia, through a long detour over the Old York Road—expected to arrive when the British were already broken, and cut off retreat. Attack was to begin at daylight on the 4th.

1777
Oct. 4

Plan of Germantown surprise

The plan was far too complicated, and too dependent on exact co-operation, for execution by troops largely raw, on a dark night and very foggy morning and over rain-sogged roads. The commanders could not see the movements of most of their own divisions, nor be sure what orders to issue; and all were much later than the calculation. The surprise was aborted at the outset by Wayne's advance, attempting to steal silently on the pickets at Chestnut Hill, stumbling instead on double sentries whose guns alarmed the whole British camp. Thus left no alternative, Wayne charged swiftly and the British light battalion broke and fled; rallied and made a stand, and again gave way; reinforced by some grenadiers, again faced about. But Wayne's men had now discovered that their opponents were the perpetrators of the Paoli butchery, and in a flame of vengeance rushed forward and broke them into a stampeding herd; "they took ample vengeance for that night's work," reported Wayne.

Overloaded

Spoiled at beginning

British vanguard routed

Sweeping down the road, they came upon Musgrave's regiment and assailed it in turn; but

1777
Oct. 4

Musgrave threw six companies into the Chew house, barricaded the doors and windows, put his best marksmen in the upper story, and through American misjudgment turned the fortunes of the day. Wayne had gone to the right, and led his men straight on; but Knox, the chief of artillery, was with the rest of the division, and had the pedantry of the unoriginal half-educated. Musgrave's men fired on the troops; Knox declared that according to the rules of war a fortified post must not be left in their rear. Most of the other officers scouted risking a great battle for the bogy of a few hundred men in a house; Knox persisted, and Washington, injudiciously yielding his own opinion, agreed to leave the decision to Conway as a brave and trained foreign officer; he could not be found, and the whole forward movement was checked to attempt capturing the house. But neither Maxwell's artillery nor torches nor storming parties—who actually penetrated a corner room, but could not force the heavy door into the centre—availed. Wayne was recalled to help, to his immense disgust—"a windmill attack" on troops only trying to "avoid our bayonets." After a half-hour, Washington did what should have been done at the outset, and might well have saved the battle—posted a guard at the house and let Sullivan with Nash and Conway push along toward the village centre.

Meantime the wings were in a maze; brigades disordered and regiments separated in the fog, and as likely to run into the enemy as their own

Chew's
house

Foolish
American
assault

Aban-
doned

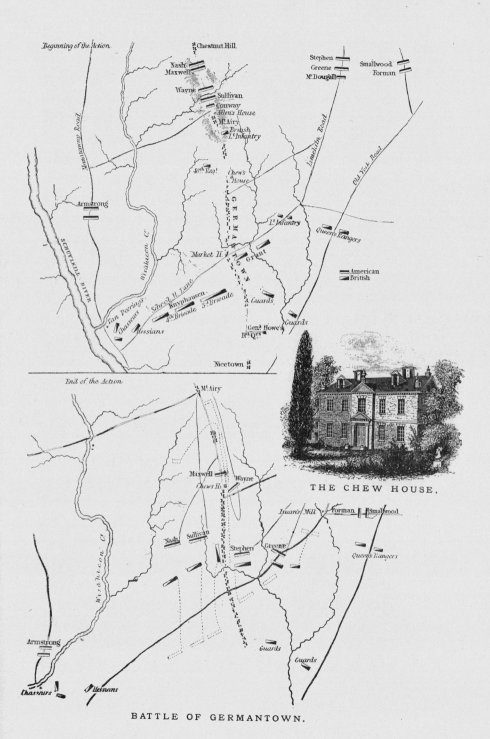

Beginning of the Action

Chestnut Hill

Nash
Maxwell

Wayne

Sullivan
Conway
Allen's House
Mt Airy
British
Lt Infantry

40th Reg^t

Chew's House

Armstrong

Lt Infantry

Queen's Rangers

American
British

Market H.

Grant

School H. Lane

Knyphausen

4th Brigade

3^d Brigade

Guards

Van Deering's Chassears

Hessians

Genl Howe's
Hd Qrs

Guards

Nicetown

Stephen
Greene
McDougall

Smallwood
Forman

Limekiln Road

Old York Road

Manatawny Road

SCHUYLKILL RIVER

Wissahicon C^t

GERMANTOWN

End of the Action

Mt Airy

Maxwell
Chew's H^o
Wayne

Luan's Hill
Forman
Smallwood

Nash
Sullivan

Stephen
Greene

Queen's Rangers

Wissahicon C^t

Armstrong

Guards

Guards

Chassurs
Hessians

THE CHEW HOUSE.

BATTLE OF GERMANTOWN.

corps, and commanders unable to reunite or direct them.   The left wing, Greene and Stephen, had formed two miles east and advanced over a country cut up by small fenced inclosures, orchards, and bogs, obliquely across the roads and therefore unguided by them, and the lines broken into extreme disorder.   McDougall did not come into the fight at all; Smallwood and Forman on the York Road not until too late.   Stephen, losing his direction in the fog (charged also with being foggy from drink, and court-martialed and dismissed for it, though a brave man), took the firing at the Chew house for the heart of the battle and marched thither; his right brigade opened a cannonade on it, his left came out on Wayne's left and startled it into a hasty retreat, the battalions and firing from the east being mistaken for a fresh British assault.   Greene with Scott's and Muhlenberg's brigades kept straight on, routed Grant's light infantry and rangers, and made a sharp attack on the main body.

Had the agreed militia assaults been made at this juncture to west and east, the British force, entirely surrounded, must have been annihilated.   It too was paralyzed by the fog, and daunted at the sudden and fierce American onslaught; the officers had selected Chester as a rendezvous and were about to attempt a full retreat upon it.   But Armstrong's men blenched at the Hessian array and refused to go forward; and Grey, thus left free, threw nearly the whole of the Hessian force upon Greene's corps, while Grant, unmolested on his

1777
Oct. 4

Advance
of
American
left

Stephen
goes
wrong

Greene
comes
near
victory

Militia
balk

1777
Oct. 4

German-
town:
British
restore
their
battle

right, closed in upon him also. Colonel Matthews
had encountered one of Grant's battalions east of
the Chew house, took 110 prisoners, and drove
the rest to Lucan's Mill; but Grant surrounded
and captured the 100 of Matthews' command left
after a desperate fight in which most of them were
killed or wounded, and then sent two regiments to
reinforce Musgrave at the Chew house. This real
British force cut up the rear of Stephen's division
marching toward the village centre, just after that
imaginary force had started a panic in Wayne's
men; and a horseman, either a fugitive American
or a British decoy, galloped to the centre shouting
to the Americans to escape, as the enemy were on
all sides. The firing so far in the rear seemed to
confirm it. Sullivan with Nash and Conway had
now penetrated to the centre, and Armstrong had
succeeded in heartening the militia to join the attack; but the former's ammunition was nearly exhausted, the whole British force was concentrated
against part of the American, and the warning
stampeded the militia in headlong flight.

It was now half-past eight, and Washington
gave the order for a general retreat. Just then
Cornwallis from Philadelphia, who had turned
out at the sound of cannon and hurried a battalion
of infantry and a squadron of light-horse northward, came on the field and fiercely charged the
retreating Americans. But Greene checked him
with severe punishment, and though pursued for
five miles, covered the retreat so handsomely—
nobly aided by Conway and Pulaski—that the

Corn-
wallis
harries
American
retreat

Checked
by
Greene

army brought off all its artillery, several pieces captured from the enemy, and its wounded. Wayne finally stopped the pursuit by planting a battery at Whitemarsh Church.

1777
Oct. 4,
etc.

The battle of Germantown lasted two hours and forty minutes. It cost the Americans 152 killed, including General Nash; 521 wounded, all but 33 being Continentals; and above 400 prisoners and missing (many being deserters in the confusion)—about 1100 in all. Howe reported a total loss of 535—not much under the American numbers aside from prisoners; and there are reasons for thinking it much understated. For once, the people appreciated that the carefully planned and bravely fought battle was in all essentials a victory; and foreigners were so deeply impressed by Washington's having narrowly missed destroying Howe's entire army three weeks after Howe had defeated him and captured Philadelphia, that technical defeat as it was, it had practically decided the French court to make a formal alliance with the United States even before Burgoyne's surrender.

Losses at German-town

Real American victory

Fruits

But in truth, this entire campaign of Howe's was in result one long victory for the Americans, irrespective of actual details. Any operations which made it slow, and prevented him from ending it and reinforcing Burgoyne, were so many nails in the coffin of the latter and the British cause; stubbornly contested defeats, and an army always to be guarded against, were nearly as serviceable as victories for this end. The campaign was

Howe's campaign saves America

parallel to Burgoyne's and every week of it was at his expense. During late July and early August, while Burgoyne's Indians were terrorizing and depopulating the upper Hudson district,—ravages which a stronger British army would have enabled the commanders to check, by being able to dispense with the perpetrators,—Howe was beating about off the Jersey shore and the mouth of the Delaware. When Oriskany was fought, when Bennington was fought, when Arnold was marching to relieve Fort Stanwix, Howe's fleet and army were crawling down the Eastern Shore of Maryland; the very day that St. Leger's force took to flight, Howe entered the Chesapeake; near three weeks later, when Howe was just forcing the passage of the Brandywine, Burgoyne was within two days of beginning his first desperate attempt to force the Hudson line, and reach Albany and (as he hoped) Howe, which was checked by the battle of September 19; the battle of Germantown, coincident with Howe's beginning preparations to open the Delaware, was three days before the final battle near Bemis' Heights which cut off Burgoyne's last hope of escape.

Since we left Burgoyne, his situation for a long time had grown steadily worse, not so much in the state of his own command as in the strengthening of his opponents. His Indians mostly left him, as stated; but they had exhausted any powers of useful service and done irreparable mischief. The wavering Onondagas had been decided by St. Leger's fiasco to join the Americans, and part of the Mohawks broke away from Brant and did likewise. The country about was a virtual desert. "We had to travel through almost impassable woods," says Madame Riedesel, " in a picturesque and beautiful region, but which was almost abandoned by its inhabitants." The settled parts had ejected most of their loyalists, and were a unit in giving help and intelligence to the patriots. Burgoyne could not communicate with his brethren in New York, even by carefully disguised messengers: two were hanged and the rest never heard of. He woke from his dream. "The great bulk of the country is undoubtedly with Congress in principle and zeal," he wrote ruefully to Germain: "wherever the King's forces point, militia to the amount of three or four thousand assemble in twenty-four hours." This meant Vermont, to which he gave a finely turned sentence that must have soothed his literary heart even for defeat: "The Hampshire Grants, a country unpeopled and almost unknown last war, now abounds in the most active and rebellious race of the continent, and hangs like a gathering storm upon my left."

Gates had succeeded to an army at last capable of effective action. Putnam had sent on two brigades from Peekskill, Washington some of his best artillery. Schuyler had gone to Albany, and was doing good service to his small-minded rival by organizing and forwarding reinforcements and negotiating with the friendly Iroquois sachems. Arnold on his return was given command of the left wing, Gates holding the right next the river;

1777
Aug.-
Sept.

Burgoyne alone in a hostile land

American army

the whole now amounted to some **7000 effective** troops.

Burgoyne was in a desperate dilemma. To advance unless Howe were to be at Albany to meet him would be suicide; on the other hand, to retreat through that forest, now sure to be alive with hostile militia instead of Indians in his own employ, would be most hazardous, and the abandonment of the campaign would be ignominious. Not having any news either way, he gave his hope and his reputation the benefit of the doubt; and assumed that Howe would keep his part of the programme, possibly even sending forward relief parties. Perhaps the considerations he put first in his letter to Germain after the surrender may really have added their weight, for he was a generous man and a patriot—that it would not be right to leave Gates' army at large to throw itself upon Howe, and that his instructions were peremptory to go forward and form the junction.

He hushed his morning and evening guns and paraded without beat of drum, to conceal his movements from the Americans, now exultant over having him trapped; but merely frightened them for fear he might slip away.[1] By immense effort, he had thirty days' provisions hauled and boated from Lake George to and down the Hudson. He called in his outposts at Fort George, Fort Anne,

Margin notes: 1777 Aug.-Sept. / Burgoyne's ruinous dilemma / Deciding reasons / Tries quiet advance

---

[1] They knew his every plan long before its execution. Perhaps Madame Riedesel's account sheds some light on it: she was astonished that the British officers' wives were informed beforehand of all movements—very different from the way in Ferdinand of Brunswick's old army. But each army swarmed with the spies of the other.

and Skenesborough, giving up all communications except Ticonderoga; built a bridge of boats over the river near the mouth of the Batten Kill; and on the 13th and 14th crossed his army, less than 7000 effectives, and encamped at the mouth of Fish Creek (Schuylerville). Thence he sent the sappers' corps in advance to repair roads and bridges; but the Americans had so thoroughly broken them up that it took four days for the British to march as many miles.

Gates had shortly before moved back from Half-Moon to Stillwater, six miles below Burgoyne's crossing. It was at first proposed to fortify there for the coming struggle; but Arnold took Kosciuszko the Polish engineer, and others, and made a careful study of the country west of the river flats to select a stronger position. This region was a plateau, heavily wooded save for occasional clearings, rising into swells and cut by ravines. A section two miles north of Stillwater, where the valley narrows to a few hundred feet and is bordered by a high bluff, sloping back to a summit known as Bemis' Heights, was fixed on under the advice of Kosciuszko. He laid out lines of fortification extending three-quarters of a mile along the bluff, with batteries at each end and one in the centre to command the valley on both sides; from its foot an intrenchment was carried to the river, with a strong battery to guard a floating bridge and enfilade the passage down river or valley; and the same was done half a mile north at the mouth of Mill Creek. The works were finished

1777
Sept.

Burgoyne crosses the Hudson

Americans at Stillwater

Bemis' Heights fortified

on the 15th. Arnold sent a scouting corps east of the river to ward off possible surprises thence.

Gates had ordered Lincoln, Stark, and all other outlying militia parties to join him; but before doing so, the first-named executed a brilliant stroke consequent on Burgoyne's calling in his outposts, and which glaringly exhibited the initial weakness of his campaign. Colonel John Brown of Pittsfield, Arnold's foe, with five hundred men burst upon Ticonderoga about dawn of the 18th; **Mount Defiance captured** and almost without loss captured Mount Defiance and the near-by works guarding the Lake George portage, with 293 prisoners (besides releasing 100 Americans), stores and arms and five cannon; seized or destroyed 200 vessels transporting provisions on the lakes, several of them armed; and thus held command of Lake George. Uniting with a party under Colonel Johnson, they besieged old **Ticonderoga besieged** Ticonderoga itself for four days; but finding it too strong to reduce, joined the main army.

On the 18th, Burgoyne had come within two miles of the American camp, occupying a more **Burgoyne forms for battle** northern range of heights with two ravines between the armies. Early the next morning—bright and frosty—he formed for the battle which alone could clear his path.[1] His left was the Germans

---

[1] Until recent years, the accepted names of Burgoyne's two pitched battles were the First and Second Battle of Saratoga; they were in Saratoga township, the final camp and surrender were near Saratoga church and ford, and the capitulation was termed the Convention of Saratoga. Later they were called the battles of Bemis Heights; still more recently, of Freeman's Farm. But the old name is still the only one known to the world in general. The battlefield is a dozen miles east of the present Saratoga Springs.

with Phillips and the chief artillery, along the flats; the centre led by himself kept the high ground west; the right was the grenadiers and light infantry under Fraser, with Breymann; the remaining provincials and Indians acted as skirmishers in front and on the flanks. His plan was to have the skirmish line hold the Americans in play, while his left wing gained a position near their centre; his own and Fraser's bodies were to make separate detours through the woods to the west and gain the American rear, and when signal guns announced their junction, a general assault should drive back or break the army already outflanked.

1777
Sept. 19

Burgoyne's array

The American force was disposed with the main body under Gates in person—Glover's, Nixon's, and Patterson's brigades—along the bluff and the flats; the centre on the plateau west was Learned's brigade; the left wing—Poor's brigade with Dearborn's light infantry and Morgan's riflemen—occupied the western summit three-quarters of a mile from the river; both centre and left were under Arnold.

American array

The moving of British bodies to form order of battle was early reported by the scouts, and about ten o'clock the full movement was developed. Arnold eagerly pressed Gates to move forward and encounter them. Gates (called by Burgoyne "an old midwife") saw no object in erecting fortifications except to have the benefit of them, wished to await the attack there, and would not suffer an advance. It is an excuse for his decision that the stock of powder and lead was nearly exhausted,

Gates refuses to attack

and in fact the battle of the day left some regiments practically unarmed; but his later conduct makes the excuse seem rather a pretext, and Arnold must have known the conditions as well as he. Arnold at last about noon secured a reluctant permission to act with his wing; and sent Morgan and Dearborn to drive in the centre skirmish lines. These, meeting the provincials and Indians at Mill Creek ravine a mile north, put them to flight; but themselves became scattered in the woods, and a reinforcement of regulars from Burgoyne's advancing columns took 22 prisoners and menaced destruction to the whole. Morgan's signal whistle collected his men, however; Arnold hurried two regiments to his aid, and after a sharp drawn fight both divisions fell back on their lines. Down the same stream on the flats, American pickets routed a body of the particolored allies working around to take them in flank.

Meantime Burgoyne had crossed a northern branch of the same ravine, and in his progress westward come to a small clearing called Freeman's farm, on the crest between the two; and Fraser, reaching a point half a mile northwest, turned south to come upon the American rear. Arnold on his part had sent three other regiments to the support of Morgan and Dearborn against Burgoyne, and now sought to bar Fraser's movement. He had asked a detachment from Gates' right wing, but Gates declared he "would not have the camp exposed." The British left was in fact within half a mile; but if their right should flank the American position, his holding Riedesel at bay would be of little avail, and what were his intrenchments for but to enable the defenders to withstand a force larger than they?

1777
Sept. 19

Arnold, however, being determined to cut off Fraser while separated from the main body, stripped his own part of the lines by taking the two regiments of Connecticut militia and part of Learned's brigade, and hurried to the left. But he could not know just where Fraser meant to strike; and as each foe pushed through the woods in ignorance of the other's movements, Arnold's right suddenly came face to face on Freeman's farm with the right of Burgoyne's division, not far from Fraser's left.

Arnold
moves
against
Fraser

A furious combat ensued. Arnold at first was borne back by the superior weight of the British battalions; and Fraser turned east and hotly assailed his left flank. But Arnold succeeded in calling four more regiments to his aid, drove the British in his front while Morgan and the others held their ground, and was fairly piercing between Burgoyne and Fraser and severing the army; Fraser saw it, and weakened his own attack by sending heavy reinforcements to strengthen the point of danger. But Arnold's whole wing, now fully engaged, made a general onslaught with such determination that the British were giving way; when Phillips, hearing the long fierce din of strife, hurried a body of fresh troops and part of his artillery from the riverside, and Arnold's corps were forced back up the slopes of their hill.

Fight at
Free-
man's
Farm

Arnold
nearly
severs
British
army

1777
Sept. 19
"Sara-
toga" 1st:

This was about half-past two, and for half an hour there was silence. Burgoyne and Fraser faced Arnold on an opposite hill-slope out of musket range, in a thin pine grove with artillery in front; the Americans were in a thick wood where artillery could not be used. The British opened a heavy cannonade; the Americans made no reply. Burgoyne then ordered the American lines to be carried with the bayonet; but as soon as his troops came within range in the open, the Americans poured such destructive volleys on them that they broke and retreated in dismay to the edge of the clearing, chased by the Americans, who captured the guns. Before they could turn them on the foe, however, the latter, again re-formed, charged and drove the patriots to their own side of the ravine, only to be once more pushed back to their lines. For more than three hours this pendulum of battle went on, the artillery taken and retaken at every charge and never coming into play, and at last being spiked by the British. Not till sundown did the general engagement cease. During all this fight Gates sent not one man to the help of his army, till towards the close he allowed one Massachusetts regiment to take part, which had a brief skirmish. One of Arnold's Massachusetts battalions remained on the field till eleven at night, and had a fight in the dark with Breymann's riflemen, recognizable as such only by the brass match-cases on their coats.

The Americans carried back to their lines about 100 British prisoners, and over 400 other British

Wavering at canon battle

Drawn at night

had been killed or wounded. The Americans had 38 missing, 64 killed, 217 wounded,—319 against over 500. About 2500 Americans and 3000 British had been engaged; but for some reason, the chief loss fell on a very few bodies on each side. It is not strange that of the 48 artillerymen serving the contested guns, 36 were struck down; one British brigade of several hundred had but five officers and sixty men left. The British officers were carefully picked off by American sharpshooters in the trees. On the latter side, Major William Hull's detachment of 200 lost over half. This heroic fighter was sentenced to death in the war of 1812 for cowardice, by the superior who had left him to destruction.

The British claimed a victory as "holding the field," sleeping on their arms all night at Freeman's farm; but it was an obvious and disastrous defeat. Not only had they failed to force the passage toward Albany, but the battle had made it very dubious whether they could ever do so, unless Howe or Clinton sent troops to make a simultaneous assault on the American rear. In fact, the next day they withdrew from the farm to their lines of the 18th, and began to intrench. The day after came a cipher dispatch successfully slipped through from Clinton, informing Burgoyne that in the exercise of the discretion allowed himself, he intended to force the Hudson forts on the 20th and come to Burgoyne's relief. Burgoyne sent two officers in disguise by different routes to assure Clinton that he had provisions only till the

1777
Sept.
19-21

Losses
in the
battle

British
calamity

Bur-
goyne's
perilous
state

12th of October, and implore speedy action; and settled down to wait for it, believing that at worst it must draw off a part of Gates' army and make a new assault practicable.

Arnold was hot with anger that Gates had not brought his reserves into action; had it been done, the closeness of the contest with much less than half the army engaged proves that the British forces must have been destroyed. The next morning he begged Gates to renew the attack on Burgoyne at once before he could intrench. Gates refused utterly. His former reasons were strengthened by a venomous jealousy of Arnold, whose former repute was now vastly augmented by the admiration for his magnificent commandership in this engagement; and his intimates believed that Arnold's friendship for Schuyler had even more to do with it. Gates in his dispatch did not mention Arnold's name, saying that the battle was fought by "detachments from the army." He also began at once a system of countermanding Arnold's orders and humiliating him before the troops, which Arnold for a day or two swallowed rather than prejudice the service; at length Gates removed Morgan's and Dearborn's corps from Arnold's command without even consulting him. Arnold went to Gates' tent and had a fierce quarrel with him. Gates heaped insolent abuse on Arnold; declared that he was of no consequence to the army and no officer of it at all, as he had sent his resignation to Congress, and that as soon as Lincoln came, he (Gates) proposed to give him Arnold's place. Arnold demanded a passport to leave the army, and received it with alacrity. But proud and sensitive as he was, he was a high-hearted patriot and the bravest of the brave. He could not bear to leave the scene of the perhaps decisive conflict for his cause; and lingered until he should be actually removed from command. His officers also not only begged him to remain, but united in an address to that effect, as they expected another battle.

1777
Sept.
22-30

Arnold
decides to
remain

Gates' very sluggishness and indecision in all but his own place-hunting, however, inefficient as it made him, and his preference for silent undermining to arbitrary openness,—the extreme opposite to Arnold,—prevented the carrying out of his threat. Probably too in his heart he knew that his own chances of success and glory were much better with Arnold than without him. On the arrival of Lincoln, who was on good terms with Arnold, the two agreed that Arnold should retain the left wing, and Lincoln as the ranking officer take the right; and Arnold privately said it would be death for any one to interfere in his command— that is, till he was officially suspended. Lincoln tried to smooth over matters between the two; but Gates, though he did not remove Arnold from the command, ignored him and admitted him to no councils. Arnold on the last of the month wrote to Gates that his conduct was doubtless due to jealousy; but that out of pure zeal for the army and country at a critical juncture, and from no desire to outshine or displace Gates, he (Arnold)

Gates
does not
remove
him

Lincoln
and
Arnold

Arnold
and
Gates

intended to sacrifice himself and remain. Gates made no answer; but blustered to others that he "only waited an opportunity to right himself with his sword." Arnold tried to stir Gates to attack Burgoyne once more; and wrote that the militia were threatening to go home, and a fortnight's inaction would probably thin the army by 4000, besides that the enemy might be reinforced or make good their retreat. Gates paid no attention.

Burgoyne planted a line of intrenchments with four redoubts on knolls, along the bluff a couple of miles north of the American position; another across the flat from the northernmost redoubt to the river, to protect his hospital and magazine, guarded by a strong body of mixed troops; from the southernmost redoubt he carried the line west across the front of Freeman's farm, turning north for some distance, and strengthened by four more redoubts. Breymann's Hessians were encamped on a rise half a mile northwest of the farm, with a redoubt and a semicircular line of breastworks, convex west; the rest of Fraser's corps, with Earl Balcarras' light infantry, on the farm; Phillips and Riedesel as before. Under Arnold's energetic direction, Gates showing no concern in it, the American lines were immensely extended, and made convex to the enemy. From the north redoubt on the bluff they were carried northwest three quarters of a mile, covered in front by a deep forested ravine, to the heights; there a log barn was turned by extra layers of logs into a formidable fortress (Fort Neilson, from the owner of the barn), encircled by a deep moat and protected by strong batteries, and with abatis (felled trees sharpened and pointed out) some way west. Thence the intrenchment was continued south to another creek ravine extending to the river south of the southern bluff redoubt. The works were thus a rough horseshoe, the open side resting on the southern ravine. Near the centre was a bomb-proof magazine to secure against another failure of ammunition, a supply of which had now been received.

Lincoln came into the American camp on the 29th, with 2000 New England militia and about 150 Iroquois, whom Schuyler had sent and Gates was better advised in not wishing. It was better to keep American skirts clear of anything to serve even as a British pretext. With former accessions, the army now amounted to perhaps 11,000 men, nearly double Burgoyne's though of course with less training. Burgoyne's foraging parties were cut off, his horses were half fed and growing weak, there were 300 sick and wounded in his hospital; the bridges rebuilt in his rear were again broken down, the forests full of foes, and a retreat would shortly become past hope. On October 1, the soldiers were put on half rations. Still no word came from Clinton. On the evening of the 4th a council of war was called. Burgoyne proposed a new flank march; Riedesel (for the first time admitted) said it would leave stores and boats at the mercy of the Americans, and advised instant retreat to Fort Edward and the restoring of communications with

Ticonderoga. Burgoyne could not bear to give up hope of Clinton and final success; but at length promised that if on a grand reconnoissance the American position could not be successfully attacked, he would agree to retreat.

On the morning of the 7th a foraging party was sent out into a wheat field. To cover it and see if the American left could be turned by a sudden movement, Burgoyne followed with all his best commanders, 1500 men, and ten cannon, all he dared to spare from his depleted camp; which was left in charge of Hamilton and Specht, the river redoubts manned by Hessians under General Gall. They started at eleven o'clock,—a purposely late hour, that if defeated night should enable them to withdraw in safety; and formed along the north brow of the west end of Middle Creek ravine, three quarters of a mile northwest of the American log fort. Balcarras' light infantry and a British regiment held the right against a wooden knoll, Phillips and Riedesel the centre with British and Germans, Major Ackland's grenadiers and Williams' artillery the left on another wooded rise. Fraser was in advance of the right with 500 picked men, to make a flank assault on the enemy's left as soon as the front was engaged. The mongrel skirmishers were to harass the American flank and rear, and divert attention from the chief movements.

The first attack was by the skirmishers near the middle ravine. They drove in the pickets, and chased them toward their lines; soon joined by a body of grenadiers, the whole pressed on to within gunshot of the western breastworks south of the fort, where a half-hour's sharp musketry fight ensued. "Order out Morgan to begin the game," said Gates; and Morgan with his riflemen and other infantry charged, forcing them about two o'clock to take refuge in the new British lines. Inspecting these, Morgan at once perceived Fraser's intent; and induced Gates to let him take 1500 men including his rifle corps, make a detour and gain Fraser's right, anticipating his flank movement, and assail him as soon as another body fell upon the British left. Poor's and part of Learned's brigade were assigned to the latter service. Marching in dead silence up the slope, ordered to let the enemy have the first fire, they heard a tremendous discharge pass mostly over their heads, the British firing too high; then they poured in volleys in rapid succession, as they pressed forward through the trees. After a long and furious struggle in front of and amid the cannon, one of which was taken and retaken five times, Ackland was severely wounded, he and Williams were taken prisoners, and the artillery was turned upon the British, who fled in utter rout, leaving the left flank of Burgoyne's centre exposed. Burgoyne's first aide, Sir Francis Clarke, was sent to call help to them; but was mortally wounded and taken by the Americans before delivering his message.[1]

*1777
Oct. 7*

Morgan opens battle

Burgoyne's left wing routed

---

[1] His memory has been perpetuated by Wilkinson, as the hero of the one recorded performance of Gates during this battle except to

At the signal of firing, Morgan threw his men upon Fraser's with such impetuosity that he drove them back to the line of the right; then making a rapid circuit through the forest, he came suddenly upon the right flank and hailed a destructive fire upon it. Almost at the same moment Dearborn attacked them in front, and they broke and fled. The forest stood their friend, however; out of sight Balcarras rallied them, and again they came on.

The British centre still stood firm, though both its flanks were laid bare; but Burgoyne, seeing that Morgan's corps was likely to surround the right and cut the British off from their camp, ordered Fraser to protect the retreat by forming a new line in the rear. Meantime Arnold could not endure his inaction longer. Mounting his horse, he galloped to the front of Learned's three remaining regiments and shouted to them to follow him; and they hastened after him to the fray.[1]

attempt recalling Arnold. Clarke was laid on a bed in Gates' headquarters, and Gates entered into a discussion with the dying man as to the merits of the rival causes; overmatched, he lost his temper, and calling an aide outside, said to him, "Did you ever hear so impudent a son of a b——h?" Clarke died that night.

[1] The accepted statement, dear to the heart of historians from its dramatic contrast, that Arnold was without command, serving as a volunteer and obeyed by the troops from mere good-will, is not true. He was still the commander of the left wing, entitled to obedience till some other was put in his place, which had not been done. It is true, however, that he felt his position ambiguous, liable to be ended at any moment by Gates' caprice (in fact Gates did try to prevent his earning any more glory, as usual assigning a false reason); was uncertain how far he could enforce orders if contested, and relied for obedience on the men's willingness more than on discipline. This explains his waiting so long before engaging in action. Gates sent a mounted aide —Major John Armstrong, afterwards Secretary of War in 1813—to order him back, for fear "he might do something rash"! This officer chased him all about the field as he rode from one point to another,

Marginal notes:

1777 Oct. 7

"Saratoga" 2d:

British right centre broken

Fraser to protect retreat

Arnold goes into action

He made so fierce an onset upon the Hessians that they recoiled; gathering again, they returned to the charge, when he delivered a second and irresistible attack and they broke and scattered.

The entire line was now engaged. Arnold seemed possessed by a demon which communicated itself to the rest, a delirium which gave him preternatural force. He rushed from regiment to regiment, plunging into and directing every attack, suggesting formations and points of vantage, and leaving no breathing-time for the British. Second only to him as director of movements, though officially but a colonel of riflemen under him, was Morgan; a tower of strength, of sure instinct in tactics and inspiring exultant confidence in his troops, and rendered the obedience due to recognized genius. Some British officers later gave him the chief credit for their overthrow; and the best proof of his transcendent merit is that Gates after the battle transferred his jealousy from Arnold to him. These two had the field of glory to themselves; neither Gates nor Lincoln left the intrenchments during the battle—there was but one Arnold to act without orders.

On the British side, Burgoyne approved himself a hero: dressed in his full uniform and mounted on a noble horse, he exposed himself with utter disregard of safety, and his hat and waistcoat were pierced with bullets. Each of his generals emulated him; but Fraser on his massive

working destruction to the British; and only delivered the order to him as he lay crippled in the captured fort.

1777
Oct. 7

"Sara-
toga" 2d:

Fraser
mortally
wounded

gray was the soul of the resistance, rallying and holding the lines to their work, restoring order, and making the American progress slow and costly. But so fierce was the assault that the second line could not be formed; and while undertaking it he was struck down by a sharpshooter's bullet from a tree, and borne off to die.[1]

Bur-
goyne
routed

Arnold
forces
Balcar-
ras' line

Carries
con-
necting
works

Burgoyne took his place; but the outmatched British were already losing heart and giving way, when 3000 fresh New York troops appeared in their front. Burgoyne sounded a general retreat to Fraser's camp at the right of the intrenchments; though covered by Phillips and Riedesel it swiftly became a headlong flight, hotly pursued by the Americans up to the very breastworks amid a hail of shot and shell. Arnold with part of Patterson's and Glover's brigades charged the abatis covering Balcarras' troops at the right of the camp, drove the defenders from it at the point of the bayonet, and tried to penetrate into the camp. Foiled in this, he dashed to the left where Learned's brigade was advancing against the lines between Balcarras and the Hessian camp,—an abatis flanked by two stockades,—and directed an assault which speedily carried the entire works, leaving the Hessian camp isolated and exposed. Meanwhile he had again hurried to the left, and ordered Morgan with his

---

[1] There are "reminiscences" that Arnold suggested this to Morgan, who directed one of his men to pick Fraser off. The tradition is of slight value, but if true needs no apology, as such action has always been held legitimate warfare. See Kinglake's *Crimean War*, where Colonel Lacy Yea at the battle of the Alma marks out a Russian officer to be shot down.

corps and two other regiments to assail the Hessian lines in front; then returning where the stockade next them had just been carried by Lieutenant-Colonel John Brooks, he put himself at the head of the regiment, found the Hessian sally-port, and rushed through it into Breymann's camp in the gathering twilight. The Hessians delivered a volley which killed Arnold's horse and shattered again the leg pierced at Quebec; then, receiving one in return, threw down their arms and fled wildly to Balcarras' camp, leaving Breymann mortally wounded. Some 200 were cut off and captured, with a reinforcement sent to them under Specht from the main camp.

Burgoyne tried to rally the remainder, but it was impossible; and, glad not to be further assailed, which the darkness rendered out of the question, the whole sought rest. But there must not be rest if they were to see another night except as prisoners. They had lost some 700 men, including Fraser and Breymann fatally wounded, Clarke likewise and a prisoner, Ackland and Williams taken also; besides much of their artillery and stores. The American loss was about 150.

At midnight Lincoln took out his division to hold the ground and be ready for a final battle the next day. Burgoyne, however, in the night drew off with silence and skill his entire remaining force to the heights a mile north above his hospital. The Americans at once took possession of the deserted camp, exchanging shots with the retreating army during which Lincoln was disabled from

1777
Oct. 7–8

Arnold
storms
Hessian
redoubt

Crushing
British
loss

Bur-
goyne
with-
draws
to new
lines

1777
Oct. 7–8

Burial of
Fraser

service. Fraser had died that morning, and in compliance with his dying request was buried the same evening in the old centre redoubt, amid a shower of cannon-balls from the Americans who did not know what the gathering of major-generals was for.

Gates
and Wil-
kinson

Gates infused his usual personality into his report of the battle. He named Arnold, Morgan, and Dearborn, as coequally worthy; but he did not recommend Morgan for promotion, asking that favor instead for his youthful adjutant James Wilkinson, of no achievements.

Clinton
forces the
Hudson

On the very day of the battle, Clinton from his side had completed a terrific counter-stroke, which should largely have neutralized it by forcing Gates to make a heavy draft from his army to protect his rear and all settled New York behind him. The Hudson had been opened to Albany; two forts stormed and one abandoned, obstructions costing over $250,000 of Continental money removed, the river fleet burned, and over 100 cannon with enormous quantities of ammunition, stores, tools, etc., captured.

Forts
and
obstruc-
tions

The passage at the Highlands was guarded on the west by Forts Clinton above, and Montgomery below, the estuary of a "kill" opposite the eminence of Anthony's Nose (north of Peekskill); to whose river-bank was stretched from Fort Montgomery's a boom of huge trees fastened together, and below that a massive iron chain; and in the river were sunk timber-frames with iron-shod projecting points. Both forts were over 100

BURGOYNE'S ENCAMPMENT AT FRASER'S FUNERAL.

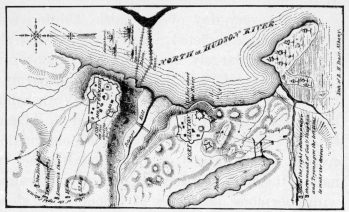

CAPTURE OF FORTS CLINTON AND MONTGOMERY.

BARRACKS OF THE CONVENTION ARMY AT CHAR-LOTTESVILLE, VA.

feet above the water, and beyond effective bombardment from it; but though commanded by Governor George Clinton and his brother James, they were wretchedly garrisoned,—not above 600 men in both, nearly all militia. In fact, Washington's draft of 2500 men had so stripped Putnam's force, at Peekskill and the neighboring Fort Independence, that though Washington could not avoid making it, he was uneasy over the Hudson. New York and Connecticut militia took the Continentals' place; but they wished to go home for the harvest, and Putnam good-naturedly allowed it, as no attack from New York seemed probable while Howe had the bulk of his army at Philadelphia. Most likely he could not have prevented it. This left him but about 1500 men. Governor Clinton in alarm ordered back half the New-Yorkers, but too late.

Sir Henry had waited for 2000 fresh troops on the way from England, which only arrived September 29. As a feint on Peekskill, on the evening of October 4 he sent 5000 men to Tarrytown on the east bank, and the next day took 3000 to Verplanck's Point not far below Peekskill. Putnam called for the local militia, and collected about 2000 troops in all; and sent for help from the forts. That night in a fog Sir Henry sent three frigates to bar any crossing from Fort Independence, and passed 2000 of his men over to Stony Point. These made their way a dozen miles north over the forested passes of the Dunderberg, to near the forts. George Clinton's scouts reported the landing, and

Ill-manned Hudson forts

Clinton's feint

Sends troops to forts

**1777
Oct. 6-7**

another party fell in with the British on their way; he sent at once to Putnam for heavy reinforcements, but the messenger was a Tory and deserted to the enemy.

By four o'clock both forts were invested. Sir Henry led the attempt on Fort Clinton, Lieutenant-Colonel Campbell with the Polish Count Grabowski and Lord Rawdon that on Montgomery.

Hudson forts stormed

The American Clintons refused to surrender; but after a struggle against overwhelming numbers till dark, the garrisons gave way and fled, half of them being captured. The American loss was 300 in all, including five regimental officers; the British 140 including Campbell and Grabowski killed. The five American armed vessels above the boom attempted to escape up the river, but adverse winds forced their abandonment and burning. The obstructions were at once cleared away. Fort

River cleared by British

Constitution opposite West Point a few miles farther up was abandoned; as shortly were Peekskill and Fort Independence, Putnam transferring his headquarters and stores to Fishkill higher up.[1]

Albany, and the entire American magazines and supporting country, were now at Clinton's

Danger of Gates' army

mercy; and the American army between two British ones would have to draw off to New England for safety, or be liable to grievous defeat if it

---

[1] Putnam of course was court-martialed, Congress demanding a scapegoat for every military disaster; and was ultimately retired from active service and set to recruiting. It is not easy to see that he was more blamable than Greene for Fort Washington, and Washington himself for being manœuvred off the road to Philadelphia; and remembering his brilliant feats gone by, we cannot but believe he was of value for other service than recruiting.

fought. On the 8th he wrote to Burgoyne implying that he would very shortly be upon Gates; refusing to advise what to do, but unless it meant him to hold out there was no object in sending it.[1] As the messenger was caught and hanged before reaching him, however, this encouragement—which would pretty certainly have caused him to hazard another battle to open the way to Clinton—was denied him. Clinton for surety sent a verbal message also by Captain Campbell, the bearer of Burgoyne's former letter to him; but this only reached the latter after his agreement to surrender. General Vaughan and Admiral Sir James Wallace were sent up the river with 3600 men— of course to make all sail to head of navigation and cut off Gates from Albany? Not at all: they merely set at work burning all the settlements and private houses along the river (the valorous Tryon was with them, and in his element), including Esopus (Kingston) the State capital; and after this worse than useless piracy, which obviously could only incense the country and scarcely diminish its fighting power, went back to New York leaving Burgoyne to his fate. The reasons for this amazing "fluke" can only be guessed.[2]

1777
Oct. 8-12

Clinton's
messages
to Bur-
goyne

Vaughan
and
Wallace
ravage
Hudson
Valley

"FORT MONTGOMERY, October 8, 1777.

[1] "*Nous y voici* [here we are], and nothing now between us and Gates. I sincerely hope this little success of ours may facilitate your operations. In answer to your letter of the 28th of September by C. C. [Captain Campbell], I shall only say, I cannot presume to order, or even advise, for reasons obvious. I heartily wish you success.

"Faithfully yours,　H. CLINTON."

[2] The current explanations are untrue and irrelevant. One is that it was too late to save Burgoyne. This was not so: besides, Clinton

1777
Oct. 9

Bur-
goyne's
retreat
for
Canada

Hard-
ships

Meantime Burgoyne at last began his retreat for Ticonderoga and Canada. But Gates, who could be active when his enemy was running away, had sent strong detachments to occupy the heights east of the Saratoga ford above Fish Creek, those near Fort Miller on the west, and those beyond on the road to Lake George; every avenue of escape was closed. Making false fires and leaving the tents standing as a blind, and abandoning his sick and wounded (treated by the Americans with a humanity which Burgoyne afterwards gratefully acknowledged), he led his army all night and all the next day through the torrents of rain and the sloughs; the worn-out soldiers sleeping as they could on the cold wet ground, too weary even to cut wood for fires. Phillips and Riedesel covered the rear; harassed by parties of Americans who had discovered the departure and pressed on their track. The main American body

---

had evidently not heard of the battle, at least when he sent his first message and presumably the expedition; and if his subordinates did so on the way, it made haste all the more urgent, and at Livingston Manor they were only five hours' sail from Albany. We are not sure what Clinton's instruction to them was; but it cannot have been peremptory to extricate Burgoyne. It is said that Campbell's message to Burgoyne was, that Vaughan and Wallace had been sent as far as Esopus; if so, Clinton himself was responsible for this petty raid instead of a military relief expedition. Whoever was so, revenge, lust of destruction, and sheer stupidity seem to have co-operated: with the peculiar English ideas of America, it may have been thought that this ravage would make the American forces stop all business and hurry down to guard the river, even after its depredators had gone. But it is hard not to believe that Clinton secretly shared Howe's feelings of not being consumed with anxiety for Burgoyne's safety. It is evident enough, from first to last, that none of Howe's following would be broken-hearted if the top-lofty Burgoyne should make a fiasco of his grand strategic scheme.

did not follow till the rain stopped on the 10th, and there was some safety for ammunition. On the evening of the 9th the British passed old Saratoga with its church, and half a mile farther on reached Fish Creek; but General Fellows with 1400 men was intrenched on the opposite bluffs commanding the ford. The next day Burgoyne crossed the creek, and planted his guns on the northern slopes where Schuylerville now stands; but the parties transferring the stores from his boats at its mouth were driven off by Fellows' artillery, and several laden bateaux captured and gutted by the Americans. All along Burgoyne's retreat he had systematically had his troops burn every building they came to; the excuse was to prevent the Americans occupying them as points of vantage to harass the British. On this ground also, they burned, on the south side of the creek, Schuyler's splendid mansion, his mills, and other buildings, worth some $50,000.

The next few days were a time of growing despair, of vain struggles against the inevitable, and of miserable suffering and terror for the women and children who had followed their protectors to share their glory. The one hope left was to secure Fort Edward, force a passage thither, and from that base clear a way to Ticonderoga. A detachment was sent to seize it, and a party of workmen to repair the bridges and open up the roads; but the fort was found in the hands of 200 Americans and the detachment dared not undertake to storm it, and the workmen were driven

1777
Oct. 9-12

Burgoyne reaches Saratoga ford

Stores plundered

British burn Schuyler's buildings

Baffled at Fort Edward

1777
Oct. 11-12

back to camp by the swarming marksmen on the
heights. This misfortune, however, nearly opened
the way for a tremendous American disaster,
which might have secured Burgoyne's escape. The
detachment trying to repossess Fort Edward was
mistaken for the main army attempting to march
to it, leaving a guard at the camp to follow later;
and Gates resolved to fall on and capture this
guard and hasten after the supposably main body.
A deserter told Burgoyne of this plan; and he laid
an ambush in the woods near the creek, of all his
army but a battery guard. The brigades of Nixon,
Glover, Patterson, and Learned, with Morgan's
corps, had been assigned to this service, and in
the fog came very near falling into the trap and
at least being dreadfully mangled. But deserters,
and the strong resistance which the British advance parties near the creek injudiciously offered,
discovered the plot in time to save the Americans.

And now the whole American army, swelled by
militia to over 13,000, had closed in around Burgoyne. His scouts brought word that every road
was impassable, and the woods alive with rebels.
Morgan's terrible corps were directly on his flank
and rear, north and west; Fellows now had 3000
men across the river; the main army was along
the creek on the south; farther back on every
height for miles was a party of Continentals or
militia. By the 12th they had drawn in so close
that every part of the camp was searched by
cannon-balls, his bordering lines were never at
rest from musket-fire, his soldiers had to sleep

Marginal notes:

Bur-
goyne's
ambush

Fails

Bur-
goyne
sur-
rounded

under arms, there was no safe refuge for sick or
wounded, for women or children, for councils of
officers. The cellar of a house in the camp was
chosen as a hospital, and crowded with sick and
maimed and the helpless families; Madame Riedesel with three little children cowered there for
days that seemed to her more than they were, with
cannon-balls crashing through the beams overhead.
There was intense suffering from thirst, for every
man who tried to bring water from the river was
shot down: finally they trusted not in vain to
American chivalry, and sent their women after it,
who were unharmed.

To retreat as a body or attempt saving artillery and baggage was now no longer possible: it
meant immediate capture or destruction. But it
was thought that the soldiers might scatter through
the woods, each with a light haversack containing
two or three days' food, and rendezvous at Fort
George, gaining Ticonderoga by boat. But this
was soon dismissed: the post and lake were in
American hands, and the fugitives would be cut off
in the woods before reaching it. The last Indians
had already stolen away, the provincials took
every opportunity to do likewise; a third of the
army that remained after Bennington had been
killed, disabled, captured, or deserted since, and
of the sound remainder a large part were Germans with no taste for martyrdom; there was not
three days' food on hand, and no more to be had;
and no word had come from Clinton. So, on the
morning of the 13th, in a tent pierced during the

1777
Oct. 10-13

Suffer-
ings in
Bur-
goyne's
army

Plans
of des-
peration

Glaring
futility

1777
Oct. 13-16
consultation by several musket-balls and an 18-pound cannon-shot, and sprinkled by the dirt thrown up by grape-shot striking near, Burgoyne and his generals held council and decided to ask terms of surrender.

Gates' first proposal was unconditional surrender. Burgoyne spiritedly refused. Gates then ordered a cessation of hostilities, and negotiation went on till the 16th, when an agreement was made, to be signed the next morning. To save the army's feelings, Burgoyne insisted that the surrender should be styled a "convention,"—a term coined for the Duke of Cumberland at Kloster-Zeven in 1757, when his Hanoverian army was cooped in by the Duc de Richelieu. This emollient was cheerfully granted, and "the Convention of Saratoga" has been a phrase of infinite comfort to British historians. The troops were to be well treated and sent free to Great Britain by the earliest transports from Boston, on parole for the rest of the war; officers to go with their corps, and retain their horses, carriages, and baggage unsearched; the Canadians of the force to be sent safe to Ticonderoga, and the Tories not to be molested; Burgoyne's dispatches to be at once forwarded to Howe, Carleton, and the British government—the latter much worse grieved at the news than the other two; and minor concessions were asked.

Gates granted all—not blamably: so long as Burgoyne's army was extinguished, it seemed to make no difference whether the men roamed in

Bur-
goyne
sur-
renders

The "Con-
vention"

Terms

GATES' LETTER TO CONGRESS ANNOUNCING BURGOYNE'S SURRENDER.

Camp at Saratoga, Oct. 18th, 1777.

Sir:

I have the satisfaction to present your Excellency with the Convention of Saratoga, by which his Excellency Lt. General Burgoyne has surrender'd himself and his whole army into my hands; and they are now upon their march to Boston. This signal and important event is the more glorious as it was effected with so little loss to the army of the United States.

This letter will be presented to your Excellency by my Adjutant-General Colo. Wilkinson, to whom I must beg leave to refer your Excellency for the particulars that brought this great business to so happy and fortunate a conclusion. I desire to be permitted to recommend this gallant officer in the warmest manner to Congress, and entreat that he may be continued in his present place with the Brevet of Brigadier General. The Honourable Congress will believe me when I assure them, that from the beginning of this War I have not met with a more promising military genius than Colo. Wilkinson, and whose Services have been of the greatest benefit to his army.

I am Sir

Yr Excellency's

Most Obt, Humble Servt,

Horatio Gates.

His Excellency, John Hancock, Esq.

GATES' LETTER TO CONGRESS ANNOUNCING BURGOYNE'S SURRENDER.

Camp at Saratoga, Oct. 18th, 1777.

Sir:

I have the satisfaction to present your Excellency with the Convention of Saratoga, by which his Excellency Lt. General Burgoyne has surrender'd himself and his whole army into my hands; and they are now upon their march to Boston. This signal and important event is the more glorious as it was effected with so little loss to the army of the United States.

This letter will be presented to your Excellency by my Adjutant-General Colo. Wilkinson, to whom I must beg leave to refer your Excellency for the particulars that brought this great business to so happy and fortunate a conclusion. I desire to be permitted to recommend this gallant officer in the warmest manner to Congress, and entreat that he may be continued in his present place with the Brevet of Brigadier General. The Honourable Congress will believe me when I assure them, that from the beginning of this War I have not met with a more promising military genius than Colo. Wilkinson, and whose Services have been of the greatest benefit to his army.

I am Sir
Yr Excellency's
Most Obt. Humble Servt,
Horatio Gates.

His Excellency, John Hancock, Esq.

GATES' LETTER TO CONGRESS ANNOUNCING
BURGOYNE'S SURRENDER.

England or were cantoned under guard in America, except that the former saved America the cost of maintaining them. And if unconditional surrender had been obtained, the first act would have been to parole them in the same way. It is invariably repeated by historians that Gates granted exceptionally mild terms from haste to close up the business before Clinton could arrive, having heard of the Hudson expedition. This is nonsense, though it probably rests on Gates' assertions later when censured by American hot-heads. The terms, as we have shown, were not in essence much milder than usual; and Gates must have heard, days before he agreed to the convention, that Vaughan and Wallace had duplicated the feat of the King of France and his 40,000 men, and did not propose to disturb him.

Burgoyne, however, heard of the expedition only through Campbell, who slipped through the guards on the night of the 16th, and supposed of course it would make all speed to reach him; and as the "convention" was not signed, he called a council of war in the morning to discuss drawing back and awaiting the diversion, for the loss of his military repute and career was exceedingly bitter. The other generals unanimously decided that their faith was pledged beyond recall: the fact was, as subordinates they had not Burgoyne's motive for periling their lives further, and they doubted whether the relief would reach them in time or would be effective if it did. Gates suspected the cause of the delay, formed order of

1777
Oct. 16

Gates
and the
sur-
render

Absurd
explana-
tion

Bur-
goyne
wants to
draw
back

His gen-
erals
will not

1777
Oct. 16

Figures
of Bur-
goyne's
sur-
render

battle, and sent word to Burgoyne that if the agreement were not signed at once he should open fire. Burgoyne dared not refuse: and the American force of 13,222 men—9093 Continental regulars and 4129 militia—became the captors of 5791 British soldiers, mostly regulars, of whom 2412 were Germans; besides 42 fine brass cannon, 4647 muskets, 72,000 cartridges, quantities of other ammunition, tents, blankets, etc. But so great had been the British losses since the campaign opened, that it cost them nearly 10,000 men in all, Burgoyne having received large reinforcements.

Gates had plenty of good feeling and tact when his mean terrors for his position were not aroused; and he behaved like a gentleman of breeding and kindness on this occasion, as he could amply afford. His soldiers were kept within their lines as the British marched out and laid down their arms, to spare the latter humiliation. The soldiers, however, were equally touched by this tremendous downfall, and gave no taunting word or even look as the British, after dinner, marched along the road between the American lines drawn up on each side. Burgoyne's sword, surrendered to Gates in usual form, was at once handed back with a courteous phrase. His generals were introduced and taken to Gates' headquarters for dinner. Riedesel brought his wife and children from their cramped and painful lodgings; and Schuyler, who had come to witness the ceremony, took them to his own tent where they might dine in more privacy, and afterwards invited them to

Thought-
ful treat-
ment of
British

The
Riedesels

his house in Albany. There also he entertained Burgoyne and his aides during their stay in the city; setting him at ease with regard to the burning of Schuyler's property at Saratoga, as justified by the rules of war. Burgoyne repaid the kindness not only by generous public acknowledgment, but by warm championship of the American cause thereafter in Parliament, where he took his seat on returning.

He would have been excusable for not doing so, for Congress broke the capitulation under the meanest subterfuges. Gates had forgotten one point of great importance—that the army was paroled only from the war in America, and once in England, could be used for home defense or other British wars and let loose that number of troops from elsewhere for the American war; while if kept in America they must first be exchanged. Congress did not forget it, and had neither sense nor honesty enough to keep its engagements when they were disadvantageous; though it might have reflected that if driven to the wall, Burgoyne could still have cost the Americans dear for their victory. When Howe proposed Newport in place of Boston, for convenience to the transports, it intimated absurdly that he meant to break faith and use the captives against New York; and when he sent the transports to Boston it refused departure till the costs for the prisoners' subsistence had been liquidated in gold, at over three for one of Continental paper—though for many months they had made refusal to receive that paper at par a high

1777
Oct.
et seq.

Schuyler
and Bur-
goyne

Con-
gress'
bad faith

Reasons

Pretexts

misdemeanor, and these very supplies had been bought with it. Washington protested against this flagrant bad faith as making exchanges impossible, but without avail: people bent on overreaching never look ahead.

Then Congress ordered Burgoyne to make out a full list of all his officers and soldiers, to keep check on them from breaking their parole; this offensive demand was not in the convention, and he yielded only after protest, and with the not overstated expression to Gates that "the publick faith is broke." Congress with insulted dignity, as if justifying the charge were equivalent to repelling it, accused Burgoyne of making it with the purpose of repudiating the convention himself; and seized this thin pretext for refusing to be bound by the agreement until its ratification was "notified by the court of Great Britain to Congress." As of course this would be recognizing our independence, it was designedly requiring an impossibility which would make all military agreements in this war mere chaff.

The officers were held for exchange, save that Burgoyne and one or two aides were allowed to go home next spring. The army remained at Boston for about a year, and were then transferred to Charlottesville, Virginia, where they lived in a barrack village and did gardening. When this part of Virginia became the seat of war in 1780, they were removed to Winchester, to Frederick in Maryland, and to Lancaster in Pennsylvania; but many were gradually exchanged, or if they wished

Margin notes:

1777-8

Breach of agreement with Burgoyne

Wolf and lamb pretext

Fate of Burgoyne's army

to return to Europe were quietly allowed to escape. Nearly all the Germans, however, and many English, Scotch, and Irish, took lands and became American citizens.

To return:—The country had such a triumph and jubilation as had not before come to it since the war began, and never came again till Yorktown. Continental paper rose 20 per cent., loyalism sunk even worse, and recruiting became distinctly easier. Gates was the hero of the hour. The stars in their courses had fought for him, not to mention the ablest soldiers and most efficient workers in the land,—Arnold and Morgan and Stark and Schuyler,—whose achievements all passed to his account without his having struck or planned one blow, or added one particle to the effectiveness of the army, from first to last. On the contrary, he had largely helped lose Ticonderoga, had spent the crucial weeks lobbying for himself in Congress, had succeeded to a decent army by virtue of Schuyler's work, had nearly lost it Arnold's services twice, had done his best to stifle Morgan's repute and had taken away his promotion. But "politics" was justified of her child, who was himself at this juncture. He reported the victory direct to Congress,—which voted him a gold medal,—not to his superior Washington; who generously echoed the chorus of praise from amid his dolors and embarrassments at White Marsh, and rejoiced that perhaps now he could obtain the reinforcements that would enable him to strike a good blow for the country.

Despite Washington's missing his stroke at Germantown, his army only twenty miles from Philadelphia, constantly menacing the British, combined with the American possession of the river, made Howe's position very uneasy and precarious. Supplies could only come by ascending the river to Chester, then debarking and going on by land, always under peril of an American raid on the convoy. The army could not be forced to a fight, probably not surprised, nor be permanently dislodged from the neighborhood so long as the State was still in rebellion; and for all the effusive loyalism it was so, and Howe had acquired for the British government little more than the ground his forces occupied. Even to make sure of that, it was indispensable to open the river to supplies and establish communication between the army and the fleet; and we have shown what steps were to be taken.

At the British approach, the Billingsport garrison spiked their guns and withdrew, leaving the lower range of chevaux-de-frise unguarded; Lord Howe brought up his fleet, and by the middle of October his workmen had opened a narrow tortuous channel through the obstructions. As to Hazelwood's flotilla, the mongrel crews had regarded its defeat as indicating the hopelessness of the cause, and many both of officers and men deserted to the British; but he filled the gaps, and being given command also of the Continental vessels there, stood ready for renewed action. He was to co-operate with the garrisons of about 400

Continentals in each of the two forts guarding the upper range—Rhode-Islanders under Colonel Christopher Greene at Fort Mercer (Red Bank), Marylanders under Lieutenant-Colonel Samuel Smith at Fort Mifflin on Mud Island. While this went on, news of Burgoyne's surrender arrived. There being no present object in holding the Hudson, and the crushing of Washington's army with the clearing of the Delaware being the one grand British objective, Howe ordered Clinton to abandon the newly captured forts and send him at least 6000 men, and began to intrench from the Schuylkill to the Delaware. Clinton accordingly dismantled the forts and retired to New York, Tryon thoughtfully burning every house within reach. The grand triune New York campaign had ended with holding in October exactly what they held in June, nothing at all except the vicinity of New York city; thanks to Burgoyne's impracticable dreams, Germain's dull incapacity, and the indifference or hostility of Burgoyne's mates to his success, in percentages needless to compute.

Donop had fretted at his subordinate place, and was convinced that with a separate command he could strike a brilliant blow; and Howe finally gave him leave to carry Fort Mercer by assault "if it could be done easily." Accordingly, Donop on the 21st took 1200 picked Hessians, crossed the Delaware, and marched inland to Haddonfield to throw the Americans off the track; thence with Tory guides they proceeded rapidly and secretly southwest all day and night. Early the next

1777
Oct.

Forts guarding the Delaware

Howe abandons Hudson forts

Sum of New York campaigns of 1777

Donop's blow at Fort Mercer

morning they reached cannon-range of the fort in a thick wood, and began to plant batteries. At half-past four in the afternoon Donop summoned the garrison to surrender, threatening to give no quarter;[1] defied, his batteries opened fire, under cover of which he led a storming party toward the southern side, while another advanced on the north across a protecting swamp. Greene's small garrison could not man the outworks, and retreated within the central redoubt, the men crouching behind the walls so that the shouting Hessians who rushed upon it thought it deserted.

But a masked battery and battalion behind an angle of the works suddenly opened at once upon front and flank of the northern party, with such volleys of grape-shot and musketry that they broke and fled; and when Donop's companies had cleared the abatis, they were engulfed in pitfalls, while two armed galleys concealed in the bushes made havoc on their flanks. Nevertheless, filling the ditch with the fascines they carried, they

crossed to climb the glacis; but the Americans rose above the parapets as at Bunker Hill and swept the whole front rank away, Donop being mortally

---

[1] It was military rule, from the Middle Ages down even to the Napoleonic wars, that defending an "untenable" post debarred the defenders from claiming quarter; and as the only possible proof of its untenability was its being captured, this amounted to, and was intended for, clearing the skirts of the commanders whenever the soldiers chose to perpetrate a massacre. This right was repeatedly claimed by the British forces in the Revolutionary War; in no case by the Americans, who were peaceable industrial workers, not hired riff-raff trained to butchery as a profession. The French asserted the same right, in theory at least: D'Estaing at Savannah threatened to make the British commandant "personally responsible" if he held out.

wounded, and his staff with more than half the other officers killed or disabled. Some brave fellows succeeded in mounting the parapet, but were shot or struck down with bayonet or lance. As twilight advanced, the whole force retreated; the wounded crawling into bushes or screaming for the quarter they had sworn not to give. They had lost 402 in all, 26 being officers; the Americans had 8 killed and 29 wounded, several by the bursting of one of their own cannon, and a reconnoitring captain was taken prisoner.

1777 Oct. 22-3

Red Bank— Terrible British slaughter

Six British vessels carrying 120 guns had made their way up, and at sound of the firing engaged the American flotilla; but received so hot a return fire that they drew off, and waiting till morning, turned their guns against Fort Mifflin, against which a battery on the Pennsylvania shore had been unsuccessfully operating. An attempt was also made to run floating batteries into the channel next that shore. But the fort with the American vessels and floating batteries foiled the effort, and so raked the British fleet that it hurried to escape down the river, during which act the 64-gun *Augusta* and the 18-gun *Merlin* grounded; the former was set on fire by hot shot and blew up, the latter was abandoned and burned.

British fleet repulsed

Two vessels lost

But the British resources were far too great to make a permanent holding of the river possible. Howe, it is true, was thoroughly sick of his task. His political plan was obviously a failure: the numbers of influential citizens who had come over did not change the fact that the country as a whole

Howe sick of his work

1777
Oct.

by their crews. The British at once cleared away the obstructions and gave the fleet free passage to the city.

Washington on the 29th of October had removed his camp to the historic position of Valley Forge, on the west bank of the Schuylkill, about twenty miles from Philadelphia among the hills of Chester County. Thence any attempt of the British to leave the city in any direction could be at once frustrated; one day's march would throw his army athwart their path. There the miserable ragged barefoot half-starved troops spent a dreadful winter: Washington planning new Trentons for which he found no opportunity; Howe once vainly attempting a surprise which might have destroyed the American army or perhaps have crippled Howe's own, but drawing back when he found it anticipated. And so the second year of independence closed. The new year was to bring startling dramatic changes in the scene, and widen the theatre of the war.

After two years of war Great Britain had reacquired, out of all the territory of its revolted colonies, a few miles around New York, Newport, and Philadelphia; and it had cost 20,000 men and £20,000,000 sterling to accomplish it. How much would the entire provinces cost? As a result of the meditations of England and France on this, within a few weeks the train was laid which shortly involved the whole civilized world in the war.

Washington moves to Valley Forge

The two armies

Summation of war thus far

CHAPTER XLIII.

POLITICAL AND MILITARY MACHINERY

We have repeatedly found it necessary to turn aside from the narrative of events to the general conditions which dictated them, and without understanding which they are not fully intelligible and are often much misunderstood. But at this point, where the war enters upon a new phase, and the results of the American system had fully developed, it seems best to avoid such interruption for a while by setting forth once for all the means and limitations of the military movements.

The Revolutionary armies were not playing a game of chess, with the satisfaction of victory for their sole aim and reward. They were not the creation of a novelist, who could supply them with means and regulate their *personnel* at his choice. Their food and clothing and munitions were not self-gathered in inexhaustible storehouses and magically transported where needed. The armies were means constituted by the civil power for attaining a political purpose, and their movements were largely subordinated to the shiftings of political feeling. The very cause of the Revolution, revolt against dangers to particularism, was incompatible with the most efficient prosecution of the war. The civil authorities of whom the military was the instrument, were human beings, limited in abilities and forecast, swayed by personal interests and feelings. The armies—in part the invading as well as the defending armies—had to be maintained out of the surplus of provinces which had no great surplus, nor any large transport facilities beyond daily use, had never been allowed to develop manufactures, and had always before drawn most of their munitions of war from the English supply departments; and whose ultimate security had not been prejudiced even by disastrous experiments on public credit. Their support was a drain not on a people of enthusiastic martyrs, contending for a principle beyond all earthly computation of profit and loss, but on practical persons who as a whole had gone to war for material interests, and must be expected to count the balance of loss or gain.

Hence even such military success as the overmatched American armies might have had, was seriously and almost fatally crippled by a political machinery constituted precisely for dead-locks and inefficiency; by the unwillingness of States to give up a grain of their autonomy, and their insistence on managing military structures and dividing military "patronage" according to the methods of civil politics; by personal ambitions, cabals, and sheer ineptitude and folly; by supply departments which as always were the chosen mark for peculation, extortion, and neglect, given full sway by the political defects noted; by a

scantiness not only of war material proper, but of
all manufactured goods, very insufficiently made
good from captures, or purchases from Spanish
or Indians or illicitly from English sources or
from France, and by running the gantlet of the
English fleets, or otherwise; by continually depre-
ciating paper money, which largely destroyed
general trade and industries, made the army's
pay almost worthless for supplying themselves or
their families, and drove the soldiers to desert and
the officers to resign; and by a steadily growing
disbelief in the profitableness of the rebellion, and
weariness of bearing its burdens, which reduced
the Continental army in the last year of the war
to less than a fourth of what it was in 1776, and
if Great Britain had persisted, would shortly have
left the country disarmed at its feet.

Some of the worst troubles were aggravated
by the action of Congress, which rapidly declined
in ability owing to its lack of any executive power.
It could only talk and advise; the States were not
obliged to obey, and as it gratified their sense of
independence not to do so, they always had a
preference for not doing it, aside from the fact
that any two bodies are sure to have different
opinions. There was in reality no officially constituted general government; only a collection of
men acting with such executive functions as were
allowed them by general recognition. Even the'
Articles of Confederation, which were little but a
formal erection of these very conditions into an
instrument of government, were only agreed to in

1775–82

Obsta-
cles to
military
success

Country
tires of
war

Govern-
mental
anarchy

November 1777, after nearly a year and a half of debate, and not ratified and in force till over three years after.

The economic history of the Revolution demands a volume in itself. The places where and the methods by which the supplies were collected, the methods of their distribution and the causes of their non-distribution, the shifts at paying for them which caused them to be held back, the almost absolute destitution of indispensable articles again and again, are essential to a full understanding of the military movements, and much mistake and injustice are due to lack of such knowledge; but we can only hint now and then at its more conspicuous phases and results.

Economics of the war

The hunt for powder, as before noted, was one of the daily and deadly anxieties of the military administration; and its incidents actually form a thrilling romance, rich in far and varied adventure and travel,—among the southwestern Indians (to buy some of the powder furnished them by the British to kill the settlers, which was done), in Florida, to the West Indies, even to Africa; smuggling, raiding, boarding war vessels. Lead was only less scarce; the chief native supply was from a small mine in Wytheville, in the mountains of southwestern Virginia. In its default, as we have said, everything small and hard was utilized, or household pewter sacrificed to chisel and hammer. Many a battle remained unfought, many a movement unplanned, for lack of the primary means of modern warfare. The lack of bayonets,

Powder and lead

apparently the easiest of things to supply since smiths' forges were everywhere, was in part due to the scarcity of bar iron, formerly imported from English iron works; partly. to the reluctance of American soldiers to use the unfamiliar weapon, useless in Indian wars—so that when furnished, for a long time they very commonly threw them away or used them for toasting-forks. But the lack of foundries appears in a startling light when we find Stark's Bennington expedition delayed because there was only one bullet-mold for his entire force.

In another department, we need to remember that there were no cloth or shoe factories in the country, nor large tanneries; that the domestic handlooms could not supply the armies' needs in clothing and blankets and tents fast enough, nor the local cobblers their shoes; that tanning was a slow process and the supply of leather ran out; that the stoppage of commerce by the war put in heavy straits the country which was dependent on that commerce for the means of waging it; and that one of the first and most grateful fruits of the French alliance was a supply of clothing and foot-gear and blankets. The shoelessness of Washington's army at Valley Forge, to the winter quarters at which their march could be tracked by the blood from hundreds of naked frost-bitten feet, prejudiced or made impossible some promising actions. To help out the shortage, he offered a reward for the best method of making shoes from untanned hide.

1775–8

Scarcity of iron goods

Of clothing and shoes

Bad results

1777
Dec.

Shocking
state of
Ameri-
can army

The other wants were even more crushing. Washington would have signalized the Christmas time of 1777 almost as brilliantly against Howe as he had that of 1776 against his outposts, but that two brigades had been two or three days without food of any kind, and were on the verge of mutiny from hunger; and his men instead of resting comfortably nights, in lack of covering had to "sit up all night by fires." According to his report, on December 23 he had 2898 men unfit for duty as "barefoot and otherwise naked," had not over 8200 in fit condition, and had lost 2000 since the 4th for the reasons above. Hungry, shivering with cold, destitute of every necessity, they lay by hundreds in log-hut or bough-tent hospitals and died by scores, sometimes from lying on frozen ground without straw or hay to put under their bodies. That the whole army did not disperse is proof of brave devotion to duty and honor which is not fairly acknowledged; we sentimentalize over its sufferings, without reflecting on the shameful proof they afford of its neglect by incompetent civil authorities.

Causes

For it was wretched administration and ignorance of economic law, much more than even scarcity of supplies, that were the chief causes of this distress. There was assuredly straw enough to keep the sick soldiers from freezing to death; the demand on the country's stock of food by the soldiers in the field was not very much greater than if they had remained at home, and not much less was raised; transport cattle, though really scarce apart from daily needs, were not altogether beyond getting at decent prices. But the owners could not give these or their services away, they were offered money in payment which did them no good, and "politics" demoralized everything. Says a historian born in the vicinity not long after, "Hogsheads of shoes, stockings, and clothing were lying at different places on the roads and in the woods, perishing for want of teams, or of money to pay the teamsters;" and the soldiers had to obtain the supplies by harnessing themselves to the carts and dragging them into camp.

1777–8

Real cause of army's distress

The responsible head of the quartermaster's department up to November 7 was Thomas Mifflin, the ardent Pennsylvania apostle of independence; of more political than practical ability, and with too many other irons in the fire to attend to his duties. He had under him a staff of assistants and wagon-masters, required to make monthly returns, but evidently not at all supervised. Washington blamed him severely for negligence; but after his resignation in November it was much worse still. Much of the trouble must be credited to Congress (of which Mifflin was one and later president), which was much more concerned—and with equal ill success—to keep the accounts in order than to get the supplies to the soldiers; and its meddling entirely demoralized the commissary department. This had been headed by Joseph Trumbull of Connecticut, son of Governor Jonathan; representing a house with extensive dealings

Quartermaster's department

Congressional responsibility

Commissary department

1777-8

in produce, in the one district of great food surplus which the British could not reach.[1] Congress, however, while leaving him the purchasing department, committed the issue of supplies to others, and insisted on appointing his subordinate officers and having them responsible to itself alone. Trumbull could not manage a business without choosing or controlling his own men, and shortly resigned; and we have seen the results in feeding the army. How much of the results in clothing it were due to similar causes, cannot be said.

Congress upsets commissary department

To prevent absolute starvation, Washington sent out parties, under the power of impressment conferred on him, to seize corn and cattle wherever they were to be found, giving certificates for their payment; but as these were only paid after long waiting, and then in Continental paper at a fraction of its face value (which the victims were obliged to accept at par under penal enactments sharply enforced), and the British paid in gold, it did not conduce to the spread of patriotism.

Impressment resorted to

This formed part of a system dependent on the finances of the Union. The war could not be carried on wholly by current taxes; no modern government except Prussia under Frederick the Great, perhaps, has ever attempted to do it—

Financial system

---

[1] The only portions of the country at this time which produced any large quantity of food for export were the valleys of the Connecticut, Hudson, Mohawk, and Delaware, and their neighboring districts; unless we except the rice plantations of South Carolina, too far from the early seats of war to be available. All these but the first were either in the possession of, or ravaged by, the British or their Tory and Indian allies during a large part of the war; so that the Revolutionary armies had to be fed very largely from Connecticut, and the first two commissary-generals were Connecticut provision merchants.

unless we except Napoleon, who made the countries he conquered pay the expenses of his wars. There were of course two methods of transferring a part of the burden to the shoulders of another generation,—paper currency and loans; the money under the latter being obtainable either from foreigners or its own people. So far as obtained from the latter, it looks like a more expensive method of accomplishing the same result as the paper money, being a loan at interest instead of without interest; but it was also an open, honest, undeceptive loan, entirely free from the inordinate hardship, injustice, and demoralization caused by the other. The other, too, was accompanied by laws attempting to force it on people at par and regulating prices and trade—an internal revolution in itself, fertile in every sort of evil, and incomparably worse than the evils against which the Revolution was a protest, save that it was temporary.

This, however, had to be taught to pretty much every one in the bitter school of suffering, and of proof so glaring that it could not be denied; even so, some of the ablest with a large part of the masses still denied it, and attributed the evils experienced to the perversity of those who refused to accept the paper. They did not consider it a loan, but a new creation of capital. It is curious that the author of "Poor Richard," the very type of cool and hard-headed business sense and supposably of philosophic sagacity, firmly believed in this: he said that

1775-8

Loans vs. paper money

Price laws

Tenacious belief in fiat money

as all money derived its value from opinion, an opinion of paper was as good as one of gold; and fully shared the sentiments of another Philadelphia Congressman, that it was absurd to lay taxes when the printing-office could turn out wealth by the cart-load. Washington thought much the same. It did not occur to either that an opinion that the paper was worthless had the same validity as one that it was not. We shall see that had it done so, circumstances might have forced the same action upon them.

Under the mixed system of government which was carrying on the war, both the Continental government and the States adopted almost at the outset the paper-money system, which had been prohibited by the English government in 1763, but the prohibition repealed in 1773. The New York Provincial Congress had advised the national Congress to follow its example in so doing; and in lieu of any power of taxation, the latter could but comply. Up to the end of 1776, $20,000,000 had been put forth by the government beside the State issues.

How soon a depreciation began is impossible to say, a slight rise in prices being assignable to other causes if debated; but it seems likely that for some months it remained substantially at par,—indicating that colonial business had really suffered and its development been restricted somewhat by the prohibition, and that the stock of bullion in circulation was insufficient for its needs. The "opinion" began to

show itself by the end of the first year, however, and by the middle of 1776 the premium on specie was fully 135. It varied somewhat with the ardency of patriotism in different localities, but even in New England it was very plain,—perhaps indeed felt soonest there because New England's trade was its life-blood. After the battle of Long Island, with the waning American fortunes and the waxing volume of paper it dropped sharply; and with the New Jersey campaign the fall became headlong.

1775–6

Rapid depreciation of paper

The patriots were very loth to admit the depreciation, and denied it altogether as long as possible; they ascribed the rise in prices to everything but inflation and bad security—chiefly to speculation and lack of patriotism. Then began the usual attempts to force it on all who had anything the government needed; those who raised prices for it or demanded payment in kind being proclaimed "enemies of the country," which meant always plunder and often tar and feathers. Washington was given power by Congress to arrest all who "maligned the public credit"; and local magistrates and mobs took in hand all who refused to yield up their goods for money which would buy much less goods.

Forced on recalcitrants

It was deemed necessary to supplement these efforts by formal legislation; and in January 1777, a convention at Providence formulated a plan for regulating prices and wages, which was shortly enacted as law by each of the four legislatures. Congress resolved that the paper should

Enforcing legislation

1776-7

Forcing
paper on
objectors

be made legal tender by the States, and be equal in all dealings to its face value in Spanish dollars, at 4s. 6d. to the dollar, refusal to accept it extinguishing the debt; and that whoever asked, offered, or received more for goods in that than in any other kind of money should be deemed an enemy to the country and forfeit the goods. Of course this increased the scarcity by making it disadvantageous for a merchant to lay in a stock, and the depreciation by making the paper price include insurance for plunder, violence, and further depreciation.

The Continental bills were issued in quotas to the States; but the latter were slack about taking up their shares, and were issuing their

Congress
tries to
work
with
States

own also, whose competition was destroying the value of both, and business as well. Congress asked them to provide a time for taking their quotas, cease issuing their own paper currency, see about redeeming previous issues, and raise taxes to pay into the national treasury. The other States were advised to follow the New England example in regulating prices; and a convention of the States from New York to Virginia was held March 26, at Yorktown, which agreed on a similar scale. As in New England, it was practically a dead letter except in furnishing another pretext for harrying loyalists, and in upsetting trade and causing distress.

A more sensible plan, however, had been attempted in the fall of 1776, that of stopping the issue of any more paper and floating direct

loans; one at four per cent. was authorized, besides the same amount by a lottery with prizes
payable in loan-office certificates. In January
and February 1777 $15,000,000 more such cer-
tificates were authorized, at six per cent.; both
Continental and State bills might be tendered for
their purchase. But the takings were slender, the
State loan offices were overdrawn by the depleted
treasuries, and Congress had to issue $12,000,000
more paper during the year; making $34,000,000
put forth in all, the value ruling at not above
25 per cent. of its face, if so much. The truth
was that American money at best was not enough
to rely upon, and the owners of what there was
had grown distrustful; and the foreign commissioners were urged to new efforts for European
loans.

Attempt to replace paper with loans

Prime cause of failure

The laws for regulation of prices had failed
utterly and at once; and another convention, held
at Springfield, Massachusetts, July 30, advised
repealing them and substituting others against
holding unused stocks of goods for a rise. It also
recommended the States to redeem all their paper,
and levy taxes instead for the support of the war.
Some were doing so already. Congress in November adopted and reiterated the judgment of
the convention, and asked the States also to
call in and replace with their own or Continental
paper all issues prior to the battle of Lexington,
because the loyalists were said to prefer the old
Colonial paper to that of the Revolution. It also
advised three sectional conventions to meet early

State legislation recommended

1777-8

Congress
recom-
mends
impress-
ment

the next year and fix a new scale of prices, to be
enacted into law by the several State legislatures;
which should authorize the Continental commissa-
ries to seize goods at such prices if the owners
refused to sell, giving government obligations for
payment.

The last day of the year, to relieve the desperate needs of the army, Congress again recommended seizing for its use all stock, provisions,
woolens, blankets, stockings, shoes, and hats kept

And lim-
itation of
trade

for sale, under penalty for refusal or evasion. To
prevent speculation, it proposed also to limit the
number of retail traders and place them under
bonds. It admitted that the laws were "unworthy
the character of infant republics," but said they
were "necessary to supply the defects of public
virtue." It alleged that a Boston dealer, after
making a contract at extortionate prices, had
refused to deliver the goods except cash down,
thereby also "wounding the public credit," and
showing unhumane callousness to the sufferings
of the soldiers defending the common liberties.
This turned out to be a mistake, however. Of

Root of
trouble

course the real trouble was the small amount of
goods obtainable, the increasingly great demand
for the waste of war and the paper issues. During
the year the war had involved a Federal expendi-
ture of some $25,000,000 (specie value), besides
State advances of at least as much more, which
had overstrained the States' credit with debts.

The northernmost of the three conventions met
at New Haven, January 8, 1778, and fixed a scale

of prices; and State enforcing laws were passed, —in sum, to prevent further depreciation of money by refusing to admit that there was any,— also against forestalling and by Pennsylvania to regulate the supply of wagons. All were to the usual effect: crippling business, harrying honest people and having little effect on the slippery, and throwing nearly all business into the hands of daring, brazen, conscienceless speculators.

It was natural also to resort for sinews of war to stripping the Tories. Congress in November recommended the confiscation and sale of forfeited properties; it had been forestalled by some of the States, and the rest obeyed with alacrity. But the age was too humane to make a sweeping enough seizure for any large gain possible. Rich loyalists who had left the country or taken service with the British were proscribed by name, and their property placed in the hands of trustees, who were to sell it, pay their debts, make provision for their families, and turn the rest into the State treasuries. Of course this forced liquidation left little surplus, and the treasuries were not appreciably enriched; but it left more legacies of ruin and rankling hate, enabled speculators to acquire some fine properties for a song, and replaced some cultivated old families by new ones generally of no very nice grain.

The States, however, paid no attention to the new request to raise taxes for the Federal treasury. Congress authorized in January, 1778, a new loan of $10,000,000, but as the old ones were not

1777-8

Laws to obviate effects of inflation

Confiscating loyalist property

New loan

half taken, it provided no funds. During the year
the Federal expenditures, aside from State ones,
amounted to some $67,000,000 in paper, or $24,000,-
000 in specie (at an official reckoning far more
favorable than the real rate of depreciation); and
as the specie was not to be obtained, the paper had
to be issued in huge fresh masses almost every
month—$63,500,000 in all, making over $100,000,-
000 issued and fully $90,000,000 outstanding.
Some of it kept coming back into the hands of
the government as payment for requisitions and
in other channels; and a little was redeemed in
interest-bearing loan certificates, but these acted
as a preferred currency and still further pulled
down both the Continental and the State bills.
The British and Tories—perhaps some alleged
patriots too—benevolently contributed to the volume of the currency by counterfeiting it wholesale, and Congress was compelled to withdraw
two entire issues of $5,000,000 each. Still the
printing-office poured out its stream of water to
thin down the milk: desperation made any cal-
culations of prudence or sound finance quite impossible.

What else could be done? Some sort of nominal payment must be made for supplies of war if
these were to be got; and if neither citizens nor
foreigners would lend cash, there was absolutely
nothing to do but force those who had any goods
to give them up on promise of future payment (the
reality of paper), or seize it without payment
which meant an instant crash of the new fabric.

Marginal notes:

1778

Floods of
new
paper

Swollen
by
counter-
feiting

No
escape
from
issuing
paper

It was not a question of the relative merit of different plans, but of using the one plan left for going on or else not go on. The rate of depreciation is variously stated by this time as six, eight, or ten to one; six in the North and eight in the South is perhaps the best accredited, though Congress in March established it as 1¾, on its policy of always underrating it. But the truth is that in such a state of currency, there was and could be no real price for anything except what each bargain established for itself; solid business was destroyed, and the depreciation could not be calculated from week to week or place to place. The final outcome will be told later.

One dangerous result, already mentioned, was in driving the best blood of the army from the service. To replace so many fairly trained officers and men with new would be most disastrous; and Washington over and over pressed Congress to balance the present disadvantage by granting bounties or pensions for service through the war. He urged half-pay for life to the officers; but Congress neither would nor dared constitute a permanent military establishment of this sort—the country would not have borne it a moment. It finally, in May 1778, agreed to a seven years' term, and even that roused bitter popular indignation at this new class of "pampered aristocracy." The soldiers were granted $80 in land bounties.

The history of the army as an organism is so intimately connected with that of an attempt to change its headship, that the latter will be dealt

1776-8 with here instead of in the sequence of events to follow.

The formation and administration of a Continental army, after one had been decided upon in June 1776, was intrusted to a Board of War and Ordnance consisting of five members of the Continental Congress, with clerks and a secretary. Its chairman was John Adams, then chief justice of Massachusetts by recent appointment, who resigned that post to accept the new one, and retained it till November 1777. His civil abilities, his energy, his capacity for labor, his utter integrity, his self-sacrificing devotion to duty, cannot be too highly esteemed. Yet he championed a policy which, had it prevailed, would have deprived the army of nearly every capable commander, and laid the country at England's feet in entire overthrow in a few months. He represented in its most intense form the dread and hate of standing armies which had roused the spirit of revolt to flame; which disbelieved in militarism altogether, but could not see that the time had not yet come, and that even the cessation of war must be won by the methods of war; which realized so deeply the horror of the still mediæval war practices in Europe, among professional fighters and ravagers, that it did not see their impossibility with a citizen army and citizen officers.

Adams was the foremost defender of the policy of dividing the army patronage among the States. He was furious at the complaints of the officers deprived of just promotion, or left junior

Army administration in Congress

John Adams

Disastrous policy

Motives

Nature

to others with less merits, or otherwise publicly snubbed after good conduct, and styled their claims "putrid corruptions of absolute monarchy" —though it might have struck him that ordinary employees of business houses ask for a similar decent recognition of service. He would have had the general officers chosen annually by Congress! if some generals resigned in consequence, let them go—they could be dispensed with. An army was only the tool of a potential monarchy; and the affection and admiration inspired by Washington was "idolatry," not only senseless but dangerous, liable to end in a military dictatorship by him. He would evidently have been immensely relieved to see Washington resign, the more that he did not believe in his military capacity; and he shortly took part in the endeavor to virtually supersede him, and humiliate him into a voluntary resignation, an enforced one not being feasible.

We have given his views special prominence, as the leader and the most outspoken; but his cousin Samuel and the New-Englanders quite generally shared the sentiments. They had always regarded Washington more as a means of drawing in Virginia than as a specially able general in himself, were not fond of planters or planter manners at best, and could not forget that their own section was doing more to sustain the war than all the rest together. James Lovell of Massachusetts was perhaps most acrid among them; but his view was held by several prominent Pennsylvanians and others quite as strongly,—Rush, Reed,

1776–8

John Adams against army claims

And idolatry of Washington

Not alone

1777–8

**Wash-
ington**

and Mifflin most notably. Indeed, the Pennsylvania leaders were perhaps bitterer against Washington than even the New England element, from anger at their home capital being given up.

**Under a
cloud**

Outside the South, his own army, and Europe, Washington at the end of the second year of the war had not by any means a brilliant reputation as a commander; and even Richard Henry Lee from his own State led the assault upon him, and Wayne from his own army thought him too sluggish in seizing opportunities. The recovery of Boston and the splendors of Trenton and Princeton had faded in the later defeats and losses; with the usual logic of the beaten, even the loss of the Hudson forts, which was blamed upon Putnam whose force had been denuded by Washington, went to swell the debit account of Washington also.

**Wrongly
blamed**

The country, in a word, wanted victory, and he was not giving it to them; they would not see that it was their own fault in not giving him the means of it, and that to have kept the war alive at all in face of the superior British resources, and preventing the enemy gaining anything but a foothold on three spots of the seaboard, was in itself an immense victory. They looked gloatingly

**Failure
con-
trasted
with
other
suc-
cesses**

toward Saratoga, and contrasted the capture of Burgoyne's army with the constant losses and retreats under Washington; though in fact it was Arnold and Morgan sent by Washington who had won the actual victories over Burgoyne, and with superior forces, while Washington had always had inferior ones. But old favoritisms die hard; the element which had always pinned its faith to Gates, as an old professional soldier, was confirmed in it by the grand success of the army he had nominally headed.

After all, it was according to rule. Every general who had failed had met with a roar of obloquy, been haled before or narrowly escaped a court-martial, and sometimes had his career broken short or ruined; St. Clair and Schuyler and Sullivan and Stephen and Putnam and Deborre— any one who could not beat five British with one American, or whose troops ran away, was held a criminal at once. Washington must take his turn with such fair and competent judges; and he was not our Washington, victorious hero and statesman and Father of his Country, but a general who in a year and a half of command had been mostly defeated, and of late always. On the whole, it is remarkable that the opposition at last proved so little rooted in general feeling, and that the real grandeur of Washington's character caused distrust to wither when brought to the light of day.

Public impa- tience at failure

Wash- ington no ex- ception

There were any number of ambitions or jealousies or grievances also which lent active leadership to the diffused dissatisfaction. Lee was still a prisoner, and not available as a nucleus of hope; but Gates more than took his place, as haloed with the glory of proved success. Mifflin resented Washington's criticisms; Wayne, Sullivan, and other officers were aggrieved at his "favoritism" for Greene, and thought him over-cautious—

Personal elements

though they had glaring evidence that defeat in attacking meant court-martials all around.

Loudest of all was Brigadier-General Conway, an Irishman but in French service from boyhood; one of Deane's recruits. He was a brave man and fair general, who had acted well at Brandywine and Germantown; but boastful, visionary, choleric, and self-seeking, and eager for undesirable promotion. Washington so strenuously objected to it—styling it an actual injustice sure to have evil results, and Conway a chronic place-beggar whose merits were largely imaginary—as to intimate that such interferences with his almost insuperable task would drive him to resign. Succeeding events show that a temporarily dominating section of Congress determined to hold him to this resolution; and the caldron of underground purpose kept seething vigorously,—Gates, Conway, Mifflin, Reed, Rush, and others exchanging letters full of detraction of Washington and "oh for one hour" of Gates or Lee or any one else.

It had been resolved in October to constitute a new War Board of persons not members of Congress; and on November 7 there were chosen upon it Mifflin as chairman, Timothy Pickering of Massachusetts the late adjutant-general, and Washington's secretary Robert H. Harrison. The latter declined, perhaps from seeing that the board was to be heavily packed against his chief; indeed, it seems by this time to have become notorious that Gates was to be made its president, and though neither he nor the other opponents dared openly

Marginal notes:

1777
Oct.–Nov.

Conway

Washington's disapproval

The Cabal

New Board of War

avow a hostile purpose toward Washington, so widespread a sentiment could not be hidden.

1777 Oct.–Nov.

Just before this, Gates' aide Wilkinson had stopped at Stirling's headquarters on his way to Congress with the news of Burgoyne's surrender (not reported to Washington); and, either from a loose tongue or drink or to sound Stirling, had quoted (not quite verbally, but nearly enough in spirit) a pungent sentence from a late letter of Conway to Gates—"Heaven has determined to save your country, or a weak general and bad counsellors would have ruined it." Stirling, who was loyal to Washington, hated underhand conduct, and probably did not love Conway, wrote this to Washington to put him on his guard; and Washington at once sent a copy of the paragraph to Conway, without giving his authority. Conway told Mifflin of it, and boasted that he had faced Washington boldly and justified the utterance; his brag is not good evidence.

Wilkinson blabs

Washington warned

Mifflin warned Gates to keep his letters safer. Gates, who like a good intriguer kept them carefully locked up, could not imagine who had pried into them, and finally decided that it could only have been Hamilton, on his visit to demand reinforcements for Washington. This was a noble opportunity to advance his own cause by discrediting Washington, as setting on his tools to rummage others' private papers; and he wrote a letter to the general of which he sent Congress a duplicate, asking how Washington came in possession of an extract from one of Conway's private letters

Gates' happy thought

1777
Nov.

to him, and insisting that the one who had "steal-ingly copied" it should be exposed, lest the British might in such ways gain valuable information. Washington replied that as Gates had for some unaccountable reason sent a copy of the letter to Congress, he was forced to do the same in reply, lest Congress should suspect him of obtaining his knowledge by illicit means. He then stated how he had in fact gained it, and that he had informed no one except Lafayette, and Conway to let him know he was watched, so that the enemy might not be encouraged by dissensions in the American camp. Further, he had not even known that Con-way was corresponding with Gates, and supposed till now that Gates had instructed Wilkinson to make the revelation in order to warn himself.

Wash-
ington
answers
Gates

Gates therefore had betrayed himself both to Washington and to Congress, though under the circumstances the latter fact was harmless. But as Washington's knowledge was confined to Wil-kinson's leakage, the simplest way out seemed to be flatly calling Wilkinson a liar; which Gates accordingly did in a fresh letter to Washington, declaring that Conway had never written him but one letter, and that contained no such passage. This was a double contradiction of his first letter; and Washington dropped the subject with a scorn-ful mention of the fact. Gates dared not produce the letter, and was left in a position of detected meanness which even he felt keenly.

Gates
tries to
sneak
out

Washing-
ton pins
him

But trifles like this did not stay the progress of the greater scheme. The appointment of an inspector-general for the whole army had been mooted, and ultimately proved of the highest service; Conway of course wanted it, but Washington disfavored him extremely. Sullivan, who tried to keep in favor with both sides, wrote to members of Congress in his favor, as having more military knowledge and better discipline than any other officer in the army; and Wayne proposed to "follow the line pointed out by the conduct of Lee, Gates, and Mifflin," the only common action of whom was thwarting Washington. Conway on the 11th wrote to Gates offering to form a plan for training the army (showing that he relied on Gates' coming headship), and sent Congress his resignation to give a pretext for advancing him. Lovell wrote to Gates on the 17th prophesying "the mighty torrent of public clamor and vengeance" for Washington; and declaring that "this army will be totally lost unless you come down and collect the virtuous band who wish to fight under your banner." Ten days later Gates was made president of the board, and therefore practically Washington's superior, with Joseph Trumbull and Richard Peters (secretary of the old board) also members, and Wilkinson secretary. In a word, it was almost solid against Washington.

Lovell wrote to Gates on the 27th that Washington collected great numbers of men solely to wear out shoes, stockings, and breeches, and had "Fabiused affairs into a very disagreeable posture," and that Gates was wanted "most near Germantown." The next day Congress voted to

1777
Nov.

Conway
wants in-
spector-
general-
ship

Gates the
rising
sun

Made
president
Board of
War

Lovell
against
Wash-
ington

1777
Nov.-Dec.

carry on a winter campaign; and sent three members to the camp to see about it. The denunciatory correspondence went briskly on; but Wilkinson

Wilkin-
son and
Gates

shortly heard of Gates' charge of falsehood against him, wrote furious letters all about, and challenged Gates. At the meeting, however, Gates had a private interview with Wilkinson, and placated him by denying that he had made such a charge; but Wilkinson on inquiring of Washington was shown Gates' letter, and at once wrote to Congress resigning his place and denouncing Gates for falsehood and treachery.

This nauseous imbroglio, with the contrast between the shallow, mean, timid, untruthful, and intriguing Gates, and the lofty dignity and up-

Congress
unshaken

rightness of Washington, should have sickened Congress of its new idol; but the members of the faction persuaded themselves that these did not affect Gates' military capacity, and Conway was taken at his own valuation by many, as usual. On December 13 he was promoted to major-general,

Conway
made in-
spector-
general

and appointed inspector-general with functions wholly independent of the commander-in-chief, to take his instructions from the Board of War alone. This was a direct blow in the face to Washington, who was now only third to Gates and Conway; but he resolved to bear it for duty's sake until some overt act forced him out.

Six days later the army arrived at Valley Forge, followed thither by protests of the Penn-

Valley
Forge

sylvania Council and Assembly against going into winter quarters at all. Washington in reply, on the 23d, censured Mifflin for neglecting his duties as quartermaster-general, gave the statistics of his men's destitution and helplessness and suffering we have already cited, and told the remonstrants that his men were not stocks and stones as they seemed to think, and that it was much easier to order marches and fights from comfortable rooms by good firesides than to make them on cold bleak hills, sleeping "under frost and snow without clothes or blankets." But the clamor did not cease; and Sullivan three days later advised Washington to risk everything and attack Howe.

On the last of the year were begun a series of anonymous attacks in the *New Jersey Gazette* of Trenton, ostensibly by a French officer but probably by Rush, extolling Gates' matchless abilities in conquering veterans by militia. Shortly afterward Rush wrote an anonymous letter to Patrick Henry in which he said that "the army had no general at its head," and that "a Gates, a Lee, or a Conway, would in a few weeks render them irresistible," and advised that the letter be made public; and he or some one wrote similarly to Laurens. The recipients only sent the letters to Washington. The Pennsylvania authorities were still insistent that the soldiers should fight at once, full or empty, clothed or naked, warm or frozen; and Congress appointed another committee to confer with Washington over it.

But the cabal could only prove a winter campaign feasible by making one, and accredit their new leaders over the old by some striking success.

1777–8
Dec–Jan.

Washington against winter campaign

Washington anonymously assailed by Rush

Winter campaign insisted on

It was also desired to strengthen the movement by weaning Lafayette, whose name and position and his probable influence with the great French families gave him much weight with the country, from Washington of whom he was the most devoted of supporters. To this end, the Board of War without consulting Washington reverted to the old chimera of invading Canada, and rousing its people to join the Revolution; and secured the authorization of Congress. Lafayette was offered the command, with Conway second: but as Lafayette was only twenty, the veteran Conway would reap all the glory, thus approving the new policy, and he might argue Lafayette into the cabal scheme.

Gates loaded the latter with glittering promises: he should find 3000 Continental regulars, amply supplied, waiting for him at Albany, while Stark and the Green Mountain Boys would already have seized St. John's and burned the British fleet. But Lafayette, who was not simple and scented the plan, insisted on having Kalb sent with him as second, thus making Conway third; and the three with twenty French officers repaired to Albany, only to find that they had been sent on a fools'

errand. There were not 1200 men fit for duty; there was no supply of clothing fit for a Canadian winter, no stock of provisions or other munitions, no transportation; no orders had been given to Stark whatever, and he wrote to Lafayette asking blankly what kind of an expedition was contemplated, how many men he was expected to raise, and for what term; and Schuyler, Arnold, and

Lincoln, who knew the whole route and section thoroughly, declared the scheme in that season sheer madness. Moreover, as the French alliance was now practically certain, a conquest of Canada might mean its restoration to France as recompense; New England had no wish for another set of Catholic French and unchristian Indian troubles, and would not help, and the rest of the country shared its feeling.

For once, the discredit of a fiasco fell where it belonged. Gates had had two years' experience in the northern district, was both civil and military head of the army and could not shirk the blame on others; and the revelation of his feebleness of judgment and executive incapacity pricked his tenacious bubble for the time. Congress saw at last that it had been worshiping a Nick Bottom with ass' ears; and Wilkinson had told everywhere the story of the plot, and of Gates' shuffling meanness and mendacity, and roused a chorus of popular disapproval and alarm. Every one concerned hastened to declare that he at least had never harbored a thought of displacing Washington—Gates as to himself declaring it a diabolical calumny of incendiaries—and admired him unstintedly; so that the affair ended in an immense accretion of repute and general trust to him.

It was then, when the impotence and factions and selfish intrigues of Congress were leading people to realize that it was a broken reed, that Washington first became the Father of his Country, the one sure bond and centre to whom all

1778
Jan.-
March

Canadian
expedition falls
through

Gates'
bubble
bursts

Cabal
blown on

Washington
rises
again

sections looked; not so much even from his massive abilities as from his lofty patriotism and unselfishness of purpose, his patient endurance of injustice and hampering conditions for his country's sake. Never again could any human being dream of being other than second to Washington while he lived.

Gates and Mifflin retired from the Board of War, and were replaced by members of Congress. Gates was sent to construct the new fortifications planned for the Hudson, and ordered to report frequently to Washington. Early in April Lafayette and Kalb returned to Washington's camp, with instructions from Congress to "suspend the irruption into Canada." Conway was left in charge of the northern department, where there was neither glory nor comfort. Not realizing the new state of feeling, he wrote resentfully to Congress and tendered his resignation *if;* and was dismayed at Congress seizing the chance and accepting it without ifs. He flew to New York and protested that his half-forgotten English had caused him to be misunderstood; but they would not listen to him. He hung about, given no employment, irritable and embittered. His boastings at last provoked General Cadwallader into charging him with cowardice at the Brandywine; a duel on the Fourth of July was the result, and Conway was desperately wounded. Thinking himself about to die, he wrote to Washington asking forgiveness, expressing "sincere grief" for all offenses toward him and the highest veneration for him. But he

1778

The Father of his Country

Members of Cabal scattered

Conway's end in America

BARON STEUBEN.

LAFAYETTE.

recovered, and after lingering around a while, returned to France.

His place as inspector-general was given on May 5 to Baron von Steuben, one of the most distinguished officers of Europe, and by far the most useful of such who ever came to our shores. He sprang from a noble old Magdeburg family fertile in able men,—scholars, mathematicians, soldiers, engineers, military inventors; had served through the mighty wars of Frederick and become one of his staff officers; later had been in other high places, and retired. The French ministers had urged him to come over and give the Americans the drill and training which was their sorest need; Beaumarchais had supplied the funds, and he arrived the 1st of December, 1777, and went to York. The Conway scheme was under full head just then, and there was no official place for him; but Vergennes had shrewdly given the grand title of "lieutenant-general" as representing his German rank, so that there was no quarrel over new rank with the American officers, and he was loyally anxious to fulfill without punctilios the duty for which he had come. Not only so, but instead of committing the practical work to subordinates, he went at once into the camp at Valley Forge, and set about training the soldiers like a common drill-sergeant, working all day month after month with musket in hand.

They were mostly an awkward squad of extreme rawness, and he mixed his drill with voluble French and German curses, sometimes calling on

his aides to damn the "blockheads" in English
which he did not yet understand; but he was no
narrow surly pedant. Americans were quick to
learn (as he was glad to acknowledge), he taught
the other officers the most approved military
science also and inspired them with his zeal; and
under all their hands the army came out by summer a disciplined body which could march and
deploy and manœuvre and stand a charge on equal
terms with the veterans of Europe, expert in all
the famed evolutions of the Prussian armies. The
despised bayonet was made so familiar to them
that a few months later they stormed Stony Point
with unloaded guns, and killed or captured its entire garrison. Steuben created an effective staff,
which Washington had never possessed. He wrote
a new book of tactics, adapted to American conditions, which for many years was the stand-by
of the army.

One instance of his inherited flexibility and in-
ventiveness of mind, not hardened out by Prussian
martinetism, has had deep effects on later wars.
The great majority of American battles were *in
the woods;* even if the forts and villages were in
clearings, most of the movements and even of the
actual fighting were among the trees. This neces-
sitated loose order, easily reunited after breaking;
and developed the skirmish lines and tactics which
had overthrown Burgoyne. Steuben wrought out
from this a system of light-infantry tactics which
became a part of the weapons of Napoleon and of
all commanders since.

[margin notes: 1778 / Steu-ben's fine success / His book / Light-infantry tactics]

The nominal size of the army was now over 60,000; in fact it numbered altogether only 36,246 during 1778, a falling off of nearly 9000 from 1777 and 27,000 from 1776. South Carolina and Georgia had to be exempted from anything but local defense, on account of their large and rebellious slave population. A new organization of the army was made, each infantry battalion to consist of 582 men in nine companies, the cavalry and artillery of 388. The cavalry had been under the command of Count Pulaski; but his ignorance of English and attempts to enforce European discipline had made him unpopular with his under officers, and he resigned. He was now permitted to raise an independent force; and recruited, chiefly in Baltimore, his famous "legion" of about 350 adventurers and dare-devils from everywhere, including deserters, prisoners of war, and miscellaneous scalawags, formed into three companies of cavalry armed with lances and three of infantry. The Marquis de Rouaire, under his family name of Charles Armand, raised and commanded a similar one; and Henry Lee, "Light Horse Harry," father of Robert E. Lee, a third entirely of cavalry. Kosciuszko, who had chosen and fortified Bemis Heights, now superintended the fortifying of the Hudson, being the first to suggest West Point for occupation.

The departments were filled with efficient men. Greene succeeded Mifflin as quartermaster-general, in which position he was of immense service; but its business, and his finally being driven to supply

1778

The army

Pulaski's
legion

Armand
and Lee

Greene
Q.-M.-G.

the needs of his soldiers from his own resources on the chance of Congress repaying him, involved him in scandal and ultimately ruined his fortune.

Trumbull was succeeded as commissary-general by another Connecticut merchant, Jeremiah Wadsworth of Hartford; and Pickering as adjutant-general by Alexander Scammell of New Hampshire, destined to be butchered by Hessians at the very close of the war. The medical department (its head called the Director-General of Hospitals) was a curious nest of broils of one sort or another from first to last. Its first head, Dr. Benjamin Church of Boston, turned traitor and

came near execution, as before noted. His successor, Dr. John Morgan of the Philadelphia Medical School, was so zealous in requiring competency and turning out the illiterate untrained quacks who, as Washington said, were "a disgrace to the army," that though he had transformed the department from chaos and emptiness to a fair state of supplies and efficiency, his enemies raised an uproar of accusations and had him summarily turned out early in 1777. He was later honorably acquitted of all charges by Congress, and Washington gave personal testimony to the condition of the hospitals under him. His assistant in the Medical School, Dr. William Shippen, succeeded him, to be in like manner forced out by charges also pronounced baseless; Dr. James Craik was made assistant, Dr. Rush surgeon-general for the middle department. Under their charge Washington had the whole army inoculated.

The commissary-general for prisoners, appointed in 1777, was Elias Boudinot of New Jersey; and this brings forward a burning question, never fully settled during the war, and fertile in lasting rancors. At the outset the British government refused to make any exchanges, because the captured Americans were not prisoners of war but rebels, liable to execution. The same policy was proposed by some members of our government in the Civil War; in both cases the barbarism could not be carried out, and logic had to give way at once to humanity and to the safety of the original government's own captured troops, who would fall victims in shoals to a policy of mutual massacre. In the first two years of the war the British captured about 5000, the Americans about 3000.

But Howe had already, on his arrival at New York in the middle of 1776, opened negotiations for exchange; this however was blocked for a time by a quarrel over making good a cartel signed by Arnold during his first Canada campaign, while commanding at Montreal. A garrison of some 400 men at the Cedars had surrendered to the Canadians and Indians; and to save them from butchery by the latter, Arnold made an agreement to exchange for them an equal number of British prisoners in American hands. Congress for some time refused to ratify it, but at last a compromise was made and a partial exchange effected. Then there were wrangles over relative rank of officers. The English were loth to admit that an

1777-8

Question of exchange

Arnold's cartel

Relative rank

American general or regimental officer was to
count as equal to a British regular one; and the
American regimental commander being a colonel
while the British was only a lieutenant-colonel
(the colonel being a titular dignitary, usually
a noble, who never went into the field), Congress
finally abolished regiments and substituted battalions to save this dispute.

The shocking treatment of the American prisoners during 1776-7 in the New York prison-ship
hells was a still worse obstacle. Howe said,
probably with truth, that he was not aware of
any ill-treatment; but he left the hulks in charge
of Tory guards, who revenged themselves savagely for their own harrying. Great numbers
died, and the survivors were mostly enfeebled
wrecks. Washington himself refused to reinforce the British army with robust well-fed
English or German soldiers in return for such.
Beneath this still again lay the fact that every
British soldier exchanged was a regular very
rarely time-expired, and who almost always resumed his place in the army, while the Americans
were invariably men whose brief terms had run
out. Exchange meant reinforcing the British
and receiving nothing; Congress therefore held off,
and the captive soldiers suffered and often died.

While these internal fluxes had been taking
place in the machinery, the country for whose
service it was designed had had its destinies shaped
from outside by crucial events to which we must
now return.

Margin notes: 1777–8 · Relative rank · Well vs. sick prisoners · Regulars vs. time-expired

PART OF A LETTER OF WASHINGTON TO HOWE ON EXCHANGE OF PRISONERS.

former it is certain but few circumstances can arise to justify that of the latter. I appeal to you to redress those several wrongs, and you will remember whatever hardships the prisoners with us may be subjected to will [be] chargable on you, at the same time it is but justice to observe that many of the cruelties exercised towards prisoners are said to proceed from the inhumanity of Mr. Cunningham, provost martial, without your knowledge or approbation.

I am Sir

with due respect,

Yr most Obt Svt,

G. Washington.

His Excl.
Sir William Howe.

Just as I was about to close my letter, two persons, men of reputation came from Phila. I transmit you deposition respecting their treatment they received while they were prisoners, and will not comment upon the subject. It is too painful.

PART OF A LETTER OF WASHINGTON TO HOWE ON EXCHANGE OF PRISONERS.

former it is certain but few circumstances can arise to justify that of the latter. I appeal to you to redress those several wrongs, and you will remember whatever hardships the prisoners with us may be subjected to will [be] chargable on you, at the same time it is but justice to observe that many of the cruelties exercised towards prisoners are said to proceed from the inhumanity of Mr. Cunningham, provost martial, without your knowledge or approbation.

I am Sir
with due respect,
Yr most Obt Svt,

His Excl.
    Sir William Howe.   G. Washington.

Just as I was about to close my letter, two persons, men of reputation came from Phila. I transmit you deposition respecting their treatment they received while they were prisoners, and will not comment upon the subject, it is too painful.

former It is certain but few circumstances can arise to justify that of the latter — I appeal to you to redress those
several wrongs, & you will remember whatever hardships
the Prisoners with us may be subjected to will be chargeable on you
at the same time It is but justice to observe that many
of the cruelties exercised towards prisoners are said to proceed from the inhumanity of Mr Cunningham provost Martial, without your knowledge or approbation   —

His Excell.   I am Sir
Sir Wm Howe
                                with due respect
                                    yr most Ob. St
just as I was about to close my   G. Washington
letter, two persons Men of reputation came from Phil: I
transmit you   Deposition respecting their treatment they
received while they were your Prisoners, I will not comment upon
the Subject, It is too painful

PORTION OF LETTER FROM WASHINGTON TO
HOWE ON EXCHANGE OF PRISONERS.

CHAPTER XLIV.

FRENCH ALLIANCE AND ENGLISH GROPING

The year 1778 marks a radical change in the British objects and conduct of the war. It had proved a costly failure against the colonies alone; and France now came openly to their aid, evidently not to be long solitary—for Spain had greater losses to recoup by war. England therefore first attempts to regain them by granting their former demands, sparring to keep a foothold while the negotiations go on; these failing, it plans to conquer and hold at least the weak and divided but agriculturally rich southernmost colonies, and ravage the others, so as to reduce the area and the strength of the new power and its value as an ally to Britain's enemies.

The salient military points of the first period are the evacuation of Philadelphia by Clinton, and Washington's effort to destroy his forces on the retreat, baffled by Lee's treachery at Monmouth; the allies' sea-and-land stroke to recover lower Rhode Island, baffled by the elements, the British fleet, and the insubordinate militia; the beginning of the war of pure ravage without military object; the Tory-Indian horrors on the border—part revenge, and part attempts to keep the *hinterland* as an Indian wilderness for Great Britain instead

1778

New phase of war

Special operations

1777–8

The year's war

of expansion ground for America; and the brilliant blow of George Rogers Clarke far in their rear, winning the whole central West for the United States, and foiling the plan—not less French than British—for restricting the new republic to the coast. The last-named and the Southern period, with the special work of the navy not a mere co-ordinate of military operations, must be left to other chapters.

French doubts set at rest

The maintenance of the war by the United States singly for nearly two years, the total destruction of one of the two main British armies of invasion, and the vigorous onslaught upon the other at Germantown by "troops raised within the year," as Vergennes said, had at length convinced France that this country was powerful and determined enough to be worth having as an ally in its age-long contest with Great Britain. Doubtless also the renewed impetus of the English friends of America in urging that the colonies' demands be met in full intensified French anxiety to forestall a possible reunion, as the French alliance hastened the British government's offers. At all events, when the news of Burgoyne's surrender came to England on the 3d of December, the foreign ministers noted North's wish to yield the points in dispute or retire from the ministry;

English division intensified

and Fox, Burke, and Richmond on the 11th urged peace at the price of giving up the colonies. North, at the King's insistence but against his own conscience, adjourned Parliament till January 20 with no offers of conciliation; but almost at the same moment Vergennes was arranging the terms of an alliance.

1777–8
Dec.–Feb.

On the 17th Franklin and Deane were told that Louis XVI. had resolved to support American independence. He promised 3,000,000 livres in January, and as much more in a Spanish remittance from Havana; but Arthur Lee's loose-tongued boast of the latter frightened Spain out of its intention, as it was not ready for war and by no means certain which side it wished to win. On the 6th of February, however, two treaties were signed: one of commerce, with the revolutionary American principle that free ships should make free goods; the other of defensive alliance, each engaging not to make peace without the concurrence of the other, nor until the independence of the United States was acknowledged, each guaranteeing to the other their American possessions present or acquired during the war. A secret article reserved the right for Spain to become a party at pleasure.

French
alliance
consum-
mated

The English government was not formally notified for a while; but the fact of the treaties being made was at once known, which meant a war with France very shortly unless England came to terms with the colonies. The King was ready to meet it by evacuating them to concentrate against France until she was beaten, then reinvading them; Hillsborough, a violent narrow man, vapored about "crouching to the vipers and rebels in America," and "giving up the sacred right of taxation." The majority in and out of Parliament supported this

English
conserva-
tives
defiant

policy heartily. We have explained that the whole
nation firmly believed the loss of political control
over the colonies equivalent to the loss of their
trade, and that in turn equivalent to the loss of
England's commercial prosperity and naval power,
and its reduction to insular isolation and insignifi-
cance; and that the mass both of leaders and populace, like that of all countries, neither understood
nor desired any method of retaining that control
except with a club. The clergy were of the same
mind. Moreover, the immense moneyed interests
built up or enriched by the war were most averse
to its discontinuance. Liverpool and Manchester
raised each 1000 men; Glasgow and Edinburgh
each a regiment, and several others were raised in
the Highlands by the old clan chiefs, who had the
appointment of officers; attempts were made to do
likewise in London and Bristol and the counties,
but in vain, though London subscribed £20,000.

But the responsible ministers were not wholly
blind bigots, and second thoughts were sobering
them. Lord Amherst, whose experience in the
French and Indian War gave his opinion great
weight, declared that carrying on the war successfully would need at least 40,000 additional men:
this before the French alliance had matured. Such
a drain could not be borne; even with the present
forces, the national debt was increasing by £10,-
000,000 a year; and where were the new troops to
come from? No more Germans could be hired,
for Frederick the Great had just refused the Hessians and Brunswickers any further passage

through his dominions, their only route to the sea; at the same time he opened the port of Dantzic to American vessels. The private and municipal levies were a drop in the bucket; and at the new session the opposition assailed the raising of them as an invasion of the rights of Parliament, while Burke again denounced the futile atrocity of employing savages. Even if these doctrinaires were voted down, their passionate onslaughts had a great effect on the country and made it harder for the government to raise forces. And the reports of the committees of the whole on the expense and loss of the war, with its notorious failure to make any impression on the mass of the rebellion after all, dismayed the ministry itself.

But the majority supposed the old policy was to be continued; when to their utter bewilderment and wrath, Lord North on February 17 brought forward two bills abandoning every claim and position for which the war had been begun, and granting everything the most radical American leaders had ever demanded for security of American liberties. One disclaimed forever all right of imposing taxes on the colonies; the other appointed five commissioners—two being the commanders of the military and naval forces—having plenary power to treat with Congress, provincial assemblies, or Washington, proclaim a truce, suspend any act of Parliament concerning America passed since 1763, grant pardons and rewards, and restore the colonial constitutions as they stood before the rebellion. He stated with truth that he had never

1778
Feb.

England's difficulties and costs

North reverses entire policy

1778
Feb. 17
et seq.

North's
defense
for
reversal
of policy

been carrying out his own policy: he had never favored either colonial taxation or the war. He merely left the tea tax as he found it, and devised no means of enforcing it; the drawback of the entire duty seemed giving the Americans a boon even above England, and no one could have dreamed of the result. The coercive acts had been meant to suppress a lawless rabble apparently disfavored by the best of their own countrymen; when the truth appeared, he had had conciliation measures passed, which had been misunderstood and misrepresented and rejected by the Americans. He had thought the war would result otherwise than it had; but he accepted facts.

Party
sneers
and
wrath

North
remains
reluctant

The scene in Parliament at the explosion of this political bomb may be imagined. There was astounded silence for a while; then volleys of taunts by the Whigs at the ministerial somersault, and a call upon North to resign and let the old champions of the new policy administer it; and fierce outcries from the Tories that North had betrayed the country. But they dared not refuse as a party to obey their leader and swallow the bitter dose; nor could the Whigs refuse to vote for their own policy in the hands of their opponent. As to North, he was as anxious to lay down a heavy and inglorious burden as any one could be to take it up; but he disliked to refuse the King who begged him to remain, and the theory of a responsible ministry was not then what it is now. He remained and the bills passed the House. David Hartley, a Whig member, sent copies of them to

Franklin, who replied that the commissioners had no need to go to America: by coming to Paris they could not only negotiate a peace with the American commissioners, but save a war with France. However, the bills passed the House of Lords also, and on March 11 were signed by the King. The French government at once notified the English that it had recognized the independence of the United States, and that its King was "determined to protect the lawful commerce of his subjects" in concert with them; that is, to consider seizures for contraband of French vessels bearing United States goods as equivalent to war. The British ambassador at Paris was at once recalled, and war was held to exist.

For Great Britain to face this new peril with a country hopelessly divided, an influential section actively thwarting the government in its defensive measures, was mad folly if united action could be secured. The Old Whigs, headed by Lord Rockingham and including Burke, Fox, and the Duke of Richmond, had long since seen that the vanished world of 1765 could not be restored, and favored letting the colonies go and securing their good-will and trade by a close alliance. But as yet such a policy was not possible: had the ministry proposed it, the country would have risen and hurled them from power.

As the concessions just offered by North were the very ones always insisted on by the other Liberal section,—that headed by the mighty name of Chatham and practically managed by Shelburne,

1778
Feb.-
March

Concilia-
tion bills
pass Par-
liament

France
virtually
declares
war

English
party
change
im-
perative

1778
March

North
cannot
have
aid of
Chatham
party

Nor make
concilia-
tion suc-
cessful

Fatal
defect
in it

which was determined on retaining the colonies,—
it would seem that this should have brought them
at once to the side of the ministry. But Chatham
would never come back to office as second to North,
and his party would not throw aside their old
leader for their old enemy. Furthermore, the
conciliation policy if fathered only by North was
doomed from the first: he had been the ostensible author of all the coercion policies, and his name
was execrated in America; one set of his offers
had already been rejected there with mockery and
utter distrust, and there was no reason why new
ones should fare better.

Still more, there was a fatal flaw even in its
terms. The troops were not to be withdrawn
during the negotiations—again the old irremov-
able rock on which all foundered: how could the
United States even relax military efforts, recruiting and arming and utilizing its forces, while a
foreign army was camped on its soil? Would any
country disarm in the presence of the foe, to be
instantly overwhelmed if the negotiations failed?
It was hard enough to keep the organization together at best in a country of farmers. Nor was
it unfair to ask Great Britain to withdraw her
troops, for she risked nothing: her military organization was a permanency always ready and supplied, and in a few weeks she could have an army
back again, in about as good a position as before,
which was little to boast of.

On the other hand, the name of Pitt was admired and worshiped throughout the colonies,

and he had been their unwavering champion: no
one there would distrust his sincerity, his friendship, or his power to have his promises kept.
Accepted or not, proposals from him would be
listened to with good feeling and seriously considered; and it was on record that he proposed to
begin by withdrawing the troops from America.
Regarding the European side, if war was to go
on, his premiership would be not less valuable.
It was he who had thrown English help to Frederick in the first part of the Seven Years' War;
Bute had withdrawn it and turned the friendship
for England to hatred. Chatham designed to make
fresh terms of amity with Frederick, and alone
of English leaders might do it and lift the ban;
furthermore, to place an allied army under Ferdinand of Brunswick and keep the armies of France
employed at home, while by expeditions over-sea
he stripped her of the last foot of her outlying
lands. Even in England itself, no one could so
rouse the national energies and assure victory as
he who had proven his ability to do both.

North himself, crushed by the new responsibility and sick of his post, was the first to urge
this action on the King; and he was followed by an
amazing stream from all parties which best shows
both the greatness of Chatham and how deeply the
peril had impressed the nation. Not only did Fox
and Richmond agree to postpone their policy and
aid Chatham in trying that of retention, but Bute
and Mansfield gave their voices for him also;
even young George Grenville, son of the author of

1778
March

Unique
position
of
Chatham

General
call for
him

the Stamp Act, had been advocating him for a month.

But George III. was rancorous with bitterness at the destruction of his semi-autocracy which Pitt's system had involved before and would again; he would accept Chatham on an open pledge to support North, and not otherwise. He would not stoop to call in "any branch of the opposition." He would "rather lose his crown than bear the ignominy of possessing it under their shackles." Shelburne said Chatham must be dictator if he came in; and there must be a wholly new cabinet and new heads of the law departments. The King furiously answered that "nothing should make him treat personally with Lord Chatham," whose party would "make him a slave for the remainder of his days." If the nation would not stand by him, they should have another king. He would "see any form of government introduced into this island" "rather than be shackled by these desperate men." It is well to note this language, as another proof that the Americans were fighting the battle of constitutional liberty in England as well as in America. Responsible government as a whole, not American liberty in particular, was what George III. was combating.

He was not quite an autocrat, however, and the call for Chatham was too universal to have been ultimately denied. But it was not to be. As the King still held out, Richmond sent Chatham the draft of a motion he was to make on April 7, for making peace with the revolted colonies on any terms they would accept; and begged his help in concentrating the national resources against France and Spain. The aged Chatham, sixty-nine and mortally stricken with the gout, despite all remonstrances came down to the House of Lords to protest against so soon giving up. Rising and leaning on crutches, supported by his namesake son and his son-in-law, his wasted form swathed in flannel but his eyes glowing with their old-time fire in his sunken face, he raised a faltering voice in broken sentences to scorn the fear of invasion by France and Spain together. "The kingdom," he said, "has still resources to maintain its just rights. Any state is better than despair. I rejoice that the grave has not closed upon me, that I am still alive to lift up my voice against the dismemberment of this ancient and most noble monarchy." Richmond with respect maintained his judgment; Chatham attempted to rise for reply, fell backward in a swoon, and was carried home, to die five weeks later.

Nothing could have happened more fortunately for the immediate schemes of the King, or more unfortunately for his final repute and his country. He at once renewed his solicitations to North, whom he was sure of keeping a puppet to his own will. North was as reluctant as ever, but from loyalty either to King or country he could not leave them without an efficient government, and no one else could do even as well. Chatham's lieutenant Shelburne, one of the most advanced economists and political philosophers of the age, the friend

1778
April-
May

Chat-
ham's
dying
protest
against
yielding

His
death

North
has to
remain

1778

North's relative primacy

of Franklin and Adam Smith, was as warm a friend to the colonies as Chatham; but he had no such prestige to gain a hearing for proposals of reunion, and the English political world never trusted him. No other of the New Whigs had any weight; and the Old Whigs were barred out by their position regarding independence. North remained, and the peace commission was sent over.

Strong chances for peace commission

Probably it would have met direct refusal even under Chatham: a nation once founded and proclaimed never voluntarily dissolves itself—pride and a hundred interests forbid alike. Yet with the troops gone it might well have so weakened resistance that the champions would have given up the fight as hopeless, or been overcome if they held out. Independence had been accepted with great reluctance by a very large and influential minority, which held it of doubtful moral right, of more than doubtful expediency or profit, and its maintenance more doubtful yet. South of New England, almost

American vacillation

as many able and sincere public men would have welcomed as rebuffed a real and reliable offer of reunion on general principles. And curiously, the military salvation of the republic, the French alliance, whose effect on the whole country was dreaded by the very men who had carried it through, was more bitterly detested in this primal seat of the rebellion than anywhere else. A league

French alliance unpopular

of Puritan republics with a French despotism, and of the dwellers on the Canada border with those who had for a century headed and hounded on hellish savageries of Indian warfare against them, might be necessary, but was a nauseous dose to swallow. And what some of the other colonies lacked in religious animosity they made up in intimate realization of the Indian horrors still close at the door.

1778

These considerations were reinforced by the miseries and losses of the war, deeply felt even in New England. Its commercial life-blood had been the West India and coasting trade and the Newfoundland fisheries, and these were virtually destroyed; 900 vessels captured by the British and the rest nearly useless. The seaports were actually scant of food, and the States were making it worse by restrictions on trade with each other. The drain of the war, the hindrance to agriculture by the constant calling away of the farmers for militia service, the waste of supplies and the outright embezzlement due to lack of decent system, had borne heavily on the people. The paper money and the laws for regulating trade had nearly ruined what business was left; and the State debts amounted to $25,000,000 besides the national debt. The loss of life had been dreadful; not so much from battle as from sickness and hardship, cold and wet and bad food and drink and unsupplied hospitals, and the intentionally foul jails and prison-ships and bad supplies of the British, where many prisoners lay from the slackness of exchange before explained. Every tenth household, perhaps, was in mourning.

American war losses. disheartening

On the other hand, this common suffering and bereavement had helped in creating a common nationality, to which England was now a foreign country; and Americans were fellow-citizens despite internal quarrels. The old English contempt for provincials, the scorn alike for their rights and their feelings so long cultivated, the social ban and the political exclusion which had made colonials an inferior caste, now met their reward: the more virile blood of the colonies could not go back to any such position again, however willing quiet and well-to-do people might be. The war, too, had left inextinguishable memories of hatred and wrong, ravage and brutality: Hessians and Indians, plunder and outrage, massacre and prison-hells, all the accompaniments preventable and unpreventable of war, made by bodies trained in methods yet hardly emerged from mediævalism.

England now a foreign country

And the results had shown that if the country unitedly chose to continue the struggle, the British could never win. The only fear was in disunion; and thus far the British had obtained only 3600 Tory recruits in the whole country, including the New York desperadoes on the border. Confidence in Chatham might not have added to the active recruits in these thirteen loyalist corps; but it might have stopped some of the ever-slackening patriot recruiting, and tied the hands of the civil authorities even beyond actual conditions.

Real danger of reliable peace offers

With North as the promiser, however, and the troops still there, it was fairly certain that the overtures would be received as not in good faith; and except by the commissioners they were not in fact meant in good faith any more than the earlier

ones. George III. two years later wrote that
the commission had no authority to make the
offers it did; so that if the United States had
accepted them and disorganized its defenses, the
King would have disallowed them. Richard Jack-
son, an old friend and agent of the colonies, refused
a place upon the board on account of its being
meant only to "reconcile the people of England to
a continuance of the war," he said later.

Its final membership does not comport with the
theory that anything was expected or desired to
come of it. To induce that vast federation to dissolve the union and forego the independence ce-
mented by thirteen years of revolt, the weightiest
dignitaries and friends of America were not too
much,—men whose very names would have guaranteed at once sincerity and plenary power, like
Chatham's; if they would not go, the heaviest metal
that would: and not only authorized but pledged
to withdraw the forces at once on a preliminary
agreement. As a fact, besides the commanders,
—even so, the really trusted Howe now replaced
by the untrusted Clinton,—it consisted of Frederick Howard, Earl of Carlisle, a dapper young
man of winning but slender personality, who
had just been styling the Americans "insolent
rebels" and "base and unnatural children" of
England for refusing to treat with the Howes;
William Eden (afterwards Lord Auckland),
brother of the loyalist ex-governor of Maryland,
and under-secretary to Lord Suffolk who was calling Congress "a body of vagrants"; and George

1778
May

The
peace
commis-
sion
a sham

Weakly
consti-
tuted

1778

Ger-
main's
unpeace-
ful
orders

Johnstone, ex-governor of West Florida, a vehement defender of America in Parliament, eager
and vituperative but not important. Its secretary, at first Henry Strachey, was finally the much-
esteemed Dr. Adam Ferguson of Edinburgh Uni-
versity; but he had no powers. It is absurd to
suppose that a political craftsman like North did
not know this board to be an embodied futility.

Germain in secret orders to Sir Henry Clinton
(Howe's destined successor) on March 8, three
days before North's bills were signed, piously
hopes they may succeed, and then puts his heart
into directing the prosecution of the war on a
new plan if they do not,—that of pure ravage
and cutting down the limits of the republic. He
is to abandon Philadelphia, untenable between a
French fleet and the American army, and retain
only New York and Newport; overrun and hold
Maine and the far South; and lay waste with the
fleet every port in Virginia and from New York
northward, destroying all vessels, wharves, ship-
building materials, and stores. Five days later
he writes to General Prevost in Florida, as he
was writing constantly to Canada and elsewhere,
to raise all the Indians on the borders, north, west,
and south, for havoc without reservation. It is

Usual
ferocity

hard not to connect his implacibility with his being
a great coward, usually the most truculent class.

Howe's request to resign had probably anticipated a removal in any case, for the campaigns
of 1777 had left no reputation to either general.
His real defense, the political scheme devised by

Lee, had been a failure and would only add to his discredit; and obviously he could not avow its origin. He had sacrificed Burgoyne and gained a phantom, for the government of the colonies went on as usual. Franklin said justly that instead of Howe taking Philadelphia, it had taken him.

At the same time, the frequent assertion that he could have destroyed the army at Valley Forge if he had seriously tried, is nonsense. That army of 8000 effectives under Washington, ill off as it was, could only have been pushed back to a slightly more distant camp, by a loss of life the British could not afford and the Americans could. Howe was at once self-indulgent and hopeless of success, and spent the winter in social enjoyments including endless gambling, and with his mistress; but the most energetic of Britain's generals in his place could only have wasted his forces to impotency by a few more fruitless victories, and made the British position that much worse. At all events, his request was granted, and he sent in his resignation April 14. Clinton received his commission early in May, and came to Philadelphia on the 8th; but not taking formal command till Howe sailed for England, which he did on the 24th, amid great emotion and even tears from his officers. Meantime on the 7th a naval raid up the river had pretty much destroyed the remains of the American fleet there, State and Continental, including an unfinished frigate at Trenton.

On the 18th a farewell diversion called the Meschianza (Medley) was given to Howe by thirty

Howe's
Philadel-
phia
situation

Victory
object-
less

Clinton
takes
Howe's
place

of his officers, staff and other. The details were mostly planned by Grey's young aide Major John André, the soul of the cantoned officers' social gayeties: a youth of great and rather feminine charm which won every heart, and caused a rapid advancement perhaps beyond his actual abilities; amateur musician and artist, fluent writer, and delightful companion. There was first a great procession of gorgeously decorated barges and boats on the river, from two miles above the city down, to the music of 108 hautboys. Landing and marching through brilliant triumphal arches— with Latin and French inscriptions in honor of Howe, and crowned by effigies of Fame—and be- tween the lines of the parading army, the company proceeded to a tournament on a lawn; where seven officers dressed in fantastic mediæval silken cos- tumes, as knights of the Blended Rose, jousted with seven of the Burning Mountain, on behalf of seven ladies in Turkish garb. Then there was dancing till far past daylight, with fireworks, a gambling table with a bank of 2000 guineas, a supper of 430 covers under 1200 wax candles, and an orchestra of over 100 pieces. It was not much like Valley Forge, and the flesh-pots of Egypt must have set many weak souls longing; but the time of vengeance and proscription for the loyal- ists was at hand.

The British purpose to withdraw was speedily rumored in the American camp; and on the very day of the festival, Washington sent Lafayette with 2400 men to occupy Barren Hill east of the

Schuylkill, twelve miles in advance of Valley Forge, to watch for such a movement and hold it in check till the main army came up. Howe learned of this isolated detachment, and laid plans to capture it entire; he invited his friends to meet Lafayette, and his brother prepared a vessel to take the notable prize to England. On the night of the 19th Grant was sent with 5300 men to gain Swedes Ford up-stream and come down on Lafayette's rear, and Grey with a strong body to hold the west bank below him; while Howe with 5700, including Lord Howe, Clinton, and Knyphausen, started the next morning from Germantown via Chestnut Hill to assail him in front or cut off escape. Grant through the carelessness of Lafayette's scouts came within a mile of him before being discovered, just as Lafayette had deployed to face Grey; but he had neglected to secure Matson's Ford below Swedes, and much nearer to him than to Lafayette. The latter sent small bodies to show themselves in the woods along Grant's and Grey's front as if heads of attacking columns, swiftly marched the main body to Matson's, and drew in his skirmishers, gaining a strong position on the west side before he could be overtaken. Howe feared that the main army was within supporting distance, and not wishing a bloody and useless general engagement, withdrew.

Clinton had a less simple problem in evacuating Philadelphia than it seems. As with Boston and any other place the British long occupied, the loyalists who had joined them or even taken their

*1778
May*

Howe tries to bag Lafayette

Cleverly foiled

Philadelphia loyalists

1778
May–
June

Plight of
Philadel-
phia
loyalists

Clinton
evac-
uates
city

Arnold
made
com-
mandant
at Phila-
delphia

Tories
hanged

protections were in a dreadful plight. They offered to raise 3000 men to still hold the city if
Clinton would leave 2000 regulars. This was contrary to orders and only leaving the troops to capture; and Howe advised the loyalists to make
terms with Congress. Some 3000 of the more stubborn or loyal or worse compromised, however,
decided to leave with the army; and were put on
board the transports which were loaded with the
stores and baggage, and sent down the river. The
defenses were dismantled. The bulk of the troops
were to march by land across New Jersey, and all
was ready May 30; but just then the commissioners
landed, apparently unaware of the intended evacuation. Waiting a while to join them in opening
negotiations with Congress, Clinton on June 18
very quietly slipped the troops from the city and
had them taken across the river to Gloucester.

The news reached Washington the same day;
and he at once sent Arnold, not yet recovered
enough to serve in the field, to take possession of
the city as military commandant, keep order till
Congress returned, and secure for the public the
goods collusively sold or given away by the loyalists. It was a calamitous choice: the weakest
side of Arnold's entire nature, both in judgment
and moral insight, was placed in a position taxing
both to the utmost. The sorrowful result must
come later. Here it need only be said that Congress returned in a fortnight, and tried twenty-
five Tories for assisting the British; all but two
Quakers were pardoned, those being hanged for

guiding the British to a night assault on the patriot lines. Many Tories were also arrested and tried in New Jersey, but all pardoned.

1778
June

Washington had already divined Clinton's line of march, and sent Maxwell with his Jersey brigade of 900 to co-operate with Dickinson and Forman's 1000 militia in obstructing his march; they did so actively, destroying bridges and causeways and filling up wells, so that the British progress was slow and tormented with thirst, the weather being excessively hot. Washington's main army was to follow when the time came, and attempt to break or capture Clinton's entire force.

Clinton's
retreat
ob-
structed

This was doubly against the strenuous counsel of Charles Lee, now in camp again with the weight of senior major-general (unluckily exchanged for General Prescott the British commandant of Rhode Island, captured the year before by a skillful night raid on his headquarters). He insisted that the British would not give up Pennsylvania, and must intend either to strike at Lancaster or move south; also that in any event the raw American troops could not safely attack the British army, whose retreat should be smoothed "on velvet" rather than hindered—all that was wanted was to clear the inland country of them. The good faith of all this may be estimated from Lee's late intrigues: it is not credible that the recent adviser of the British how to conquer the Americans was sincerely trying to help the Americans conquer the British. Yet all the officers save Greene, Wayne, Lafayette, and Cadwalader sided with

Lee
wants it
smoothed

Probable
purpose

1778
June
18–26

him as to a general engagement, despite the stubborn fighting and skillful retreats of the past months; but most of them favored harassing the enemy and trying to cut off detachments.

Washington, ever leaning to the side of Hannibal rather than Fabius, on hearing of Clinton's departure moved his army to the Delaware, crossed it June 22 sixteen miles above Trenton, and sent Morgan with 600 men to act against Clinton's right. On the 24th he held a council of war at Hopewell, northwest of Princeton. Again Lee was for total inaction; but the general opinion was as before, and Washington sent Scott and Poor with some 2000 men to hang on the British rear, while Morgan operated on the right flank and Maxwell on the left, and Cadwalader's Pennsylvania militia joined Dickinson. With the main body he moved southeast to Kingston on the Millstone River, where he would be close to the flank of a march to the Raritan, which Clinton was to cross at Brunswick and put his men on transports for New York.

Washington threatens Clinton's march

Clinton, however, had less than no object in fighting. Moreover, he had a baggage and provision train twelve miles long (there being but one road for it), impossible to protect during such a crossing against an army equal to his own; Maxwell and Morgan had already so endangered it from Crosswicks (southeast of Trenton) onward, that he had transferred it to the head of the lines. Finding the Americans almost in front, therefore, he turned more eastwardly at Allentown, to march

Clinton tries to evade assault

instead to the Neversink Highlands and take boats thence. On the 26th he reached Freehold, the seat of Monmouth County, and encamped. His left (rear) under Cornwallis, about half the army, which would bear the brunt of attack, he accompanied in person, stationing it north of the courthouse some three miles along the road just traversed, strongly covered by woods and marshes and ravines; the right, largely Knyphausen's Hessians, was in advance with the baggage train a mile and a half on the road to the Highlands.

Washington heard of this change, and on the 25th at Kingston held another council as to a general engagement. The former militant group, with Steuben and the chief engineer Du Portail, were strongly in favor of it; and he decided to form the various advance bodies and another under Wayne into a corps 5000 strong, a third of the army, to assail Clinton's rear. Lee's rank entitled him to head it; but he refused what he thought a hopeless attempt, and Washington gave it to Lafayette, who had approved his skill, energy, and boldness of temper. Lee took the alarm: he must not let the control of affairs go out of his hands, nor let another in his stead win a possible success; and he could find plenty of excuses for failure. The next morning he begged Washington to restore him the command: of course Washington could not so affront Lafayette. Then Lee wrote to Lafayette, "My fortune and honor are in your hands: you are too generous to ruin the one or the other." Washington added a courteous appeal

1778
June
25–6

Clinton
at
Freehold

Washington
decides
on attack

Lee
refuses
to head it

Then
takes
command
from
Lafayette

1778
June
26–28

which Lafayette could but honor; to save the appearance of displacing him, Lee was to go forward with two brigades and assume command by virtue of his superior rank.

Washington plans attack on Clinton

A heavy rain prevented either army moving on the 26th; the next morning Lafayette moved to Englishtown five miles northwest of Freehold, the main army lying three miles in the rear beyond Cranbury. Clinton made dispositions for the assault. Washington was anxious to prevent his reaching the strong position of Middletown Heights a few miles ahead; and early in the afternoon summoned his chief officers, told them he should engage the next morning, and ordered Lee to prepare a plan of attack with his chief officers unless there were strong reasons to the contrary. There was one,—that Lee was resolved to carry out no one's plans but his own, whatever they were; he could not tell that, but told Lafayette, Wayne, and Maxwell that he could not form any plan until the field was reached. However, he ordered Dickinson and Morgan toward morning to throw out corps of observation.

Lee dawdles

Ordered to make attack

At sunrise the next morning, Sunday, Knyphausen with the baggage train began the march toward the Highlands, followed at eight by the rear columns. Dickinson on the first movement sent word to Lee and Washington; and the commander ordered Lee to make a vigorous attack at once unless for imperative reasons, and he would bring up the rest of the army to his support. The discretion allowed was necessary in any military movement; but to Lee it was a loophole for disobedience.

He advanced, however, past a meeting-house three miles back of the village, across the swampy and wooded broken country to the northern verge of the fields around Freehold, on high ground. Seeing a large body of British troops deploying on his left,—in fact Cornwallis' rear covering body, some way northeast of the village,—he professed to intend cutting it off while detached; and sent Wayne with 700 men to assail it in rear, while he hastily proceeded to the left with a larger force to take it in front, and held the flanks in check with small detachments in the woods. A feigned American cavalry attack and retreat drew part of the British body within range of Wayne's skirmishers; as it retreated after a volley from ambush, Wayne pushed forward his artillery across a swamp to a height, opened upon the whole corps, and hastened forward to charge it with the bayonet. But Lee ordered him to hold back, as he would drive it to retreat on the main column and ruin the design of capturing it. Wayne with chagrin refrained, hoping Lee would make good the movement on his own side.

Lee's
plan to
cut off a
detach-
ment

Wayne
held back

Meantime Lee's left, Scott and Maxwell, had pressed on and were forming in the edge of the woods on Cornwallis' north flank; and he learned at the same time that Lee's right under Lafayette was marching on his rear from the court-house. It seemed evident that they intended to cut off his baggage train. He faced his front to the north

Lee's
wings
move
forward

1778
June 28

to meet the danger, moved vigorously forward to charge Wayne and force the American flanking parties to reinforce him, and sent a large force of cavalry toward the court-house, where was Lee's right with Lafayette. This last movement if successful would sever Wayne from Lafayette; but it also offered a fine opportunity to crush the detachment, and Lafayette asked permission of Lee. Lee said, "You don't know British soldiers; we can't stand against them." Lafayette replied that they had been beaten before and could be again; but he knew Lee's career, was convinced that either treachery or cowardice was at work, and took the first opportunity to tell an aide of Washington that his presence on the field was sorely needed.

Lee at length allowed him to move, even weakening Wayne to reinforce him; but almost immediately ordered him back, on the ground that he had seen a huge body of British marching toward the court-house. He also ordered Scott to retreat, form in the woods, and wait for further orders. Scott noted the retreat of the right, and slowly withdrew westward; Maxwell and Wayne, left unsupported and without orders, and certain to be captured, followed him; Lafayette to his astonishment and mortification found a general retreat of Lee's wing under way, and could only join it; and the whole corps gained the high ground northwest of Freehold, where they halted, the British also halting at the court-house. The temperature was 96°, both sides were worn out and

Side notes:

Lee holds back Lafayette

Who sends for Washington

Lee orders partial retreat

Which becomes general

many died from sunstroke, and all were choking with thirst.

Thus far, though Lee's conduct was very suspicious, it was defensible or at least honestly explainable—though only on the theory of a timidity and forgetfulness most improbable in Lee; but what followed was not. The corps had lost its stroke, and had no power to seriously endanger Clinton's army; but it was in a strong position itself, in perfectly good order and morale, and able to punish the enemy dreadfully for an attack. But when the British resumed their movement, instead of awaiting it, he ordered a retreat down the slopes and across a broad marsh in the rear, crossed by a log causeway. Abandoning so strong a position without assignable reason started a panic: the men thought there must be some terrible unknown danger imminent. They fled in a huddle through the loose deep sand of the road, wherein many sank exhausted and were trampled to death by the mob behind them, while the shouting foe pursued; some were crowded off the causeway into the swamp and suffocated.

Meantime Washington had reached the meeting-house with the rest of the army, and prepared to support Lee's supposed general attack. Greene was to go by the court-house, Washington himself directly in Lee's rear; the men had thrown aside their knapsacks for better speed. Just then a countryman galloped up with the news that Lee's whole force was flying with the British on their heels. Washington had heard but few shots, and

1778
June 28

it was evident that Lee was making a hasty retreat without even a battle. Spurring forward, he met the head division of the rout half-way from the marsh to the meeting-house; ordering the commander to halt on high ground, he kept on and met Lee himself on the eastern side of the swamp, just descending. "Sir, what is the meaning of this!" thundered Washington. It was not a question to answer in a sentence; and while Lee hesitated, Washington repeated it with a crashing oath. Lee impudently replied, "You know the attack was contrary to my advice and opinion." "You should not have undertaken the command unless you intended to carry it through," rejoined Washington sternly. Lee answered that he "did not think it prudent to bring on a general engagement"! Washington wrathfully told him that his opinions did not matter—"I expect my orders to be obeyed;" and left him, for there was no time to bandy words—the enemy were within two or three hundred yards of them.

Washington and Lee

Washington hurried to the rear regiments, and the winter's drill at Valley Forge now showed its quality. In a few minutes after his appearance the panic ceased, the retreat stopped, two regiments were re-formed and posted in a wood and a small battery was in position, and the exultant British advance was slackened by a heavy fire. Two more brigades took cover behind a hedgerow in a field nearer the swamp. Washington then crossed the morass and lined the western eminence with his divisions: Greene—fallen back on hearing

Washington stops the retreat

of the retreat—on the right, with a battery far south on a height commanding both sides of the ravine; Stirling on the left; Lafayette in the rear. Wayne was brought east of the ravine and placed in an orchard south of the hedge, with a strong battery on his right.

1778
June 28

The British overwhelmed the rear American line and drove it out of the wood into the field; then after a stubborn resistance, a simultaneous cavalry and bayonet charge forced the brigades from the hedge line. They and their companions retreated across the causeway in good order and passed around to Washington's rear, while the British moved down on Wayne. Here raged the bloodiest conflict of the day. Again and again the British attempted to turn Wayne's flanks to right and left; each time they were enfiladed by the well-placed American batteries and riddled by musketry fire. At last the British commander, Colonel Monckton, made a desperate attempt to break Wayne's line by a frontal charge in solid column. Wayne reserved his fire till the enemy were within a few rods, then delivered a volley which swept away most of the front rank with nearly every officer, including Monckton.

The chief Monmouth battle

British bloodily checked

The Americans now took the offensive, and part of the divisions on the west moved across the morass and assailed the British force at every point; driving it, still fighting bravely, to a point half a mile southeast, where it made a stand. Washington sent for Steuben, two miles in the rear, to bring up three brigades and aid the attack.

Driven back

1778
June
28–30

Lee's last
treach-
ery

Steuben came upon Lee (whom Washington had again met, and finding him in no more promising mood, had ordered to the rear) sitting on horseback assuring a group around him that "it was mere folly to make attempts against the enemy"; and Lee vainly tried to delay him on the ground that he must have misunderstood Washington's orders. The British were driven back to the position occupied by Lee when he began his needless retreat; a natural fortress, flanked by swamps and heavy woods, and with only a narrow road for approach in front. Washington nevertheless made preparations to surround and capture them; but the difficult ground made movements so slow that the attack had to be postponed till morning. In the night, however, Clinton silently slipped all his troops from the grasp of the sleeping Americans, leaving part of his wounded behind, and gained the Middletown heights, where attack in such weather and over such roads was impracticable. On the 30th he reached Sandy Hook, where Howe's fleet—just arrived from Philadelphia—was waiting to carry the army to New York; and Washington kept on to the Hudson.

Clinton's
night
escape

The Battle of Monmouth was in every respect, technical and moral, an American victory, though Lee's action prevented it from being nearly as crushing a one as hoped;[1] Frederick the Great

American
victory

---

[1] Lee's part in this battle, from a creditable desire to be just to the unpopular side, has repeatedly found defenders. Some accept his own assertion that he was trying to extricate his men from a trap, as the swamp would have cut off retreat; one able writer thinks he was trying to toll the British across the ravines into one, and "his men could

said the reports showed that Clinton had merely reached New York with the remains of his army.

not understand his strategy." The extreme opposite view is that he was deliberately trying to effect a defeat for the army and consummate the ruin of Washington's military reputation, in order at once to succeed him and discourage the Americans; and thus carry out through the new commissioners his old plan of negotiating a peace, which the Americans would not consider if flushed with victory. A middle view is of honest misjudgment and distrust of his forces. These "safe" views are as likely to be wrong as extreme ones, for human nature is not so flabbily lukewarm; and both this and the wholly favorable one not only leave out of account Lee's previous character and conduct, which cannot be omitted in judging the special case, but ignore or distort the details of the latter.

He knew perfectly well what Washington wished him to do, and his own words are witness that he took the command with the express intention of not doing it, away from Lafayette who he knew would do it. That he did so in fear lest Lafayette might do harm by over-confidence in his troops is too innocent to propound; that it was to watch developments and win a dazzling victory for himself if circumstances favored, is belied by his neglect of its means when they lay to his hand. He left Morgan three miles off out of the fight altogether, giving him no order to move, when he might have flung him on the British rear and accomplished the result for which he is credited with luring them on; he held back Lafayette from an assault that would have accomplished the very purpose his defenders claim for him—destruction of isolated detachments. He left Maxwell and Wayne to their fate. He withdrew over 4000 almost fresh men without a blow, not as he asserted from an unsafe position without retreat, but from one so strong that Washington needed hours to prepare for assaulting the British in it, and with a peculiarly strong way of retreat; and if even his generals and Washington did not understand his purpose, it adds to his discredit that he did not inform them. Now, he was neither muddle-headed nor timid, and he was an experienced regular officer. To attempt whitewashing Charles Lee's honesty, of all men's, at the expense of his intelligence, is absurd.

Then if he did not intend to win victory for Washington in his way, or for himself in his own while he was subordinate to Washington, so that it would support the latter's credit; and after refusing a command, took it on second thoughts from another who might do one of the two,—what other rational hypothesis is left us than that he still held the purpose for which he had before sacrificed Washington's army, and acted as Howe's adviser to crush the rebellion? That his purpose was purely selfish is beyond question: but there were only two sources to gain anything for himself, America and Great Britain; and only one of two ways to gain it, victory for the former while its

The American loss was 67 killed and 160 wounded, with 130 missing many of whom rejoined later; the British considerably above 400, of whom 59 died of sunstroke unwounded. But many hundreds of Clinton's men deserted on the march,— most of them Germans, a large part returning to wives or sweethearts in Philadelphia,—so that his army was depleted by some 2000 in its course.

Lee knew the almost unlimited possibilities of "bluff," and one fairly admires the example of it he gave the day after the battle, by demanding an apology from Washington for his words on the battlefield. Washington replied with a scathing letter, telling him he should have an opportunity as soon as feasible of proving to the world that he was not "guilty of a breach of orders and of misbehavior before the enemy . . . in not attacking them," and of "making an unnecessary, disorderly, and shameful retreat." Lee wrote a grossly insolent reply to this, welcoming "the opportunity of showing to America the sufficiency of her respective servants," and sneering at the "temporary power of office and the tinsel dignity attending it."

He was at once put under arrest, and a court-martial convened July 4, with Stirling as president, to try Lee on the two charges stated by

commander-in-chief or betrayal of her to the latter—or both. Even to gain a chance for the one, by displacing Washington, involved the other as a preliminary. At the same time he would not have called it betrayal,—merely compulsion to the Americans' own ultimate good, as Arnold thought later. But that he is not entitled to the favorable view we take of Arnold's purposes, his whole history is witness.

LORD CARLISLE'S MEMORANDUM OF WHAT ENGLAND WOULD HAVE LEFT AFTER MAK-ING THE CONCESSIONS TO AMERICA.

Q--What left after the concessions:—

—They would still acknowledge the same King

—They would not be enabled to make any alliances or treaties hostile to G Britain

—The appointment of the Gov^s would still be with us

—The appointment of their officers still with us

—The interests of the two nations would still be intimately connected

—The Americans would still consider G Britain as their home

—The arrangement of the P C [paper currency] would put them in our debt

Q—How was any act of P to touch them?

LORD CARLISLE'S MEMORANDUM OF WHAT ENGLAND WOULD HAVE LEFT AFTER MAKING THE CONCESSIONS TO AMERICA.

Q.—What left after the concessions?—

—They would still acknowledge the same King

—They would not be enabled to make any alliances or treaties hostile to G Britain

—The appointment of the Gov^S would still be with us

—The appointment of their officers still with us

—The interests of the two nations would still be intimately connected

—The Americans would still consider G Britain as their home

—The arrangement of the P C [paper currency] would put them in our debt

Q—How was any act of P to touch them?

On what left after the concessions —

- They would still acknowledge the same King
- They would not be enabled to make any alliances
  or treaties hostile to G Britain
- The appointment of the Govr would still be
  with us
- The appointment of their officers still with
  us
- The interests of the two nations would still be
  intimately connected
- The Americans could still consider G Britain
  as their home
- The arrangement of the ƒ C would
  put them in our debt —

2 — How was any act of P to touch them

Washington, as also "disrespect to the commander-in-chief" by the two letters. On August 12 it found him guilty of all, but imposed the petty sentence of suspension from any command for a year; because, bad as his conduct was, his motives were leniently judged. His intrigues with Howe were not known for nearly a century later, and he was believed to be merely unbalanced and cranky.[1]

Meanwhile Lord North's peace commission had set to work. Clinton was ordered to join it in place of Howe. But it was looked upon by patriot America simply as an irritating and time-wasting bore; and the commissioners as mischievous incendiaries, who could offer nothing wanted and only unsettled people's minds. Its essential powerlessness and intentional inefficacy were as clear to the patriots as to the King or Germain or North; though doubtless not so to the entirely well-meaning gentlemen themselves. Even had success been within their reach, the method must have been not through formal submission from the constituted government, spineless and degrading

1778
July-
Aug.

Lee's
court-
martial

Futile
peace
com-
mission

---

[1] He was rancorous, however, at a sentence that put a permanent end to his schemes of treason; if he could not hope for a command enabling him to sell out the cause, he wanted none. He wrote bitter communications to newspapers, vilified Washington to all who would listen to him, and drew on himself a duel with Colonel John Laurens, son of the president of Congress, in which he was wounded. In 1779 Congress censured him for obtaining money from British officers in New York; he wrote an offensive letter to it, and was dismissed from the service in January 1780. He then became openly a loyalist, consorted only with such, advocated rotation in military office to exclude Washington, and was dismal in predictions of anarchy and despotism. He was stricken down with fever in a shabby Philadelphia tavern in October 1782, and died without a companion near; but his still magnified reputation drew many distinguished people to his funeral.

1778
June,
et seq.

surrender and violation of its pledges in face of the world, but the dissolution of organized effort from the melting away of popular support. In fact, however, they received no more private than public favor.

Washington refused to meddle with the business, even to the extent of granting their secretary a passport to Congress at York. Thereon they sent it their official authority under flag June 13, before Clinton's evacuation, and proposed a suspension of hostilities; and as a rough draft of an agreement, greater freedom of colonial trade, no military force to be maintained in any colony without the consent of its Assembly, the existent Continental paper money to be floated at face value and ultimately redeemed, the colonies and the British government to be mutually represented in Parliament and the Assemblies, and the colonial governments to be virtually autonomous.

Peace commissioners' proposals

Congress briefly refused to treat unless the fleets and armies were first withdrawn, or the independence of the United States acknowledged. Its report and resolutions, with previous ones on the same subject, were printed together and circulated everywhere.[1] Its confidence was justified: they were jeered at everywhere, and at least one

Refused by Congress

---

[1] One of these resolutions, of April 23, was a mockery of the King's proclamations of pardon, recommending the States to offer the same to all loyalists in arms against the Continental government who would come in before June 10. Tryon had impertinently sent Washington the "deceptionary bills," as the commissioners' proposals were called in America, with a request that he help circulate them; and the above with others were now sent to Tryon with a similar request.

copy burned under a gallows specially erected. Washington said, "Nothing short of independence can possibly do. A peace on any other terms would be a peace of war." British injuries and American dignity made "a coalition with them as subjects" impossible. Robert Morris used similar language, and said truly that our independence would not harm Great Britain, which "would still enjoy the greatest share of our trade." George Clinton said, "Lord North is two years too late with his political manœuvre." Jay found not a single American "willing to accept peace under Lord North's terms."

Until October the commissioners labored with every resource of diplomacy and glittering personal lures; but to no purpose, while the war went on unchecked. Johnstone—doubtless with good motives, but with that universal British confidence in the venality of American leaders which the fact of their scarcely ever being able to buy any seems never to have been able to shake[1]— undertook by letter and messenger to engage

Margin notes:
1778
June-
Oct.

Peace
offers
scouted

Bribery
under-
taken

---

[1] British archives and correspondence are full of this stuff; lists of the colonial leaders are drawn up for the ministry, with the confident assertion that most of them are to be bought. Captain John Montressor, a British "chief engineer," who had served with Putnam under Bradstreet in 1764, says in his journal that the "rebel generals" were generally for sale, and that even Putnam "might have been bought, *to my certain knowledge*, for one dollar per day." In that case, it is most discreditable to the sense of the British that they did not close with so cheap and valuable a bargain. A distinguished New York military writer, in one of our foremost historical works, kindly observes that this statement is "very likely without warrant"—a remark which is not without bearing on the feud of the New-Englanders against Schuyler.

Joseph Reed in the cause of conciliation by the promise of 10,000 guineas and high office; Reed in wrath laid the offers before Congress, which refused to have any further dealing with Johnstone, and he had to be dropped from the commission.

At last the others gave up, venomous with hate and chagrin; and published on October 3 a farewell manifesto, addressed not only to Congress but to the Assemblies and the people. It declared that all the points in dispute had been conceded by Great Britain, and Congress was alone responsible for continuing a needless war, whose miseries the people should not allow a few ambitious men to inflict upon them; denounced the papistical French alliance; offered the proposed terms to the State Assemblies separately; granted forty days more for submission, and proclaimed that the desolation of the country should be the leading object of the war thereafter. Congress had it published in the newspapers, with a counter-proclamation and comments upon it and advising that all who circulated it be seized as traitors. Lafayette, in resentment of the references to France, sent a challenge to Carlisle, who refused to be accountable to any one but his own government. At the end of the forty days the commission left for home.

The manifesto was not different in tone from most of the other British menaces to the Americans through the war; but significant in admitting that the government had wholly abandoned the idea of conquest and political reunion, and would

By the CONGRESS of the UNITED STATES
of AMERICA.

MANIFESTO.

THESE United States, having been driven to hostilities by the oppressive and tyrannous measures of Great-Britain; having been compelled to commit the essential rights of man to the decision of arms; and having been at length forced to shake off a yoke which had grown too burthensome to bear, they declared themselves free and independent.

Confiding in the justice of their cause; confiding in Him who disposes of human events, although weak and unprovided, they set the power of their enemies at defiance.

In this confidence they have continued, through the various fortune of three bloody campaigns, unawed by the power, unsubdued by the barbarity of their foes. Their virtuous citizens have born without repining, the loss of many things which make life desireable. Their brave troops have patiently endured the hardships and dangers of a situation, fruitful in both beyond former example.

The Congress, considering themselves bound to love their enemies, as children of that Being who is equally the Father of all; and desirous, since they could not prevent, at least to alleviate the calamities of war, have studied to spare those who were in arms against them, and to lighten the chains of captivity.

The conduct of those serving under the King of Great-Britain hath, with some few exceptions, been diametrically opposite. They have laid waste the open country, burned the defenceless villages, and butchered the citizens of America. Their prisons have been the slaughter-houses of her soldiers, their ships of her seamen, and the severest injuries have been aggravated by the grossest insult.

Foiled in their vain attempt to subjugate the unconquerable spirit of freedom, they have meanly assailed the Representatives of America with bribes, with deceit and the servility of adulation. They have made a mock of humanity, by the wanton destruction of men: They have made a mock of religion, by impious appeals to God whilst in the violation of his sacred commands: They have made a mock even of reason itself, by endeavouring to prove, that the liberty and happiness of America could safely be entrusted to those who have *sold their own*, unawed by the sense of virtue or of shame.

Treated with the contempt which such conduct deserved, they have applied to individuals: They have solicited them to break the bonds of allegiance, and imbrue their souls with the blackest of crimes: But fearing that none could be found through these United States, equal to the wickedness of their purpose, to influence weak minds they have threatened more wide devastation.

While the shadow of hope remained, that our enemies could be taught by our example to respect those laws which are held sacred among civilized nations, and to comply with the dictates of a religion which they pretend in common with us to believe and to revere, they have been left to the influence of that religion, and that example. But since their incorrigible dispositions cannot be touched by kindness and compassion, it becomes our duty by other means to vindicate the rights of humanity.

We therefore, the Congress of the United States of America, Do solemnly declare and proclaim, That if our enemies presume to execute their threats, or persist in their present career of barbarity, we will take such exemplary vengeance as shall deter others from a like conduct. We appeal to that God who searcheth the hearts of men for the rectitude of our intentions. And in his holy presence we declare, That as we are not moved by any light and hasty suggestions of anger or revenge, so through every possible change of fortune we will adhere to this our determination.

DONE in Congress, by unanimous consent, the Thirtieth day of October, One Thousand Seven Hundred and Seventy-eight.

HENRY LAURENS, President.

Attest. CHARLES THOMSON, Secretary,

henceforth conduct the war not for the objects of civilized states, but for those of a tribe of savages. But as we have already shown, that was what the government had determined upon before the commission was sent out at all.

Johnstone, enraged at the ban upon him, had changed his position to the other extreme and raved like a child. "No quarter ought to be shown to their Congress," he said: "if the infernals could be let loose against them, I should approve of the measure. The proclamation certainly does mean a war of desolation: it can mean nothing else." Other opinions divided along political lines. Rockingham said that "since the coming of Christ war had not been conducted on such inhuman ideas" as in the "accursed manifesto." Coke proposed an address to the King disavowing it; Germain of course defended it—the Americans had become French and should be treated as Frenchmen. Chatham's political legatees could have no sympathy with it; yet Shelburne's declaration, following his dead chief's lead, that he never would serve with any one who would consent to American independence (in fact his ministry carried it through a few years later), amounted to upholding it, for it was the ministry's proclaimed machinery of continuing the war.

Just after Clinton had escaped a destruction only less complete than that of Burgoyne, Britain's loyal subjects and savage allies struck for her one of those hideous blows in which Germain and the King seem to have taken more satisfaction and

1778

Indian ravages futile

pride than in the victories of their regular armies, as a triumph of acute statesmanship rather than expected routine. Yet the former were fruitless of any military effect, and in effect on the temper of the colonies fruitful only in nullifying any possible achievement of the peace commission.

Wyoming

We have narrated the settlement of the valley of Wyoming on the Penn lands, by Connecticut emigrants; and the wars for it, which ended in favor of Connecticut because the Penns' own subjects had no sympathy with their attempt to keep the region a wilderness. But after the Revolution had put Pennsylvania in control of her own property, she took up the old feud as her own, and only waited a chance at once to extend her jurisdiction over the district, and oust the settlers from their property in favor of her own citizens. This front-

Isolation

ier county of some 3000 people, therefore, was in one respect the most isolated settlement in the country, since it looked for no protection from its white neighbors against its savage ones. Moreover, it was intensely patriotic; and when some dozens of the ejected Tories from the Mohawk Valley came down and settled thereabout, they were sharply repressed and some of them deported to Connecticut. This furnished at once a fresh cause of enmity and an excuse for invasion. Yet though their men were needed for home protection, in the winter of 1776 they furnished two companies of soldiers to the Continental armies,

Patriot-ism

which were enrolled in the Connecticut line, and re-enlisted in 1777.

This flourishing New England outlier, thus doubly exposed and stripped of its defenders, hated on one side as intruders and as Yankees and on the other as patriots and as expellers of Tories, was a shining mark for the particolored gang which had its stronghold at Fort Niagara, and made its business to carry arson and massacre and ravage and the torch along the fringes of civilization. The Butlers had retired thither from Fort Stanwix as they had come, and around them gathered a crowd of borderers little less savage than the Indians, and often far flintier of heart; again and again we find Indians granting mercy which their white allies denied, and the foulest murders both at Wyoming and Cherry Valley were done by Tories. Some of these were known to be exiles driven from Wyoming by the patriots. Brant and his Mohawk band made their headquarters there also.

In the spring of 1778 the desultory outrages on the edges of Wyoming grew so numerous, and Indian runners from a large band at Conewawah (Elmira) so constantly coming to the Tory residents and returning, that in deadly fear the inhabitants half suspended their farm work to fill the valley with stockades; a military company of a few dozens was raised and drilled, and placed under Colonel Zebulon Butler, a Continental officer who chanced to be at home; and the Wyoming companies in the Continental service besought Congress in anguish to let them go home. But Congress was busy, did not believe the danger imminent, had too

1778

Butlers
and
Brant

Tories
worse
than
Indians

Wyoming
in peril

hard work in finding soldiers to part with them easily, and at length allowed one company to go just too late, only five officers reaching home in advance with the news the very day of the catastrophe.

Meantime Major John Butler with his rangers and his merciless son Walter,—escaped from custody and burning with revenge,—a regiment of Greens, and several hundred Senecas, about 1100 in all, threaded the forest to the Susquehanna, took canoes down the river, and two days after Monmouth swarmed through the pass and entered the valley. Every straggler was murdered, and the northernmost blockhouse shortly captured; most of the others, garrisoned by a few old men, must soon follow; and the Tory leader demanded the surrender of Forty Fort, the chief defense, where the women and children had been collected. Had this been made, it would not have prevented a frightful massacre and orgy of torture, for the Senecas were determined to soothe the shades of their warriors slain at Oriskany; and it would have been best to defend the fort, which could probably have been held till the rescuing Continental company arrived. The commander and some of his chief officers counseled this; but many families had not yet reached the protection of the fort, and the majority took counsel of chivalry and resolved to attempt driving off the enemy by a swift blow.

On the afternoon of the 3d the entire male force of the community, some 300, ranging from slight boys to aged men, marched north and gave battle to the infernal allies. They fought with such vigor and skill that it seemed as if victory might be theirs; but the great numbers of the foe out-flanked them, and in attempting a change of position they fell into confusion, and soon fled for life. A few including Colonel Butler escaped to the forts or the mountains; but in half an hour 225 scalps were in the hands of the Indians, and a large number were saved for a night of unspeakable atrocities, a Fourth of July Indian festival. In the ears of the helpless inmates of the forts rang all night the shrieks of their tortured dear ones and friends, slowly mutilated or burned alive, one captain held down with a pitchfork on the burning embers of a fort. John Butler, himself a humane and honorable man, listened with shame and agony, and said agitatedly to those who begged him to interfere, "I can't restrain them—I can't restrain them!" as if the fact were novel to him, and he were under no obligation to keep out of affairs sure to involve such devil's work. This was what loyalty to England meant. Many prisoners were more mercifully dispatched with tomahawk and maul by an old French-Indian hag said to have been Frontenac's granddaughter—Catherine Montour, also called "Queen Esther."

The next day the fort surrendered, and all lives were spared thereafter. The wretched survivors, mostly women and children, toiled on foot through the vast lonely forest, almost without food, to reach the nearest settlements. They underwent sufferings only less than those of the victims of the

1778
July 4-5

Wyoming
butchery

And
Indian
tortures

Sufferings of
the
helpless

Indians, and many scores perished miserably of hunger and hardship in the great swamp of the Pocono Mountains still called the Shades of Death, and in struggling through the Wind-Gap and Water-Gap to the Lehigh and Delaware.

Every building in the valley was burned after plundering, and the whole surrounding country laid waste. Butler in his report boasted that his party had burned a thousand houses and every mill, and Germain praised him for it. Wyoming was temporarily restored to the wilderness—of course a much happier fate than to be the haunt of Englishmen not acknowledging English sovereignty.

Clinton's withdrawal from Philadelphia was well advised: less than three weeks later a French fleet under Count Charles Henry d'Estaing arrived off Delaware Bay. It comprised eight ships of 74 to 90 guns and four other heavy ones, and four frigates, against Lord Howe's six ships of 40 to 64 guns, eight frigates, and some armed sloops; English seamanship was a heavy odds in itself, but Howe was much overmatched, and D'Estaing carried 4000 land troops. Philadelphia might well have anticipated Yorktown. Finding his prey escaped, D'Estaing transshipped Gérard the new French ambassador and Silas Deane, and made all haste for New York. Anchoring off Sandy Hook and making prize of unknowing British vessels as they came in, he had a speedy conference with Washington's aides, Laurens and Hamilton, while Washington moved his army to White

1778
July

Wyoming
made a
desert

D'Es-
taing's
arrival

British
gone
from
Philadel-
phia

French
follow
them to
New York

Plains (July 20-21). They planned to effect the same stroke there; but there was much less water on the bar then than now, and the two largest ships could not be safely got over,—certainly not in a fight,—and the scheme had to be given up.

D'Estaing, evidently not in his country's secret counsels, wanted to capture Newfoundland and make it the fourteenth State of the Union; but Washington more wisely decided to employ the new force in aiding to recover "Rhode" Island at whose southern end lies Newport. It had been in British hands for the past eighteen months; blocking up Narragansett Bay, besides keeping Boston and the Connecticut coast towns constantly insecure. General Spencer of Connecticut had been put at the head of an elaborate and expensive expedition to recapture it the year before, but failed and was forced to resign; he was succeeded by Sullivan, who still kept a force at Providence to prevent land raids into New England. Redeeming it, and capturing one of the two British corps still encamped in the United States, would not only be an immense gain both practically and morally, but enable the other army to be blockaded into its holding and probably forced to surrender. In fact, Clinton on the 27th wrote to Germain that he should probably have to abandon New York and retire to Halifax.

It would also relieve the occupied district from almost intolerable conditions. General Richard Prescott, the commandant, the same who had treated Ethan Allen so brutally, was one of the most offensive tyrants ever inflicted on America by England; a close parallel to Sir William Berkeley in his old age. The worst type of English aristocrat, hard, greedy, irascible, fiercely contemptuous of provincials, he let his soldiers plunder and deface property at will, and aided them in it,—for instance, making a private sidewalk out of the citizens' door-stones,—besides the destruction of lawns and shade-trees for barracks; assaulted citizens, imprisoned them on suspicion, refused them communication with their families, and treated their wives with dastardly insult. As before said, he had been kidnapped by Americans in 1777, two bad jobs being done at once when he was exchanged for Lee, and resumed his post in April.

Washington ordered Sullivan to call on Massachusetts, Connecticut, and Rhode Island for 5000 men; fully 8000 were promptly furnished, the enthusiasm rivaling that after Lexington. Hancock headed the Massachusetts men, many of them prominent citizens from all over the State. Washington sent on two of his best brigades and commanders,—Greene who knew the whole district, and D'Estaing's kinsman Lafayette with Glover's famous Marbleheaders: about 1500 together, later increased to 2000. On the 29th D'Estaing arrived off Newport; on the 5th of August he attacked the British fleet there, and to prevent its capture most of it was burned or scuttled,—ten vessels mounting 212 guns. But the American forces, though plentiful and eager, had been slow in equipping

1778
July-Aug.

General
Prescott

And
Charles
Lee

Forces
for
Rhode
Island
campaign

ADMIRAL LORD HOWE.

COUNT D'ESTAING.

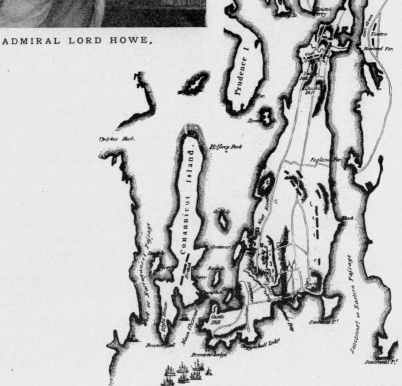

OPERATIONS AGAINST RHODE ISLAND IN 1778.

themselves and arriving; and it was still several days before Sullivan was ready to leave Providence, a delay which ruined the expedition.

1778
Aug. 5-10

About this time a heavy British reinforcement arrived under General Robert Pigot, one of the commanders at Bunker Hill; a humane accomplished man, the extreme opposite of Prescott, and under whom Newport was well treated. He took over the command, his troops numbering about 6000; the main body at Newport and the strong intrenchments for some three miles north, and a detachment holding Butts Hill at the north end of the island, on the Bristol channel. It had been concerted with Sullivan that on the 10th the French marines should land on the west and the Americans on the east of the island, at the unfortified part north of Newport, cutting off the Butts Hill detachment before assailing the rest. On the 8th D'Estaing ran the Newport batteries and commanded the harbor, and on the 9th began landing his men on Conanicut Island west of Newport, to cross over the next day. Pigot, however, seeing the danger, drew in the Butts Hill garrison to the Newport works; and Sullivan, without waiting for the French, very properly crossed his troops from the Bristol side and moved down to Quaker Hill, ten or eleven miles from Newport. D'Estaing was vexed at this unnotified movement, though without reason; but it did not affect his conduct.

Pigot
replaces
Prescott

French-
American
move-
ments

The
Butts
Hill
garrison

In the afternoon, however, Lord Howe's fleet, reinforced by four vessels which had come in a few days after D'Estaing left New York, came off

Point Judith; though still inferior to the French, like a brave captain he had resolved to attempt relieving the point of peril. D'Estaing was obliged the next morning to re-embark his troops and sail

French
and
English
fleets
scattered
by storm

out to give battle. Howe drew him off to the southward, each trying all day to gain the weather-gage. The morning after, there gathered a two-days' hurricane, the most terrific for generations before and after, remembered for near a century as the "Great Storm" of fearful wreckage along the coast. Two French ships were totally dismasted, the Count's flag-ship losing her rudder as well; others were badly damaged. For three days afterward there were a few ineffectual duels between members of the scattered squadrons; then they sheered off, and on the 20th D'Estaing brought his injured fleet again to Narragansett Bay.

Meantime the American forces after serious damage from the storm, which killed men and horses and ruined all the powder outside the chests, had gone forward and begun to bombard the British works, hoping for a speedy return of the French. When D'Estaing arrived they urged the immediate carrying out of the original plan. The conditions were not changed except for the better: Pigot having now no hope of relief, his surrender could be easily forced by their 14,000 men against his 6000. The Count, it is said, would have com-

D'Es·
taing's
officers
force
with-
drawal

plied; but his naval officers, angry from the first at being commanded by a land officer, and resolved that he should not have a chance to gain distinction, gladly seized the pretext for insisting that according to government orders, the fleet if damaged was to refit at Boston.

1778
Aug.
20-25

A protest against this, signed by every general officer except Lafayette, argued that this was only a suggestion for convenience, and the Bay was full of ship-yards; that if unseaworthy, the storms and shoals around the Cape were the worst things the fleet could encounter; that in any case the soldiers need not be taken along; and that it was most unjust, and injurious to French honor and American interests alike, to wreck without actual need an expedition collected at such cost and effort in reliance on the French, and would disaffect the Americans to the French alliance. D'Estaing, perhaps a little ashamed, professed to be affronted by this, and answered tartly; and Sullivan in his general orders retorted by assuring his soldiers that though they might be discouraged by this departure, there was no reason to suppose themselves endangered by it, and America would do for herself what her allies would not assist in. Much recrimination followed; but the United States could not afford to quarrel with her one ally, and the affair was smoothed over.

American
protest
against
French
desertion

But the French had only given the enterprise a very ugly wound, and made it slower and less certain; the militia proceeded to give it a death-blow. Disheartened and not knowing how long it might keep them from their harvests, from two to three thousand of them went home on the 24th and 25th. The Americans without the intrenchments were now little more numerous than the British

Militia
go home

1778
Aug.
25-30

within; this made an assault mere suicide. Rational hope of success was at an end; for before D'Estaing at earliest was likely to be back, Howe's fleet would certainly be, with reinforcements for Pigot. Washington advised leaving the island.

Lafayette
appeals
to
D'Estaing

But Sullivan could not endure to give up an enterprise so vital, if success could yet be wrested from fate; and on the night of the 28th retreated to Butts Hill, to await the result of an application to D'Estaing by Lafayette. The latter had counseled abandoning the business; but he rode the seventy miles to Boston in seven hours, and begged his relative for a speedy return. The Count as a land officer could do as he liked, and offered to bring the troops on by land if requested. It was too late. Pigot at once started in pursuit; occupied Quaker and Turkey Hills south of Butts; and the next morning attempted to cut off retreat by flanking Butts Hill from the left, in co-operation with a bombardment from some armed vessels and the southern hills. After a furious fight in the plain between the north and south hills, the British were driven back to their own works, with a loss of 222 to the American 206.

Butts
Hill
battle,
Aug. 29

It was wasted bloodshed. The next day Sullivan was informed that Howe's fleet would probably be at Newport before night, with Clinton and a heavy reinforcement (4000 in fact) for Pigot. He therefore with the invaluable assistance of Glover's amphibians took the troops and supplies off the island without loss, just as Lafayette arrived and skillfully drew in the rear-guards. The next day Howe reached Newport; but hearing of Sullivan's retreat and D'Estaing's going to Boston, he sailed thither to attack the French fleet while still out of order. The harbor being impracticable for such an operation, he returned to New York; Clinton on the road having Grey burn the chief part of New Bedford and Fair Haven (September 5), and plunder Martha's Vineyard.

1778
Sept.

New
England
coast
ravaged

The whole country, and New England especially, was bitter against the French for this fiasco, which even now must be pronounced wanton; though Congress for reasons of policy passed a resolution approving D'Estaing's course. At Boston, the American sailors provoked a fracas with the French ones. D'Estaing increased the ill feeling by an address to the French of Canada urging them to return to French allegiance. The Americans were not fighting to make a new French and Indian War necessary, and were exceedingly irritated over it; Vergennes guessed that fact and discountenanced the manifesto.

Before D'Estaing's fleet was entirely refitted, another English fleet was close upon it. Admiral Byron, grandfather of the poet, had been sent on its track as soon as its destination was known; but encountered the persistent storms which gave him among sailors the name of "Foul Weather Jack." Coming to New York for Lord Howe's orders, he found that Howe, sick of his futile politico-military task, had followed his brother's example, resigned, and returned to England; and he therefore kept on to Boston to strike at the

French. But his fleet was scattered by a storm which wrecked one of his vessels on Cape Cod; and D'Estaing took his squadron to the West Indies, the chief seat of the French war with England.

This again roused anger as a desertion; though of course France must defend her own interests first, and Clinton had to send 5000 troops to the West Indies also the same day, which simply made an effective campaign from New York impossible. The most he could do was raid and burn here and there, as per Germain's orders, and in connection with foraging expeditions. Grey was an enthusiastic agent in this business, especially when it enabled him to perpetrate massacres, his notion of energy in military operations. In a foray against Little Egg Harbor (New Jersey) the latter part of September, he surprised Baylor's cavalry regiment while lying unarmed in camp, and bayoneted the greater part in cold blood, 67 out of 104 being killed. Pulaski's legion were also surprised and forty killed; the village was burned and the neighborhood thoroughly ravaged.

In November, however, Brant and Walter Butler delighted Germain's heart by wiping out another nest of happy rebel homes in fire and blood. A dozen miles east of Otsego Lake and fifty west of Schenectady lay Cherry Valley; the largest and wealthiest settlement around the headwaters of the Susquehanna, and noted among frontier towns for the unusual cultivation of its inhabitants. It had been fortified in the spring by Lafayette's orders, being so shining a mark for

Clinton
power-
less save
for raids

Grey's
butch-
eries

Cherry
Valley

Indian assault; and was now garrisoned by some 250 Continentals, placed by reason of sectional claims under Colonel Ichabod Alden of Massachusetts, none of them knowing anything of Indian warfare. The officers slept in a house outside the works; and when authoritatively warned on the 8th of a large force on the way against the place, Alden discredited it and dissuaded the families from moving inside the fort with their goods, saying his scouts would give them full warning.

1778
Nov.

Cherry
Valley's
reckless
garrison

But the scouts were as skeptical and reckless as he; built fires and went to sleep nights. One party in the night of the 9th was captured by some 200 Tories under Butler and 500 Indians, chiefly Mohawks under Brant, with a band of uncommanded Senecas furious as wolves. Learning from their terrorized prisoners the fact of the officers' outside lodging, on the 10th in the rain they hid in a swamp thicket in rear of the house, and early next morning crept on to capture them and cripple the defense. The Senecas broke orders and rushed on for first plunder, fired on and wounded a stray settler, who escaped and gave warning; the officers hurried toward the fort, but several with Alden were overtaken and slain. The garrison held the fort against some hours' assault that day and the next, 16 being killed including the above; but the allies burned every building in the settlement and carried off the cattle and the inhabitants, save 32 butchered on the spot.

Brant kept his own warriors from this massacre; but he could not control the Senecas nor

1778
Nov.

Cherry
Valley
massacre

the still worse Tories, and some of the murders were the most shocking in the history of the Revolution.[1] Most of the captive settlers were shortly set free and let go where they would or could, by Butler, who took credit to himself for compassion and not warring against women and children; but the Indians kept several of both and

Walter
Butler's
belated
scruples

murdered some on the way, and it seems probable that his own family's being in American power stimulated his not enervating humanity.

But there was no further campaign in the North worth calling such from now till the end of the war. Washington and Clinton merely neu-

Washing-
ton and
Clinton

tralized each other, neither one able to cease vigilance or draw off his troops till Washington's grand stroke at the last, neither able to strike at the other. Washington's army held in the British by a girdle of cantonments from Danbury, Connecticut, to Elizabethtown, New Jersey. It was in much better comfort than formerly, as Beaumarchais had succeeded in getting a fair supply of clothing to it, and the commissary department was at last decently managed; on the other hand, the dreadful depreciation of currency had practically annihilated its pay, and there was great distress for almost every necessary of life but the barest needs of food and clothing.

---

[1] The most dastardly crime was by a Tory, who found a father trying to revive the spark of life left in his mangled little girl, the only one not dead of several murdered children, and at once finished slaughtering her. On the other hand, one of Brant's Indians saved an old man's life out of compassion.

CHAPTER XLV.

THE WEST AND THE REVOLUTION

The dozen years after the conquest of Canada were an era of extraordinary growth in American population. Freed from the constant dread of war with the French, and of their inspiring and aiding the murderous outbreaks of the savages, the colonists began to spread out and occupy regions previously regarded as too dangerous. The swarming sons of the prolific New England families, virile, ambitious, and stinted, irresistibly overflowed the chartered limits of their provinces.

1763–75

Spread of colonial population

Those of Connecticut were far in the lead: they had less territory than those of Massachusetts or New Hampshire, and outnumbered manyfold those of Rhode Island. They moved by hundreds into the green valleys of that northwestern region named by the French the Verdant Mountains, with lesser bodies from the other provinces, and laid the foundations of the future State of Vermont, under the royal grant to New Hampshire. By royal selfishness and ignorance combined, this was later taken away and given to New York; and the authorities of that province, not content with endeavoring to extend its jurisdiction over "the Grants," which was its legal right and would not have been resisted, undertook to force the existent

Connecticut leads

The New Hampshire Grants

settlers to buy their properties over again or yield
them up to New York grantees. This the Green
Mountain Boys resisted to the death, or rather

the Beech Seal over the backs of the New York
surveyors and claimants. We have told of their
declaration of independence.

But the lands even of this section were too
limited and hard to satisfy the needs of the Connecticut farmers. They had an eye to the superb

lands west of the Pennsylvania settlements, kept
a wilderness by the Penns in order some time to
lease it in great feudal manors. With the real
though not avowed help of the colony, they sent
an organized emigration thither, so solid and resolute that the trivial bodyguard the Penns could
call to their aid was a straw against a torrent—especially as it had the passive sympathy of most
Pennsylvanians themselves and the active help of

a good many. Its story has been briefly told under
Pennsylvania; and the story of its horrible fate
and temporary extermination in the Revolution
has been given only a few pages ago.

But the overspill was not confined to New
England: it was general throughout the colonies.
A universal tide set in toward the west. Georgia,

the Carolinas, Virginia, Maryland, Pennsylvania,
and New York, all participated. European emigrants also came over, and swiftly melted into
the mass of citizens. Many British officers had
become infatuated with America and its opportunities while serving against the French, and now
resigning their commissions, organized colonies

mainly of time-expired soldiers, and formed new settlements. In the Revolution these men very generally took sides with the Americans, forming themselves into battalions for the protection of the border.

Of these westward impulses, that ultimately most important was the one which led to the peopling of Kentucky and the Illinois country. The policy of the English government for the decade after the treaty of 1763 was to confine white settlement in perpetuity to the Atlantic seaboard. The pretext was to keep order and do justice to the Indians; the actual reasons were to keep the colonies "in a due subordination to and dependence upon the mother country," and to prevent a decrease of the fur trade, "to the prejudice" of which "all colonizing in its nature operates." Thus the Board of Trade and Plantations in 1772, by its president Lord Hillsborough, in refusing a land grant on the Ohio. But Franklin wrote a pamphlet in reply, so powerful that the Privy Council allowed the grant and reversed the government's long-time policy.

Still the government wished to keep the control of the new territory in its own hands; and Lord Dunmore when appointed governor of Virginia was specially instructed to veto the colony's claims west of the mountains. But in 1773 he became himself a partner in two huge purchases from the Indians, at the Ohio Falls (Louisville) and opposite Cincinnati, and stretched Virginia's bounds indefinitely westward.

Pittsburg, well within the Pennsylvania char-
ter, was made the rallying-point for western emigration and the central depot of the vast Indian
trade thereabout. Dunmore was rapidly becoming
an empire-builder of boundless vision. Suddenly
he extended Virginia's jurisdiction over a large
well-settled section of Pennsylvania; and through
his land-jobbing agent, John Connolly, a native of
the province, ordered the assembling of the militia.
This was done with the entire good-will and probably at the suggestion of the annexed inhabitants,
who always chafed at the Quaker championship
of the Indians; and Dunmore treated the Pennsylvania protests with haughtiness. The Virginia
Burgesses, however, would not sanction this aggression, which England would be sure to disallow;
but they supported the extension west, which
interfered with none but Indians.

Meanwhile, despite the failure of ambitious
schemes for organized colonization, hundreds of
pioneers were squatting singly or in settlements
not only in Kentucky, but beyond the Ohio and
on the Illinois plains. Among others employed
and encouraged by Dunmore was a young man
named Daniel Boone, a Pennsylvanian of Quaker
family. He had removed at eighteen with his
father to the banks of the Yadkin in North Carolina, became a noted huntsman, and married Re-
becca, daughter of William Bryan, a prosperous
neighbor farmer. Three of her brothers later
founded Bryan's Station (near the present Lexington, Kentucky), which became the centre of

DANIEL BOONE.

COTTAGE BUILT BY BOONE WITH HIS OWN HANDS. FRONT VIEW.

COTTAGE BUILT RY BOONE WITH HIS OWN HANDS. REAR VIEW.

SIMON KENTON.

KENTUCKY RIVER VALLEY FROM BOONE'S COTTAGE.

attack from the British and Indians during the
war that followed. For some years he farmed and
hunted uneventfully—except for "cilling bars"
and the like; but the gradual influx of well-to-do
slaveholding planters formed an aristocracy and
reduced his class to the status of "poor whites,"
a degrading and unbearable distinction to men of
any spirit.

1764–73

Slavery
degrades
free
planters

In 1764 Boone and three or four others, two his
brothers-in-law, in the interest of a land scheme
penetrated as far as Rockcastle Creek, a branch
of the Cumberland, within the present Kentucky;
the first white men to set foot on this forbidden
Indian ground. Their glowing accounts of land
and springs and timber and game enkindled immediate desire to verify them; numbers of others
followed, and declared their descriptions far
understated. But Boone's work and his increasing
family prevented him from making another trip
west till May 1769, when as the chosen leader of
five companions he gained central Eastern Kentucky, in the present Morgan County. It was
nearly two years before he again reached home.
In that time he had tasted neither bread nor salt,
had lost six companions (others having joined),
been captive to the Indians, and spent many
months alone in the wilderness. This might have
satisfied him; but he was fully determined to take
his family to, and make his future home in, the
new rich region of glorious hunting, fertile soil,
and no contemptuous upper class. On September 25, 1773, he and his brother Squire and their

Boone
visits
Ken-
tucky

Second
trip and
hard-
ships

Goes to
settle

1773
Oct.-Dec.

families set out from the Yadkin, with a drove of pack-horses carrying their stores, and themselves driving several milch cows.

Massacre
of part of
Boone's
band

At Powell's Valley they were joined and heartened by five families and forty well-armed men; but at Cumberland Gap a shocking disaster fell upon the little colony and drove them back to civilized security again. The defile was notedly perilous; but the Indians thereabout had committed no outrages for some time, and seven youths and boys attending the cows were loitering in the rear of the party to let them graze. Suddenly a rifle volley blazed from a hazel thicket; six of the boys fell dead and were immediately scalped, while the seventh, a little fellow without gun or hatchet, ran screaming along the trail till he met the armed men summoned by the firing and the Indian yells. The Indians had disappeared when they came up; but the bereaved families dared go no farther into such dangers, and retreated to the Clinch River settlements in Virginia.

Re-
venged

This massacre directly brought on the famous Dunmore's War, one episode of which is immortal in popular memory. It was found to have been committed by a roving band of Cherokees; as that nation was not at war with the whites, Dunmore demanded the surrender of the perpetrators for punishment. The chiefs shuffled the responsibility to other tribes; at length one of the culprits was pointed out at a frontier horse-race to the father of one of the murdered boys, who at once shot him dead. The whites upheld the act, and the Indians began murdering stragglers all along the frontier. They killed eight men in a few weeks; and the Shawnees in February 1774 murdered the crew of a trading canoe on the Ohio and distributed the goods among themselves. Shortly afterward they stole several other such canoes; and Michael Cresap (cres'-op), a noted Indian-trader with a post on the Ohio near Wheeling, recovered them by a battle with one killed on each side.

By this time it was known that the Cherokees and other western tribes were exchanging messages for a combined attack on the white settlements; and a general warning was sent out by Connolly from Pittsburg. This was taken by Cresap and his company for authorization to forestall the savages, especially as the latter had been carrying on war for months; and on the 26th of April some of them stalked a canoe on the Ohio containing two Indians and a white man, and killed the former. On the 30th five Delaware and Shawnee warriors and their women, encamped near Yellow Creek at the present Wellsville, Ohio, were enticed across the river to a trading post, made drunk, and all butchered; two others coming to look them up were shot on landing; five more following in a canoe turned to flee, but were fired on, two killed and two wounded. A race war without quarter was begun: in the last ten days of April thirteen Indians were killed in that locality alone, and sometimes their corpses buried by their friends were dug up, torn in pieces, and flung up in the trees.

1774
Jan.-
April

Shaw-
nees and
Cresap

Indians
com-
bining

General
war

Massacre
of Ind-
ians at
Yellow
Creek

1774
April

Murder of
Logan's
family

Among the murdered women were several relatives of the famous Mingo chief Tahgahjutè; son of the Cayuga chief Shikellamy, and given the English name Logan after William Penn's friend James Logan, whose visit to the Indians of Conestoga had made him greatly beloved and revered. About the same time Logan's cabin on Yellow Creek was burned in his absence and the rest of his family murdered, by a gang of worthless drunken whites. No more insane or unprovoked outrage could have been committed than this cowardly crime. He was the stanchest of friends to the whites, and had steadily thrown his powerful influence to restrain his race; in this very war he could and would have saved immense loss and bereavement. He had been reared on the Susquehanna under Moravian influences, and educated in their school; settled near Reedsville, Pennsylvania; was chosen chief by the Mingoes; and became not only of great Indian consideration, but a high favorite among the whites in western Penn-

Logan's
career

sylvania and neighboring Virginia, distinguished for ability, character, and generosity. One old frontiersman declared that Logan was the best man he ever met, red or white.

It was this noble man and unwavering ally, —settled on the Ohio for a few years past,—whose household was now exterminated by the whites.

Turns
against
whites

He laid the act to Cresap, and sent him a challenge; then, his friendship for the whites changed to deadly hatred, went on the war-path, a brand of destruction. At the head of a like party he burst

into the heart of the settlements, taking no less
than thirty scalps with his own hands. His allies
were even more successful. A Shawnee chief on a
raid from the Allegheny to the northwest corner
of Tennessee brought back forty scalps personally
taken from men, women, and children. Great
numbers of the pioneer families fled from the border to the older settlements.

Dunmore ordered all the border militia under
arms. Boone was made a captain and placed in
command of several frontier stations. Other men
subsequently famous were called into service.
Daniel Morgan, part of his distinguished career
already told, was one. A teamster who had saved
many helpless wounded at Braddock's defeat,
serving through that war and then in Pontiac's,
he had settled on a farm at "Soldiers' Rest" near
Winchester, and now came in at the head of a
company of riflemen, to be world-famous a little
later. Another celebrity was General Andrew
Lewis; the son of a Donegal farmer of Huguenot
blood who had killed his landlord in resisting eject-
ment, and fled to America. He had been a major
in Washington's regiment in 1754, surrendered
with him at Fort Necessity, was with him at Braddock's defeat, headed the "Sandy Creek expedition" of 1756, and was taken prisoner in Grant's
attempt to capture Fort Duquesne. He was now
commissioned brigadier-general of the Virginia
forces. Later he was to defeat his present chief
Dunmore at Guynn's Island, and fill other important posts. John Sevier, Evan Shelby, and

1774

Frightful
Indian
raids

Daniel
Morgan

Andrew
Lewis

James Robertson, the latter a companion of Boone, were among the other Revolutionary notabilities who served here.

In September 1774, while the clans were gathering from the southwest, Dunmore repaired to Pittsburg and renewed treaties of peace with the Delawares and the Six Nations. Then, without waiting for Lewis' command, he proceeded down the Ohio with about 1200 men including Morgan's, and invaded the territory of the formidable Shawnees; they who boasted of killing ten white men to the other tribes' one, and under their celebrated chief Cornstalk were now preparing to make a clean sweep of the border settlements, and restore them to the deer and the buffalo. He found their villages all vacant—a gloomy omen. The admirable strategy of Cornstalk, whose generalship throughout would have done credit to any civilized commander, had led them with the Mingoes and the Delawares through the forest far in his rear, to fall upon Lewis' army before it could join him. Under this skillful chief the divided forces might well have been separately wiped out, and the settlements for the time obliterated.

On the 6th of October Lewis' command, close upon 1100 men, encamped on the wide densely wooded peninsula where the Kanawha joins the Ohio. Its fat deer and wild turkeys and other game won it directly the name of Point Pleasant. Lewis had expected to meet Dunmore there, and was grievously disappointed at having no word from him; presuming that he was approaching on

Dun-
more's
reckless
invasion
of Shaw-
nees

the Ohio, and totally unsuspecting any Indian assault, the men remained carelessly in camp for four days, hunting for sport, scarcely guarding the camp at night, and scattering at their own will. It was blind luck added to native skill and courage that saved them from annihilation.

On the night of the 9th Cornstalk's savage army crossed the Ohio unsuspected, formed themselves in military order, and early in the morning stole through the woods on the mostly sleeping camp. When almost within rifle range, they came suddenly upon two youths ranging the Ohio banks in quest of deer; one was instantly shot, the other escaped and alarmed his comrades. About the same time Robertson and Sevier, self-posted sentinels, discovered and reported the danger; the shot had already roused the army, and Lewis hastily formed his force into two divisions under his brother Charles and Thomas Fleming, and sent them forward to engage, holding a strong reserve in camp—a wise precaution. The advancing troops were shortly met with a volley from the timber that mortally wounded Charles Lewis and killed several others, and the men fell back in a panic. Soon reinforced from the reserve, they held their ground and the battle became general and unflinching, both sides fighting behind trees scarce sixty feet apart; Cornstalk alone came into the open with disdain of cover, encouraging his warriors. Whenever one of either side fell, some from the other would rush out to take his scalp, for the borderers were as fierce as the Indians;

and to save it others would spring out, and desperate encounters took place with the knife and tomahawk.

Until noon the battle raged without cessation; then the Indians gave back and formed a new line across the point from river to river. Fleming's men pushed close after them, cautiously thrust forth a number of caps on the ends of rifles, let them fall when shot through, and instantly shot or knifed the savages who leapt forward to secure the scalps, adding many such ghastly trophies to their own belts. But they had advanced beyond their own lines, and were soon hemmed in by superior numbers. The Indians made wilder efforts than ever to destroy them; twice Fleming led desperate charges to break the inclosing circle, and was three times wounded and carried from the field. But in the afternoon both sides slackened their fire, which ceased at sunset, and in the night the savages recrossed the Ohio and fled westward.

The victory of the frontiersmen was not only complete, but it was one of the decisive contests of America; it was the last pitched battle for the frontiers till Tecumseh's time, and it gave the central West to civilization, though it was Clark who gave it to the republic. It was purchased by a loss of fifty killed outright and eighty wounded, some of whom died later. That of the Indians was never known, for they carried away all their dead they could to prevent their being scalped. So dismayed were they at their dreadful decimation that they did not cease flight till the Scioto was between themselves and the foe, and they had no further heart for war or hope of reclaiming the land.

A day or two later Lewis received a reinforcement of 300 men; and having orders at last from Dunmore, left a garrison there and marched to meet his chief at Camp Charlotte (seven miles south of Circleville), where Dunmore received a delegation of chiefs suing for peace. The Shawnees agreed to surrender all their prisoners and stolen horses and other property, give hostages, molest no more boats on the Ohio and hunt no more south of it, and regulate their trade by the instructions of the King's officers. This treaty—which the Indians neither kept nor intended to keep—extended the territory of Virginia to embrace all Kentucky, a part of Tennessee, and the great northwestern region.

Dunmore
makes
treaty
with
Shaw-
nees

Logan had fought bravely and taken several scalps at Point Pleasant, but he would take no part in the peace proceedings. His brother-in-law John Gibson, who had fought against him in the battle,—an Indian-trader subsequently a Continental general and governor of Indiana,—was sent to ask his attendance at the council; Logan led the way from his cabin to the woods, seated himself on a log, and gave his answer in a strain of eloquence and pathos that are of undying memory.[1]

---

[1] "I appeal to any white man to say if he ever entered Logan's cabin hungry, and he gave him not meat; if he ever came cold and naked, and he clothed him not. During the course of the last long and bloody war, Logan remained idle in his cabin, an advocate for peace. Such was my love for the whites that my people pointed as they passed, and said, 'Logan is the friend of white men.' I had even thought to

1774

This stamping out of the organized Indian resistance, though isolated murders were still thick, gave new life to the western settlements,

Ken-
tucky
founded

which soon began to expand with greater vigor than ever. Within a few months a new commonwealth was born, the new settlements in which soon attained an importance sufficient to make their influence felt during the war for independence. On the 1st of April, 1775, Boone with his family and an emigrant party reached the Kentucky River northwest of the present Richmond, Madison County, after being twice assailed by Indians and four killed besides some wounded; decided to settle there, and built a palisaded log

At
Boones-
borough

fort. This first permanent Kentucky settlement was called Boonesborough; a small town grew up, and the first legislative Assembly of the West was held there. But it gradually vanished, and the site of Kentucky's first capital is now farm land.

Shortly afterward Colonel Robert Patterson with a party chose a site for a settlement; while the surveyors were at work came the news of the

have lived with you, but for the injuries of one man. Colonel Cresap, the last spring, in cold blood and unprovoked, murdered all the relations of Logan, not even sparing my women and children. There runs not a drop of my blood in the veins of any living creature. This called on me for revenge. I have sought it; I have killed many; I have fully glutted my vengeance; for my country I rejoice at the beams of peace. But do not harbor a thought that mine is the joy of fear. Logan never felt fear. He will not turn on his heel to save his life. Who is there to mourn for Logan?—Not one."

This undoubtedly owes some of its exact wording to Gibson, as two reports of it from his memory vary a good deal; but that in substance it is genuine cannot be doubted. The Biblical sentences are natural to one educated in Moravian schools. Logan, however, was mistaken about Cresap's agency in murdering his family at Yellow Creek.

battle of Lexington, and its name was given to
the town. Others rapidly followed, not only in
Kentucky, but in the territory now embraced
within Ohio, Indiana, and Illinois, nearly all then
claimed by Virginia. Most of these not only maintained their existence throughout the Revolutionary War, but assisted materially in that contest,
and remained afterward as a nucleus around which
the great States of the Mississippi Valley were
built. The pioneers of this region have been unfairly left out of account in the struggle for
liberty; very much of its glory belongs to them.
Their battles with the British and Indians were
not only of high importance in their bearing on
the final result,—as keeping a formidable horde
of mingled savagery from falling on the flank of
those engaged on the main theatre of action,—
but they kept the whole country west of the Alleghanies from being a new set of English colonies, to bar United States expansion and breed
a new war.

To the Kentuckians belongs also the honor of
taking an early step in the direction of American
independence. This interesting measure was enacted by a convention or "legislature" of eighteen
pioneer delegates—among them Richard Henderson, Daniel Boone, Richard Callaway, Thomas
Slaughter, John Floyd, James Harrod, and William Bryan—at Boone's Fort on May 23, 1775.
It assembled under a large elm-tree overhanging
the unfinished stockade; organized by an Anglican
clergyman's reading a prayer, and appointed a

1775
et seq.

First set-
tlement
of the
West

Import-
ant
work of
pioneers

First
inde-
pendent
American
republic

committee to draft resolutions, Richard Callaway
chairman—a man of education, probably their
chief author. These, unanimously adopted, asserted their purpose to organize a new province;
declared that "all power is originally in the people, and therefore no doubt should be felt as to
the efficacy of any laws they may be pleased to
make"; and that "we have a right as a political
body, without giving umbrage to Great Britain
or any of the colonies, to frame rules for the government of our little society." It was named
Transylvania—later changed to the better because
native name of Kentucky; rules for its government were enacted on "the happy pattern of the
English laws"; courts of justice, and militia bodies for defense against British and Indians, were
formed. Annual elections, sole popular control of
raising and disbursing taxes, salaries fixed by
statute, land-offices to be always open, judges appointed by the proprietors but responsible to the
people, entire religious freedom, were other details. A government was at once organized, with
Henderson president, and Boone's Fort the capital.

Henderson had been an associate justice of the
North Carolina Superior Court, driven out of the
Hillsborough court-house by the rioters in September 1770, and soon after resigned; elected
judge of the State Superior Court when the province revolted in 1775, he declined on account of
having organized the Transylvania Company and
removed thither. The company, through Boone,

Margin notes:
1775
May 23,
etc.

Ken-
tucky
embodies
itself
indepen-
dently

"Tran-
syl-
vania"

President
Hender-
son

GEORGE ROGERS CLARK.

(From the Chicago Historical Society.)

bought from the Cherokees in March 1775 all the
land south of the Ohio and between the Cumberland Mountains and River,—nearly all the present
Kentucky; Virginia disallowed it as an invasion
of her chartered rights, but indemnified the Company and its actually settled pioneers by a tract
twelve miles square on the Ohio below the mouth
of the Green River, where Henderson town and
county were established. Neither the Cherokees
nor any of the various other tribes north and
south who claimed it, however, ever occupied a
foot of it, even as a recognized hunting preserve;
for they fought each other for its possession as
ferociously as they afterwards fought the whites.
The Cherokee chief Oconostota is said to have
remarked to Henderson, after the purchase, that
he had bought a fine country, but might find some
little difficulty in occupying it.

We now come to the world-famed expedition
of George Rogers Clark, by which he gave his
country an empire. Clark was a Virginian, a
schoolfellow of Madison and through life a warm
friend of Jefferson. He followed Boone into Dunmore's War in 1774, and into Kentucky in 1775;
became a major of militia the next year, and was
sent to Williamsburg to ask the very moderate
supply of 500 pounds of powder for the western
settlements. The Virginia authorities would not
give it up; and Clark angrily said that "a country
not worth defending was not worth claiming,"
whereupon they furnished the powder. It was
carried on pack-horses to the Monongahela, thence

1774-5

The
Transyl-
vania
Company

Ken-
tucky
unowned
territory

George
Rogers
Clark

Gets
powder
from
Virginia

down the Ohio to Three Islands (near Maysville), and again packed to Harrodsburg as a distributing point. Part of it helped Clark to repel an Indian attack on the fort there in 1777, with such skill that he was made a Continental lieutenant-colonel.

Clark now conceived the idea of conquering the Illinois country, and breaking up the British force with its den at Detroit, whence were organized and sent out nearly all the Indian plundering and **Clark investigates old French posts** scalping expeditions against the western settlements. During the next winter he sent two spies to visit the chief Illinois settlements and report. This old French district—with towns and trading posts at Vincennes on the Wabash, at Kaskaskia, St. Louis, and Cahokia on the Mississippi, and smaller ones elsewhere—had nothing to hold it to Britain but small garrisons at the chief points; and those often composed of French ex-officers and privates, who would risk no blood for her. As in Canada, England had let the French population manage their own affairs, and they would not personally fight against her, but they did not **Favorable for conquest** like her and neither would they aid her; they would welcome the Americans as deliverers, and a small force of determined men could easily sweep the whole district, was the report of the agents.

Clark at once set out for Virginia and laid his plans before Patrick Henry, just re-elected governor, who warmly approved them; as did Mason **Virginia leaders favor it** and Jefferson, who had the House authorize the governor to aid "any expedition against their western enemies." Clark was also given ample

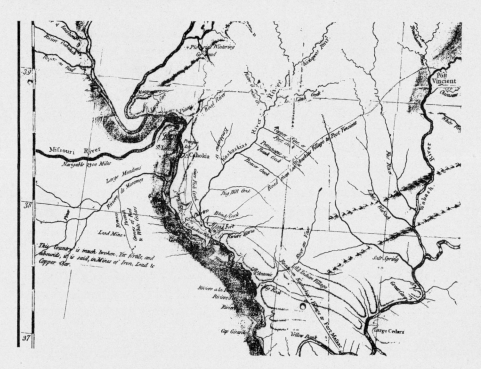

THE MISSISSIPPI, ILLINOIS AND WABASH
COUNTRY IN 1778.

MAGAZINE AT OLD FORT CHARTRES.

funds; proceeded to the Kanawha district, and soon enlisted 150 hardy volunteers, another hundred shortly coming from Kentucky. The whole were gathered on an island opposite Louisville, drilled and kept in barracks built for them, and corn and vegetables planted for fall and winter food—whence the name "Corn Island."

On the 24th of June, 1778, leaving a small garrison at the island, Clark set out with 130 men to conquer the Northwest; they canoed down the Ohio to the deserted French Fort Massac, in southern Illinois, then marched overland to Kaskaskia. There was not a white or even Indian settlement on the road, and during the latter part of their six-days' journey they were wholly without food save what they shot. On the evening of the Fourth of July they came in sight of Kaskaskia; waiting for darkness, they rushed into the town and captured it without opposition or bloodshed. Rocheblave the commandant was a Frenchman, he had but a handful of men, and for both reasons had no disposition to resist. The people welcomed the Americans with open arms; feasted them royally, and the conquerors crowned the victory by paying liberally for everything they wished. From that moment the French were Americans heart and soul. By their mediation also Clark was enabled to make treaties of amity with the principal Indian tribes of the region. He sent Captain Bowman with a small company to take and hold possession of Cahokia, and the same scenes were enacted, as everywhere that the French dwelt. He probably

1778
June-
July

Clark's
campaign
at Corn
Island

Captures
Kas-
kaskia

And
Cahokia

1778
July
et seq.

also visited St. Louis, founded fourteen years before, now under Spanish control; and regarded as of little importance by Kaskaskia and Cahokía, who could not see why a town should be built on a bluff, instead of a plain where the streets had not to be graded. Carondelet—later called "Empty Pocket"—was thought to have much better chances from its room to grow along the Des Peres.

St. Louis despised

But Clark's main thought was of putting an end to the infernal work concocted and engineered at Detroit. Henry Hamilton, its commandant, lieutenant-governor of Quebec, was Germain's and the King's most dutiful and thorough-going agent in America; he paid (though with nice logic he injuredly denied offering) high rewards for scalps without distinction of age or sex; hounded on the savages to burn and slaughter; and the cruelties upon settlements and prisoners by his sanction, if not order, almost exceed belief. Clark in his own words "felt as never again in his life a flow of rage," and resolved to move at once on Vincennes as a base of action. But Father Gibault, a French priest at Kaskaskia, who gave zealous co-operation and wise counsel, dissuaded him; proposing to go himself with a small party and secure the submission of the Wabash towns without violence, as they would share the general French feeling. He did so; and the people after hearing him not only repaired to the church and took the oath of allegiance, but entered heartily into the plans for capturing Detroit. This message was sent to all the tribes: "The King of France is come to life.

Hamilton's deviltries from Detroit

Gibault secures Wabash towns to Clark

"We desire you to leave us a very wide path for us to pass through your country to Detroit, for we are many in number, and we might chance to hurt some of your young people with our swords."

Hamilton was not destitute either of courage or ability, and he put forth all his efforts to counteract Clark's sweeping success. By October he had four or five hundred regulars and volunteers ready, with 350 picked Indian warriors from thirteen different tribes, and several cannon; on the 7th he started for Vincennes, and on the 15th with this overwhelming force took possession without a blow, compelling the people to renounce their late oath and take a fresh one to England. He repaired and armed the fortifications, and set about collecting a still larger body of Indians, to recover the lost settlements in the spring. Within a few days he had 700 more miscellaneous savages, of tribes from Michillimacinac to Louisiana, his whole force amounting to some 1500; and to keep them busy, he sent out parties to burn every settlement and cabin and kill every settler found unprotected. It was a fearful winter for the colonists, and large tracts were deserted. Gangs of the savages hovered around Kaskaskia and Cahokia, and Clark had all the trees cleared away for a wide circuit to prevent their gaining cover, besides mounting several cannon. The Indians therefore left that section to strike an easier mark.

Meanwhile both the French inhabitants and the Spanish across the Mississippi zealously supplied them with provisions, and with information

1779
Jan.-Feb.

Hamil-
ton's
tempo-
rary
weakness

Clark
starts to
over-
throw
him

Terrible
winter
march to
Vin-
cennes

of the enemy's movements. A number of young
Frenchmen volunteered to fight, and Clark armed
and drilled them for garrisons, to leave his own
force free for emergencies. Late in January a
Spanish merchant from Vincennes arrived at Kaskaskia, bringing news that Hamilton's numerous
bands sent out to maraud and block the Ohio had
left him not over eighty men, with three cannon
and a few small swivels; but that in the spring he
meant to call them in and clear the West of the
Americans. Clark at once dispatched a company
of riflemen in a small galley he had mounted with
two four-pounders and four swivels, to proceed by
the Mississippi, Ohio, and Wabash to within a few
miles of Vincennes, allowing nothing to pass them
westward. This done, he called in his Cahokia
riflemen, left the volunteer militia to guard that
place and Kaskaskia, and set out straight across
the southern-Illinois peninsula through the unbroken wilderness for Vincennes, nearly 180 miles,
with 130 men of iron.

The rivers were in flood and the bottom-lands
under water; yet in eleven days the company were
within nine miles of Vincennes,—fifteen to sixteen miles a day loaded with rifles, ammunition,
food, and blankets. Thence on, the entire distance
was across the "drowned lands" of the Wabash,
and finally the swollen river itself, wading every
step, often up to their arm-pits; six days it
took them, almost without food, sleeping at
night on hummocks of earth. Only the unusu-
ally warm season saved them from perishing; the

boats accompanying them picked up those exhausted and likely to drown, and carried those unable to march further. On the afternoon of the 23d they reached dry land, recruited their strength from the meat and corn found in a captured Indian canoe, and rushed into the town; the citizens received them joyfully and united with them in assailing the fort, which was taken completely by surprise. But the garrison fought obstinately through an incessant fire of eighteen hours; and Clark's galley having not yet arrived with his artillery, storming the fort was impossible.

About one o'clock of the second night, however, the moon went down; in the darkness Clark threw up and manned with picked shots an intrenchment within rifle range of their strongest battery, and within fifteen minutes after daylight had silenced two guns and disabled seven men, without losing a man of his own. No gunner could serve a piece under the unerring fire; and Hamilton hung out a white flag and asked for terms. Several fruitless conferences were held; Clark declared that if compelled to storm the fort, he would give Hamilton the treatment due to a murderer. One of Hamilton's Indian scalping parties came in meantime; Clark's men tomahawked them in front of the fort and flung their bodies into the river, and the good Hamilton was shocked at this "barbarity." At length Clark demanded an unconditional surrender on pain of immediate assault; it was yielded (February 25). Clark captured 79 men besides Hamilton, and a large quantity

1778
Feb. 23–5

Clark
enters
Vin-
cennes

Assails
the
forts

Negotia-
tions

Hamil-
ton sur-
renders

of munitions, at a cost of but one man wounded, he having cautioned his small band not to expose themselves unnecessarily and unprofitably.

*1778
Feb. 25
et seq.*

Scarcely was the battle over when Clark learned that a strong party of British and Indians was descending the Wabash, convoying goods from Detroit to Vincennes. He at once armed some boats with the captured swivels, and sent sixty men to push day and night up the river and fall on the party before news of Vincennes could reach it. It was captured without a blow, and forty prisoners and more than $50,000 worth of goods were brought back to Vincennes.

*Clark
captures
Hamil-
ton's re-
inforce-
ments*

Clark's prisoners, now nearly man for man of his own, had to be mostly paroled; but Hamilton and his principal officers were sent to Williamsburg, where they were jailed in irons on the three grounds of retaliation for general English treatment of American prisoners, his and his savage allies' atrocities on the frontier, and his individual barbarities on American citizens. Washington, to whom it was referred, ordered them released on condition of not talking against the United States till exchanged; they insisted on freedom of speech and were remanded to jail without irons, but in a few days accepted the conditions and were released.

*Hamil-
ton and
his offi-
cers im-
prisoned*

Paroled

Before news of Vincennes had reached Virginia, Clark had been made a brigadier-general and placed in command of all the Western troops. Governor Henry in his letter suggested the capture of Detroit, to end British savageries in the West.

*Clark
com-
mander
in the
West*

Clark received it a few days after his victory. He replied April 2 that with 500 men when he first arrived in the region, or 300 and ability to secure his prisoners after taking Vincennes, he should have attempted it; and doubtless succeeded, for he learned that Detroit and its surrounding country held a three-days' festival in honor of his success, and provided handsomely for his expected coming there, the garrison of only 80 men not daring to interfere. But they were now building a stronger fort (Le Noult), he feared too strong for any force he could raise out there. In fact it was, and Detroit remained in British hands; ceded with the present territory of Michigan to the United States in 1783, it was not surrendered till 1796.

Picturesque though not directly important during this time were the operations of Captain James Willing in West Florida. It will be remembered that by the treaty of 1763, Great Britain held all the former Spanish territory east of the Mississippi except New Orleans and its environs, but including Natchez, Baton Rouge, and Mobile. Upon the opening of the Revolution the British posts there—with a mongrel population of Spaniards, French, British traders, and floaters of various nationalities, and slender garrisons—were in a ticklish posture, which led to their easy capture by Governor Galvez of Florida in 1779. The Spaniards in British and Spanish Florida sympathized naturally with the Americans, from dislike of the British interlopers; and

1778, etc.

Clark
unable
to take
Detroit

British
West
Florida

In
danger

1777–8

Span-
iards
furnish
American
arma-
ments

Willing
as
unofficial
diplomat

Forces
neutral-
ity oath
on
Natchez

their trade with the new West via the Ohio to Pittsburg being large and lucrative there was a double reason why they should furnish a chief source of arms, ammunition, and other military stores for the patriots. With the help of Galvez, governor from February 1, 1777, the river boats carried on an active trade in these supplies.

Among the agents sent up the river in 1776 by the American merchants in New Orleans, with the goods they had collected, was one James Willing, a resident on the river for some years; perhaps related to Robert Morris' partner in Philadelphia, where he appears in the following winter. The next spring he was back from Fort Pitt with several canoes on the same errand; but added the political one of a visit to Mobile with some of his followers, to induce the English residents there to join the Revolution. He was unsuccessful, but evidently determined to enforce at least neutrality on the English in this region. In January 1778 he was back in New Orleans with a Continental commission as captain, and perhaps made some arrangement with Galvez to help regain the district for Spain if he could not gain it for America, in consideration of help in depriving England of it on some terms.

Engaging new men to work the boats back, he took a party of chosen companions and descended on Natchez; where he told the authorities an American army of 5000 men was close behind, and terrified them into calling a public meeting which took an oath of neutrality. He then went to Manchac with the same success; but while he was gone the Natchez citizens had thrown their oath overboard and formed an association for mutual protection, electing officers, and it would seem ousting a small garrison Willing had left in the fort. Stories coming from this citizens' association tell that he and his band plundered plantations, seized a vessel and sold it to the Spaniards and spent the proceeds in a carouse, and made the scattered settlers take an oath of allegiance to Spain. At any rate, it seems certain that he returned to Natchez and had a battle with the citizens, in which he was beaten and some of his men killed, and he returned to Manchac; then visited the Tensan settlements above Mobile on the same political quest. Late in 1778 or early in 1779 he was captured and put in irons as a freebooter, but exchanged later in 1779. The Natchez people or the British soldiery recovered Manchac in April; but shortly afterward Galvez overran the whole district and recovered it for Spain, retaining it at the end of the war.[1]

Early in 1779, a little before Clark left Kaskaskia for Vincennes, about 1000 Cherokee and other Indian warriors assembled at Chickamauga, in pursuance of Hamilton's assignment of them to the work of massacre and fire among the

1778-9

Willing foiled at Natchez

Galvez reconquers West Florida

Evan Shelby strikes Cherokees

---

[1] This account has been extracted from a number of not very consistent recitals, after careful comparison and as far as possible harmonizing. The Natchez affair has evidently suffered from British anger and distortion, and it is not possible to be sure in detail what happened. Especially, what was the British garrison doing?

1779-80

Chero-
kees
crushed
by Evan
Shelby

Our debt
to Clark

Fort
Jefferson
built

Kentucky and Ohio River settlements. To break
up this gang at its central rendezvous, Colonel
Evan Shelby was placed in command of 1500 men
by Virginia and North Carolina: 1000 volunteer
frontiersmen, and 500 one-year men enlisted to
reinforce Clark. About the middle of April they
embarked on the Tennessee, and made such speed
that they fell on the encampment without even
the supposably vigilant Indians suspecting their
approach. The warriors were dispersed to the
woods and hills, many followed and killed, their
towns burnt, their crops destroyed, and their
cattle driven off. Their time for long thereafter
was so fully occupied hunting to keep themselves
and their families alive, that they had little time
left for excursions of murder, and the British
agents found their occupation gone.

This expedition with those of Clark cleared
the West of British influence. The cause was at
a very low ebb in the East when they took place,
and they greatly heartened the patriots there;
and but for them, the boundary of the United
States in 1783 would have been the Alleghanies
instead of the Mississippi. To Clark especially
we owe the empire of the Ohio and Mississippi
Valleys. Clark's friend Jefferson foresaw rich
settlement in the former; he underrated the value
of the latter, but having become governor of Virginia in June 1779 to succeed Henry, he wrote
to Clark early in 1780 to build a strong fort on
the Mississippi near the mouth of the Ohio, to
command both valleys above for the Americans.

Clark in the early spring moved down from Kaskaskia, with a strong body of riflemen and French volunteers; selected a commanding and wonderfully picturesque site on a high bluff, which overlooks the broad mouth of the Ohio to the north and more than twenty miles of the Mississippi's course to the south, and built a stockade which he called Fort Jefferson. It was well armed and manned by a permanent garrison, and for a number of years was the chief military station on the western rivers. Thence Meriwether Lewis and Clark's brother William started on their epoch-making trip to the head-waters of the Missouri. But now no relic remains except the graves of some of its soldiers.

That spring a grand raid was fitted out by Lieutenant-Governor Sinclair of Michillimacinac, as part of a scheme of the English ministry to capture the entire line of Spanish and American posts along the Mississippi from New Orleans up. He collected 1500 Indians, led by a Sioux chief named Wabasha, and 140 English and Canadian traders and their men, and sent them down the river to sweep the posts from St. Louis south. They murdered or carried off a number of settlers; assailed Cahokia but were repulsed in a sharp engagement; crossed and attacked St. Louis, were defeated there also, and then dispersed and made for home. It is beyond question that Clark was in these two fights and the chief agent in the victories. Why so large an expedition fell so flat is not wholly explainable.

1780

Fort Jefferson built

Formidable British-Indian expedition

A fluke

1780
June
et seq.

Meantime Colonel Byrd had started from Detroit on June 1, with 600 Canadians and Indians and six cannon, his objective the Licking settlements. On the way through Ohio some 400 more savages joined him, making up the largest Indian army yet in that section. Reaching the forks of the Licking, they landed at the site of Falmouth and built huts as if for a permanent station; but soon left it to assail Ruddell's Station on the south fork in Bourbon County (probably near Ruddell's Mills). None of these stations had any artillery; and even had this one, it was utterly overmatched. Ruddell surrendered on agreement that men, women, and children should be prisoners of war to the British, and saved from Indian treatment. But on opening the gates, the savages rushed in and divided the whole population among themselves as prisoners; tearing children from their mothers' arms, and perpetrating all sorts of outrages which horrified Byrd, one of the most humane and honorable of British officers, naively surprised at the unheard-of fact that he "could not control them." All movable property was carried off, and the place burned to ashes.

*Byrd
moves
from
Detroit*

*Byrd's
Indians
destroy
Rud-
dell's*

The elated savages now demanded to be led against the remaining stations between the Licking and the Kentucky,—Martin's, Bryan's, and Lexington,—which would probably enable the capture of Boone's and Logan's forts. Byrd, sick of their performances, tried to dissuade them; but they insisted, and agreed that all prisoners taken hereafter should be under his control. Martin's

*And
Martin's*

Station was thereupon captured, and exactly the same scenes re-enacted. Byrd at once abandoned the expedition, leaving the other places unharmed, and returned to Detroit via the Great Miami, hiding the cannon on the bank where he started overland. The Indians carried away 240 prisoners, mainly to their towns in Ohio, some to Detroit and distributed among Canadian tribes; some men were tortured to death, many women and children died from hardship.

Clark heard of this raid, and leaving his riflemen to protect the Illinois settlements, started on foot with two companions to the scene of war. Too late for help, he was not too late for exemplary punishment. He enlisted about 1000 pioneers, invaded the Indian country in Ohio, defeated and slaughtered the warriors, destroyed the crops, and swept the towns with fire. For many years his vengeance was remembered. Some of the prisoners were rescued; but most who survived were not restored till the close of the war, and many severed families never met again.

Immediately after this, Clark interviewed both Jefferson and Washington on the subject of capturing Detroit, and outlined a plan that met their approval, Jefferson arranging for Virginia to furnish him men and means; but before it could be executed, Benedict Arnold's invasion intervened, shortly followed by Cornwallis' campaign. Clark had raised 240 riflemen for the expedition, and tendered them to Steuben for service against Arnold; assigned to special duty, he ambushed

1780

Byrd abandons his expedition

Clark revenges it

Plans capture of Detroit

1780-2 and nearly annihilated a party at Hood's on the James, and so dispirited Arnold's marauders that only large parties ventured inland thereafter.

Kentucky Kentucky was now to suffer the most terrible loss of the war, revenged by a quick and fearful retribution at the hands of Clark. Its people had begun to feel fairly secure against Indian raids, from their strength and organization. It had grown so much that the Virginia Legislature organized it into three counties, each with a civil and military government; and each with a regiment of militia, the three formed into a brigade **Clark commands its brigade** under the command of Clark, now living at Corn Island. One was commanded by Colonel John Todd, Clark's second in the Illinois campaigns; who organized a civil government there, and two years later returned to Virginia as a member of the Legislature, shortly securing land grants for public schools, and vainly introducing an emancipation act. Boone was his lieutenant-colonel; he had removed his family from North Carolina to **Todd and Boone** Boonesborough in 1780, and in October was ambushed by Indians with his brother Squire, who was killed, himself escaping.

The chief agent in the horrors to follow was Simon Girty, the second of four sons of a sot and **The Girtys** a drab on the Pennsylvania border. His mother married again; the whole family were captured by the Indians after Braddock's defeat, and his step-father burned at the stake. James Girty was adopted by the Delawares, and as usual in such cases, became worse than any of them; Simon was among them awhile, then with the Ohio Indians, and won a name for special ferocity toward women and children, being a coward as well as a brute. During Dunmore's War he served as a nominal spy against the Indians, but quite probably played false. In the Revolution he naturally took the British side, and displayed all a renegade's fury added to his own savagery.

During the summer of 1777 he organized 400 Indians at Sandusky, and after a feint against Limestone (Maysville), Kentucky, appeared before Fort Henry (now Wheeling) on the 1st of September. It was the usual frontier stockade, garrisoned by thirty-five men and boys under Colonel Sheppard, and with a number of women and children within. The savages' approach was discovered, and a small reconnoitring party under Captain Mason sent out; they ambushed it and killed over half. A rescuing party was sent under Captain Ogle, ambushed in turn, and only four escaped. Twenty-three had now been slain, and the garrison was reduced to twelve. There seemed no hope; but a horrible death was sure if they surrendered, and resistance could win no worse than an easier one. For this and heroic resolve to protect their helpless charges, when Girty came forward with a white flag and demanded unconditional surrender, Sheppard replied that it should never be surrendered to him or any other renegade while an American was left to defend it. Girty at once ordered an assault, under cover of some log cabins within rifle range; but their indifferent

1774-7

Simon
Girty

At Fort
Henry

His am-
bushes

Assails
fort

muskets were outclassed by the steady fire of the rifles within, kept loaded by help of the women and children, and after severe loss they withdrew out of range at noon.

Then the appalling discovery was made that they were almost out of powder. One man, Ebenezer Zane, had a keg hidden in his cabin sixty yards outside; more than life depended on their obtaining it, and Zane offered to try. Each of the others promptly volunteered for the desperate chance; the contention was finally settled by Zane's sister Elizabeth insisting on going, as too much for all of them hung upon every male life. Covered by the fire of all the rifles she made the journey, and returned with the keg in her arms, unharmed by a solid volley from the entire Indian force.

In the afternoon the assailants again took cover in the cabins, and a storming party attempted to batter down the gate; six fell dead and the rest ran back in dismay. Then they bored a hole in a maple log, bound it with iron chains, filled it with powder, stones, and scrap iron, and touched it off within sixty yards of the gate; it burst in fragments and killed several Indians without harming the defenders. At dark they withdrew, but lay in wait to cut off any relief parties that might come. About four in the morning a party of fourteen under Captain Swearingen did come, and were fired upon, but escaped harm in the darkness and fought their way into the fort. A few hours later another band of forty under Captain McCullough did the same, except their

Margin notes:

Powder
runs out

Elizabeth
Zane

Indians
draw off

Rein-
force-
ments

commander, a noted frontier Indian-fighter whom the Indians were especially anxious to capture alive for torture. In the running fight he was separated from his men and forced to take refuge in the forest. Surrounded on three sides, the fourth was a sheer precipice 150 feet high with Wheeling Creek at its base. They thought him their prey and would not shoot him; but of course even that death was far better, and there was a faint chance of escape. Rifle in hand he spurred to the edge of the cliff the powerful blooded horse he rode, and leapt with it into the air. The water broke their fall, and they disappeared in the forest as the baffled savages came to the brink and fired a futile volley after them.

Further attack being now useless, Girty and his gang burnt the cabins and fences, killed the 300 head of stock they found, and withdrew. Aside from those killed in the ambushes, not a person in the stockade was hurt; while the Indians lost over sixty, and were so disheartened that they could never again be induced to make an attack in the neighborhood, foiling Girty's intention to destroy Pittsburg in revenge for his imprisonment there. This defense of Fort Henry was one of the most brilliant minor affairs of the Revolution.

Girty was soon after sent by the British through the Indian country as far as Detroit, to stir up the Indians to fresh assaults on the whites; aided by two other renegades named McKee and Eliot, not less vicious than himself, if of less ability and influence. They assured the savages

1777, etc.

Fort Henry: McCullough's desperate leap

Girty foiled at Fort Henry

Tries to incite further ravages

that the Americans purposed wholly to exterminate them, and their only safety lay in joining the
King's troops and the tribes already in the field.
This was generally successful; but one Delaware
chief, White Eyes, an old and firm friend of the
whites, sent a message to the Shawnees which kept
them out of the war for some time. As an
authentic specimen of Indian literature, it is
worth preserving: "Grandchildren, ye Shawnees:
Some days ago, a flock of birds that had come on
from the east lit at Gaschochking, imposing a song
of theirs on us, which song had nigh proved our
ruin. Should these birds, which on leaving us
took their flight toward Scioto, endeavor to im-
pose a song on you likewise, do not listen to them,
for they lie."

On the morning of August 14, 1782, Girty at
the head of over 600 of the fiercest Ohio savages
laid siege to Bryan's Station, Kentucky. The
garrison was not over 50, and the stockade was in
decay. First a small decoy party of Indians was
set to yelling and hooting and gesticulating and
firing toward the fort, to draw the garrison out to
disperse them. The experienced members knew
better, and soon saw that the fort was surrounded
by large Indian forces. Runners were chosen to
ask assistance from Lexington, Boonesborough,
and elsewhere; and by stealing into the standing
corn that grew close up to the stockade, they succeeded in escaping the savage cordon. Meantime
it was discovered that, as curiously common in old
American forts, there was no water inside—the

nearest supply a spring some way off; thence the women brought some under cover of the rifles.

Then the garrison tried a decoy of their own, with shining success. Thirteen young volunteers undertook a sally against the Indians still making demonstrations in the woods, on the side of the fort opposite the main Indian body; Girty supposed the major part of the garrison engaged in it, and a horde of yelling savages with him at their head rushed to burst in the gate. They were met by a volley that laid a great number low, and the rest fled back in panic. Unfortunately Girty escaped, and soon brought them back to a fresh assault. Again they were driven back by a withering fire. By this time the thirteen had returned in safety; and the Indians drew off to a safe distance and kept up a desultory firing.

In the afternoon a party of fifty, part mounted and part on foot, arrived from Lexington, and of course had to run the gantlet of an Indian ambuscade. The horsemen passed unscathed, for Indians were never good shots; the foot party might have done so through the cornfield they had entered unperceived, but the firing drew them out into the road to take a share in the fight, and they fell into the ambush and lost six men. The rest gained the fort. Other reinforcements were known to be probable by the savages, who besides had lost heavily; and they began to retreat. But Girty wished first to try stratagem: crawling on a stump within hailing distance of a bastion, he called for a parley. With luckless honor toward

1782
Aug.
14-18

Girty's
aged
trick

one who had none, the older men kept the younger from shooting him. He announced that a large white reinforcement for him was near with artillery, when they must surrender, and he might not be able to restrain his Indians' ferocity; whereas if they would yield now, he guaranteed protection "on his honor." This hoary trick on such a guarantee, Bardolph's security, was refused even an answer.

Rein-
force-
ments
flock to
Bryan's

By night reinforcements began to arrive from various directions: Colonel John Todd, with the militia from Lexington, including Majors Harlan, McGary, McBride, and Levi Todd, all prominent citizens and noted Indian-fighters; Daniel Boone with a strong party from Boonesborough, including his brother Samuel and his eldest son Israel; and Colonel Stephen Trigg from Harrodsburg. Colonel Benjamin Logan was also known to be coming with a strong force: but having sixty miles to march, he could not arrive for a day or two. On the 17th the principal officers held a council. After leaving a small garrison at the fort they would have 182 men, and the majority were hot for immediate pursuit. Boone advised waiting for Logan, and was called a coward by Todd, who said if they wanted glory and reputation they must push on at once. It was so voted; Todd was made commander with Boone second, and they started on the morning of the 18th.

Insist on
chasing
Indians

Indian
lure

The Indians had blazed the trail and trodden the path with glaring plainness, obviously eager to draw their foes along it; but not till next day was one seen, two or three then being noted leisurely moving on a ridge beyond the Licking ford just reached. Todd, a little uneasy, called another council, and seemed inclined to side with Boone, who held to his opinion. Logan would be with them in twenty-four hours, giving them a force fully equal to the enemy and an assured victory; the Indians could not escape, for the Ohio was between them and their country, and they could be caught before being able to cross. But if a present fight was resolved on, the party should divide, and one detachment cross a horseshoe bend of the river above where the Indians were seen, and gain the Indian rear while the other attacked in front. This wise counsel would have saved a horrible catastrophe; but Todd's coarse taunt at Boone now wrought destruction. McGary, his warm friend, eager to turn the tables on Todd, spurred his horse into the ford and shouted, "All who are not cowards, follow me and I will show you where the Indians are." This deplorable act of insubordination carried the young men, and they hastened after him; the others could only follow, and in a few minutes the whole force was on the same side as the savages.

The ground bore a striking resemblance to Braddock's field: two ravines starting together near the summit of the ridge ran diverging to the foot, forming the fatal "V." The savages were hidden in these ravines, between which the Kentuckians must march, with an open ridge between for a clear sweep of the Indian fire.

1782
Aug. 18

Boone's
sound
advice

Hot-
heads
scorn
counsels
of safety

Girty's
ambush

Two experienced scouts went forward half a mile and were allowed to return safely, reporting no Indians in sight. The company moved forward in three columns, Todd supposably commanding the centre, Trigg the right, Boone the left; but there was very little authority in this independent militia. Well within the jaws of the ambuscade, a spurt of fire burst on both flanks at once; Trigg's column, being in the rear not over forty yards from the right ravine where the bulk of the Indians lay, received the heaviest discharge; some fifteen including the commander fell from their saddles, and the Indians rushed out in their rear, tomahawk in hand. The Kentuckians were completely surrounded, and being so greatly outnumbered that they could not spare men to load while others fired, were unable to check the volleys that rained upon them. Todd soon followed Trigg. The Harrodsburg men were the heaviest sufferers; the vanguard under Major Harlan stood their ground until only three remained, the commander falling among the first. McGary, the author of the calamity, fought bravely but remained unhurt. There was no cowardice; but against such fearful odds and a hidden foe they could do nothing. The savages rushed upon the broken columns with gun and hatchet, and the slaughter was horrible. The wounded were at once tomahawked; seven prisoners were reserved for torture. Out of the 182, 77 were left dead on the field.

Boone was as calm as if in a hunt, and to his firmness and judgment most of the survivors owed

their lives. He was among the last to yield, but
when he saw that the rout was hopeless, he bent
his energies to securing safety for the living. Collecting a few of the bravest, he held the swarming
foe at bay a few minutes while the remainder
reached the ford. But by this time all order or
pretense of resistance was at an end. The men
broke madly through the line of savages and waded
the river, many being killed in the water. Far
heavier slaughter was saved by the coolness of a
soldier named Netherland, who halted ten or a
dozen as they came ashore and had them fire on
the Indians, keeping them back till the fugitives
got across. Some Indians, however, swam over
below the ford and continued the pursuit more
than twenty miles, killing several who had lost
their horses and were making their way on foot.

The day after they left Bryan's, Colonel Logan
arrived with 450 men, and foreboding some disaster, set out at once on the old trail. Within a
few miles he met the first fugitives, who thought
themselves the only survivors; and he returned to
the station to await fuller news. By the night of
the 20th all were in, and the ghastly story known;
and Logan with Boone started for the battle-
ground, where they had the mutilated bodies of
the dead laid to rest.

This was the last important battle with the Indians on Kentucky soil. When the news reached
Clark, he repaired to the scene of action, and in
a few days had nearly 1000 men collected at the
mouth of the Licking opposite Cincinnati. Most

1782
Aug.
18–20

Licking
ford:
Boone
protects
retreat

General
panic

Logan
comes
too late

Clark's
punitive
expe-
dition

1782
Sept.-
Nov.

Clark's
ven-
geance
for
Licking
slaugh-
ter

of the survivors, and the militia under Logan, many with relatives to avenge, made part of this force; and Boone accompanied it as a volunteer scout. Simon Kenton, another famous Indian-fighter, was there also, in command of a frontier company as brave as himself. Crossing the Ohio, this army hot with vengeance skirted the banks of the Scioto with such rapidity and secrecy that they came within half a mile of Girty and his returning savages before the existence of such a force was suspected; it being revealed by two stray Indians, the whole band scattered to the forest. Runners alarmed the Indian towns everywhere, and Clark found only deserted lodges; at Old Chillicothe smoking meat was cooking over the still burning fire. The Kentuckians were resolved to make thorough work: they remained in the Indian country till November before dispersing to their homes. Five towns were burnt, and every stalk of corn cut down. So wide-spread and complete was the ravage that the Ohio Indians never again invaded Kentucky in force, confining themselves to prowling about unprotected settlements burning cabins and murdering single families.[1]

In the previous spring there occurred a shocking massacre from the side of the whites, which

---

[1] This was Clark's last important service during the Revolutionary War. What it meant to America we have shown. Yet he was given no Continental command, his property was virtually confiscated to the public, and he remained poor, soured, and alone till his sister drew him to spend his last days with her near Louisville. When Virginia sent him a handsome sword, he listened in gloomy silence to the address of the committee, exclaiming at its conclusion, "When Virginia needed a sword, I gave her one; now when I need bread, she sends me a toy."

illustrates the darker side of the frontiersman that accounts for many of the hideous Indian revenges. The Moravians, almost alone of North-American missionaries, had succeeded in making the Christian religion sink into the inner natures of a large body of stout Indian warriors. On the Muskingum River they had planted three villages of Delawares,—Salem, Gnadenhütten, and Schonbrünn,—with schools and churches and improved agriculture, models even for white settlers and widely noted. Their prosperity, and the repute of their Moravian heads David Zeisberger and Joseph Heckewelder, drew in many of the remaining Delawares, and it was hoped that the whole tribe would finally join them.

But the war placed them in an impossible position, neutrals in the heart of a war district. As peace Christians they could not take sides, and both sides held them enemies. The Indian bands who raided the white settlements forced them to contribute supplies going or returning, and the borderers believed them secret allies and spies of the immemorial savage foe, besides hating Indians of any sort as part of a frightful constant danger. On the other hand, the British considered them American spies who gave secret information of their own Indian allies' movements; besides, it was desired to bring over all the Ohio tribes, and the Moravian missionaries secured the neutrality of the remaining Delawares.

Both sides, therefore, set out to resettle them under their own control. Matthew Elliott, already

1775-81

The Moravian Delawares

Between two fires

1781-2

British
force out
Moravian
Indians

mentioned, came there with the Huron chief Half-King and 300 Indians and whites, and urged them to remove to the head of the Sandusky for protection against the borderers; they declined, and the gang plundered their houses and shot their cattle till they were forced to comply, leaving their crops ungathered. An American party from west Pennsylvania under Colonel David Williamson was already on the way to move them to Fort Pitt, but came too late. They were now held a part of the British-Indian alliance. After a wretched winter, ill-fed and ill-sheltered, about a hundred returned to the old farms to pick the standing corn; the borderers heard of it, supposed them coming back to live, and a band under Williamson started to root them out. They were found in the fields, told they were to be carried to Fort Pitt, ordered into a house, and by nearly unanimous vote, all butchered the next morning (May 25).

Amer-
icans
slaugh-
ter them

An expedition was soon organized to extirpate the survivors on the Sandusky, and the Wyandots there; no quarter to be given. Colonel William Crawford, an experienced Continental officer, valued friend and surveyor of Washington, reluctantly accepted its headship. The Indians had been warned, secured reinforcements from Detroit, and in two battles in early June drove them home in rout, with heavy loss, capturing Crawford and exhausting ingenuity in torturing him to death.

Crawford
defeated
and
tortured

We have far anticipated chronological order, and must now return to the central field.

CHAPTER XLVI.

THE BRITISH GAIN A SOUTHERN FOOTHOLD

From November 1778 to November 1779 is one of the most firmly marked periods of the war. With the former begins a new phase, pursuant to the ministerial policy resolved on before the pinchbeck peace commission started, but openly heralded as the result of its predesigned failure. One part, that of devastation for its own sake and without bearing on specific campaigns, had been fitfully practiced from the first by the more brutal and passionate underlings—especially civilians—unchecked by their superiors; but it now becomes more wide-spread and systematic. The other, that of "carrying the war from the south to the north," in the official phrase,—saving the southern provinces from the colonial wreck and using them as a basis for future reconquest,—is now for the first time undertaken; but experimentally and with a petty corps. Its result, however, the conquest of East Georgia and the edge of South Carolina, is so encouraging that much larger though still insufficient forces are embarked in it.

But the year is fruitful in other important or striking events. Within the original field, where none affected the general status, the most brilliant is the storming of Stony Point, the most extensive

1779

Settlement of the West

Paul Jones

Spanish alliance

Paper currency

the unsuccessful attempt to end the border horrors by crushing the Iroquois and capturing Detroit. Farther on, as already detailed, the central West and Northwest are added to the Union by the capture of Vincennes, Kentucky is effectively redeemed from the savages, and western Tennessee is begun at Nashville; the swarming of peaceful settlement over new lands going on almost without check from the war. On the sea, as told in the following chapter, the declining American navy, under a hero and seaman of the first order, strikes a blow of immortal brilliancy and of enormous ultimate importance though no immediate military effect, proclaiming the advent of a sea-fighting power ranking with England alone on the globe. In the political field, Spain joins France against England, but not directly for the United States; and both the first-named powers endeavor to bring about peace, but on terms too injurious to this country's future to be considered, while Spain reconquers West Florida for herself. In the administrative field, the national paper money works its own annihilation, and teaches the teachable part of the people its first great currency lesson.

Though each of these items acts and reacts on the others, some of them strongly, an attempt at unity and chronological sequence would only confuse that of each within itself; and it seems best to take up each in the order indicated above, save those dealt with in other chapters.

Germain's plan for the southern campaign was minutely specific. Pensacola was to receive an additional thousand troops from New York; a new post was to be established on the lower Mississippi to preserve communication with the Indians; from New York also were to be sent men enough to beat down resistance in Georgia and South Carolina, which were to be held thereafter by Tory militia (sure to flock to the King's standard if protected) backed by some regulars; the Florida Tory rangers with the Indians were to carry devastation along the southern frontier. Then the old Stuart scheme was to be revived: the British agent to bring down a large savage force toward Augusta; 5000 British troops to capture Charleston and a small corps to land at Cape Fear; and the lowland Carolina planters to be crushed between the Indian and Tory hordes from the mountains and the British forces from the coast—the same plan balked at Fort Moultrie. Diversions were to be made in Virginia and Maryland,—the Lee-Howe scheme,—and all the country south of the Susquehanna would soon return to its allegiance. Cornwallis, however, who had a dormant commission to succeed Clinton and was much more trusted, was the one relied upon to accomplish this; Clinton's failure would lead to his suppression.

Granting an initial right of the British government to the colonies so entire as to justify it in wasting them with fire and sword and unbridled savage atrocities if they resisted its supremacy, the new plan can only be approved both politically and militarily. It was the most judicious and practical of any since the war opened. As before

1779

Germain's specific action

Cornwallis

Merits of plan

explained, Great Britain had not and could not raise troops enough at any time to hold down the country, without more loyalism in it than existed; and in this year it had so many military irons in the fire, from the East Indies to the West Indies and from Canada to the Falkland Islands, that no less than 314,000 soldiers and marines were needed to handle them. Even the insufficient 40,000 men formerly allotted to the American war had now to be cut down by half. But such being the case, the long attempt to crush the rebellion in precisely its strongest fortress was blind fatuity. New England had no loyalism worth a regiment or a thousand pounds to the Crown; and the campaigns in the Middle States, where that element was stronger, were made futile by the men and supplies with which New England reinforced its neighbors. And the sections from Virginia north were the richest and most populous of the Union.

Now, in every respect the case for a campaign beginning at the other extremity was far more favorable. There was a military chance for conquering and holding part of the colonies at one end of the line with the slender forces available, even when the entire line could not be taken. As to the southernmost colonies, their loyalism, although proved by experience not to be dominant, was of a much fiercer and more militant type than elsewhere: partly from the nature of its constituents,—largely recent Highland Scotch immigrants, full of the contentiousness of the race and the semi-savagery of the clans; partly from the

1779

Immense
British
arma-
ments

Previous
military
mis-
judgment

Better
chances
in South

fanatical savagery of the patriot element itself,—largely North-Irish of Scotch and English blood, with some of Huguenot stock,—who seem to have begun the outrages which long paralyzed their efficiency by a ferocious civil war. Georgia had but a few thousand people in all, and lay next British Florida, a secure base for expeditions and retreat. South Carolina's relatively immense slave population, hating its masters worse than anywhere else in the South, kept them nervously busy guarding against insurrection; and these lowland planters with the Charleston citizens, nearly all of English-Huguenot stock, were exactly the element most unmixedly patriotic. In the western uplands of both Carolinas, the two factions counterpoised each other as said. The Quaker and Moravian elements would generally not lift a finger for either side. Lastly, the whole district was out of reach of any great help from New England. And its value to keep was out of all proportion to its immediate strength: the priceless ship supplies from the pine forests, the tobacco and indigo and rice; while the planters and towns were opulent in wealth to plunder.

East Florida was held by a British force under General Augustine Prevost, with headquarters at St. Augustine. It was also the refuge of the many loyalists ejected, and too often shockingly misused, by the Georgia and Carolina patriots at the outbreak of the Revolution; corresponding exactly to Canada and the expulsions from the Mohawk Valley, though their class largely maintained its

1776–9

Both Southern parties barbarous

Slavery in South Carolina

Value of Southern colonies

Tory refugees in Florida

hold in the east-Alleghany highlands as it could
not in upper New York. These refugees were
organized into the Florida Rangers; commanded

by the Tory Colonel Thomas Browne, who had been
tarred and feathered and his feet roasted for
refusing to take an oath of allegiance to the Revolutionary government, and by Lieutenant-Colonel
Daniel Girth, said to have been publicly whipped
by order of an American officer to have him dismissed from the militia and seize his valuable
horse. Both avenged themselves amply and fright-
fully in these bloody years.

Aided by some of Prevost's regulars, these
refugees raided and ravaged the Georgia rice

plantations and settlements with a thoroughness
needing no suggestion or authorization from the
ministry: they looted and burnt every building
they reached, carried off the negroes (for sale),
horses, and cattle. Charles Lee, after the victory
of Fort Moultrie, organized a secret expedition
against St. Augustine to put a stop to this—re-
minding one of Oglethorpe's days, with the contestants oddly reversed (for the Spanish inhabitants would at least not have aided the British);

but was recalled just after starting, and left part
of his troops to die by scores in the Ogeechee
swamps.

Prevost then built a fort at the St. Mary's, as
a basis for more effective preying on Georgia.
To put an end to this, in the autumn of 1778 General Robert Howe, who was in command of the
southern department, repeated Lee's expedition,

GENERAL LACHLAN McINTOSH.

THE SAVANNAH-CHARLESTON CAMPAIGNS.

with 1100 Continentals and several hundred militia. They met with little opposition from the enemy, but none was needed. Heat and malaria, bad water and salt junk, soon had half the men on the sick list, the country was so destitute of any green thing that many of the horses died and the rest were too weak to drag the wagons and artillery, the militia officers would not take orders from a Continental officer, and after more than 500 men had died of sickness Howe ordered a retreat. One of his officers, Colonel Elbert, however, by a very brilliant action with three small galleys captured three British armed vessels at Frederica, and relieved the Georgia coast for the time.

This wreckage and insubordination left south Georgia at Prevost's mercy; and to pave the way for Clinton he was ordered to invade it, capture the important port of Sunbury, and advance upon Savannah, Clinton's first objective. He sent one party to seize Sunbury; but being told by the commandant, Lachlan McIntosh, to "come and take it," they retired. Prevost with the other detachment marched through lower Georgia to devastate it and join the first at Sunbury; but failing to do this, and meeting first the Georgia militia under General Screven,—whom having wounded and captured his men murdered in cold blood, to avenge the alleged murder of one of their own officers,— and then an intrenched body of Continentals under Elbert whom he dared not engage, he retired to Florida, laying the country entirely waste, and

1778

Robert
Howe's
Florida
fiasco

Prevost
invades
Georgia

Retreats

burning the buildings. So far from this advancing British interests, it probably harmed them like the Hessian maraudings in New Jersey.

The American-French fiasco at Newport, the disbanding of the colonial forces assembled for its recapture, and the departure of D'Estaing's fleet to the West Indies, enabled Clinton to begin the ministerial scheme. On November 27 Lieutenant-Colonel Archibald Campbell, in a fleet with 3500 men, commanded by Hyde Parker, sailed from New York, reaching the Savannah River December 23; an eloquent testimony of the difficulties of naval expeditions in those days, and explaining many failures in co-operation ignorantly misjudged. Campbell was in all respects one of the best Britons sent to America during the war: not only of high abilities, but of high character, honor, judgment, and humanity. The patriots dreaded these latter qualities more even than his military capacity; but they need not have feared—such men were not the sort Germain and the King wished, but "energetic" men of the stripe of Tryon and Dunmore. They received their reward.

Howe's failure had produced the same result with the State and national authorities as the Northern failures. The Southern delegates had already procured his replacement by General Lincoln, a New England favorite who had shared in the halo of Saratoga, with almost as little direct share in the victory as Gates. Lincoln had arrived in Charleston on the 6th. Campbell had been ordered to wait for Prevost, who was to join the

Campbell's expedition south — marginal note

His character — marginal note

Howe to be replaced by Lincoln — marginal note

expedition and take command of it; but he may
well have known that Howe was awaiting his
successor and on bad terms with the local authorities,—a disadvantageous condition,—and most
probably that his own numbers were overwhelmingly superior. Howe in fact had but 1200 men,
half militia, and was in doubt whether not to
retreat; but his officers determined to fight, hoping
to hold out till the arrival of Lincoln, who had been
notified and was hastening thither.

The ground was strong enough to make this
seem feasible; a lagoon in front, a wooded swamp
on one flank and the river swamps on the other,
and intrenchments in the rear. But Campbell
anchored off the town on the 28th; the next morning his Highlanders carried the half-mile causeway through a rice-field on the four-mile road from
the river to the city bluff, and a negro guided a
party to Howe's rear by a swamp path; and the
American force was at once routed. Howe was
pursued through the town, losing his artillery and
baggage and 550 men, the rest escaping across
the river. Campbell had lost but 7 killed and 19
wounded; and at this trivial cost had secured not
only the capital of Georgia, with over fifty cannon
and much food and munitions, but the control of
the entire province for the remainder of the war.
Yet Germain excoriated him for not having called
in the Indians to assist, even securing the results
he desired not satisfying this truculent dastard
unless part of the credit could be assigned to his
savage favorites.

1778
Dec.

Howe's
disad-
vantages

Routed
by Camp-
bell

Georgia
restored
to
British

1779
Jan.

Early in January Prevost marched across the lower Georgia to Savannah, this time capturing Sunbury on the way, while Campbell went up the river and took Augusta, placing Browne in command. The strongholds having been thus reduced and Georgia assured as regained for the Crown, Campbell issued a proclamation (evidently under strict orders from Germain) offering protection to all inhabitants who "would support the royal government with their arms"; thus forcing all who remained neutral to fly to the interior or South Carolina. Most submitted. In ten days there was no further opposition; great numbers came in and took the oath of allegiance, and military companies were formed from them and used for general patrol and scouting duties. But there was a considerable exodus of the rest, while all prisoners who refused to enlist in the British service were crowded into prison ships to rot. The property of the patriots was thrown open to a riot of plunder by the troops.

Georgia conquered

People mostly submit

Others punished

On his way, Campbell had detached 200 mounted infantry under the Tory John Hamilton, a Scotchman of wealth and position who had fought at Culloden, and was much esteemed and respected, to march along the frontier, receive submissions and urge the inhabitants to return to loyalty. Thus encouraged, a force of some 700 North Carolina Tories under one Boyd started to march across and join him; many of them mere blacklegs calling themselves loyalists, who pillaged all the inhabitants they met on the way. Colonel Andrew Pickens, a remarkable man who now

Raising the Tories

comes to the front,—Indian-fighter, Assembly-man, and militia commander,—collected some 500 men from the Ninety-Six district and assailed Hamilton; this failing, he turned and marched rapidly against Boyd, and in a sharp fight at Kettle Creek killed him and captured or dispersed his force, of which some 300 reached the British, the rest of the survivors scattering through the Caro-linas. The prisoners were tried, and some seventy of the worst desperadoes sentenced to death; not however as such or for crimes, but for treason to the Revolutionary government. Five of the worst were executed, the rest pardoned. Very likely the deaths were richly earned, but the alleged reason was criminal folly: it gave the enemy a terrible justification for any atrocities they chose to perpetrate thereafter. Browne at Augusta promptly hanged an equal number of his own prisoners; this had to be revenged by their kin and friends; and the vendetta thus begun scarcely fell below the Indian mark in ferocity. It was not helped by the hanging of two men in Charleston soon after, under a State law punishing with death all who attempted to join the enemy. Two could— and did—play at such games.

Lincoln found a little over 1100 Continentals in his department altogether. Unable to succor Savannah, on January 5 he took post at Purrys-burg up the river from Savannah, on the South Carolina side, to watch the enemy. Reinforce-ments slowly came in, and by the end of January he had perhaps 2500 men. Part of them were

Marginal notes:
1779 Jan.

Pickens routs Boyd

Tories hanged as such

Savage feud started

Lincoln in Georgia

1779
Jan.-Feb.

North Carolina militia under **John Ashe** and Griffith Rutherford,—ultimately over 2000,—sent on condition of South Carolina furnishing them arms; this was done, but the ten days' delay for it in Charleston perhaps cost Savannah. Prevost did not feel able to advance on Charleston; but having the command of the water, he sent 200 men to capture Beaufort. This would furnish a base for penetrating into the Carolina lowlands, menacing Charleston, and even making the American positions on the Savannah perilous, as liable to be struck from there and Savannah at once. On the 2d of February, however, Moultrie with nine Continentals and about 300 militia, but a part of the superb Charleston battalion of artillery, drove the enemy from the island where they had landed, with the loss of nearly all their officers, having only eight of his own men killed.

Prevost tries to take Beaufort

Driven off by Moultrie

Meantime in January South Carolina had done as great a service to the Continental cause as many such victories, by once more putting John Rutledge at the head of its State government, in succession to Rawlins Lowndes. He had been its president under its first constitution, and was now governor under the new; and for four years remained such, during two of them being absolutely the only government the State had, and during its occupation by the British constituting officially the entire State as a member of the Union.

Rutledge and his State

By the middle of February the militia from various Southern quarters had swelled Lincoln's army to about 7000 men, along the Savannah on

both sides. Nevertheless he was in a very distressing and almost alarming position. All the insub-
ordinations and democratic fractiousness of the
militia at the North together were feeble compared
with those of this ungovernable body, which considered almost any order an impertinent humiliation, disobeyed any and all they did not like, left
their posts or watches when they pleased, and
utterly refused to submit to any discipline whatever, in the very face of a disciplined enemy. Why
the British did not scatter them to the winds is
unintelligible yet. Lincoln at last refused to have
anything more to do with the militia, and turned
over their command to Moultrie, thinking they
might obey a Southerner better; but they did not.

1779
Feb.-
March

Lincoln's
unruly
militia

Nevertheless, Lincoln could not refrain from
attempting some stroke to loosen the enemy's hold.
Pickens' victory, despite Hamilton's baffling him,
had made Augusta too dangerous to hold; and
Campbell called in Hamilton and slowly retired
down the river, returning to Savannah to establish civil order before returning to England, a
harsher man being wanted in his place. Ashe with
some 1400 North Carolina militia and 100 Continentals followed his force along till it halted at
Hulston's Ferry; then he took a strong position on
the Georgia side at the junction of Brier Creek
and the Savannah. Rutherford on the other side
had 700 to 800; and Lincoln resolved to join these
with the main force at Purrysburg and assail the
British advanced post. Prevost learned of the
move, and made a swift march to overwhelm Ashe

Campbell
retreats

Ashe
follows

Prevost
turns

before the others could reach him. Making a demonstration of crossing the Savannah in Ashe's front, he sent 900 men under his brother to cross Brier Creek fifteen miles above, and take the American rear on its unguarded right flank (March 3). The destruction was far more complete than even Howe's: only 450 of the 1500 reached Lincoln across the river; 150 fell on the field and in the pursuit, several hundred were drowned in the Savannah, 227 were captured, and seven cannon with nearly all the small-arms and all the baggage were lost. The British lost five killed and eleven wounded. Augusta was at once reoccupied; the British had a clear path now from the coast to the frontier; the old colonial government with Sir James Wright at its head was reinstated.

Ashe's force destroyed

Georgia's colonial status restored

The patriots would not resign hope of recovering the State, however. Rutledge ordered 1000 militia to be embodied, to make incursions into it and carry off all live-stock or provisions they met, to distress the British. On the 20th Lincoln left 1000 men to guard the lower Savannah, and set out with about 2000, hoping to collect 4000 altogether, cross near Augusta, cut off the enemy's supplies and prevent their junction with the Indians, and then drive out the new British government and convene a popular convention there. This would have a great moral effect and raise the patriots' spirits. Moultrie was to remain at Black Swamp with some 1200 men, hold Purrysburg, and if the British showed an intention to move on

Lincoln plans to recover Georgia

Charleston, occupy the passes and delay the enemy till Lincoln could return. Lincoln tried to keep the march secret; the British knew of it before it started.

1779 March-April

Prevost made a feint of the Charleston move, to draw Lincoln back and prevent his gathering up the detachments; but finding the road open, he turned the feint into earnest. On the 28th he crossed the larger part of his troops, some 3000 men, and McIntosh withdrew from Purrysburg. Moultrie sent word in haste to Lincoln, and took up a good position; but was soon forced to abandon it in face of overwhelming forces. Lincoln refused to believe the movement anything but a feint, and for several days would send no troops. Prevost pressed on, wasting the country with fire and ravage, sacking and laying waste the estates and burning the slave cabins. He executed Germain's orders in the full spirit. He took a band of Cherokees with him, and gave them their will.

Prevost moves toward Charleston

Ravages country

Moultrie had committed a tactical error of the worst kind, which, compulsorily repeated by Lincoln the next year, lost the town and army; leaving Prevost to cross the Ashley unopposed, not even seizing the boats to delay him, and falling back at once on the peninsular town. There, if defeated, he must surrender his whole force as well as the place, and expose it to the horrors of a storm likewise; while above, were the river forced in his despite, he could retreat safely toward Lincoln, and Prevost dared not coop himself up in the town with liability to capture. As it was, Prevost on

Moultrie's blunder

1779
April

the morning of April 11 appeared with some 2400 men before the town lines.

These were unfinished; the 2500 troops of all sorts there were mostly militia, disorderly and mutinous; there was no single command, the governor **Anarchy at Charleston** claiming the right to command the militia, and Moultrie being chosen full commander only after the enemy were on them and some loss had occurred by an unauthorized attack of militia; and even then the governor and Council were to have control of "parlies and capitulations"—the right to stop the fighting any time they chose. Naturally the responsibility of protecting the town from sack weighed heavily in their minds, and Prevost's forces were grossly overrated—seven or eight thousand it was said, and even a private scout estimated them at 3600, known to be the flower of the British army. Pulaski lost most of his infantry in a skirmish with the advance guard, and **Panic over Prevost's advance** this disheartened them. No word was heard from Lincoln, whose letter of the 10th that he was advancing to their aid—he having been finally convinced—was intercepted by the British.

There was a further reason which made the authorities inclined to purchase safety for the State rather than risk such treatment as Prevost **Grievance against general government** was according: they felt that the general government had left it to work out its own salvation. Their applications for reinforcements had been denied by Washington, on the ground that before a detachment reached there, the hardships and losses of the long march, over some of which they must fight their way, would have nearly or quite destroyed it. Lincoln had come without troops. Then one of the State's delegates in Congress, Henry Laurens, had conceived the plan of turning its chief weakness into a source of strength, by enrolling regiments of negroes as Dunmore had done in Virginia on the other side. Hamilton favored this. Washington scouted it: if it was begun the British would do the same with better resources for equipping them, so the patriots would not be profited; and after the State for generations had been anxiously disarming them, it would now be arming them for an internecine slave war. Congress, however, approved it, and sent Laurens' son John, of Washington's staff, to recommend enlisting say 3000 of them. It merely added fresh fuel to the South-Carolinians' grudge at being "abandoned." Furthermore, they had never been enthusiastic for the Declaration of Independence. Their delegates in Congress had voted against it; then reversed their vote merely for the sake of casting in their lot with the others, but without instructions, and frankly admitted that it was doubtful whether the State would support them. This, they thought, was their thanks for imperiling themselves.

The decision of the authorities was suggested by Prevost himself. Moultrie after consulting the Council, but evidently sharing their feeling, speedily asked for terms. Prevost offered to allow all citizens who did not choose to join the British to become prisoners of war on parole, their fate

Margin notes:
1779
April 11

Negro regiments advised

Feelings balanced

Prevost's offer

1779
April 11
et seq.

to be decided by that of the other colonies. Rutledge and the Council asked that this be extended to the entire State, and Charleston Harbor be neutralized; which of course would nullify the chief object of the expedition, a naval base for the conquest of the South. Prevost's brother, for the general, refused to have any dealings with the Revolutionary government: they had not "come in a legislative capacity," and had business only with Moultrie. Thus loaded with the responsibility of surrendering the State government and the inhabitants of Charleston as well as his army for prisoners of war, Moultrie recovered his resolution and said, "We will fight it out."

Moultrie
refuses
sur-
render

This was on the 12th. But Prevost had been playing a game of "bluff." He knew that Lincoln was approaching: in fact, that over-cautious general with a little more energy might easily have caught him between his own army and Moultrie's, and "Burgoyned" him, as Moultrie expressed it. Prevost therefore decamped that night, and after remaining some days beyond the Ashley, moved down and occupied John's Island; an immense island a little below the harbor, separated from the mainland by the tidal inlet Stono River, to which from the Ashley ran Wappoo Cut just opposite Charleston. Lincoln planned an attack on this, but it was too strong. This failure, and his leaving Charleston to so near destruction for a wild-goose chase after Augusta, had roused general dissatisfaction with him; and Congress gave him "permission" to retire and be replaced by

Prevost
retreats
from
Charles-
ton

Lincoln
dis-
credited

Moultrie. Moultrie urged him not to do it; and
Lincoln in fact did not, remaining for a wholesale
catastrophe the next year.

1779
April-
June

Meantime he learned that Prevost was gradually withdrawing the John's Island force to
Savannah; and again arranged to attack the
weakened post in co-operation with Moultrie, who
was to cross over to James Island below the town,
have boats on Wappoo Cut, and take the enemy
in the rear. Had this been done, beyond doubt
Prevost's entire force would have been killed or
captured. But Moultrie was as sluggish and careless as he was brave; he dawdled about collecting
the boats, and did not approach the scene of action
till the battle was over. Lincoln on June 20 made
a strong and well-planned assault on the lines at
Stono Ferry, commanded by a remarkable man,
Lieutenant-Colonel Maitland. But his men disobeyed his orders to charge bayonet, and stopped
to fire and reload instead; the lines could not be
carried in front; and after an hour's fight he
retreated with the loss of 150 men, against the
enemy's 129. Prevost soon evacuated the island
and retired by way of the coast islands to Beaufort,
where he left Maitland with 800 men. This and
a supply of provisions and live-stock were the
fruits of the expedition for government account.

Plan to
cut off
Prevost

Battle
of Stono
Ferry

American
defeat

British officers and soldiers, however, enriched
themselves plentifully, perhaps ultimately at the
government's expense. All through the advance
and retreat they ransacked the country in parties,
thoroughly looting every house of its valuables,

Private
plunder
by
British

1779
March-
June

Pillage
and
ravage
of South
Carolina

stripping the inmates of their money and personal ornaments, emptying the feather-beds for ticking to make bags to carry off the plunder, and even breaking open vaults and digging up graves to search for treasure; not only so, but they systematically destroyed and ruined whatever they could not carry off. They killed all the remaining live-stock and poultry, often even the dogs and cats. They smashed the windows, mirrors, china, and bric-a-brac. They girdled the shade-trees, and trampled the lawns and gardens into ruin. All this did not stimulate loyalty; the struggle to the death finally carried on by the people may have been intensified by this hideous devastation, and the frightful distress and even starvation it caused.

Negroes
aid
British

They were helped by the slaves, who pointed out places of concealment, and co-operated in the plunders and outrage. Over 4000 slaves were lost by this incursion, of whom 3000 were carried off by the British and a large part sold to the West Indies. Great numbers also, gathered near the army, died of camp fever. Many were left behind in the retreat for want of transportation; and having been told horrifying stories of the certainty of cruel deaths if reclaimed by their masters, some of them clung to the sides of the boats and their hands were chopped off, while guard lines kept the

Their
reward

mass of them away with sword and bayonet. Many, fearing to return, died in the woods. Those carried off were herded at Otter Island, where hundreds died and were left to the wild animals and carrion birds.

Prevost was able to hold Savannah and Beaufort solely from the British control of the sea; and the prime hope in the French alliance had been to break that control. If the French fleet could now be utilized, Georgia might be recovered and the thorn in South Carolina's side removed. D'Estaing in July conquered the islands of St. Vincent and Grenada from the British, then went to Hayti; and Rutledge, Lincoln, and the French consul at Charleston wrote him, urging him to escape the hurricane season there by coming to the American coast and making a joint attack with Lincoln. He eagerly accepted the idea, sent two ships to Charleston in advance, and with twenty more and eleven frigates appeared off Georgia, both so unexpectedly that two British vessels mounting 74 guns and two store-ships fell into his hands. This was in the first days of September; and the Count sent a message to Lincoln urging haste, as at that season he could not remain long on the coast. The South Carolina Legislature adjourned at once, and the authorities set at work zealously to co-operate, drafting militia, furnishing boats, and so on.

On the 9th D'Estaing anchored off Savannah bar; by the 12th his 3000 troops were debarked some miles south. Without waiting for Lincoln he advanced on Savannah, and on the 16th sent a summons to surrender, couched in the braggadocio terms then thought likely to strike terror, including a threat of putting Prevost to the sword if he held out. This at once aroused suspicion and

1779
July-
Sept.

D'Es-
taing be-
sought
to come

Arrives

Aided by
local au-
thorities

Sum-
mons
Savan-
nah to
sur-
render

1779
Sept.-
Oct.

jealousy in the Americans, for fear D'Estaing meant to hold Savannah for France if captured; but the Count explained. Prevost, to gain time for his Beaufort detachment to join him, asked for twenty-four hours to consider it and prepare terms of capitulation; the vain Frenchman, who could have captured the place easily had he attacked at once, granted it in assurance that Prevost would not dare resist him; and before the time was up, Maitland, though fatally sick with bilious fever, had brought in his forces through marshes where the men had to wade up to their waists and drag their boats through the mud. Prevost, having now some 2500 men, sent a message that the place would be held to the last.

Prevost hood-winks D'Es-taing

Rein-forced and defiant

On the 23d Lincoln joined D'Estaing with about 4000 men; and for a week and a half siege works were pushed forward, mounted with 53 guns. But from the French arrival, when only ten or twelve guns were on Prevost's works, the garrison and their impressed negroes, under the able engineer Moncrieff, had worked night and day throwing up and arming new works, and had now nearly a hundred cannon in position. On October 4 the allied bombardment began: it is not pleasant to record that Prevost's request to place the women and children on vessels in the river, under D'Estaing's protection, was rejected by him and Lincoln. Till the 8th the cannonading went on. Then D'Estaing told Lincoln he must raise the siege or attempt a storm. He had expected and been told that the reduction of the place would not

Siege works

Bombard-ment— women and children

take over ten days; and but for his own folly it would not have taken one day. But he had been there a month, found that the autumn storms would shortly endanger his fleet, the British fleet might descend upon him and cut off his from his army, and the West Indies demanded him. The engineers were positive that in another ten days the approaches would penetrate the British works; but D'Estaing was peremptory, and on the 9th the assault was made.

1779
Oct. 8-9

D'Es-
taing
insists
on storm

The night before, the sergeant-major of a militia regiment deserted to the British and disclosed the plan of attack; he was afterwards captured and hanged by his comrades. It illustrates a situation that prevailed increasingly through the war. Said a British officer, "We fought our last battles with their deserters, and they fought their battles with ours." Prevost consequently was ready with his strongest defense for their point of strongest attack. A feint was made along the river by a body of militia, but it fled in a panic at the first fire. Count Dillon's column on the right, which was to skirt the redoubts and storm their rear in the morning dimness, became entangled in a swamp, and emerging in broad daylight, was so cut up by a hot fire that it could not even form. The main attack was by D'Estaing and Lincoln in person; the former with his 3000 Frenchmen, the latter with 600 Continentals and 350 militia. The assailants were swept away by a murderous front and cross fire, which cut down among others Sergeant Jasper, the hero of Fort Moultrie; yet

Mutual
deserters

Fiasco of
flanking
parties

Frontal
assault

1779
Oct. 9
et seq.

with heroic valor they pressed on, and at last the American and French colors were planted side by side on the redoubt. Lachlan McIntosh had cleft the British line. But Maitland threw the grenadiers and marines upon the column, already riddled by musketry and artillery fire and now raked by an armed brig in the river. The standards were torn down; the assailants thrown into the ditch and slaughtered like cattle, till a portion scrambled out; and Pulaski, trying to pierce between the redoubts with his legion of 200 cavalry and take the British in rear, was mortally wounded from an armed galley in the river and the horsemen driven back. D'Estaing was twice wounded. After an hour's combat the allies were definitely repulsed with a loss of 594 men,—337 French, 257 Americans,—to a British loss of 55.

Allies
repulsed
from
Savan-
nah

One-sided
slaugh-
ter

There were bitter recriminations among the allies: the French were voluble in their contempt for the "insurgents," and blamed them for the refusal of terms to the Savannah non-combatants. But in all fairness, pretty much the entire fault lay in D'Estaing's vanity, impatience, and instability. He would not take his American staff officer's word how easily Maitland's detachment could be cut off and captured; he lost the immediate possession of Savannah through conceit; would not wait for siege operations, and insisted on a storm precisely when the place had been strengthened almost to impregnability. Lincoln has been also blamed for slowness in coming up; but from his previous experiences it is doubtful if he could

D'Es-
taing in
fault

have got his unruly mob along much earlier than he did.

D'Estaing re-embarked his troops, shortly met the storm he feared, and though nearly wrecked, succeeded in getting part of the fleet to the West Indies and returning to France himself. Lincoln slowly returned to Charleston, and on the breaking out of small-pox in the army the militia dispersed. And thus stood matters in the South at the end of 1779. Georgia was effectively recovered by the British, because it was only a fringe of settlement dominated by two or three posts. South Carolina was awaiting its turn, after a terrible example of what was in store for it. Yet its chief provision for the coming onslaught was a militia law which divided the militia into three drafts, each to be relieved by another in two months and ten days at the longest, so that no militiaman could be kept out longer than that whatever the exigency!

Clinton in the North fretted at his inglorious confinement to holding a few miles of lines; yet as he wrote to the ministry, his resources would permit no more. His subordinates fretted still more, longing for chances to win fame and promotion. The Tories fretted more yet, declared that the rebellion could be crushed by a little more activity, that the wealthier rebels should be executed or exiled and their property confiscated, and especially that the Indians should be much more freely employed. Thus was civilization to be improved. This chimed exactly with the ideas of Germain and the King, who fretted most of all,

1779

British
govern-
ment
grumbles

keeping an idle army at enormous expense to hold two villages on the coast of a half-continent, and never ceased insisting on the use of the means so felicitously at hand from "God and nature."

Meantime it was possible to give his men some adventure, secure some plunder and prizes, and put in operation Germain's and the peace commissioners' plan of devastation. Especially the immunity of Virginia, which escaped both the Northern and Southern operations, and was quietly flourishing, irked the British exceedingly. Since Dunmore's final expulsion it had peacefully raised tobacco, exporting it through Norfolk (partly risen from its ruins) and Portsmouth, or by a land carriage to Albemarle Sound; and had established a navy yard at Gosport, to have a long and famous career. To spoil these goods for British behoof, and make the rebels quake, Clinton sent General Matthews with 2500 men to raid the region; and on May 9, at the very time Prevost was carrying destruction through South Carolina, Matthews entered Hampton Roads, passed up Elizabeth River, and began a ravage that left Prevost's tame. So sudden was the attack that resistance was impossible. He seized Norfolk and Portsmouth; burned every house but one in Suffolk County; carried off or destroyed all movable property, taking to New York 3000 hogsheads of tobacco; sent parties all along the Chesapeake to bring away or burn all tobacco on its banks, and burn all the planters' houses; kept seventeen vessels as prizes and burned 113 more in the Elizabeth

Virginia

Mat-
thews'
devastat-
ing raid

and James, besides nine unfinished vessels on the stocks; and gave his troops free rein to murder and violate at will. Virginia lost $2,000,000 worth of property by this expedition, and the private wrongs helped to create some of the bitter hatred of England that lasted so long.

When Matthews returned at the end of the month, Clinton executed another plan of more immediate military importance. After his abandonment of the conquered forts on the Hudson in 1777, Congress had ordered new and much stronger works begun at West Point, some miles higher up the river, with obstructions in the channel as before and a more massive chain. These, constructed by Kosciuszko, were approaching completion at this time, but still vulnerable. About as far below the old forts, at Stony Point on the west and Virplanck's Point on the east, works had been erected to guard King's Ferry, the great road from New England to the Middle States while the British held New York; as cutting this line of communication would compel a long circuit, Clinton hoped that Washington would draw so large a detachment from his main camp at Middlebrook to defend it that the camp could be seized, and Washington compelled to fight in the open. He therefore took 6000 men and a strong naval squadron, and made a swift movement on Stony Point, which was abandoned at his approach; then he planted heavy cannon to command the Verplanck's Point redoubt (Fort Fayette), invested it from the land side also, and forced a speedy surrender.

1779
May-June

Virginia's losses

American works on the Hudson

Clinton captures lower range

1779
July

Washington in alarm placed his army so as to guard West Point more effectively, and hurried on the works, which were finished during the summer.

Raid on
Con-
necticut
coasts

Clinton early in July sent a naval squadron under Sir George Collier, with 2600 men (largely Hessians) under Tryon, to make one of those expeditions of ravage in which Tryon's soul delighted, and which he therefore assured Germain would "make rebellion totter" if persistently carried on. It was to do what Germain had suggested to Lord Howe, and he had ignored,—thoroughly dismantle the southern New England coast; no open orders were given to burn houses, but that was not necessary with Tryon. On July 4 it came off New Haven, and the next morning two parties invaded the place from either side and began a sack of the place; also burning the wharves, the warehouses near them, public stores, and vessels in the harbor. Tryon's intention was to burn the entire town; but

Towns
to be
burned

the soldiers were too busy looting and drinking, and the morning after were driven out by the Connecticut militia. The same performances, ended in the same way, went on at East Haven, where he had begun burning the dwellings; and some of the inhabitants were murdered and others carried off as prisoners. On the 7th the pretty old village of Fairfield was gutted for a night and a day, and burned to the ground. Green's Farms and Nor-

Towns
burned

walk were next laid in ashes. Collier and Tryon issued an address to the people of Connecticut, saying, "The existence of a single habitation on your defenseless coast ought to be a constant reproof to your ingratitude;" and no doubt the expedition stimulated a lively sense of English favors past and to come. New London was next marked for destruction, when the banditti were suddenly recalled to New York by a move of Washington the exact reverse of what Clinton had counted on.

1779
July

Connecticut expedition recalled

Stony Point, lately captured by Clinton, was a rocky triangular hill washed in front and on two sides by the Hudson; its western base lay against a deep marsh overflowed at high tide, making the hill an island, and crossed on the north from the river by the King's Ferry road, over a causeway also overflowed except at low water. The British had fortified this hill with a strong redoubt garrisoned by 600 men, heavy batteries which commanded the entire morass and the river around, and a double row of abatis outside; and armed vessels held the river and raked the hill and approaches. Along a rather firm spot on the southern morass also they had dug pits filled with sharpened stakes, to impale the Americans if they attempted that path.

Stony
Point

Fortifications

Washington believed a night surprise feasible when low tide should favor; even if the post could not be permanently held, the blow would stop the New England devastation, and perhaps alarm Clinton into keeping his forces at home thereafter. "Mad Anthony" Wayne had been put in command of the light infantry, stationed near the Dunderberg a considerable distance in advance of

Washington plans recapture

1779
July
15-16

the main army. Wayne, like his great chief, was as cool and careful in preparation and execution as "mad" in the field; and he had full confidence in himself, his men, and Washington's strategic sagacity, all amply justified. "General," said he,

Wayne
prepares
to take
Stony
Point

"I'll storm hell if you will only plan it." On July 15 he collected 1200 men at Sandy Beach fourteen miles below; sent out parties to reconnoitre thoroughly, and also to kill all the dogs within several miles of the fort, who might ruin the enterprise by barking; and for a similar check on heedless or nervous firing, and to prevent delay from stopping to load, had all the guns left unloaded, the reliance to be on the bayonet.

At half past eleven at night he began the march. A negro slave of a local Whig, who sold

Strata-
gem

fruit to the garrison and acted as a spy for the patriots, had craftily pretended that his master would not let him come daytimes, as it was corn-hoeing season; and had been given the countersign to come at night. He went in advance with two stout soldiers disguised as farmers, gave the countersign ("The fort's our own"), and his companions seized and gagged successively the sentinels west of the causeway. Waiting for dead low

Sentinels
seized

tide, just after midnight Wayne led 900 men across the causeway, leaving Muhlenberg with 300 as a guard; and divided them into two columns at the foot of the hill. Both marched swiftly and solidly up undiscovered, to within pistol shot of

March on
the fort

the pickets on the summit, who then fired to alarm the garrison. These hastily sprang up from their

ANTHONY WAYNE.

HENRY LEE.

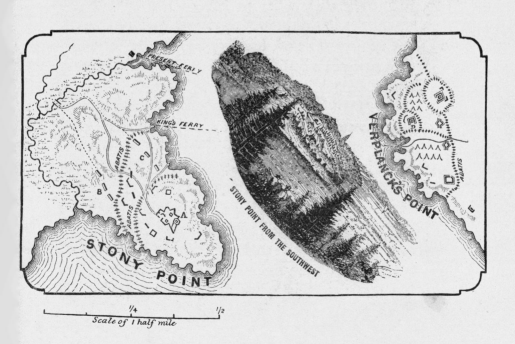

heavy sleep, and in the darkness trained a fire of muskets and cannon upon the assailants. But a forlorn hope of twenty picked men for each col- umn pulled away the abatis for its advance, seventeen of one being struck down; and in the teeth of the volleys both columns gained the walls, swarmed over them, and forced their way to the heart of the works with the bayonet, the van of each column meeting in the centre. Wayne was struck on the head by a bullet, but only stunned, and resumed his place in the assault. In a short time the entire surviving garrison of 543 men and the commander (Johnson) surrendered. The bloody military usage of the time, often put in practice and pleaded as full defense by the British, justified a wholesale butchery; but Americans did not perpetrate cold-blooded massacres, and not a life was taken after the surrender, though 63 had been killed in the fight (Johnson says 20). The Americans lost 15 killed and 83 wounded.

The artillery was at once turned on Fort Fay- ette at Verplanck's Point, and General Howe from North Carolina was sent to attack it by land; but from some misunderstanding this was not done till Clinton had sent reinforcements, and the attempt was abandoned. Clinton at once prepared to move up the river in force, and reinvest Stony Point, hoping that Washington would throw so many troops into it that a victory might put West Point in his hands; but Washington was too wise. He could not spare troops for such a contest at such a risk, and ordered the place dismantled and

1779
July 15

The
storm

American
human-
ity

Clinton
moves on
post,
Washing-
ton dis-
mantles
it

the garrison and stores drawn back nearer the main body. Clinton reoccupied and refortified it, but abandoned it not long after.

Wayne's exploit excited the emulation of "Light Horse Harry" Lee, and with Washington's approbation he undertook an even more daring enterprise against Paulus Hook (Jersey City opposite the Battery), at Clinton's very gates; and for just that reason, though it was very strongly fortified, the garrison of 500 men were careless, not dreaming of assault, as Lee had found out. It was a low-lying peninsula joined to the western lands by a narrower isthmus, nearly severed by a creek, and entirely so by a deep ditch inside, flooded by the tides and crossed by a drawbridge. On the Hook were two lines of intrenchments and abatis. Lee took 300 picked men, and on the night of August 18 boldly forded the creek, the sentinels supposing his men one of their own foraging parties returning, waded the flooding ditch, found the entrance to the main works, rushed past a fire from the blockhouses, and gained possession of the fort before a cannon had been fired. Of course succors were quickly summoned from New York and the fleet, and Lee had to retire toward morning; but he took 159 prisoners with him, his own party losing but two killed and three wounded.

A week later began in full force the great expedition which it was hoped would end the Indian atrocities on the borders. Wyoming and Cherry Valley had made it impossible longer to leave the fringing settlements to the mercies of "God and nature's" self-constituted legatees. On February 25 Congress directed Washington to protect them and punish the Indians: two bodies of troops, one of 3000 Continentals on the Susquehanna and one of 1000 or more New York militia on the Mohawk, were to unite and penetrate to the country of the Senecas. It had been hoped that Fort Niagara, the stronghold of the Tory-Indian forays, might also be taken; but this was given up. Washington asked Gates to head the expedition; Gates refused as too hard for one of his years, and Sullivan was assigned to it, while James Clinton collected the New York forces. While equipment was preparing, Colonel Van Schaick from Fort Stanwix descended on the Onondaga villages and destroyed them, with their remaining stores; it was too early for crops. Brant and his Mohawks with the Tories continued the raids of old: on the night of July 19 they laid Minisink in ashes, and three days later ambushed a pursuing band and took forty scalps; they beat up and ravaged the vicinity of the very armies collecting against them, capturing on July 28 Freeland's Fort on the West Branch of the Susquehanna, and shortly cutting up a party sent to its relief.

The Mohawk Valley was at first intended as the main route, but later the Susquehanna was decided on. Sullivan got together about 2300 troops in the Wyoming Valley, and remained there over a month waiting for stores; the delay saved the expedition, for when all in they were not

1779

Plan to
punish
Iroquois

Sullivan
takes
command

Brant's
work

Sullivan
collects
force

1779
July 31-
Aug. 31

Sullivan
on the
Chemung

Clinton
boats
down
Susque-
hanna

Battle of
Newtown

Sullivan
begins
ravage

enough to subsist the army for the expected time
(more administrative helplessness), and but for
having now come to the season of growing crops,
Sullivan could not have moved. On July 31 he
started up the river, and about the middle of
August fortified the narrow peninsula formed by
its junction with the Chemung, to wait for Clinton.
That general had gathered about 1500 men at
Canajoharie by June 16; wagoned 200 boats and
three months' provisions across the hills to Otsego
Lake, the source of the North Branch of the Susquehanna; dammed its outlet, and on August 9
broke the dam and floated his boats down the
swollen brook; and on August 22 joined Sullivan.

On the 26th the united army of nearly 4000
moved forward, and on the 29th reached Newtown,
now Elmira; where Brant, the Butlers, and Mc-
Donnell had collected some six to eight hundred
Indians and Tories to bar their advance, and
thrown up a log fort masked with brush and sap-
lings. They made a stand, but Poor's brigade
outflanked them and they soon gave way and scattered, with probably more loss than the 11 dead
they left behind, the Americans losing three killed
and 33 wounded. There was no further organized
resistance, though the allies hovered around to
cut off stragglers, who met a hideous fate. On the
31st Sullivan sent back all the baggage and all
artillery but five small pieces; put the men on half
rations in reliance on the crops; and began a march
through the Seneca country with systematic destruction of everything the Indians had done to

redeem the land from the wilderness, justified only by the need of preventing them from turning the still higher white civilization into one.   The Iroquois had long passed out of the stage of mere huntsmen and berry-pickers, with incidental corn-patches; indeed, one leading cause of the terrible dominance which enabled them nearly to exterminate all other northeastern tribes was their developed agriculture, which gave them stores of winter food when others were dispersed grubbing up roots and gnawing putrid bones.   They had great apple, peach, and pear orchards, large fields of corn, beans, and pumpkins, often framed houses with chimneys in place of wigwams with smoke-holes.   This growing dependence on semi-civilized comfort was now to become their bane.

The main army swept the eastern side of Seneca Lake, crossed its foot and skirted those of lakes Canandaigua, Honeoye, and Hemlock, and turned southwest across the lower end of Conesus. Meantime detached parties had ravaged portions of the western sides of Cayuga and Seneca.   On September 13 a scouting party under Lieutenant Boyd fell into an ambush of Walter Butler; fifteen were killed and eight escaped; Boyd and a sergeant were taken, ordered by Butler to reveal Sullivan's plans, and on their refusal given over to the Senecas for a torture awful even in the fiendish records of savage cruelty.   The next day the army reached Seneca Castle, the chief seat of the Senecas, "the western door of the Long House," on the west side of the Genesee River

1779
April.
Sept.

Iroquois
civiliza-
tion

Sullivan
devas-
tates
their
lands

Butler's
cruelty

across the valley from Geneseo. It was far the largest of the Indian towns, containing 128 houses, many of them well built; with its orchards and smiling cornfields and gardens it was extirpated from the earth.

1779
Sept.-
Oct.

Seneca
Castle
de-
stroyed

Sullivan's provisions were running out, there was some sickness among the soldiers, and he thought best to turn back. He had sent to the Oneidas to furnish him warriors; they sent excuses instead, and begged for mercy on the Cayugas. None the more inclined to leniency, he detached parties to lay waste such portions of the Cayuga and Seneca shores as had escaped before, and the Tioga Valley; sent Gansevoort to Albany, to destroy on the way the lower Mohawk Castle, which was not done; razed the Chemung fort; and regained New Jersey late in October. He had destroyed forty Indian villages, ranging from a few houses to the great Seneca "city."

Sulli-
van's
return
and
fresh
ravage

Meantime a co-operating movement was carried on by Colonel Brodhead along the Alleghany from Pittsburg. With 605 men he left there on August 11, took a month's stores by boat to Mahoning and then on pack-horses, and in a 200-mile march obliterated the Indian villages and cultivation extending for eight miles on the Alleghany.

The Iroquois League was permanently broken. The homeless and foodless Senecas and Cayugas took refuge at Fort Niagara; but in the winter of almost unparalleled severity that followed, they were terribly thinned by famine and attendant disease, never regained their numbers, and had

neither heart nor strength to remake the achievement of centuries. The Oneidas, in fear of the
vengeance of their fellow tribes, abandoned their
villages and dispersed, some 400 taking refuge
with the Americans at Schenectady. The Onondagas had sustained a crippling blow. But the
immediate design of the expedition was foiled:
the New York and Pennsylvania borders were a
scene of horror and misery till the end of the war.
In the Mohawk and neighbor valleys, under the
tireless energy of Brant and Johnson, supplied
with means by the British, torch and tomahawk
never ceased their work. In April 1780 Harpers-
field was obliterated. In the summer the lower
Mohawk was swept with fearful ravage by Johnson. In August Brant uprooted Canajoharie and
several settlements adjoining, and even Norman's
Kill not far from Albany, and devastated part
of Schoharie Valley. In October another invasion of this by Johnson, Brant, and Cornplanter
left scarce a building or a stalk of corn standing. The upper Mohawk followed. The conditions were like Europe's in the Middle Ages
when the northern and eastern hordes were pouring on it. Every settlement clustered around a
blockhouse where the women and children flocked
at the first alarm, and the farm work was done by
bands of neighbors, with weapons close at hand
and scouts and sentinels ever on the watch.

But the destinies of the United States were
perforce to be determined outside itself: alone
with an unmolested England, it must ultimately

1779-80

Upper
New York
and the
Indians

be harried into exhaustion and passive acquiescence in reconquest. Its salvation lay in the fact
that the very system which had driven it into
revolt made the dominant sea power the natural
enemy of the rest of the world.

We have seen that Spain had long been half
inclined to join France in its American policy,
yet unable to decide. Her dilemma was most
painful, between two sets of considerations each
nearly decisive in itself. She hated England on
every possible ground, national, commercial, and
religious; of interest, pride, and duty. England
had wrested from her the dominion of the seas
and half her ownership of America; colonizing it
in her teeth, absolutely barring her expansion in
it, taking from her some of her own ancient colonies, and making her tenure of others dubious.
Its help to her own revolted Netherland provinces
had lost them to her. It was the bulwark of Prot-
estantism and political freedom. It had ravaged
her own home coasts and sacked her towns and
burnt her shipping, and as perpetual thorns in her
flesh, retained not only her largest home island
close on her border, but a fortress on her home
mainland that took from her the control of the
gates of the Mediterranean. There were gains and
revenges without end to be had from humbling it.

But to humble it to the behoof of the American
colonies was merely to strengthen a foe as hated
and only less formidable, to the probable loss of
much and the possible loss of all she had left in
the New World. It was precisely these colonies

which represented English infringement of her
monopoly of America; their growth was exactly
what militated against that of her own; to help
them to a successful revolt was to set the worst
possible example to her own; and they were as
Protestant as England and much more democratic. Commercially, also, her interests were
directly opposed to the French. Her great colonial possessions made her cling even more firmly
than England to the policy of trade monopoly
embodied in the Navigation Laws; while it was
France's loss of hers that had converted her to
the policy of open trade. Lastly, more might be
stripped from Spain in case of failure.

The last two considerations were really but
one, and dictated the respective attitudes of the
two powers. France had little more to lose, and
only wished to cripple England and unfetter
commerce; Spain had very much to lose, and was
quite as anxious to cripple America and keep
commerce fettered. "I observe with pain," wrote
the French ambassador at Madrid to Vergennes,
"that this government singularly fears the prosperity and progress of the Americans." Florida
Blanca the Spanish foreign minister had advised
Vergennes against the league, and when made,
wrathfully styled it "worthy of Don Quixote,"—
a war with neither an object in view nor a plan
for termination. He succeeded in making the
French government very uneasy over its precipi-
tancy; economists like Turgot rightly argued that
common language and old habit would keep

1778-9

Spanish
dislike of
United
States

France
vs.
Spain

Spain
resents
French
alliance

1778-9

United States commerce mainly English, letters from there reported still tenacious attachment to England, and Vergennes began to doubt their

France will not desert United States

constancy. Still, France for pride and honor could not break her solemn engagement; and there was a large real element of generous and disinterested enthusiasm for America among her influential classes, which affected even her cool governmental heads. So, feeling herself overmatched with but one weak ally against England, she bid steadily for Spanish aid.

The basis of negotiation was threefold: what would France secure for Spain, what would she ask for herself, and what would she limit the

Bids for Spanish help

Americans to. Her offers on the first two points are a striking proof of her anxiety and her new commercial outlook: she would make the restoration of Gibraltar to Spain an absolute prerequisite to peace (on which Spain was inflexible), and do her best to regain for her Minorca, East Florida, Honduras, and Campeachy Bay; for herself she asked only part of Newfoundland and its fisheries, and freedom to restore her own harbor of Dunkirk. As to the United States, Spain early in 1778 had proposed forcing them to make a

Spain's wishes for America

treaty with England substantially *uti possidetis* —that is, leaving to the latter New York, Newport, Philadelphia, and perhaps some other ports; thus preventing a united coast power from being formed, and keeping the two English branches neutralized by a perpetual broil. Vergennes would not hear of it: the treaty made independence of the existing colonies a *sine qua non*. But France had not agreed to enforce their claim to the West; and like every other European state for a century, it was loth to see the new republic "remain the exclusive mistress of that immense continent." Spain should be at liberty to get what she could from them as the price of her help. And by simply allying herself with France against England, she would not have to acknowledge American independence till England herself did by the peace, and thus would escape setting her own colonies an evil example. Accordingly, on April 12, 1779, a treaty was concluded for a joint war against Great Britain; a French army to invade it with the help of a Spanish fleet, the Newfoundland fisheries to be shared between the two powers, and other terms as stated. But for a couple of months it lay dormant.

What Spain modestly wished of the United States was merely the St. Lawrence basin and the Great Lakes, the territory from the Alleghanies to the Mississippi, and the sole right of navigation on the latter; the last she absolutely insisted on. France had a treble reason for urging the republic to be compliant: it would make her new ally more likely to be liberal with help, it chimed in with her own preferences, and she wished an early peace to relieve her finances, upon which the strain of war was telling badly. Gérard the French minister, and his successor Luzerne, pressed Congress long and earnestly to moderate its territorial ambitions for the sake of enlisting Spain's

1788-9

Spanish
dilemma
solved

France-
Spanish
league

Wish to
have
down
United
States

warm help: to give up the Mississippi navigation and territory to her, be content with a tacit and not formal acknowledgment of independence like Switzerland and Holland, not to ask for Canada or Nova Scotia, and not to insist on the fishery rights off Newfoundland.

There was a strong party in favor of acceding to the territorial limitation. One potent consideration was true of conditions then though not now, and affected most thoughtful Americans as well as Europeans: before railroads and telegraphs existed, authority was too weak to stretch over great spaces, and the choice seemed despotism or monarchy. A vast orderly republic was thought a contradiction in terms. Jay said, "Our empire is already too great to be well governed," and favored the concession; Gouverneur Morris, though wishing Canada and Nova Scotia added, favored giving up the Mississippi and adopting a fixed limit to the republic's expansion. Indeed, from this very lack of communications, it was thought that the country so far west would never be really settled, and that its value in bargaining was all it ever would have. Twenty years later, Jefferson was ready to yield up the right of navigation for a half-century, on the ground that the region would not be populated for five times that. Again, for military considerations, the war had converted the country to a preference for Spain rather than Great Britain in Florida: she could not be more savage and would be far less powerful for harm.

But on the other points there was a bitter contest for six months. To forego acknowledgment of independence was to forego the very and sole object of making the distasteful alliance; and now in breach of that treaty, without consulting them, the cession of Gibraltar had been made as indispensable a condition of peace as that independence, so that they were to refuse terms of peace and freedom till Spain got back her citadel. Aside from that, they would not consent. The fisheries, the North would not give up; the western lands already settled must not be given up, and demanded the Mississippi for an outlet,—at worst, full navigation down to Spanish Florida and a free port in that province. The French envoys argued, expostulated, threatened to withdraw from the alliance: France, they said, could not break with Spain, and waste her own resources for years, to profit a few shipmasters or gratify "an unjust desire of conquest." But with fortunate contumacy the interest of one American section balanced the "broad-mindedness" of another, and prevented the republic being heavily maimed of its growth. France could not decently allege America's refusal to buy a new alliance as a ground for breaking the old; and Spain had so huge a stake to win by a gambler's chance that it was worth risking.

It was finally decided to insist on acknowledgment of independence; to claim as a western boundary the Mississippi down to 31° (present southern limit of Mississippi), as a southern

1778-9

French-
Spanish
treaty
objected
to

Or
sacrifice
of
interests

Allies
angry

But
cannot
withdraw

1778-9

United
States'
basic
demands

the 1763 north boundary of Florida, as a northern
the 1763 south boundary of Quebec, but if necessary giving up the peninsula between Erie, On-
tario, and Huron—the garden and industrial heart
of present Canada; not to make the fisheries a
sine qua non—though in separate instructions for
a commercial treaty with Great Britain they were
made so; and to send a minister to Spain to
negotiate the Mississippi question and a loan of
$5,000,000. Jay, who had succeeded Laurens as
president of Congress, was appointed as such
minister, his place being taken by Samuel Huntington of Connecticut; John Adams was sent to
England; and Laurens shortly after to Holland
for a loan, with the result of being captured by the
English and flung into the Tower.

Ever since the French alliance, Spain was
really trying to sell its services to the power which
would pay most; it is not to be blamed for consulting its own interests, but relatively the charge

Spanish
diplo-
macy

of "Quixotism" against France was true—it
would never have bargained with England to
crush the colonies. Florida Blanca in the spring
of 1778 proposed to Lord Weymouth, the foreign
secretary, a "mediation" to restrict the United
States to the Alleghanies, and secure to England
the basin of the St. Lawrence and the territory
northwest of the Ohio—the same later asked for
Spain. Weymouth refused to negotiate till
France withdrew from alliance with the rebels,
and told him that since United States independence meant Spain's losing her American colonies

(as it did), she had best ally herself with England. In the fall came the French offers already recited, and thenceforward the Spanish government fully determined to accept them, the next six months being occupied in wrangling over details; but to mask the purpose, the farce of proposals to the English government was kept up, completely deceiving it. A generation's truce with the concurrence of Spain and France was proposed; Vergennes protested vigorously, but Weymouth contemptuously rejected it as yielding up the British rights in America not even to the Americans, but to the French. If they were to be given up, Great Britain should secure what advantages were to be had in return. No action was taken by Spain for a while, however; and more than a month after the treaty with France was signed, Maria Theresa was writing to Charles III. of Spain, and her minister Kaunitz to the French and English governments, to preserve peace. Charles refused the overture, and on June 16, 1779, declared war against Great Britain, without mentioning the American war.

England had now three other powers pitted against her, and shortly had nearly all the rest of Europe; and on the surface was so enormously overmatched that her emergence unharmed is not so much a marvel as a miracle. A striking proof of power and constancy it is; but miracles do not happen, and something of the wonder vanishes when we note the conditions of the problem. When a power is assailable by land and by sea,

1778-9

Spanish
pretense
to
bargain
with
England

Declares
war

English
con-
ditions

1779
June-
Aug.

not only has it a double risk of overthrow in war, but the need of perpetual huge defensive land armaments absorbs a part of the resources that could otherwise strengthen its sea force. But

Great
English
advan-
tages

England was and had always been practically unassailable by land; she could pour her whole vitality unafraid into her shipping, which therefore could be made supreme in Europe, and was the only one really native to the sea. She was like an army with flanks and rear unapproachable, and able to intrench invulnerably in front. We do not forget the intrinsic vigor and resourcefulness bred by old free institutions; but the very circumstances which enabled them to develop were a part of those which dictated this special result.

During the months just detailed, both France and Spain had been preparing a new Armada, equipping their fleets while France gathered an

Fiasco of
the new
Armada

army at Havre; and in August the allied squadrons entered the Channel, to destroy the English fleet and let the land force across. It was a far more complete fiasco than the one of 1588, for there was no battle. Their vessels numbered fully half as many again as the English; but the admirals fell out and the crews fell sick, the fleet withdrew and the army likewise. The English militia had been called out, but was not needed, and the allies had a costly and ridiculous failure to quarrel over. Gibraltar was besieged for four

Gibraltar

years, but never captured. Outside, each ally by itself had somewhat better success. D'Estaing, as noted, captured two islands in the West Indies;

but his American campaign ended in the discreditable failure before Savannah. Galvez, the able and energetic Spanish governor of Louisiana, at New Orleans, succeeded best of all. He at once set about recovering British West Florida for Spain; collected 1400 men,—Spanish regulars, American volunteers, negroes,—and speedily captured in succession Fort Bute at Manchac, Baton Rouge with the chief British force of the province (400 regulars and 100 militia), and Fort Panmure near Natchez; Mobile was taken a few months later, leaving only Pensacola in English hands, to be moved upon later; and Spain kept the province at the close of the war.

1779
Summer-
Fall

Galvez
retakes
West
Florida

While the country was thus holding its own in the North, losing some ground in the South, winning a vast but unrealized empire in the West, covering itself with glory on the ocean and exciting a British rage never yet cooled, financial chaos and helplessness had reached the climax. We have shown how its creation of paper wealth had wellnigh dried up its sources of real wealth, and menaced not only the continuance of any supplies for the army, but the existence of the army itself. In September Congress resolved not to have more than $200,000,000 in circulation, and not to emit the remaining $40,000,000 if possible; but there was no place for pause. The States had been asked to pay $60,000,000 in taxes into the national treasury; up to the middle of September they had paid in $3,000,000. Before the year closed the assigned limit had been reached, and even this miserable

American
finances

1779

Paper currency experiment

substitute for gratuitous impressment closed—to the dismay of Washington, who could see no other way of obtaining any supplies whatever for the army. In utter desperation, Congress now began to throw off all restraints, and began a reckless effusion of paper which finally cured the evil by annihilating the value of the currency altogether, and compelling a new start on a sound and non-illusory basis.

Issues in first half of 1779

In January it emitted $50,000,000 at a single issue, "on the faith of the United States," redeemable in 1797—an eighteen-years' loan without interest, on security for which no man would give a year's purchase. By June it had issued $35,000,000 more—$186,000,000 in all, $160,000,-000 outstanding.

Depreciation

The value had now sunk to an acknowledged five cents on the dollar; as the depreciation was always grossly underestimated and postdated, it was probably worth not above two or three, which means that it had no real value at all except for speculation. But the more utterly the bottom dropped out of it, and it failed to discharge any of the functions of a medium of exchange, the more stubbornly the people and their representatives shut their eyes to the facts, and the more fiercely

Anger of experimenters

they blamed and penalized the "speculators" and "enemies of the country" to whom they attributed the evils.

Jay, in a report drawn up for Congress, voiced the general feeling by laying the blame on "want of confidence," the circular argument which had an odd power of confusing all but a few of the best reasoners in those times. He attempted to restore this confidence by an argument more extraordinary still, but which has had a vigorous life in our own day: that the paper was the best of all currencies, because it was the only one which "will not forsake us," and "is always at hand for the purposes of commerce." As to the speculators, there was some truth in the idea, but only as a foul drain breeds disease-germs: the paper system had driven the old decent merchant class almost wholly out of business, and thrown it into the hands of sharp vulgar unprincipled adventurers; in this welter of speculative values constantly dropping, only such could keep their footing as were willing to take the chances of gain or ruin. Then, too, this paper worth two cents on the dollar was still lawful tender at a hundred for debts: those unwary enough to give credit were always liable to be legally defrauded by their debtors, unless they had taken the precaution to exact a manyfold price at the outset. The honorable, the kindly, those of mediocre business talents or small means, were the victims; the greedy, the cunning, the knavish, and those with cash in hand, were the gainers, as always under an unstable currency.

But nothing could more clearly show the absurdity of identifying business sagacity with treason than the affair of October 4 in Philadelphia, where the attempt to subvert natural law by force produced a miniature civil war. Here the State, national, and town administrations were so

1779

Arguments for paper money

Sharpers bred by system

Philadelphia riot

largely identical in personnel as to give them unusual local power; and the laws against engrossing and refusal to take paper money, and fixing the prices of various food-stuffs, were

Paper-money laws in Philadelphia

enforced as in other cities by a committee of citizens. The chief dealers refused to comply; headed by Robert Morris, a great merchant and true patriot, whose credit and ability were the absolute salvation of the cause over and over, and legally aided by James Wilson the Signer, a leading lawyer who had made himself obnoxious to the narrower patriots by defending the Quakers accused of treason. A mob gathered to drive him

Riot against objectors

and the other recalcitrants out of the city; the imperiled persons armed themselves and collected at his house, reinforced by Mifflin, George Clymer the Signer, and other patriots of unimpeachable stripe. The mob came up with beat of drum and two cannon, and opened a musketry fire on the house. The defenders returned it, but one of them was killed and two were wounded; the mob were just breaking in the doors, and the whole might have been slaughtered had not Reed and a few of the town cavalry guard opportunely come up and charged the assailants, killing one and wounding several. It was days before the furious mob were wholly quieted. The mutual prosecutions were dismissed by the Assembly.

One good effect it had, however: it showed the folly if not iniquity of attempting longer to preserve the grisly fiction that the currency could be legal tender at par. A convention of New

England and New York delegates, held at Hartford on October 20, proposed a regulation of prices at twenty to one, and advised a general convention to adopt this; which Congress amended by asking each State to adopt it at once. But by the time the full $200,000,000 was issued, the depreciation was at least thirty to one, and there was not enough of even such money for the daily outgoes. The year's expenses had been $160,000,-000 in paper. This was less than $10,000,000 in coin value, showing how empty the system of mere requisitions on States was keeping the national treasury, and how intense was the need of a stronger government even to keep the Union and its indispensable machinery alive; but it had been enough to disorganize the whole business system of the country under the paper régime. Congress, at its wits' end, drew six-months' bills of exchange for £100,000 on Laurens and Jay, to be met by the proceeds of the loans they were to negotiate in Spain and Holland respectively; though Laurens did not even start for months after and was captured before reaching Holland, and Jay was not recognized by Spain as minister of an independent nation, and the bills were of infinite torment and prejudice to him. These were sold for paper at twenty-five to one, the buyer having to loan the same amount additional; that is, for a $100 draft the buyer paid $5000 in government paper, of which he was to have $2500 back some time if the government lived and was solvent. As for the next year's outlays, the resources were

1779
Oct.-Dec.

Tremendous depreciation of paper

National treasury empty

Expedients of Congress

1779

absolutely nothing except to call the States to pay up the taxes already pretty much ignored.

American discour- agement

The year closed in gloom and despondency. Nearly four years' war seemed to have brought independence no nearer. Our military position was on the whole more encouraging than ever, and England's was worse as new foes joined against her; but even so, England had apparently resources enough to wear us out. The French alliance seemed a broken reed: both the expeditions undertaken in reliance upon it had been fiascos, and both from reasons that seemed likely to affect all future ones—the unwillingness to spend more than a few grudging days here at any time, and the consequent impatience of necessary operations or holding captiously to the letter of instructions. Yet its existence made the country laggard in efforts to recruit its own army, which was dwindling rapidly: unpaid, ragged, suffering, sick, disheartened. The government was out of money, had never had any power, was discredited in counsel. There were ominous signs that the public feeling was leaning toward asking a renewal of Great Britain's offers to come back to her fold; but for the doubt whether George III. would not exact a bloody toll of the leaders, it might have been stronger. The real present grievances of the colonies had never been intolerable, only their apprehension of the future—well-founded enough, but would it have been worse than this? And there was worse to come. But for the moment we will turn to another field.

CHAPTER XLVII.

THE NAVY IN THE REVOLUTION

The action of the naval force on both sides in the Revolution, as in any war, is not wholly separable from that of the land armies; and where it formed part of a combined military operation, or a British fleet engaged an American land armament, it has been described in its place—as in all those about and upon Lake Champlain, those at the siege of Boston, the capture of Newport, the assault on Fort Moultrie, the defensive fleet at the Hudson Highlands, the contest for the Delaware River, the French movements at Newport and Savannah, and so on. Others have been alluded to when they bore on political events or feeling. But there is much in the naval warfare of this period, as of all periods, which forms a world apart, and can only be treated as an individual whole; bearing of course on the general result, but not on specific land campaigns. And the fortunes and misfortunes of the little American navy, adorned by one of the greatest heroes and seamen of the ages as well as by a great natural military genius (his part already told), must not be left without commemoration.

As a part of the effort at a military reduction of the colonies, the British government began

Navy as auxiliary

Independently

without delay to seize their shipping and threaten their coast towns; laying requisitions on the latter, and bombarding them if refused, as with Bristol in Rhode Island—Narragansett Bay being much annoyed. Some of the prizes were made against all law or equity, the vessels having cleared under the English navigation acts. One of these was chased into Gloucester harbor; the British commander, Mowatt, was repulsed in trying to capture it, fired on the town and tried to land, but was again driven off and thirty-five men captured.

The colonies were much more helpless thus than by land, for a double reason.

First, courage and ability to shoot can make a formidable army in a short time out of the rawest rustics; while seamanship is a trade, and a navy a machine that cannot be improvised. It is true that a century and a half of adventurous seagoing had trained up a race of seamen and fighters noway inferior to the British except in numbers and resources; but thus inferior they were, and the naval preponderance of England far outweighed its military preponderance. Further, while each colony could arm its shipping for defense, none dared at first recoup themselves as later, by reprisals from their privateers. They were still ostensibly loyal subjects of Great Britain, and Congress gave strict orders to both land and sea forces to avoid aggression—the Ticonderoga expedition was not authorized, and its results were accepted with reluctance. Thus they could only strike back when already struck. The most extraordinary instance of this was a cruise of two Massachusetts vessels, the *Lynch* and *Franklin,* off the Gulf of St. Lawrence in the fall of 1775; they captured ten prizes and the governor of St. John's, and released them all, as the colony was not waging war "against our most gracious Sovereign"!

This could not go on. Early in October the news came that a fleet of British transports was on its way to Quebec, with a mass of military stores sadly needed by our own troops. To cut out some of these was an enterprise most desirable, but transcending either the power or the rights of any single colony; and while Congress was meditating the use of its general powers by sea as well as land, it learned on the 13th that Falmouth, now Portland, had been bombarded and burned by the revengeful Mowatt, who however was beaten off in attempting to land.

We have noted the weighty political effect of this. Its instant result was that Congress voted to fit out two armed vessels, of 10 and 14 guns each besides swivels, to cruise "eastward" and intercept any store-ships met; and appointed Silas Deane, John Adams, and John Langdon an executive committee to see it done. Adams was shortly replaced by Christopher Gadsden. On the 30th it was voted to fit out two heavier vessels, of 36 and 20 guns; the naval committee was doubled and given supervision of all marine affairs, but final decision rested with Congress; and this board, with changing personnel and repeatedly renamed,— Marine Committee, Marine Board, and so on, with various subordinate boards,—constituted the Navy Department throughout the war. On November 9 two battalions of marines were voted, and on the 30th separated from the Boston army. The curse of Congressional "patronage" and meddling, however, was on the navy as on the army: it appointed all officers down to third lieutenant, the naval board choosing the rest.

The colonies had already begun to grasp their natural weapons: New England, in the forefront, could not let itself be ravaged without retaliation.

All its colonies but New Hampshire armed one or more vessels; Massachusetts passed an act encouraging and authorizing privateers, and established a prize court; and Washington, then besieging Boston, fitted out six State vessels to intercept British supplies. Most of his officers and crews were a duplicate of the poorer side of the land force, the former being incapable and the latter mutinous; but there were some brilliant exceptions. Captain John Manly with the 8-gun schooner *Lee* kept Massachusetts Bay patrolled amid the autumn and winter storms, and captured

in November an ordnance brig loaded with immense quantities of arms and ammunition; in December three transports; outwitted and damaged a British cruiser pursuing him: and was made a captain in the Continental navy. The *Lee* will be heard of again. The astonishing loyal cruise of the *Lynch* and *Franklin* we have mentioned; but in the spring, James Mugford with the latter made a capture of surpassing value—

a transport with 1500 barrels of powder and a quantity of intrenching tools and other munitions. Pennsylvania armed some vessels to defend the Delaware; Maryland, Virginia, and South Carolina established naval boards and small armed fleets.

To hold back longer from full recognition of a state of war with England was not caution but stupidity, and giving ourselves into the enemy's hand. Five days after the savage edict of North's ministry (page 2484) to outlaw the colonies and hang their seamen, Congress declared all armed vessels employed against them, and the accessory tenders and store-ships, lawful prizes; authorized privateering, and colonial courts to try prize cases; and drew up rules and regulations for a Continental navy. On December 13 it ordered thirteen vessels ranging from 32 to 24 guns to be completed by April, costing $866,666.66, and the work of construction divided among all the chief ports north and south; and shortly authorized the purchase and equipment of still other vessels for cruisers.

On the 22d Captain Esek Hopkins of Rhode Island (brother of Stephen Hopkins the governor, chief justice, and Signer), an old and noted seaman, was made commander-in-chief of the navy; the senior captain was Dudley Saltonstall; and among a number of other officers appointed, the senior first lieutenant was John Paul Jones, a Scotch seaman of 28 lately settled in Virginia. On March 23, 1776, Congress issued letters of marque, and authorized all colonial cruisers and privateers to capture any vessel armed or unarmed carrying the British flag. At the Declaration of Independence, the United States had six regular-built war

vessels and nineteen armed merchantmen, with 422 guns altogether; while nearly three-fourths of the entire British navy, seventy-eight war-ships and frigates with 2078 guns, were stationed off the coast of America.

With eight cruisers of 24 to 8 guns, the heaviest 9-pounders, including the 24-gun flag-ship *Alfred* (an English merchant ship previously named the

Black Prince), Commodore Hopkins left Philadelphia early in January for a secret cruise—in fact against Dunmore's piratical fleet; but was held in the river six weeks by the ice, and only got clear February 17. He did not find Dunmore, and two of his vessels became strayed and did not rejoin; but learning that at New Providence in the Bahamas was an important magazine of British stores, he sailed thither, and with four vessels and a party of marines stormed the place.

Sacks
New
Provi-
dence
maga-
zines

He held it some days, and carried back the governor and several leading citizens as hostages for Americans in British hands (the governor exchanged later for the American Lord Stirling), towards 80 cannon, and a great quantity of ammunition and stores.

Near home Hopkins captured two ordnance store-ships; but in the night of April 6-7 the squadron ran across the English 20-gun ship *Glasgow,* and in an hour's fight was badly mishandled, with

10 killed and 14 wounded, while the *Glasgow* lost only one killed and three wounded, and escaped. This is far the heaviest relative American loss in any battle in the history of the navy, and was due to raw men; but it discouraged them, and of course angered Congress, which held an inquiry into Hopkins' conduct, and censured him for exceeding his instructions in leaving the United States coasts. Later, he was ordered to protect the Southern coasts; but it took time to get the vessels ready— especially with so little money—and he was again in bad odor. Ignoring an order to attend on Congress the next January, he was dismissed from service. Thenceforward no commander-in-chief of the navy was appointed.

The service was unpopular, and a large part of the useful work by American war vessels was increasingly by privateers, fired by the chance of a fortune at a blow. In part, to be sure, this was because the navy rapidly lessened in its numbers at large from losses and blockades, which the national resources were too small to make good. Yet there were many spirited actions for a while, which showed what might happen with more training and more and heavier vessels; and very valuable prize-making. During 1776 alone, the Americans captured 342 vessels; 44 were recaptured and 18 released, but a London paper estimated the damage to the West India trade alone at nearly $2,000,000, and doubtless much correspondent damage was saved to American ports by keeping British cruisers busy.

1776
April
et seq.

Hopkins
cashiered
for
failure

The
privat-
eers

American
prizes in
1776

1776

General
work of
American
navy

The *Lexington* under Captain John Barry captured an armed tender in April; under William Hallock in October, bringing ammunition and stores from the West Indies, she was captured by a frigate of double her armament, which put a prize crew aboard her; the captured marines rose on the crew, took them prisoners in turn and ran the vessel into Baltimore. Captain Nicholas Biddle in the *Andrea Doria* captured during a four months' cruise ten prizes, two being transports containing 400 Highland soldiers for the British army, and returned to port with only five of his own crew, the rest being in charge of prizes. The *Cabot* under Captain Elisha Hinman in about the same time captured seven prizes. The *Columbus* under Captain Abraham Whipple took four in a three months' cruise. The eight-gun schooner *Wasp* under Captain Charles Alexander took an English bark, and under Lieutenant J. Baldwin took three prizes during a short cruise in October. The *Sachem*, Captain Isaiah Robinson, took a British privateer July 6. The captain then took command of the *Andrea Doria;* while returning from the West Indies early in 1777 with ammunition and supplies, it was overhauled by the British

Good
fighting

brig *Racehorse* sent to capture it, but after a fierce two-hours' fight captured its assailant, whose commander was mortally wounded. The *Andrea Doria* was one of those later burned in the Delaware to keep it out of the hands of the British.

State vessels shared in these fine deeds. We have mentioned Manly and the *Lee*. Towards midnight of June 17, the same vessel and the Connecticut State cruiser *Defense*, in an hour's hard fight off Nantasket Roads, captured a transport with some 200 British regulars from the crack 71st regiment, killing 18 and their commander; and the next morning another with 100 more of the same regiment.

The magnificent resistance of Arnold to a vastly superior force on Lake Champlain has been told in its place; but not the beginning of Paul Jones' career, which deserves a notice by itself. Returning from Hopkins' expedition, he was put in command of the 12-gun brig *Providence* to convoy troops and supplies; and soon began to display his marvelous seamanship. He lured a frigate off from the chase of his convoy, and then escaped himself—a favorite performance. He closed in on the 28-gun frigate *Solebay* by mistake for a merchantman, was chased against a head wind and almost overhauled; tacked to let his pursuer get nearly astern; then suddenly turned, threw out every rag of canvas he had, and sailed past her within pistol shot, the astounded Englishmen not gaining their senses to open fire till he was out of range; and in the renewed chase outsailed the frigate. Escaping still another and heavier frigate (the *Milford*), in a month's cruise as far north as Cape Canso he took or destroyed fifteen vessels and several fishing stations.

Transferred to Hopkins' old flag-ship *Alfred*, early in November with this and the *Providence* he slipped adroitly through the British squadron

1776

Hard fighting at Nantasket

Paul Jones

Crafty seamanship

Commerce-destroying

off Block Island, took four prizes, and off Cape
Canso on the 13th fought and captured three more
British vessels, one a 10-gun transport carrying
150 soldiers, 10,000 suits of clothes, and other
supplies for Carleton's army in Canada. Starting to convoy this precious prize and his others
to Boston, he captured shortly after a 16-gun
privateer; on the way home was closely pursued
by the *Milford* again, sent ahead all but the
privateer with instructions to pay no attention to
his signals, took another tack with this one prize
and glaring signals out for the rest to follow, lured
the *Milford* off on a long chase after him, then
dropped the privateer, outsailed the frigate, and
went to Boston, where the seven prizes were safe.
For the moment he gives place to others, but soon
to reappear more grandly, displaying not merely
alertness and energy but the noblest type of heroic
action.

To the surprise perhaps no less of the Americans than of the rest of the world, the astonishment, admiration, and meditation of continental
Europe, and the immeasurable wrath and fury of
the English, the greatest glories of American
naval heroism were won not in defense of our
own coast, but in wresting from the English the
control and almost the maritime occupancy of
their own. The American fleet were nearly as
much masters of the English Channel for a while
as the English themselves were against the French
a generation later, though the Americans never
had more than three or four vessels there at any

1776–7

More of
Paul
Jones'
seaman-
ship

America
seizes
control of
English
Channel

one time. England with all her enormous superiority of armament, her mastery of the European waters against European competitors, could not protect her own commerce at her own doors against her own despised colonists. France just across the strait had never been able in centuries to disturb the effecting of marine insurance; but now for the little run across the Channel it rose to prohibitive rates, and at last the companies refused to insure English bottoms and their cargoes at any price. The Thames was crowded with French shipping, or English masquerading as French to make the voyage with any chance of safety. Not only merchantmen, but even privateers, took the passage from London or Southampton or elsewhere not by the Channel and the south of England, but around the north of Scotland in fear of the American cruisers.

No chagrin since the foundation of the English realm has sunk so deeply into the English heart as this unforeseen and astounding humiliation; it rankles to this day. The trading class had favored the war, as certain to restore to them the monopoly of colonial commerce half broken up by smuggling; the cost would be manyfold repaid by the permanent stream of profit. Now to have their own commerce destroyed and their own coast blockaded by the petty armaments of the rebels was infuriating, and it hurt the complacent pride of ages more even than their pockets. They indemnified themselves by barbarous misusage of officers and crews when captured,—and by styling

1777

English commerce at American mercy

Permanent English rancor

1775-6

them "pirates" then and since;[1] finally they recovered control of the Channel by the virtual extinction of the American navy.

The first American war-vessel to display the flag in foreign waters was the 16-gun brig *Reprisal*.

The "Reprisal"

First used as a transport of military stores from the West Indies, and once beating off a British vessel of equal armament, under Captain Lambert Wickes it carried Franklin to France in the fall of 1776 and took two prizes on the way, as already recited; then went to the Bay of Biscay and took two more, one the royal packet from Falmouth to Lisbon. Stormont demanded their surrender;

Prizes sold in Spain

but they were secretly sold for American behoof. Meantime Franklin and the other commissioners had always urged that a small fleet be sent into English waters—Franklin suggested, to take post in the German Ocean and intercept the northern fur or whaling vessels. So in April 1777 the

A companion

Reprisal was reinforced by the 16-gun (4-pound)

---

[1]How lasting was the rancor it excited is best shown by the epithet of "notorious pirate," which is the favorite description of Paul Jones by a section of English writers even yet. There is of course the same truth and decency in this that there would be in Americans speaking of "Lord Cornwallis, the notorious English thug," or "Admiral Rodney, the notorious English mock-auctioneer." Jones was a lawfully commissioned naval officer, who warred only against the enemies of his adopted country; no more a pirate than Nelson, and much less so than Rodney, who even turned pirate against his own people. If the validity of American commissions is denied, the same reasoning would justify calling Washington a brigand. It is like the digging up and gibbeting of Cromwell's bones by the royalists, and degrades only the perpetrators. The truth is, the English, though magnanimous to those they have beaten, are coarsely vindictive to those who have beaten them. Besides, a defeat on land could be borne; a defeat on sea was unforgivable and has never been forgiven, either of those in the Revolution or the War of 1812.

Lexington; [1] in June Wickes swept through the Bay of Biscay and around Ireland, took fifteen prizes and threw the whole British Islands and environs into panic. The *Reprisal* was so hotly pursued that she had to throw her guns overboard and cut away her bulwarks to escape; but saved her prizes, which were sold secretly.

England was so wild with anger that France, not yet ready for war, ordered prizes and captors to leave, and held the latter a short time till bond was given for it—during which they refitted, and the prizes were sold underhand as before. The *Lexington* left September 18, for some reason very short of ammunition; was soon overhauled by the English *Alert* with more guns than herself, and after using up her ammunition and temporarily crippling her foe, was overtaken again after the latter had made repairs, and by an hour's unreturnable fire compelled to surrender. Her crew were imprisoned on charge of high treason and shamefully maltreated, dug themselves out of prison after some months, and were caught again by a press-gang while embarked for France. The *Reprisal* had left France shortly after her mate, but foundered off the Banks of Newfoundland and only one of her crew escaped.

In the spring the commissioners had bought and fitted up a 10-gun cutter which they renamed

Marginal notes:
1777
The "Reprisal"
England tries to coerce France
"Lexington" captured by "Alert"
"Reprisal" sinks

---

[1] We are told that a 10-gun cutter, the *Dolphin*, bought and fitted out by the commissioners, was added to these and sailed with Wickes. But nothing is heard of it again; the cutter renamed *Surprise* (see later), was bought by them about the same time, and we incline to think *Dolphin* was its original name, and the two have been confused.

the *Surprise,* and commissioned Gustavus Connyngham as captain. Unable to man or arm it
under the angry vigilance of the British agents,
he had sailors and armament shipped out separately under a false pretense, leaving Dunkirk
May 1; took a merchant ship but apparently plundered and let her go; then a packet with which he
returned to Dunkirk. Stormont threatened to
leave the country if captor and prize were not at
once surrendered; and the government, in a corner,
turned them over to the English without trial,
threw Connyngham's bondsmen into the Bastile
for a few weeks, and imprisoned him and his men.
The British government demanded them as
pirates; but the American commissioners secured
their release, and hastily sent them on another
cruise in the famous *Revenge,* a cutter armed with
14 6-pounders and 22 swivels, with a crew of 106
men.

It was this which first made the tremendous
havoc in the British shipping, and caused the
frantic alarm and destruction of security even
close at home. The *Revenge* held the swarming
commerce of England at its mercy, and almost
daily sent off prizes to Spain to be sold for the
commissioners, the moneys thus received being
priceless to the cause. Not daring to refit at a
French port when in need of it, Connyngham
coolly did so at an English one without being suspected, provisioned at an Irish one, and went on
for weeks with his depredations. Now it was that
the English had to take refuge under **French**

Margin notes:

1777

"Sur-
prise"
sails

Returns
and
handed
over to
England

Same
captain
goes in
"Re-
venge"

Master of
the seas

colors. The great fair at Chester could not be held. Connyngham was the master of the seas. The English government again proclaimed him a pirate, and ordered him delivered up to them. The next year they captured and so misused him that Congress officially demanded an explanation, ordered a sufficient number of prisoners to be closely confined if it were not given, and later ordered one to be so kept as a hostage for him.

In August 1777 the 32-gun *Raleigh* and 24-gun *Alfred* sailed for France as transports and commerce-destroyers; came upon a British fleet of four vessels convoying the Windward Island merchant fleet, and attempted cutting out some of the latter by using the enemy's code. Totally unsuspected, but unable to break their line, Captain Thomas Thompson with the *Raleigh,* the faster vessel of the two, boldly sailed through the British fleet giving orders and answering signals as one of their own vessels; then suddenly opened fire on the 16-gun *Druid* till she was a wreck, with 6 killed including her master and 26 wounded. The other vessels at first crowded on sail to escape the supposed hostile fleet; finding there was but one vessel, they closed in upon her, but Thompson rejoined the *Alfred* almost without harm, and finding no safe opportunity for attack, went on to France. On their return in February 1778, the *Alfred* was captured by two English ships of war; the *Raleigh,* too far off to help till too late, escaped with its precious stores, but Thompson was dismissed and tried for abandoning his mate.

"Ra-
leigh"
and
"Alfred"

Thomp-
son
destroys
one of
fleet

Usual
fate

1777

For the first time in its history, even including the wars to the death with France and Spain, England had now to furnish convoys for its coasting trade. The linen-vessels between England and Ireland were not safe. Off Guernsey, almost within range of the Castle guns, a 12-gun American privateer took a £7000 brig and carried it to Cherbourg. During this period also the most valuable part of England's outside commerce, the West India trade, was almost destroyed for a while. Fourteen merchant vessels were captured and taken to the French port of Martinique in one week of April 1777. Of sixty vessels that left Ireland for the West Indies early in the spring, not over twenty-five reached there, and the rest were believed to have been captured by American privateers; great scarcity and famine prices ruled in the islands. The slavers from Africa, laden with negroes, gold dust, and ivory, were also keenly watched for, and one at least was captured, estimated as worth £20,000. In all, the Americans captured 467 vessels in 1777.

English home coasting trade unsafe

West India trade half ruined

The work of bearding England in her own lair was now taken up by a far greater man; not with greater success in the immediate task of destruction, but greater in elevating the whole status of America in foreign consideration, displaying grand qualities and furnishing an undying name for American emulation and enthusiasm. John Paul Jones sailed from Portsmouth November 1 in the 18-gun ship-sloop *Ranger;* slow, ill-fitted, with scant and sleazy sails, and short of stores.

Paul Jones again

JOHN PAUL JONES.

Capturing two prizes and eluding sharp pursuit on the way over, he convoyed some American merchantmen to the protection of the French fleet, and secured the important recognition of having the admiral salute the American flag; refitted, and started on April 10 for the English and Irish coasts. Sinking several trading vessels on his path, sending an important ship as a prize to Brest, baffled by a storm in a swoop on Whitehaven in Cumberland,—a populous seaport full of shipping,—cruising up the west side of Scotland and crossing to Ireland, he made an attempt upon the British 20-gun sloop-of-war *Drake* in Carrickfergus Roads, in the night, amid a violent gale, intending to board; but the wind nearly drove the *Ranger* aground, and it took all his seamanship to extricate it.

He then resumed his onslaught on Whitehaven on the night of April 22, "to put an end by one good fire in England, of shipping, to all burnings in America." But his boats took till daylight to reach the pier; and his chief lieutenant, Wallingford, sent to fire the shipping on the north, with inopportune humaneness "did not see the good of destroying poor people's property," and made an excuse of his candle's giving out to do nothing. Jones seized two forts and spiked their guns; found on return to the first that those candles had somehow given out too, secured candles and tinder from a house, and set fire to a large vessel with some 150 others about it, grounded at low tide. It was broad day; a crowd

1777

Jones
in the
"Ranger"

On Irish
coast

Narrow
escape of
White-
haven

had collected warned by a deserter,—perhaps treachery in his varied crew helped in the fiasco of the candles, though not with Wallingford. Jones held the crowd at bay with his pistol till the fire was well started, then took to his boat; but they rushed aboard the ship and put out the fire. Jones took away three prisoners, and had no loss except the deserter.

Jones then tried to kidnap the Earl of Selkirk at his country seat, on the Isle of St. Mary at the mouth of the Dee, as a hostage for American prisoners in British hands; and would have succeeded had the earl been at home. Jones' men stole some of the family plate, which he returned with a note of regret—very little like English looters in America. By this time the waters were swarming with war-vessels sent to capture him; but Jones was bent on a fight against odds to test his powers, and by moving off Carrick-fergus again, tolled the *Drake* into mid-channel. Five vessels followed, full of passengers curious to see a naval battle. They saw it; one decided not by skillful manœuvres, but by sheer compe-tition of skill in gunnery. The *Ranger* had 18 guns and 123 crew, the *Drake* 20 guns and 160 to 190 crew. In a little over an hour the *Drake* was put *hors de combat*, her captain and first lieuten-ant mortally wounded and forty others killed or wounded, against two killed and six wounded on the *Ranger*; and surrendered. The next day the *Ranger* sunk a large brigantine in the intervals of making her prize seaworthy; then passed around

1778
April–
May

Jones
fires
ships at
White-
haven

Misses
Earl of
Selkirk

"Ranger"
and
"Drake"

the north of Ireland and by way of its west shore returned to France. Jones had been gone twenty-eight days, and earned an eternal hate and vilification by his foes surpassing that of all other Americans together from that day to this. The one unforgivable offense was that of defeating and capturing a vessel of the English navy better armed and manned than his own; a prelude to greater glories still of the American navy. They could only solace themselves by inventing falsehoods about him.

The fate of the *Randolph* in 1778 is a sad but splendid episode of the Revolution navy. She was the first to be utilized of the 32-gun frigates ordered by Congress in 1775. Leaving Philadelphia in February 1777 under Captain Nicholas Biddle, she was forced into Charleston by injuries from a storm; then took six prizes in one week, one of them a 20-gun war vessel; but was blockaded in the harbor until March 1778. Starting with four State cruisers to look up some English ones off the coast, on the 7th they came upon the 64-gun ship *Yarmouth;* and to save the rest of the fleet, Biddle had them take to flight while he engaged the monster, of double his armament. For an hour he and his crew of 315 fought so bravely and skillfully that the *Yarmouth* was seriously injured, five Englishmen killed and twelve wounded; then a shot struck the *Randolph's* magazine, and vessel and crew were scattered to the winds by an explosion. Four of the men were found five days later on a piece of the wreck, kept alive by the rain that had fallen on a piece of blanket; no others were saved. But the sacrifice won its purpose: the *Yarmouth* was unable to overhaul the fleet.

Another episode of the year illustrates the ex-action of invariable success from both army and navy commanders, under penalty of dismissal and perhaps punishment, by judges both uninformed, inexpert, and unreasonable. In May the second of the new frigates, the 32-gun *Hancock* under Captain John Manly, set out from Boston on a cruise, with the 24-gun ship *Boston* under Captain Hector McNiel. Four days later she captured, after an hour's hot fight in which she lost 8 killed and wounded against her antagonist's 32, the 28-gun frigate *Fox,* which was manned with a prize crew and taken along. On June 1, having gone too near Halifax, the three were chased by three British vessels of 44, 32, and 18 guns; the *Hancock* and the *Fox* were caught by a sudden failure of wind; the *Boston* was far enough to sea-ward to escape. Had she tried to assist the others, the fight would have called out the whole fleet of the chief British naval station in America, and there would have been one more vessel lost; but there was an uproar against McNiel for "desert-ing" his mates, and he was cashiered in disgrace, like Thompson of the *Raleigh* for a similar escape.

An interesting portion of the year's naval war-fare was the invention of the first submarine boat, by David Bushnell of Saybrook, Connecticut. It was shaped like a double tortoise-shell, and was

Cruise of
the
"Han-
cock"
and
"Boston"

ballasted with lead; had a valve to admit water for descent, and force-pumps to eject it again for ascent; a rowing oar in front, another at top for ascent or descent or remaining stationary, and a rudder behind; in the centre sat the operator, with a half-hour's air supply under water and a ventilator for the surface.   A wood screw could be twisted into a ship's bottom by an iron rod, and was fastened to a hollowed oak log containing 150 pounds of powder, with a time apparatus for exploding it by a flint-lock.   He called it the American *Turtle;* the current name for the attached torpedoes was "kegs."   They gave great promise, one of them blowing a schooner in pieces; and a fleet of them was launched to blow up the British squadron in the Delaware, but freezing, ice, and darkness confined their success to blowing up one boat.   The incident was commemorated in a once noted comic poem, "The Battle of the Kegs," by Francis Hopkinson the Signer.

By February 1778, before the French alliance, the American State and national navy and privateers had captured or destroyed 733 vessels, 559 not being retaken; English authorities estimated their value with cargoes at £1,800,000 to £2,200,000. The insurance, which had been 2 to 2½ per cent., was now about 5 with a convoy and 15 without.

American activity was not slackened during the year.   The handsomest exploit was against the same New Providence which Hopkins had taken two years before, and which that experience and the importance of the depot had not taught

1777

Bush-
nell's
"Amer-
ican
Turtle"

The
"Kegs"

English
losses
from
American
vessels

New
Provi-
dence
again

1778

New
Provi-
dence
stores
again
sacked

the British to protect.   Captain John P. Rathbourne in the little *Providence* descended on it
in the night of January 27 with twenty-five men,
was joined by some thirty escaped from the prison
ships there, captured the forts, turned their guns
on the shipping, and became master of seven vessels including a 16-gun privateer.   But the populace rose, and the small party were in peril;
Rathbourne spiked the guns, took off all the other
arms, ammunition, and stores, burned two prizes
and carried the others off with him.

But privateers grew more and more the main-
stay; for as the public vessels were lost by weather
or foes, blockade or destruction to keep them from
Deple-
tion of
American
navy
the enemy, the treasury was too poor to replace
them.   One fleet had been locked up in Narragansett Bay when Newport was taken, another
burned on the upper Hudson when Clinton captured the forts, a third blockaded in the Delaware
and soon to be burned—though the latter had a
sting yet, Captain John Barry of the *Effingham*
with a small party destroying a British 10-gun
schooner and four loaded transports.   To replace
New
vessels
this fleet, Congress ordered three 74-gun ships,
five large frigates, and several smaller vessels;
but the money ran short and most of them never
were finished.   The 32-gun *Raleigh,* now under
Barry, was overhauled September 27 near the
mouth of the Penobscot by a 50-gun and a 28-gun
Loss of
"Ra-
leigh"
British ship; and after a hot fight with the latter,
losing ten men and the enemy probably thrice as
many, had to be run aground, Barry and his men

escaping. She was raised and used by the British. By 1779 the national navy consisted of only fourteen vessels with 10 to 32 guns, 332 in all.

This memorable year was to be forever made glorious by Paul Jones. But other work was done of much immediate value.

John B. Hopkins, son of the ex-commodore, left Boston April 18 with the 32-gun *Warren,* the 28-gun *Queen of France* (bought in France by Franklin and Deane), and Jones' famous *Ranger;* captured a 14-gun privateer, and learned that nine armed transports and store-ships had lately left New York with munitions for the troops in Georgia and South Carolina; hastened after them and shortly captured seven at a blow—three having 44 guns and 279 men, including Lieutenant-Colonel Campbell and twenty other officers. The next month the *Queen of France* and *Ranger* with the 28-gun frigate *Providence* put to sea, in July cut out eleven merchantmen from a fleet convoyed by a 74 and a number of frigates, and got eight of them to port, valued at over $1,000,000,—the most lucrative cruise of the war. In August the 32-gun *Deane* and the 24-gun *Boston* (now under Captain Samuel Tucker, a seaman and fighter of immense ability and success, who had taken several dozen prizes and had some fierce engagements) took six prizes in a short cruise; among them two privateers and a packet with 54 guns. Tucker was afterwards captured at Charleston, exchanged for the captain of one of these privateers, and took seven more prizes in 1780.

Of a much higher type in valor and determination were two actions in the spring. The 14-gun Massachusetts State cruiser *Hazard,* under John F. Williams, in an hour's desperate battle with a loss of 8 men forced the 18-gun privateer *Active* to strike, badly shattered and with 33 men killed or disabled. Williams was transferred to the 10-gun State cruiser *Protector* (on which was Edward Preble), and the next year had an hour's fierce combat with a large English privateer, which then blew up. On May 7, 1779, the 12-gun brig *Providence,* now under Captain Hoysted Hacker, engaged the English 12-gun brig *Diligent,* and in an hour compelled her surrender, with 27 men killed or wounded out of a crew of 53,—over half, —the *Providence* losing 14. The *Diligent* was made a United States war vessel.

But the whole sea armament sustained a heavy disaster in August. The English had established a post near the mouth of the Penobscot, to curb New England from the north; Massachusetts to break it up sent General Solomon Lovell with 1500 militia in thirteen transports and privateers, and the *Warren* (flag-ship), *Diligent,* and *Providence* (the late contestants), under Captain Saltonstall. Unable to reduce the fort, they awaited reinforcements; but hearing of the expedition, Sir George Collier sent seven vessels including a 64 and three 32's to reinforce the three small ones already there. The privateers scattered in panic, some of them and of the transports running up the river, whither the three Continental vessels had to follow them, the whole being burnt to save them from the enemy. The crews and militia escaped.

1779

Meantime the fast dwindling navy had received an important accession from France. Paul Jones, since his return from the cruise of 1778 in May, had been appealing to the French court by letters and messages for a better ship than the small slow *Ranger,* and some others with it, as a squadron to operate on the British coasts; but was put off month after month. At length his eye chanced to fall on the sentence in a *Poor Richard's Almanac* advising a man to attend to business himself if he wishes it performed; he acted upon the hint, went to court, and on February 4, 1779, was granted a worn-out old India merchant ship, the *Duras* or *Duc de Duras,* which in gratitude for what had secured it he renamed the *Bonhomme Richard.* It was an old-fashioned high-pooped affair with high sides; and Jones took advantage of this to cut a lower row of port-holes, six on a side, half of them mounted with old 18-pounders— unfit for use, and the ports having to be closed anyway in a heavy sea. The main deck had 28 12's (18's not being procurable); the quarter-deck and forecastle eight 9's—42 in all, or a broadside of 21.

Paul Jones' efforts

Secures the "Bon homme Richard"

Two more merchantmen, the *Pallas* and *Vengeance,* were bought and armed, the former with 30 guns, the latter not stated; the 18-gun cutter *Cerf,* a regular war vessel, was added; and still another from America, the 32-gun *Alliance,* one of the frigates built to replace the lost Delaware fleet, and named in honor of the French

Her consorts

alliance. She was sent to France in January to carry over Lafayette; and for his sake, the command was given to the French captain Pierre Landais. The latter was reputed to have good professional skill; but Franklin afterwards wrote to him personally that he was "so impudent, litigious, and quarrelsome, even with his best friends," that peace, order, and subordination were impossible with him, and if he (Franklin) had twenty ships, he would not give one of them to Landais. This in fact had shelved him in the French navy; and he was worse yet—a traitorous scoundrel exactly parallel to Charles Lee.

The vessel was manned by a medley of Americans, French, and captured English seamen given their liberty if they would undertake the cruise, it being so hard to raise seamen and especially for service under a Frenchman. The English Parliament had recently passed a bill offering large rewards to crews of American vessels who would mutiny and bring them over to the British; that of the *Alliance* naturally plotted to do so, and would have succeeded but for an American seaman mistaken for an Irishman disclosing the plot. And even this mongrel gang was homogeneous and harmonious compared with the offscourings of the civilized and uncivilized world with which Jones had finally to man the rest of his vessels. The *Bonhomme Richard* had a majority of American officers; but her crew hailed from every country of western Europe except Holland, from Malta, India, Fayal, Malay-land, and Africa.

Margin notes:
1779
Pierre Landais
Motley crew
Attempt at mutiny
Crew of "Bonhomme Richard"

I do hereby certify that John Paul Jones was duly
commissioned and appointed to command the armed
vessel Sloop called the Providence and that
this Sloop is now employed in the service of the thirteen
United States of North America Witness my Hand
October 29th 1776

John Hancock Presid

The first objective was Liverpool, to burn it or hold it to ransom, and let the English know that the game was not confined to one power. Lafayette was to head a land force; but he was called off and assigned to the command of the royal guards—not impossibly because the French government did not wish to set England the dangerous precedent of laying each other's home cities in ashes. Jones was reduced to his naval armament; and on June 19, 1779, sailed from L'Orient. Landais at once showed his hand, and claimed to rank Jones and command the squadron, as commissioned by Congress direct while Jones was commissioned by Franklin—a double falsehood, as Jones' commission was from Congress, and Franklin with plenary power had made him commander. The same night the *Alliance* and *Bonhomme Richard* fouled, with so much damage that they had to return to port. It was August 14 before the squadron again set out; but the delay was of perhaps decisive advantage, for while at L'Orient 119 exchanged American prisoners came to Nantes, and most of them enlisted on the *Bonhomme Richard,* giving Jones a force he could depend upon. Richard Dale, late master's mate of the *Lexington* and afterwards noted in the Barbary wars, not long escaped from prison, also joined him and was made first lieutenant. Jones now had 380 men on his flag-ship.

The squadron sailed again, accompanied by two French privateers, the captain of one of which rifled the first prize captured and put his own prize

1779

Plan to
seize
Liverpool
blocked

Landais
quarrels
with
Jones

Fresh
start

Fresh
crew

crew on it; Jones disallowed this, and the privateers left him. Some days later, the English crew
of a towing barge of the *Bonhomme Richard* cut
the line and escaped to the Irish coast in a fog,
which also led to those of another barge pursuing
them losing their course and being captured. Landais fell to berating Jones with the utmost inso-
lence, and proclaiming that he should do what he
pleased. Skirting the west coast of Ireland and
Scotland, the fleet was scattered by a gale, and
the *Cerf* did not reappear during the cruise; while
Landais refused to obey any signals from the flag-
ship, then to obey written orders and finally a command to come on board for a council, and at last
disappeared altogether for a fortnight.

The rest of the fleet stood around the north of
Scotland and came down the east coast; and about
the middle of September Jones came off the Firth

of Forth, where lay a British war vessel. He resolved to capture it, and do to Edinburgh as he
had intended for Liverpool; but was foiled by a
gale which blew the cruisers out to sea and sunk
a prize vessel. The captains of his consorts began
to grow nervous over the gathering of English
war-ships to intercept this expedition, which had

roused the whole of Great Britain to a frenzy of
panic and venomous fury. "The pirate Jones"[1]

---

[1] This term of abuse seems to have been taken in literal earnest
even by many of the upper classes; for a member of Parliament—apparently supposing the vessels carried black flags—sent a boat to the
Bonhomme Richard for powder and shot to defend his place from Paul
Jones. Jones sent him some powder, but professed to have no shot of
the right size.

was the official English description; and the officers had good reason to dread falling into British hands, for every ill-usage short of murder would be theirs. They declared that if Jones did not leave those waters in a week they would abandon him; meantime they went cruising down the Northumberland coast, at their own will and doing what they chose with the prizes. Jones followed. The *Pallas* disappeared, and the remaining two entered the Humber and took several vessels.

1779
Sept.

Jones'
consorts
alarmed

The expedition had taken seventeen prizes, and the prize crews put aboard them had reduced those of the fleet so that the *Bonhomme Richard,* which had lost 24 men in the two barges also, had only 320 left. Jones for safety again moved north; and was rejoined by the *Alliance,* unluckily enough, and the *Pallas.* The *Vengeance* here drops out of the accounts. About noon of the 23d, while chasing a brigantine toward Flamborough Head just north,—a pilot boat with Jones' second lieutenant and fifteen men in advance,—they were suddenly confronted by a great merchant fleet bound for the Baltic; forty craft, convoyed by two war vessels, the *Serapis* and the *Countess of Scarborough.* Such an opportunity for crippling a whole section of English commerce at one gigantic blow would never occur again; and Jones ordered an immediate onslaught. But the English fleet was speedily warned; the merchantmen began to scud away in every direction, some under the guns of Scarborough Castle; while the naval pair advanced to protect their escape.

Cruise on
Northumberland
coast

Baltic
fleet rout

Scatters

The *Serapis,* Captain Pearson, had only been built a few months; the *Bonhomme Richard* was so old and rotten that the shipmasters said she would not stand the needful repairs. The *Serapis*

"Serapis and "Bon-homme Richard"

had 20 18-pounders on the lower gun deck against Jones' six, 20 9-pounders on the main deck against his 28 12's, and 10 6-pounders on the quarter-deck and forecastle against his eight 9's: 50 guns against his 42. His "pounds," however, were French, much above English weight, and his broadside was 278½ pounds against her 300. He had to abandon his pilot-boat, leaving him 304 men

"Countess of Scarbor-ough"

against her 320; and he had several hundred prisoners in his hold to be guarded. The *Countess of Scarborough,* Captain Piercy, had 22 6-pounders and 150 crew.

Jones signaled the *Alliance* to fall astern; instead, Landais went ahead to tell Captain Cottineau of the *Pallas* that if the *Serapis* had over

Landais and Cot-tineau

50 guns, there was "nothing to do but run away," and drew off. Cottincau, however, at last closed with the *Countess of Scarborough;* but after a long hesitation, or at least delay, which left it near nightfall when Jones was able himself to move down on the *Serapis.* The latter headed landward, apparently to reach the cover of the Castle guns; Jones turned the same way to get between her and the land; Cottineau thought Jones' prisoners had risen and captured the vessel and were running it into Scarborough, and headed off shore.

Jones closed up to the *Serapis* in the heavily gathering darkness, towards 7 P. M., refusing to answer her hails; and when within pistol shot both vessels poured their full broadsides into each other at the same moment. Two of Jones' old 18's on the lower deck exploded at the first fire, killing most of the gunners and shattering the upper deck, and the men refused to work the others; thus reducing Jones' broadside at a blow by over 58 pounds and all his heaviest guns, thinning his force, and still worse, leaving his lower deck deserted so that the gunners of the *Serapis'* lower tier were able to pour their broadside into their foe unmolested. Jones moved landward across her bow, and she in turn moved obliquely so that each fired with the opposite broadside from the first, Jones from the port side. They closed to within half the former distance, and each manned the upper rigging with sharpshooters to pick off the enemy's gunners. Before an hour was up the *Bonhomme Richard* was in a horrible state. The carnage had been such that her decks were astream with blood, which was trickling from the scuppers; she was leaking badly from several shot that had struck below the line, and the enemy's 18's below were tearing her whole middle into a wreck; the entire broadside of 12's was dismounted or otherwise silenced like the 18's, and two of the four 9's on the quarter-deck and forecastle; one of the 9's from the starboard was dragged over, and the *Bonhomme Richard* now had three 9-pounders for her whole broadside, against seven or eight times that number in full play, mostly much heavier. Jones, however, directed them in person and did heavy

1779
Sept. 23

"Bonhomme Richard" fares ill at first

execution along the *Serapis'* deck; then double-shotted them and aimed at her mainmast.

The moon now rose. Pearson tried to gain a raking position, but got in line instead, and Jones ran his vessel's bowsprit over the *Serapis'* stern; each gathered to repel boarders, and Pearson sent a hail to know if the other vessel had struck. "I haven't begun to fight yet," returned Jones, and backed away. Pearson again tried to turn and rake, but amid the smoke entangled the *Serapis'* jib-boom with the *Bonhomme Richard's* mizzen-shrouds; and Jones, who saw that his one salvation was to keep close and silence the enemy's upper guns by musket fire on the gunners, at once lashed the vessels together, the *Serapis* now on his starboard. Her bowsprit broke off; Jones threw a hawser around its stump and his vessel's mizzen-mast, and they held close despite Pearson's efforts to separate. The *Serapis* had closed its lower ports to keep the Americans from boarding through them; now they could not be opened, and the British shot them away to reach the foe. The gunners of each vessel could only load by stretching the rammers into the ports of the other; the *Bonhomme Richard* was set on fire in several places at once by burning wads, but was extinguished. Pearson tried to board between nine and ten, but was daunted by the resolute bearing of the Americans.

Jones' policy now began to bear fruit, and the frightful odds to turn. The *Serapis'* 18's had so utterly shot away both sides of the *Bonhomme*

"Bon-
homme
Richard"
grapples
"Sera-
pis"

Richard that the upper deck rested only on a few stanchions, too close to the guns to be raked; but for that reason this heaviest broadside was now useless, having no one to kill and merely shooting into the sea. On the other hand, every man of the *Bonhomme Richard* being on the upper deck and rigging, and one or two of the 12-pounders set up again, their concentrated fire shortly killed or drove below every human being on the *Serapis'* upper deck and shrouds, and silenced its 12-pounders, so that it in turn was reduced to its five forecastle and quarter-deck guns. To keep the deck cleared, one of the *Bonhomme Richard's* men with a bucket of hand grenades clambered to the end of its overhanging main yard, and began tossing them down whenever any one showed himself; then aimed at the hatchways, and killed or injured several standing there; finally he stretched over and flung one down the main hatchway into the gun-room. A great quantity of 12-pound cartridges had been brought there from the magazine and strung along the deck, and left unused by the silencing of the guns; the grenade set them off, and a fearful explosion killed or injured 38 men.

Now Landais with the *Alliance* came into view, and the Americans thought victory secured. But to the utter amazement of all, she fired her whole broadside into her consort; and while Jones and his officers frantically hailed her and hung out lanterns in fear of a possible mistake, she "passed round firing into the *Bonhomme Richard* head,

1779

"Bonhomme Richard" begins to have vantage

Frightful carnage on "Serapis"

Landais fires on his ally

1779
Sept. 23

Landais'
treach-
ery

stern, and broadside," as Jones reported, a single volley killing or wounding ten or twelve of the best men in the forecastle, including "a good officer," and several of the shot striking below the line and increasing the already heavy leakage. This was no mistake: not only was the identity of the vessel clear, but Landais was told by several of his own officers that he was firing on his mate, and some of his gunners refused to fire; and he said later that he would not have been sorry to see the *Bonhomme Richard* strike, so that he could rescue her and capture the *Serapis* himself. To such a depth of execrable villainy could mean ambition lead a man insane with egotism. It was of course believed that the British had captured the *Alliance* and was reinforcing the *Serapis;* and Jones at last prepared to strike, but for some reason Landais drew off.

"Bon-
homme
Rich-
ard's"
dreadful
state

The *Bonhomme Richard* was in such condition as no other vessel in history ever approached which yet came out victor. It had six feet of water in the hold and was settling; the crew had for some time been vainly trying to put out a fire which was now within a few feet of the magazine; the master-at-arms had liberated one to two hundred prisoners confined below decks, to give them a chance for life, and one of them escaped through a port-hole and informed the *Serapis'* crew of the desperate American plight, at which they cheered and took fresh heart. At the same time the mas-

Panic
started

ter screamed that the ship was sinking, and set the crew into a wild panic to lower the boats;

while several officers, in the absence of Jones and Dale looking over the pumps, tried to strike the flag but found it shot away, and the quarter-deck head gunner cried for quarter to the *Serapis*. Pearson prepared to come aboard, but his party received a volley from the *Bonhomme Richard's* rigging that drove the survivors down the hatchways; and Jones himself came up to answer Pearson's fresh inquiry if he had surrendered, as curtly as before.

Jones' remaining officers counseled surrender; but Sir Richard Grenville himself was not farther from such thought under any circumstances. He had it bruited around that the *Serapis* was sinking, and that every man on both vessels would drown unless the *Bonhomme Richard* was kept afloat; and the prisoners, instead of rising on their captors, manned the pumps at their order with the energy of terror, gang relieving gang, and under Dale's supervision not only floated the ship, but left their guards free to fight. Jones forced his men to their guns at the point of a cocked pistol; and a fresh storm of missiles swept and tore the *Serapis,* gradually silencing her few remaining serviceable guns, penning the sound crew helplessly between decks, and setting her on fire in various places. Holding out further seemed to mean total destruction, and at 10:30 P. M. Pearson hauled down his flag with his own hands, just before his mainmast fell overboard carrying the mizzen topmast with it. Dale at once went aboard and took possession, and Jones had the lashings

1779
Sept. 23

Divided
counsels
on "Rich-
ard"

Jones
still firm

Prison-
ers help

"Sera-
pis"
strikes

1779
Sept. 23
et seq.

cut. The wounded and prisoners were hastily transferred to the *Serapis,* while the *Bonhomme Richard's* crew worked without ceasing all night and the next day to keep above water that splintered and burning wreck on which they had fought and conquered, a mere skeleton of rotten and mangled wood, with the very magazine in danger; though a number of her men in fear swam to the other ships, and ten English seamen escaped ashore in a boat. But about 10 A. M. of the 25th she sank to the bottom.

"Bon-
homme
Richard"
sinks

The losses in this unique naval engagement were marvelously equal: the *Bonhomme Richard* lost 49 killed and 67 wounded, the *Serapis* 49 killed and 68 wounded—each over a third of its force; but some of the former's loss must be credited to Landais' treachery. Cottineau and the *Pallas* also had borne their part handsomely: after a two-hours' fight in which the *Countess of Scarborough* had a third of her guns dismounted, four men killed and 20 disabled, and her sailing gear mostly shot away, Piercy surrendered. The remaining American squadron sailed for the Texel, arriving October 3; the *Serapis* and *Countess of Scarborough* were refitted and presented to France, and Jones took command of the *Alliance.* Landais was dismissed from both the French and American services, and ordered out of France. The commissioners feared to prejudice the alliance by pressing his rightful punishment.

Losses

"Coun-
tess of
Scarbor-
ough"
taken

Landais
dis-
missed

This amazing cruise resounded through Europe. The final victory over an English war-ship of the first quality, by a crazy hulk with a smaller armament and an undisciplined casual riffraff of a crew, many traitors outright, and his own consort taking part with the enemy, placed Paul Jones on the pinnacle of fame: in England as a sort of Antichrist among pirates, much like the view taken by the Spaniards of Drake; on the Continent justly as a naval hero of the foremost rank. The nations whose commerce was incessantly interrupted and plundered by England under the right of search were overjoyed at her humiliation: the King of France made Jones a knight of the Order of Merit, presented him with a sword, and offered him a captaincy in the royal navy, which he declined; Catherine of Russia gave him the ribbon of St. Anne, the King of Denmark gave him a pension, the other nations lauded him, and the Dutch were proud to give him harborage. But the British ambassador to Holland, Sir Joseph Yorke, ordered that the ships and crews taken by "the pirate Jones, a rebel subject and enemy of the state," be given up; refusal meant instant war, for which the Dutch burghers were not yet ready; and after remaining nearly three months, Jones was compelled on December 27 to take the *Alliance* out in the teeth of a number of cruisers eager to intercept him—not singly, however. But the English expected him for prudence to go north around Scotland, and the main body waited for him on that path; instead, slipping through the blockading fleet, he sailed straight down the Channel in view of several heavy British

1779

Paul Jones famous

Honors given him

Holland forced to thrust him out

Sails through Channel

ships, skirted close to Dover and Spithead, reached and cruised in the Bay of Biscay, returned to France in June 1780, and on September 7 again sailed in the 20-gun *Ariel,* royal French vessel. Nearly wrecked in a storm, he was unable to sail again till December 18. About New Year's he engaged an English ship, but she escaped. On February 18, 1781, he reached Philadelphia, was publicly thanked, and assigned to the 74-gun ship *America* then building; but the war was over before she was ready, and she was presented to France to make good a French 74 accidentally lost in Boston harbor.[1]

Despite all this glory, the American navy was fast thinning out. Four more of the Continental vessels, all of historic name,—the 28-gun *Providence* and *Queen of France,* the 24-gun *Boston,* and the famed 18-gun *Ranger,*—were lost by the fall of Charleston in May 1780, leaving only six —three 32's, a 28, a 20, and an 18. This made it extremely difficult for the few to slip through the swarming English cruisers and get to sea. It was also increasingly difficult to man them, the English refusing to exchange the captured officers and seamen for that very reason,—a loss they could bear and we could not, contrary to the conditions in the

---

[1] The American navy being wholly dismantled at the close of the war, there was no further employment for Jones; and he entered the Russian service,—with liberty of resuming the American if he was ever needed,—did good work against the Barbary corsairs, and rose to be rear-admiral. In 1792 he was appointed United States consul to Algiers, but died just before setting out. His burial-place, long unknown, was recently discovered, and his body removed to the United States in 1905.

army, for in 1780 their assignment to the navy was 85,000 men. When they finally did offer to exchange, it was because their prisoners were mostly privateersmen, and would return home without advantaging the American cause, while the American prisoners were British regulars and an immediate reinforcement—as set forth in a previous chapter.

The 28-gun *Trumbull,* Captain James Nicholson, escaping her watchers in May 1780, by ostentatious carelessness decoyed a 36-gun privateer, the *Watt,* into an engagement of nearly three hours, almost as deadly as Jones', at so close range that the *Trumbull* was twice set on fire by the other's wadding; then all her masts and spars but the foremost came down in a ruin, and the *Watt* made her escape with a loss of 92 killed and wounded, the *Trumbull* losing 39 but barely able to reach land. On October 8 the *Saratoga,* under Captain James Young, cruising from Philadelphia, decoyed a heavily armed English merchantman with 90 men into its toils; then chased and captured its two mates, armed brigs of war. But a 74-gun ship overhauled her and recaptured the prizes, and she was never seen again after her own escape.

The *Alliance,* now with 40 guns and under John Barry, left Boston for France in February 1781, conveying Colonel John Laurens; whose father, the ex-president, was a prisoner in English hands, threatened with death as a rebel. She captured a privateer, reached her destination,

sailed again with a heavy French privateer, captured with her two English privateers of 26 and 10
guns and 167 men, and went on alone. On May
28, in very light wind, two English brigs of 16
and 14 guns overhauled her, secured raking positions with sweeps, and discharged broadsides into
her for an hour without her being able to respond
save with a few guns; Barry was badly wounded
and the frigate was about to surrender, when a
breeze sprang up, she stood between them and
poured full broadsides into both and compelled
them to strike, with 11 killed (including the commander of one) and 30 wounded, the *Alliance* losing 11 killed and 21 wounded. One of the two was
recaptured.

On June 22 the *Confederacy,* one of the new
1778 frigates, was captured by two heavier Eng-

lish ships while laden with military stores. In
August the *Trumbull,* while escorting to the Delaware a large merchant fleet, and with an excessively small crew largely made up of British
volunteers, was badly damaged in a storm which
scattered the fleet; the next night in a squall, while
the wreckage of her masts and spars was tangled
in the rigging, along the deck, or dragging in the
sea, she was closed on by two British ships of
heavier armament, one the captured *Hancock* renamed the *Iris.* The deck hands put out the lanterns and scuttled below; Captain Nicholson and
some fifty Americans, including Dale from the
Bonhomme Richard and C. H. Perry, the father of
the victor of Lake Erie, fought bravely, but to the

CAPTAIN JOHN BARRY.

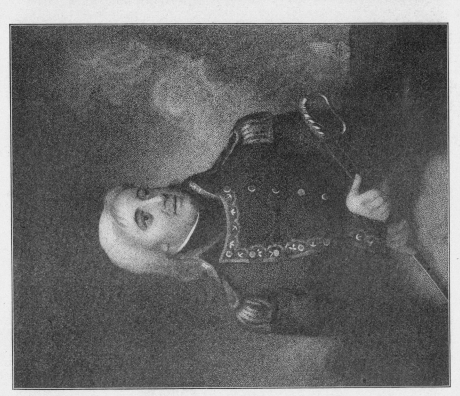

CAPTAIN JOSHUA BARNEY.

enemy's superior forces was soon added the *General Monk,* and she had to strike.

In the remaining months of the war, the two most brilliant actions were fought by other than Continental vessels.

The month after the *Trumbull's* capture, on September 6, the 20-gun Philadelphia cruiser *Congress,* privately armed and manned almost wholly by landsmen under Mr. Geddes, overhauled the British 16-gun sloop-of-war *Savage,* of the regular navy and manned by trained seamen. Ranging so close to her that the gun flashes scorched the men, and shells were thrown by hand into the hostile vessels, the *Congress,* in a couple of hours' fierce fight—interrupted for a half-hour while she repaired her shattered rigging—shot off the *Savage's* mizzenmast and almost the mainmast, killed or wounded 32 men while losing 30 herself, cleared the upper works, and forced her foe to surrender.

In April 1782 the Pennsylvania State cruiser *Hyder Ally,* with 110 crew under Lieutenant Joshua Barney, and carrying 16 6-pounders, while doing convoy duty at the Delaware Capes was approached by two English cruisers, one of which chased the merchant fleet up the river. The other was the *General Monk,* Captain Rodgers, a sloop-of-war with 20 9-pounders and 136 crew. While attempting to follow her mate she was forced to a fight by Barney. Rodgers moved up to board. Barney told his helmsman to do the exact reverse of whatever he was ordered; shouted orders which brought on a move from Rodgers that entangled the *General Monk's* jib-boom with the *Hyder Ally's* fore rigging, enabling the latter to rake the former with a full broadside; lashed them together; and in half an hour had laid low two-fifths of his enemy's crew—20 killed and 23 wounded—with a loss of but 4 killed and 11 wounded of his own, and compelled it to strike. He then rescued his convoy, and retired out of reach of an English frigate approaching.

About this time the Continental *Deane,* under Captain Samuel Nicholson, captured four armed vessels with 48 guns in a two-months' cruise. The *Alliance* closed a checkered career with the last naval action of the war, fighting on the way to Havana a battle with an English ship, which finally drew off.

The United States during the war lost of its regular navy 24 vessels with 470 guns; the British 102 vessels with 2622 guns—this of course including losses from the French and Spanish, but much the greater part from the Americans. The latter through all their sea forces captured some 800 British vessels. Privateers alone captured sixteen English cruisers, of 8 to 20 guns each, and mounting 226 in all, while British privateers did not capture one Continental vessel.

The ocean warfare between England and other powers, which deeply affected the issues of America and the world, belongs to the political history of the Revolution and not to that of the American navy, and will be treated in its proper sequence.

CHAPTER XLVIII.

THE BOTTOM REACHED

The first nine months of 1780 brought the patriot cause in America so low that its recovery is one of the marvels of history. Disaster thronged upon disaster, with deeper gulfs seeming to yawn behind, and scarcely a source of recoupment showing anywhere; and internal disorganization kept pace with external defeat and loss.

Two crushing blows won for the British not only the chief Southern seaport but all South Carolina except its mountainous northwest, annihilated in succession the only regular American forces in the South, and made prisoners a third of the entire Continental army. Charleston and Lincoln's troops surrendered together in May, Gates' corps was destroyed at Camden in August. The hope from the French reinforcement which landed in July was speedily darkened by the blockade of its naval part in Narragansett Bay. The narrow escape in September from losing the whole Hudson to the British without a blow, by Arnold's treason, was far more ominous than its loss by battle could have been; for it seemed to show that the best and bravest had abandoned all hope and were ready to save their necks by the most infamous means. And besides a strong

Charleston, Camden, Narragansett Bay, Arnold

1780–1

Deser tion and mutiny

civil element always opposed to separation, and growing more influential as patriot zeal ebbed, a herd of little soldiers were following the example of the great one as far, perhaps, as impotence sometimes rather than honesty enabled, and deserting a score a week. Those too honest for that were often resorting to law for a discharge, often growing as dangerous to their own government as to the enemy: besides petty mutinies, three months after the turn of the tide more than a thousand rose in a great one to extort their rights from Congress.

Resour ces ex hausted

The existent national currency was virtually repudiated, though the belief in ability to create monetary confidence by law was not yet quite given up. There was no other money, and the States would not pay their taxes; and specific supplies were made almost impossible of obtainment by the very law that authorized them.

Why ruin did not happen

What then prevented utter dissolution of the patriot mechanism?—The element of luck cannot be left out of account; but also a few great general causes left enough organized power in the Union to wait the opportunity for one of those considerable destructions of British force which the struggling and party-rent empire could not retrieve.

No choice but per- sistence

First of all, it had to fight whether or no, as there was no longer an olive-branch held out to accept. A really sincere peace commission in the early fall of 1780 would have been a dire temptation to the Middle States at least. But even the simulacrum of the year before was abandoned;

that gathering of second-rate men secretly disavowed by their superiors, the British army couched to spring, and the war carried on while the offers were making in such a way as to render their acceptance a shame to self-respect—imagine voting to dissolve the Union and break the French treaty in the teeth of Wyoming! The government had never meant them except as ammunition for its party in Parliament, so it gladly dropped them and threw its whole soul into inflicting injury purely for injury's sake. With not even colonial autonomy offered,[1] and nothing beyond reunion but a hard-bridled existence under the heel of exultant and contemptuous foreigners and their own loyalists inflamed with revenge, it was harder at the very worst period to go back than forward. There was nothing but wearily and stubbornly to hold out till the last, for subjection offered no worse than submission.

This policy was enabled to succeed by the open or secret banding together of Continental Europe against Great Britain heretofore referred to. England thus compelled to make war all over the globe at once, its forces assignable to wear out America were so slender that commonplace casualties of war crippled the active corps, and the first

*1780
Jan.-
Sept.*

Nominal British concessions withdrawn

America forced to fight

Reasons of success

---

[1] It is true that Clinton, in his instructions to Cornwallis before leaving South Carolina, promised that as soon as feasible after the war was ended, the Southern conquered colonies should have practically the autonomy offered by the peace commission. But this was unofficial and not binding even morally on the British government, and local in its application at best; and the steady ruining of the great indifferent middle class that went on under it was sufficient warning to others not to lay down their arms.

serious mischance left the extreme party unable to carry the country with it in replacing them.

The never-dying English hope was that of "conquering America by the Americans,"—enlisting the Tories. The rear of the Carolinas was still believed so dominantly loyalist that at the approach of a British army the major part would rise in a body, and with a small nucleus of regulars would furnish force enough to hold down the provinces. Special faith was pinned to Cross Creek (Fayetteville), North Carolina, a noted settlement of Highlanders. There was a basis of truth in the conception: but it overrated the proportion of Tories: it overlooked the ideal conditions of the Southern country and climate for guerrilla warfare, impossible in the North; and—the chief element in its failure—it presupposed a wish to understand and an effort to gratify colonial feeling and interests, which even as to loyalists were foreign to the temper of the government and its leading agents, and still more, ran counter to the latter's interests.

The scheme was in fact baffled by the logical consequences of the government's own policy of spite and hate, which kept aflame in very desperation the untamable spirit and unquenchable patriotic zeal of the Carolinians and their children the Tennessee borderers. These carried on more than a year of incessant Lexingtons amid forest and swamp, mostly fighting without pay and furnishing their own supplies from their or the loyalists' war-wasted farms; fighting the British and

1779-81

The Carolina scheme

Why it failed

A boomerang

waging a ferocious civil war with their own Tories both at once, till victory and defeat which alike drained their foes made final victory possible. And the new but equally illusory American currency was eked out by foreign specie, and the larger work of life and war enabled to go on.

The prizes to be won, however, account for visionary hopes that forgot means. The capture of Charleston alone would impair the patriot strength incalculably: it was the chief supply station for the whole South, the grand rendezvous of foreign vessels and of privateers with their prizes. The wealth of the province as a whole we have noted, and the flaming greed it inspired.

Admiral Arbuthnot in August had brought Clinton 1500 fresh men; the next month 1500 more came from Ireland; in October Clinton evacuated Rhode Island and the Hudson forts altogether, concentrating his whole force at New York; and on the 1st of December he had 28,756 soldiers there. Washington had not 10,000 in the flesh, and Clinton could easily spare troops enough, with the 3930 already in Georgia and Beaufort, to capture Charleston during the winter months when a Northern campaign against him was difficult. He estimated that he could take a force to Charleston by sea in ten days, and he now had Arbuthnot's extra fleet for a convoy; while Washington must send reinforcements by land, a three-months' journey in winter. Clinton therefore on the day after Christmas left Knyphausen in command at New York, and sailed south with ample

1780–1

Clinton's delay an American disaster

artillery and stores and 8500 men, including 250 cavalry with their mounts. But the vessels were scattered by storms, some sunk with most of the artillery and all the horses, some captured by the American cruisers; and it was the 11th of February before the refitted remnant arrived at John's Island thirty miles below Charleston. The delay doubled his prize. Had he been a month earlier, Lincoln would have evacuated the ill-fortified town without blame; the long warning enabled the construction of works just enough better to excuse the civil authorities for compelling Lincoln to keep his army in the trap.

Rutledge made dictator

The South Carolina Assembly was in session at Charleston; it at once adjourned, the military officers included in it rejoining the army. But previously it conferred on Rutledge, "and such of the Council as he could conveniently consult," "till ten days after their next session," dictatorial power of the most sweeping kind, extending to everything needed to carry on the war except taking citizens' lives. As it held no more sessions while the British occupied the State, and the other leaders were nearly all dead, fled, or captive, Rutledge for the next two years after Charleston surrendered practically constituted the entire government. He now issued a call for the 2000 or so militia of the ten-weeks' draft, as well as the townsmen, to join the garrison at once, "under pain of confiscation." Clinton issued a counter one, and the British threats were much the more formidable. The militia did not respond; those

Threat and counter-threat

CHARLESTON IN 1780.

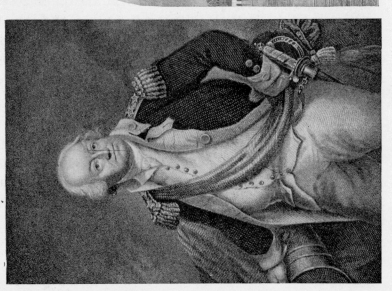

BENJAMIN LINCOLN.

from the camps at Augusta and Camden alleged fear of the small-pox which had repeatedly desolated Charleston; though Lincoln indignantly denied that there was any.

1779–80

Militia
hang
back

Washington had guessed the objective of the expedition when he heard of its fitting out; and early in December sent Lincoln his North Carolina brigade of 700, of whom 600 reached him March 3. Long before Clinton started, Lincoln had also sent Colonel Laurens to Washington for help; and Washington on December 14 denuded his petty force still further by dispatching the entire Virginia Continentals, something over 3000. He urged their going by water from Head of Elk on Chesapeake Bay, because their native State lay on their road and probably many would desert; which added to fatigue, sickness, and time-expiry on so long a land march, would leave but a small band on arrival. Congress instead sent them by water only to Williamsburg; and for some reason three-fourths never went forward, only 750 under General Woodford arriving April 7, after a march of 500 miles in 28 days. About 100 cavalry had joined him under Colonels William Washington (a second cousin of the General) and Anthony White. But the promised Virginia militia never materialized, nor the North Carolina save a few: while the term of the latter's brigade expired March 24, and only 170 of 1000 could be induced by liberal bounties to remain, even the general decamping. Some South Carolina militia, overcoming their fear of the small-pox,

Deple-
tion

partly made good the loss; but even at the last
Lincoln had under 5000 men, and till Woodford's
arrival little over 4000, more than half militia
who would take no orders from him.

Clinton, hearing of Lincoln's expected reinforcements, called 1200 more from Savannah, and
sent on to New York for Francis Hastings, Lord
Rawdon,[1] to join him with 3000 others. Even before these came, he had about 10,500 splendid
troops, or two to three times Lincoln's largely raw
and insubordinate numbers; and Lincoln should
not have cooped up himself in face of such overwhelming odds. The extreme value of the town
and its stores to the patriots, and his orders from
Congress, were pleaded by him in justification for
a forlorn defense; and were such for making his
best fight within the limits of safety, but not for
losing army and town both when the latter became
untenable. The chief culprits, however, were Congress itself, which had disgraced St. Clair for
doing exactly that after its own laches had forced
him to it, and by its uproarious unreason was
terrorizing every officer into reckless follies to
save professional ruin and public shame; and the
local leaders, as will be seen.

This granted, Lincoln did in most respects the
things he should not have done, aided by able
coadjutors. Clinton blocked the harbor with his
fleet, and sent detachments to take possession of

---

[1]Afterwards Earl of Moira and Marquis of Hastings, and Governor-
General of India, as Cornwallis had been. Both figured to much better advantage on the larger field, and left a good name as statesmen.

all the channels and cut-offs and gradually surround the peninsula; but acted with such caution,
intrenching as he went, that it was March 29 before
he crossed the Ashley and lay athwart the main
line of retreat to the north, even then leaving one
open. Lincoln had more than seven weeks to
make the best defense possible and still escape.

1780
Feb.–
April

Congress had sent three frigates under Captain
Abraham Whipple to co-operate with Fort Moultrie in defending the harbor. Heavy ships could
not cross the bar without taking off most of their
guns and being at his mercy; but he and his
captains declared the inner shoal so broad they
could not lie near enough to command the bar,—
which seems odd, as the enemy had to cross the
same shoal before re-arming,—and advised moor-
ing opposite the fort, for both to rake the vessels
after they were across and in fighting trim. It
still seems incredible that Whipple shortly became
frightened even to do that, and on his representation Lincoln allowed the frigates to be drawn up
to the Charleston docks and their 152 guns used
in the city intrenchments. One feels a pang yet
to think of the many Vikings at that moment
afloat on American vessels, full of dauntless pluck.
On the 7th of April Arbuthnot's fleet ran past
Fort Moultrie—which alone could not much harm
a squadron that did not stop to bombard it—with
only the loss of a store-ship and a few men.

Unheroic
American
seamen

British
fleet
occupies
harbor

Washington on this news saw at once that the
town was no longer tenable; and Lincoln should
have seen it. Before this, indeed the game was

up. His natural defense was at Ashley Ferry, where a broad deep river and impassable flanking swamps gave enormous vantage; but if he stripped the Charleston lines for this, the British numbers enabled part to detain him while the rest crossed below and captured the town. Even so, however, it would have been no worse off and he would have saved the army. In a word, he had not force enough to hold it. The investment was so far completed on April 10 that Clinton sent a summons to surrender; Lincoln refused, though now his only retreat was across the Cooper, here an estuary four miles wide.

On the 13th, however, Lincoln sent Rutledge and some of the Council out of town, Lieutenant-Governor Gadsden and others remaining; then he called a council of war and told them the works could hold out but few days longer. Even the fiery McIntosh was warm for evacuating; but Lincoln came to no decision, and for six days could get no business done in the councils he repeatedly called, they were so interrupted—a uniquely eloquent portrayal of utter insubordination, showing the reverse side of the intractable Southern independence which held out so tenaciously. It must be remembered all through that Lincoln was allowed authority only over his Continentals, not the militia; those were under the orders of their State governments, and Gadsden *vice* Rutledge claimed command of the South-Carolinians.

On that very night (13th) the one retreat was nearly closed up. Communication with the

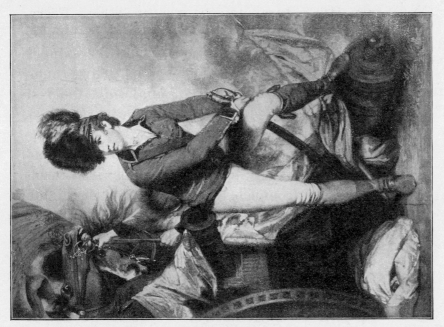

TARLETON.

(Print from the New York Public Library.)

LORD RAWDON.

interior was maintained by a force under General Isaac Huger, with William Washington, Major John Jameson, Pulaski's Legion under Major Vernier, and some militia. It was now lying at Monck's Corner, at the head of the Cooper. Against it were dispatched a group of officers later to become widely famous or notorious: Lieutenant-Colonel Banastre Tarleton, with his "British Legion" of cavalry and light infantry (regulars but raised in New York), and a body of marksmen under the Scotchman Major Patrick Ferguson, slain at King's Mountain; while Lieutenant-Colonel James Webster, another Scot also of much worth, brought more troops and took chief command. Tarleton with Ferguson in a night surprise entirely dispersed Huger's force with great loss,[1] Vernier being refused quarter and savagely mangled (for "Tarleton's quarter" was begun at his arrival). The roads from the Cooper were at once guarded, though not very tightly, and the investment steadily pushed on.

1780
April
3–19

The
Monck's
Corner
force

Broken
up by
Tarleton

---

[1] Some of Tarleton's dragoons broke into the house of a rich and titled loyalist and outraged (or attempted it) several ladies of high position, cutting them with swords to force submission. Ferguson would have had the brutes hanged, but Webster turned them over to Clinton, who let them off at most with a whipping, even that dubious,—a fine method of stimulating loyalty. Tarleton's spirit was not likely to make women safe where his men were. It was reported in England after the war that he boasted of having "killed more men and abused) more women than any other man in America." This if true was of course mere brutal mess-room brag, but it gives the measure of the man; and even if pure invention it shows his repute among his companions—no one can fancy such a story invented about Cornwallis. Tarleton was one of "the Prince of Wales' set" (afterwards George IV.), as were Rawdon and Hanger. He was in essence a typical English squire of the coarser type—energetic, narrow, violent, and gross.

1780
April
19–21

Civilians
will not
permit
retreat

On the 19th a council was finally got to stay together. The best officers were for attempting a retreat still; but Gadsden and his Council were allowed a share as commanders of the militia, and Lincoln engaged to do nothing without their permission. They declared that the militia were utterly averse to giving up, and Gadsden's brother-in-law blustered that if the Continentals attempted to leave the place, he and the other citizens would open the gates to the enemy and help them assault the Americans.[1] Colonel C. C. Pinckney from Fort Moultrie came over and stormed in like manner. Lincoln's life during these days was in fact one long torture of insult and bullying from almost every official native to the State. Washington and all the Continental forces together could hardly have held the town under such conditions, unable to obtain obedience or even outward decency.

Lincoln on the 21st, after proposing terms of capitulation which Clinton flatly refused, held a council which gave up the idea of evacuation on account of the civil hostility, and because for lack of boats the British would overtake them before

---

[1] The most curious and significant feature of the whole business is, that from first to last even the most patriotic of the civilians, like Gadsden, were determined that if the town had to surrender, the army should stay and go with it. They looked on the latter apparently as a self-seeking body who were proposing to sneak out of a trouble they had engaged to share with the town, and must take their punishment like the rest. Over and over this fact is brought out, that the citizen body would consent to capture, but not to the army's evacuating. They seem hardly to have looked upon the Union as their own, but as a semi-foreign body which had long refused to help them in a scrape it had dragged them into, and now was about to save its own interests harmless from the wreck of theirs; and they were bound it should not.

they reached the Santee; and the hopeless fight and sorties went on. On the 26th the French engineer Duportail came from Washington, examined the situation, and said the British might have taken the town ten days before. A council of war again proposed evacuation; again citizens came and told Lincoln that if he attempted it, they would smash his boats and open the gates to the British. The State authorities, however, were making strenuous efforts to collect the militia, who with the North-Carolinians were to gather on the Santee and try to effect a diversion. Lincoln's hopes rose; but on May 6 Tarleton routed a body at Lenuds' Ferry, and the next day Fort Moultrie surrendered with 200 men.

During the 8th and 9th Lincoln obtained a cessation of hostilities to discuss terms of surrender; but those with regard to the militia and citizens were too hard for the civilian authorities to swallow, and the next night a fresh and terrific bombardment was opened. On the 10th they yielded; and on the 11th, just as the British were preparing to storm, Lincoln sent a flag agreeing to Clinton's terms. On the 12th the surrender was effected; and the British came into possession of the virtual capital of the South, with 157 cannon, some 50,000 pounds of powder, and large stores, and 5684 prisoners comprising all the adult males in the place, Tories and invalids included. Perhaps 2700 were Continentals, of whom 245 were commissioned officers—not so absurd a disproportion as it seems, for the final success of the war was largely due

1780
April 26–
May

Hopeless
struggles

Charleston sur-
renders

Forces
taken

1780
May 1
et seq.

to the ability of the many officers, who kept their men up to the mark.

The Continental troops were of course regular prisoners of war, subject to exchange. The terms

Terms of citizen surrender

of surrender for the militia and other citizens are of vital importance, and to be carefully noted; since both the legal and the practical aspects of the Southern war turned upon their wanton alteration by Clinton, after he had gained the conquest by granting them. They followed the old policy of putting the entire populations out of the field of war as fast as conquered, by constituting them prisoners of war on parole, to be *neutrals* as long as they refrained from resuming part in it.

Clinton remained there to reconstitute the civil government, and sent Cornwallis into the interior

South Carolina overrun

to seize and fortify the chief remaining posts, put down attempts at resistance, and capture Rutledge and the rest of the Council if possible. Cornwallis sent one division up the Savannah to Augusta, the patriot capital of Georgia, just over the State border; another to Ninety-Six on the Saluda (ninety-six miles from Keowee, the easternmost Cherokee town), the chief frontier fortress of the northwest, on the main Indian trade line; Tarleton to Georgetown, on the coast north of Charleston; and himself marched to Camden on the Wateree, the great centre of the roads from the North above the swamps and wide rivers of the lowlands.

No resistance was encountered anywhere: the people sent out flags and similarly surrendered on parole. Clinton's task, though it had taken him months instead of the expected weeks owing to his extreme caution, seemed crowned with fulfillment: the State was again a British colony, and a large and probably controlling body of citizens under heavy bonds against fresh revolt. To a great extent this was so with their fair good-will; and it needed only moderation, tact, and above all good faith, to retain it, and permanently deprive the Union of its two southernmost members at least. And now a series of rough-shod violations of all at once—the results of brutal passion, sectarian rancor and ignorance, greed, over-confident impatience, and contempt for the colonies' right to exact the keeping of promises—undid the whole, and drained the life-blood of the British invasion.

Lieutenant-Colonel Abraham Buford, with some 400 Continentals, had been waiting at Nelson's Ferry on the Santee for a chance to reinforce Lincoln; on the surrender he retreated in all haste toward Salisbury, North Carolina, via Camden. Tarleton, kept informed by Tories, made forced marches toward him; and after accomplishing 154 miles in 54 hours, came up with him on the 29th at the Waxhaws, near the North Carolina border. By a furious charge he cut down Buford's rear-guard to a man, the commandant being mangled as Vernier had been. Buford sent forward a white flag, but the bearer was instantly butchered.[1] The

Margin notes:
1780
May

What British policy should have been

And was not

Buford

Attacked by Tarleton

---

[1] Tarleton's defense—for even he came to realize that it needed one —was that his horse was shot under him just as the flag was raised, and his men thought him killed and killed the bearer in revenge. He does not say that he tried to check the massacre which followed.

Americans, taking it as a signal that quarter was refused, attempted to resume the arms they had grounded; this was the excuse Tarleton had been seeking, and with his dragoons he plunged among
them and began one of the most atrocious massacres in modern history. Not a man who could be caught was spared, nor a cry for quarter heeded; 263 were felled on the spot, the American-British searching the ground and bayoneting any who showed signs of life, even lifting corpses off living men to murder the latter. Of the whole, 150 were still breathing when paroled on the ground by Tarleton, but mostly died afterward; 53, rounded up later, were able to be taken along as prisoners.

"Tarleton's quarter" became a byword still remembered, and that rang through the Union.
If its object was to intimidate the patriots,—probably it was mere unthinking delight in "energy," like Grey,—it had the reverse effect. The population there was mainly recent Scotch-Irish immigrants, who having no State representation were not afflicted over the State's lack of Parliamentary representation, and whose most abhorred tyrants were the horse-thieves: generally they were either indifferent or preferred the British government. But this monstrous butchery under their own eyes roused them to horror and fury, and created a patriot district where there had been none. The density to political common-sense of many English leaders is shown by Clinton's outspoken delight in the affair, and Cornwallis' tacit approval.

Another embodiment of unintelligent British violence had even deeper effects: it resulted from dull men's adherence to a catchword without examining facts. For a century and a half "Dissenter" had been to the Anglican Briton a synonym of rebellion; it was so in Scotland, and in the northern colonies the Dissenters were the originators and mainstays of the Revolution. It was assumed that the same must be the case in the South, though there the Dissenting immigrants were largely passive and often the very backbone of loyalism, and the British made systematic war against all implements or belongings of the sects: burning their meeting-houses, their pastors' dwellings, their books, especially all Bibles with the Scotch Psalms in them; and making a stable out of their meeting-house in Charleston, as they had a riding-school of the Old South Church in Boston. No more senseless folly was perpetrated in the whole Revolution. Of all enmities, that of desecrated and insulted religion is the deadliest; and this outrage in the South was oftenest against friends.

Now too arose the dazzling vision of loot, to close the eyes of the commanders to any political ends whatever. The booty gained in Prevost's short raid had been so enormous that it set the whole British army on fire with cupidity. Whether a campaign succeeded or not in its ultimate purposes, there were fortunes for officers and soldiers in its course; and Clinton, and Cornwallis after him, turned theirs into sheer organized gutting

1778–82

Foolish
outrages
on
South-
erners

Visions
of
pillage

1780
May–
June

South
Carolina
plun-
dered on
system

British
forces a
vast
looting
asso-
ciation

of the province of all its movable wealth, not forgetting pure destruction to cripple the patriots.
The almost mediæval ravage and outrage it involved turned masses of the neutrals into active
patriots, for they could hardly suffer worse, friend
and foe being despoiled impartially. The outspoken loyalists, it is true, were given "receipts,"
orders for payment on the paymaster-general at
Charleston. But the suspected or neutrals were
given only "certificates," payable at the end of the
war if they behaved themselves; and as the divi-
dends of the looters depended on the difference
between what was taken and what was repaid,
most people were accounted suspects, and the
amounts receipted for to either class were perhaps
apt to be auction rates. As the pillaged families
could not afford to wait, they sold the certificates
at a great discount to speculators, and were often
practically ruined.

Tobacco, indigo, and general stores, were seized
and sold in open market for the army account at
knock-down prices, yet to such extent that a major-
general's share was over £4000; and the entire
amount distributed was over £300,000. The army
and navy quarreled bitterly as to their respective
shares of spoil, and carried the question up to the
government. The individual plunder was often
greater yet; and households were sacked as described under Prevost. Thousands more of negroes were carried out of the province and sold,
over 2000 at a single shipment. Numbers of others
crowded around the British encampments, and

LORD CORNWALLIS IN LATER LIFE.

LORD CORNWALLIS IN YOUTH.

SIR HENRY CLINTON

from hunger, exposure, and an epidemic of small-pox were carried off by hundreds, lying unburied in the woods. All industry was crippled by this enormous depletion of the laboring class.

1780
May-
June

All this was bad enough: Clinton and his sub-ordinates within three weeks had turned a great share of the neutral population into fierce and im-placable foes, compacting all but the hide-bound Tories into irreconcilable and despairing hostility to everything British. But now Clinton—with that heaven-sent thickness of perception which dominated so much of British action in America, and saved or rounded off the great Union despite its own weakness—capped the climax by releasing the entire neutralized population from their pa-roles at a blow, and forcing all patriots not only to fight him, but "with a halter around their necks."

British
rouse
swift
reaction

Clinton was anxious to return to New York. It had taken so much longer to capture South Caro-lina than he forecast that it was now June, and the heat would make the projected campaign up into Virginia dangerous; with the warm weather Wash-ington might venture a stroke against New York; and a French fleet was known to be on the way, which would make the sea voyage perilous. He therefore on June 1 issued a letter of instructions to Cornwallis, of the most proper and sensible kind to anchor the province to its new loyalty: promis-ing full pardon for rebellion, protection to all who avoided active participation in it for the future, and holding out the hope of colonial autonomy as soon as the situation would permit. But the next

Clinton's
outlook

Instruc-
tions to
Corn-
wallis

1780
June 1-3

Clinton
revokes
terms of
neutral-
ity
two days, either by his own meditation or the advice of some evil genius, worked an entire revolution in his mind. It came to him that this policy of neutralizing the people was directly incompatible with the primary one of "conquering America by the Americans," and compelling all who would avoid expulsion or ruin to aid actively in holding down the irreconcilables. On June 3, two days before he sailed for New York, he issued a proclamation that all civilians under parole should be thenceforward restored to the rights and duties of citizens,—that is, liable to military service,—and all who should refuse allegiance should be treated as enemies and rebels.

The excuse for this was, that there being no longer any rebellion in South Carolina, the state of things contemplated by the paroles had ceased, and the province must be regarded as on its old status. But this was a shabbily dishonorable pretext for breach of faith. The paroles were for the war with the Continental government, which was still going on; and the present claim would make them a farce from the start, as the very fact of their being taken would invalidate them as soon as given. In a word, Clinton, having saved a bloody contest by giving terms for a surrender, at once broke the terms on the ground that the surrender ended the status to gain which the terms were accepted by the vanquished. The effect was speedily visible.

Cornwallis was left with some 4000 men to occupy the State. The line of seaports, Savannah,

Beaufort, Charleston, and Georgetown, was firmly garrisoned, the latter with Tories. The rest of the troops were disposed mainly in a line through the north, to hold down the border and form nuclei and protections for the Tory sentiment to group around. The main body was at Camden under Rawdon, with Tarleton and Hamilton. Northeast at Cheraw, near the North Carolina line, a body under McArthur kept open the communication with Georgetown, and held out a hand to the coveted Highlanders at Cross Creek. A post under Turnbull at Rocky Mount above Camden on the same stream (there called Catawba), with Ferguson's corps and some loyal militia on the move, preserved the communications with Ninety-Six under Balfour. Browne commanded at Augusta. Rawdon with a detachment went forward to the Waxhaws where Buford's command had been massacred, expecting an eager welcome; naïvely astonished at not finding it, he withdrew to Camden, establishing a post at Hanging Rock as a half-way house.

To effect the object of the proclamation, Cornwallis sent parties through the State, under officers with full military and civil powers, enrolling the inhabitants to draft a British militia force. Some of the quieter patriots submitted under duress; to the disgust and wrath of their Tory neighbors, who complained that rebels fared as well as loyalists. The latter acted as informers and volunteer servants of order, and roved about in bands, plundering, committing murders, wreaking old grudges

1780
June

Disposition of British troops

Rawdon disappointed in Waxhaws

Cornwallis' registration parties

(often deadly enough, for the patriots had given them awful measure during their own ascendency), and compelling their foes to defend themselves for life and property and honor; this was counted rebellion as had been desired, estates were confiscated, Tory debts discharged, patriots' dwellings burned, and the country plunged into anarchy and civil war.

It is hard to tell which were the aggressors in many cases: the patriots certainly did their share of murders, tortures, plunders, and so on, not only on active British agents, but on those who refused to join the patriot side. But the primary guilt was on Clinton and Cornwallis and their under officers, who were after spoil instead of the legitimate objects of the campaign; and could have kept decent order, and saved the worst of the anarchic savagery and desolation of the next two years, if they had honestly and single-mindedly set themselves to the task. Back of them still lay the ministry, who had ordered them to conduct just such a warfare, and even a worse one than they actually did (for the Indians were not much called into it in this period), and on whose heads the blood must finally rest.

Now began a new and thrilling period of the war, full of romance and deeds imperishably dear to memory. It was a guerrilla warfare unsurpassed for picturesqueness, tenacity, and ultimate decisiveness; suffering many defeats, sometimes reduced almost to the last straits, yet winning frequent victories, always important in such a field, often considerable, sometimes of crushing and vital magnitude, and opening the way for the final triumph. It was headed by men of sterling patriotism, matchless resource, heroism, endurance, and power of leadership, sometimes the highest qualities of lofty and generous knighthood;[1] seldom daunted by odds, never dismayed by defeat, never discouraged by utter inadequacy of means. With commands scant of numbers, of ammunition, of clothes, of shelter, sometimes of food, rarely having artillery, not often having bayonets, they cut off the British supply convoys, ambushed or openly assailed their detachments, broke up their outposts or kept them helpless, harassed or delayed the greater movements; hiding in forests and swamps and mountain fastnesses, issuing for night surprises and long forced marches and sudden onslaughts wherever advantage could be obtained.

The chief of these in popular memory, chief also in strategic capacity and craft and resource, was Francis Marion. Yet he had far the smallest means, rarely commanding over seventy men and often not a third that: with ammunition so short that more than once they went into a fight with but three rounds to a man, glad to eke out their bullets by the waste shots of the enemy lodged in trees, or slugs hammered from pewter dishes; with swords forged from the cross-cut saws of

1780-1

*The great
partisan
leaders*

Marion

---

[1] It is odd that the greatest of these leaders belonged to the moderate section; one of the two greatest (Sumter) being even suspected and nearly refused a commission as a Tory at the outset, and none of them having taken any part in the violence against the Tories.

1780–1

Marion

the dismantled sawmills. He was a planter of Huguenot stock from near Georgetown, and an actor in the Indian wars; now forty-seven; short and slight; reserved, modest, tender-hearted, and sympathetic, the soul of honor and courtesy, with feminine and masculine characteristics mingled in the rarest harmony. He would not burn a house, nor destroy a growing crop, nor take provisions save for absolute need; he hated "distressing women and children," and he kept his commands from all ill conduct as did few either of British or American leaders: but his alertness of mind and quickness of action, his unerring perception of where and when to assail the enemy and his lightning energy and tireless endurance in doing so, and his power of warding blows from his own long inaccessible hiding-places, were unparalleled. "The Swamp Fox," his friends called him in exultation and his foes in admiring anger.[1]

Sumter

Thomas Sumter was esteemed even above him by Cornwallis, who styled him "our greatest plague in the country," and said that "but for Sumter and Marion, South Carolina would be at peace." He was as unlike Marion as a brave man and stout soldier could well be: tall, powerful,

---

[1] By a strange chance, Marion was saved to the cause by what seemed likely to end his usefulness for a while. While commanding a body of horse before Savannah while Clinton was investing it, he had left it and gone into town; and while at a party, the host, after the jovial usage of that hard-drinking time, turned the key on the crowd to keep them in till all were drunk. Marion was delicate, disliked such bestialities, and thought it incompatible with his duty; he jumped from a window, dislocated his ankle, and was sent out of the town, escaping capture with the rest.

THOMAS SUMTER.

WILLIAM RICHARDSON DAVIE.

FRANCIS MARION.

stern in manner, rough and somewhat ruthless in his methods; "less inclined to plan than to execute," said his companion Henry Lee, but of tremendous force in execution; suffering great disasters from haste or recklessness, but always retrieving them; as unconciliatory as Arnold, but like him in his best days a whole-souled patriot and a generous man, willing to submit himself to broader plans. He was forty-six; had been at Braddock's defeat, and with Thompson at the battle of Fort Moultrie, and till lately was living as a retired planter; lived to be United States Senator and minister to Brazil, and attain the immense age of ninety-eight.

Another distinguished leader of this new warfare was William Richardson Davie, of English birth and Scotch blood, now twenty-four, reared in America since five; a graduate of Princeton and a law student; a tall, graceful, handsome, high-souled young knight, magnanimous, daring, vigilant, active, and enduring; a superb horseman and consummate orator. To equip a body of troops he had sold a considerable estate just inherited. Davie's corps, though fitted out by himself, was regularly commissioned by North Carolina; the immortal bands of the others were pure volunteers without pay, coming and going as occasion served. Some of their lesser helpers bear still noted names. The Horrys,—Daniel, Hugh, and Peter, to the last of whom we owe a most entertaining account of Marion's career,—the Hamptons, the Taylors, the Postells, James and Lacey and Witherspoon, and

1780-1

Sumter

Davie

others, with their great chiefs formed a body of
partisan warriors never surpassed.

With these were other men of power and leadership who joined in tremendous blows at the
enemy here or farther north on the border: Elijah Clarke, James Williams, William Campbell, Isaac Shelby, John Sevier, Charles Mc-
Dowell, Benjamin Cleveland, Andrew Pickens;
some constantly in the field, some as called on.

Fortunately for the cause, the first effort of the
North Carolina Tories to gratify the British hopes
was premature, and its defeat by the patriots discouraged them so utterly that they never again
organized during the war. This is a measure of
the respective energies and determination of the
parties; for the loyalists' defeat was not nearly so
severe as those suffered by the patriots over and
over. But it was the third for the North-Carolinians; and while Moore's Creek and Kettle
Creek had daunted the Scotch part, Ramsour's
Mill daunted the Germans, who had had no idea
of entering on a war, and only meant to return
to their duty as required by Cornwallis' agent.

Cornwallis, however, had expressly charged
them to stay at home till his forces were ready to
come to them, about the last of August. But his
messenger Lieutenant-Colonel Moore, fired by
chasing a patriot band who were after the Tory
leaders, collected some 1300 men at Ramsour's.
There on June 20 they were attacked by Colonel
Francis Locke with about 400 patriots, knowing
themselves immensely outnumbered, but resolved

Margin notes:

1780–1

Other
leaders

Battle
of Ram-
sour's
Mill

Its
effects

Prema-
ture
rising

to risk it rather than leave the patriot families exposed. After a disorderly engagement in which each side lost about 35 killed and 100 wounded, the Tories were crowded off their first position but formed a new line. The Whig remnant waited for General Rutherford, who had gathered a force to oppose Rawdon's march to the Waxhaws, and was hurrying toward them a few miles off; but the Tories, who did not know this, sent a flag for a suspension of hostilities, and meantime took to their heels or horses and dispersed. About 50 were captured, but some 800 under one Bryan made their way to the British camp in the Cheraws. That very draining off of the hot blood kept the home district quiet.

1780
June 20

Battle
of Ram-
sour's
Mill

The South Carolina Scotch were of different mettle. Those in Charleston remained generally passive; but the traders and their retinue in the Piedmont country, with many others loyalist from tradition, conviction, or interest, rose with the British advance as had been expected, and enlarged the scope of the sanguinary civil war.

It must be remembered also that while a great part of the Tory element were as respectable citizens as the patriots, it included practically the whole of the blacklegs and outcasts who infested the borders; so that in this district "Tory" and "robber" were almost synonymous. Fugitives from justice, the bohemians and lawless, all the scum and wreckage of society, naturally gravitated to the districts too far from organized legal force to be reached by it; and in the Revolution of course this class sided with foreign authority which could not control them, against local autonomy which would make that its business. Many of both sides disgraced the cause they professed by using it as a pretext for pillage and revenge, like the Skinners and Cowboys of the North; nevertheless the patriots as a whole represented the cause of civilized order and a respectable future.

Southern
Tories
vs.
patriots

The special actions in this mêlée of confusion are rich in interest, and some were of much consequence. In one month, from July 12 to August 12, the improvised bands of patriots with their voluntarily chosen leaders, with not a Continental soldier in the State except prisoners, fought twelve engagements worth calling battles, killing and wounding some 300 British and Tories and taking about 200 prisoners, with less than half that loss to themselves. But our space will allow only a brief mention of the most significant, and their result in sum. In fact, their importance is as a whole rather than individually. They cut down the British strength and crippled its action; they kept the Tories broken up and the inner sections either Whig-ruled or in anarchy, preventing the organization of that civil district dominated by loyalism which was the centre of the British scheme; they kept alive the hope of redemption, and made a promising field for the coming Continental army. Moreover, they organized and kept in action an invaluable body of cavalry scouts as auxiliaries to that army, and developed a host of leaders with abilities rising to genius.

Early
partisan
battles

Results

Just before Tarleton's massacre, two attempts were made by Tories to organize west and north of Rocky Mount; the Whigs dispersed them. Turnbull, to reduce the latter and back the Tory assemblings, sent Christian Huck, a Philadelphia lawyer in regular British service, who had accompanied Tarleton's Legion to the South and made good its reputation for violence and cruelty. With 115 men he marched along sacking and burning houses and desolating the country,—burning as a Whig rendezvous one settlement entire, with the only iron works which made farm tools for fifty miles around; men were wantonly murdered, and women beaten and all but murdered for information; and Huck with Tarletonian folly banded the deep religious feeling of the people against him by blasphemous scurrilities.

Some 500 Whigs gathered to drive him off. About dawn of July 12 they burst on him at Williamson's Plantation just below the Waxhaws: after an hour's struggle in which he was slain, his men took to flight, and the Whigs in a pursuit of fourteen miles exacted a terrible revenge for Tarleton's massacre, though they granted quarter when asked; 30 to 40 of Huck's force were killed and some 50 wounded. This action was of pivotal importance for the cause. The Whigs, enrolled under penalty as loyal citizens, had risen and defeated a regular British detachment and slain the commander: for their very lives and families they must cast their lot with their country now, without retreat, and the result of the battle heartened the

1780
June–
July

Huck
sent to
put down
Whigs

Force
de-
stroyed
at
William·
son's
Plant·
ation

timid. Within a few days Sumter's little camp was swollen by 600 volunteers.

Patrick Ferguson with 150 or so of his "American Volunteers" [1] had gone to Ninety-Six. Bearing a full civil and military commission, he set up a camp at Little River, sixteen miles beyond Ninety-Six, and announced a policy of conciliation and grace. He won the hearts of all classes by his condescension in talking and arguing loyalty with endless patience and gentleness, and urging on the people considerations of mingled duty and interest. Great numbers of Tories flocked to him, and were enrolled in regiments and companies, and officers commissioned from them; one Tory leader placed sixty-two commissions. Hosts of the outlaws and blacklegs and shiftless or poverty-ridden of the district, as well as ambitious youth and honest zealots, came to his standard; and he drilled and trained them as sedulously as he explained their loyal duties. By August 20, according to Cornwallis, Ferguson had "formed seven battalions of militia consisting of about 4000 men,"

*1780
July*

Ferguson's successful policy

---

[1] Ferguson was regarded as the best marksman in the army, perhaps in the world; invented the breech-loading rifle; was given command of a picked rifle-corps which did good service at Brandywine, Germantown, and Monmouth; demolished Pulaski's Legion at Little Egg Harbor; and came south with Clinton, at the head of a regular British corps of 300 raised in America and hence styled "American Volunteers," with 200 Hessians under Major Hanger, a brave but profligate man. He was as dashing, as resolute, and as firm in repressing enemies, as Tarleton, and carried on a war of ravage with as little wavering or mercy. But this to him was war, or the sort of war to which he was committed; outside it he was no brutal dragoon, but a man of character and humanity. He sternly repressed wanton murder and outrage,—witness Tarleton's ravishers,—and he was of statesmanlike insight and policy.

of whom 1500 could be collected at short notice. At the same time he and his detachments kept on the move, beating up the country from the Saluda to the Catawba and around, and putting down the Whigs with merciless pillage and devastation.

But the Whigs had burned their boats behind them and were rising all through the north-northwest, near the North Carolina line and the mountain region. For four nights and the next day in succession, beginning with the signal engagement at Williamson's, there were Whig victories and severe British losses.

At Fair Forest Creek southeast of the present Spartanburg, on the night of the 13th, a British party of 150 attempting to surprise a Whig band rushed headlong into an ambush and were routed with heavy loss. The next night the remainder were dispersed, 32 captured and one killed, by an onslaught of Colonel John Jones with an advance party (35) of Elijah Clarke's coming to join the patriots, and who by pretending to be loyalists induced a Tory to lead them to the camp; they then joined McDowell on the Pacolet. From Prince's Fort twenty miles south, 70 dragoons and some loyalists under Major Dunlap, a twin spirit of Tarleton, started after Jones and surprised the combined body on the night of the 15th; but were driven off, though with heavy American loss. Before sunrise Captain Edward Hampton and 52 men, on picked horses, were on Dunlap's track; they overtook his force fifteen miles farther on and routed them with many killed and wounded, pursuing them to near the fort and capturing 35 horses and much baggage without losing a man.

This utterly unlooked-for rekindling of insurrection was counted by the British commanders as "treachery" from those who had submitted, regardless of the fact that they had freed every one from obligation by their own treachery. They were disappointed and enraged beyond measure at their easy glories and flattering triumphs being dashed in this way to their home discredit; and kept no measure in their punishment of it when they got hold of those thought to be ringleaders. The Whigs on their part hanged any number of those who had taken the oath to the Revolutionary government and then joined the English. Neutrality was annihilated: hundreds were between two fires, liable to execution by either side if they joined the other. The savagery of a warfare under such conditions may be imagined.

Mutual rancor of British and Americans

The folly of the British officers, and the truculent passion to which they felt safe in giving rein, was not even yet spent. Rawdon, in pursuance of Clinton's proclamation, ordered the citizens in and around Camden to take arms against the expected Continental army; the bulk of the substantial patriots refused, and in the blazing summer heat over 160 were shut up in a Black Hole of a little jail, twenty or thirty of them chained down. This infamous and silly outrage, for "intimidation," nerved their kin and friends to spend their last drop of blood in resistance. Rawdon too was intensely exasperated at the incessant desertions of

Rawdon's foolish outrage

his favorite regiment, the Royal Volunteers of Ireland, which he had organized in Philadelphia. He offered five guineas for a deserter from them alive, or ten for his head; and gave orders that not only every person aiding in any way a soldier straggling without a pass, but every one who should fail to secure him or spread an alarm, should be imprisoned, whipped, or sent to the King's service in the West Indies, as he judged fitting. That is, every South Carolina gentleman was liable to be flogged or crimped to foreign service if he would not act as spy and bailiff to keep the British troops from desertion; and that on the evidence even of his own slaves, which the British encouraged. A race of sheep would have revolted at such freaks of Oriental despotism.

But few days at a time now intervened between one sharp patriot blow and another. On July 20 Davie destroyed a convoy of provisions a few miles from Hanging Rock, took the escort prisoners and carried them off on the captured horses; and the garrison, attempting to rescue them by ambuscading their captors, killed most of them by a blundering fire while the captors escaped. Sumter and others from South Carolina and Irwin from North Carolina soon joined Davie on the Catawba, making some 800 in all; and joint attacks on Rocky Mount and Hanging Rock were planned. On August 1 Sumter made several fruitless assaults on the former; but Davie by stratagem surrounded three companies of Bryan's loyalist regiment in sight of Hanging Rock, killed or wounded nearly

1780
July–
August

Raw-
don's
ferocious
order

Ameri-
can
victories

the whole, and escaped with all their horses and arms before the garrison could reach him.

On the 6th a joint attack was made on Hanging Rock, garrisoned by 160 of Tarleton's Legion and 340 loyalists. The Americans drove them out of their camp with terrible slaughter, over 200, themselves losing about half that; but the pursuit, plundering the camp, drinking the spirits found there, and exhaustion of ammunition, scattered or incapacitated the victors, and on a British rally supported by artillery they leisurely withdrew, dispersing on the way a detachment from Rocky Mount trying to intercept them.

Meantime Ferguson was advancing through the Spartanburg region, around the head-waters of the Catawba, Broad, and Pacolet; and Charles McDowell and Isaac Shelby of North Carolina (the latter from the Tennessee settlements), Clarke with the rest of his Georgians and others, and Sumter with his South-Carolinians, late in July, had collected 900 to 1000 marksmen at Cherokee Ford on the Broad. Some 600 were sent to root out a nest of Tory plunderers who were leaving the Whig families far around without the means of life—Fort Anderson or Thicketty Fort, a strong old Indian-fort two or three miles from Thicketty Creek, an affluent of the Broad. Invested on July 30, its garrison of 94 with 250 stand of loaded guns surrendered without firing a shot.

On their return, the 600 with some changes were sent to watch and harass Ferguson; and by moving about in the Fair Forest Creek region, eluded his

persistent attempts to disperse them. On the
morning of August 8, however, his van under
Major Dunlap came up with them at Wofford's
Iron Works on the Pacolet, not far from Cedar
Spring; they were ready for him, and in a half-
hour's running fight drove him back a mile with
some 30 killed and wounded. On the advance of
Ferguson's main body they had to retire, but the
thunderbolt was forging which was soon to strike
him and his corps into annihilation together.

The eastern part of the State, afterward the
scene of Marion's exploits, was having also its
full share of ravage and brutality, and consequently of growing hatred to the English name.
Major James Wemyss (Weems) had gone on a
raid north from Georgetown to the Cheraws along
the Pedee, and not Tarleton himself left a more
detestable name for wanton and remorseless cruelty. Especially he loved the torch as Tarleton
did the sword, and burned everything in his track.

Not impossibly for this reason, and that Mc-
Arthur at Cheraw used the parish church as a
barrack and let the soldiers do what they liked,
McArthur's attempt to raise a Tory regiment
in the section failed, though the broil of neighbors' vendettas was as ferocious as elsewhere. His
Highlanders, however, sickened and died fast
under the summer heat; and he drew back to
Lynch's Creek. In the latter part of June he sent
about 100 of the sick down the Pedee to Georgetown, with an escort of loyal militia under Colonel
Mills. The Americans waylaid it at Hunt's Bluff

1780
August

Dunlap's
defeat
at the
Iron
Works

Wemyss'
raid

McAr-
thur
fails to
raise
Tories

and captured the whole without resistance, by collusion with the escort, many of whom had taken
British service only to save themselves and their
families from ruin.

The last week in June a British naval officer,
Captain Ardesoif, came to Georgetown to enforce
Clinton's proclamation; and the people in the
neighborhood mostly complied. But the section
just northwest, between the Santee and Pedee, was
settled mainly by Irish, as hot against the British
government as the Scotch in its favor; and with
the tact and regard for decency that characterized
so much of British conduct in the South, two very
disreputable Tory officers had been set over them,
one a thief and the other a profane libertine. They
sent to Ardesoif their military leader and representative in the Assembly, Major John James, to
urge that they be not required to serve actively
against their countrymen. Ardesoif said haughtily
that they must. James replied that the people he
represented would not submit to it. Ardesoif, a
typical sea bully, roared out, "Represent, you
d—d rebel!" (or a fouler epithet). "If you talk
that way I'll have you hanged. You must take
up arms for his Majesty!" and raised his cutlass
threateningly. Major James, a powerful man,
snatched up a chair, sent Ardesoif sprawling,
rushed to the back door and escaped on his horse.

Marion's brigade dates from this warning.
Anger, disgust, and zeal were reinforced by hope:
Gates was approaching from the North with
a Continental army, and they would not be left

unprotected. The district resolved to join the patriot cause, raised six companies under approved leaders, and sent to Gates, now near the State border, to appoint a commander for them. He appointed Harrington; but meantime Marion, who had joined the national army in North Carolina, and on his own suggestion been sent back to his State to scout, seize boats, and otherwise annoy the British, arrived and was at once given the command. Meantime the men had made prisoners of their thief and his sub-officers, and under Major James taken post at Witherspoon's Ferry on Lynch's Creek. Tarleton advanced against them with 70 men, burning settlements along his road, where the Tories were committing atrocious murders under a couple of desperadoes with British commissions; but on 50 militia (whom he was told were 500) coming forward to meet him, he hastily retreated, pursued by them. Lieutenant-Colonel Hugh Horry came with a party from Georgetown and took command of the whole; but on August 10 gave it up to Marion, who arrived with Peter Horry and other officers. On the 12th Marion surprised and cut up a large body of Tories under Major Gainey; another under Captain Barfield was decoyed into an ambush and routed.

The situation in South Carolina which Gates found awaiting him, then, was as follows: The whole northeast and northwest were in full insurrection, with death and ruin facing them if they retreated no less than if they advanced. Nearly 2000 men were in arms, officered by some of the

1780
August

Marion commander of insurgent militia

Tarleton's check

Marion's first fights

General review

1780
August

General
situation

ablest partisan leaders of the world, and holding
a rough line from Georgetown through the centre
and north to the mountains beyond Spartanburg.
On the extreme northwest, McDowell, Shelby,
and Clarke had checked Ferguson's advance; in
the centre, Sumter and Davie were operating
from the Broad across the Catawba to Lynch's
Creek, capturing or threatening the northern outposts; in the east, Marion from the Pedee was
reaching out toward Charleston's communications
with Camden. If Gates could drive the British
from this, they would at once lose every foot of
their conquests except Charleston and Savannah.

The
Northern
relief
army

Let us now trace the previous history of this
relief army. More than a quarter of the entire
Continental force in the field outside of South
Carolina and Georgia had been sent thither to be
engulfed in Charleston; but when it was known
late in March that another British detachment
(Rawdon's) was to sail, Congress at Washington's
request authorized matching it by the Maryland
and Delaware line under Kalb [1]—about 1400 men
including three companies of artillery, making up

---

[1] John Kalb, already mentioned, was a German soldier of fortune
born in 1721; he entered the French service in 1743, served in the War
of the Austrian Succession and the Seven Years' War, and became
lieutenant-colonel (*i. e.* really colonel),—practically the highest position
a man without high connections could attain in Continental armies.
His title "Baron de" Kalb was fictitious, to obtain a commission
otherwise virtually impossible. He was the Duc de Choiseul's secret
agent in the colonies 1767-8, to report on the probabilities of their re-
volting from England, and their condition and resources; retired from
active service, but was sent over by Deane as brigadier-general, ultimately major-general. He was not only of eminent abilities and experience and splendid physique, but of the highest probity and loyalty.

the relief forces to near half the effective army. As the rumor might be a trick to decoy part of the army south and fall on the rest, however, no movement was made till Rawdon actually sailed April 7. Washington thought it probably too late to save Charleston, but hoped it might rescue the remainder of the Carolinas.

The division broke camp at Morristown on the 16th, marched to Philadelphia, and were equipped and dispatched to Head of Elk on the Chesapeake; thence on May 3 the infantry embarked for Petersburg via the James,—the seventeen guns and baggage following by land in fear of the British fleet. The whole force was collected by the 23d. But the State of Virginia was floundering in the same financial chaos that was fast ruining the Union as a whole; the transport wagons promised Kalb straggled in so slowly that he could not start the last brigade till June 8, and then only by making the soldiers carry their own baggage.

The news of Charleston's fall May 12 had reached him before he set out; but his instructions contemplated that. The needful supplies for his march were so slow and meagre that he reached North Carolina only on June 20; resting the worn-out soldiers some days at Hillsborough, the capital, on July 6 he came to Deep River. Here he was absolutely stalled for lack of provisions: the State furnished no supplies, and the district was barren. Kalb camped at Buffalo Ford, and began a little magazine. He had been promised large reinforcements of North Carolina and Virginia

1780
April–
July

Rescue
army for
Carolina

Reaches
Virginia

Halted in
North
Carolina

**1780
June–
July**

militia, respectively under Richard Caswell and Edward Stevens, but almost none came; while sickness, expiry, and desertion thinned his regulars. He had already left nine of his seventeen guns behind as too many for so small a corps. He was joined from Wilmington, however, by Armand's "legion" of about 120 horse and foot, composed chiefly of British and German deserters, with a keener appetite for plunder than fighting (though the commander was a man of honor and courage); and by a wretched-looking body of some twenty mounted men and boys, black and white, under Francis Marion, which the soldiers considered a farce but whose commander the sagacious Kalb treated with respect.

**Kalb
joined by
Armand
and
Marion**

But an American successor to Lincoln as head of the Southern Department was desirable; and there was a general cry for Gates, "the hero of Saratoga," whom the Canada collapse had but temporarily discredited. Prominent men showered letters on Congress recommending him; [1] and Congress, with a chorus of thanks from North and South but without consulting Washington (who wanted Greene), appointed him on June 13—this time formally independent of Washington, to take

**Gates
placed
over him**

[1] One of these was Daniel Morgan, who had fought under him, *not* been slated for promotion by him, and withdrawn from service through not receiving it, and was assuredly a competent judge of military capacity. The truth seems to be that Gates had some talent in beaten tracks, but little originality, and that neither he nor most others appreciated the fact that he had a simple task at Saratoga with the ground thoroughly cleared for him; and he took and was allowed credit for devising what he merely accepted. It is hard to blame him for thinking as well of himself as others did of him, but his naturally overweening vanity had been wofully inflated by this piece of work.

orders from and make reports to itself only, take any military measures he thought proper, appoint his own officers, and make requisitions directly on Virginia and the more southern States. He could not complain of not having a free hand.

1780 July

Gates passed through Petersburg, visiting Charles Lee, who is said to have shouted after him the parting salutation to beware lest his Northern laurels turn into Southern willows; arrived at Hillsborough about July 10, and on hearing from Kalb, wrote dismally appealing letters to the governors and to Congress: no magazines to enable the army to reach the Pedee, often no meat or corn and only unripe vegetables even at hand, no medicines or hospital stores, no bayonet belts, arms out of repair, many without cartridge boxes, no money in the State treasuries to pay his warrants on them. But the executives knew it all and were powerless: his successor fared worse yet.

Gates' dismay at condition of the army

On the evening of the 24th Gates arrived at Kalb's camp and took over command. Here he was shown letters from Sumter on the Catawba, urging the most rapid advance possible to forestall British concentration: they had only 3200 men scattered over twelve posts,—not over 700 at Camden and 600 at Cheraw,—could not draw them together in less than twelve or fifteen days, and could easily be overwhelmed in detail; while if allowed to retreat slowly on Charleston, embodying the compulsory militia as they went, they would add 10,000 men and hold the State. This was advice from the reputedly ablest partisan leader on

Sumter urges swift advance

the ground, and Gates accepted it as conclusive. Finding that Caswell, Rutherford, and Harrington were already at or on the road to the Pedee, he ordered an advance on the 27th by the shortest road to Camden, from which he boasted he should never deviate; without waiting for Stevens, who wrote that he should be at the camp on the 28th.

Gates
orders
bee-line
march

The leading officers were both astounded and alarmed; and Colonel Otho H. Williams, his deputy adjutant-general and an old friend, took him a note from them and remonstrated in person. The army had not food for one day's march, and the road lay through sand-hills and pine barrens, sterile by nature, sparsely settled, and already ravaged by the civil war there (Peter Horry said afterwards it would not have subsisted "a forlorn hope of caterpillars"); and as it traversed the Fayetteville region, the very heart of Southern Toryism, the people would carry off the rest as the army advanced. On the other hand, a route by Salisbury and Charlotte, through Mecklenburg and Rowan counties, crossed a well-settled country of active Whigs: safe for supply convoys, the sick and wounded, and the women and children who gathered to the army for protection or to be with their natural protectors, and for a sore need, a repair shop for arms. The enemy's outposts could be turned, and Camden attacked with the Wateree at the right and friends in the rear.

Officers
remon-
strate

Gates drew on his hopes for promises of supplies he said were near, and would not delay the marching orders, though two more cannon had to

WILLIAM WASHINGTON.

OTHO WILLIAMS.

JOHN KALB.

be dropped for want of horses. It is bare justice to him to say that he was right and his officers wrong, *if* he used his opportunity when he reached it: by their route it would be too late. Later he said that a roundabout one would look like retreat, and dishearten the troops and the patriot inhabitants. This was foolish: the first reason was the only defensible one; and as he pushed on, Rutherford and Caswell sent him word that the British were concentrating at Camden, increasing his desire for speed.

The prophecies of evil were more than verified. The dismal desert they crossed had been utterly abandoned, the people fleeing to partisan bands for protection; and the army would literally have starved or had to disperse had the distance to the Pedee been much longer. On the other hand, four days brought them to its fertile banks; but even there his own auxiliary bodies had taken everything there was left, Caswell and Rutherford stripping both sides; while Stevens stopped the supplies coming up in the rear. The men in despair resorted to the unripe crops, and ate unsalted green corn boiled with the meat of the scrawny cattle wintered in the woods, with half-green peaches for dessert; the result in dysentery and cholera morbus may be imagined. The officers, more sensible, confined themselves to the meat and thickened their soup with hair powder.

The Pedee was crossed August 1-3 at Mask's Ferry; and Lieutenant-Colonel William Porterfield's Virginia Continentals, a body of about 100

1780
July 27
et seq.

Gates'
reason
for the
desert
march

Hard-
ships

Rein-
force-
ments

1780
Aug. 1-6

Gates
loses
other
reinforce-
ments

who had been skillfully saved from capture after Charleston fell, were picked up. But Gates lost the invaluable reinforcement of White's and William Washington's cavalry by refusing to lend his influence to help them recruit their mangled regiments; this because he believed cavalry of no value in the Southern field, though it was the deadliest need at Camden. Marion's scrubby band, as before said, had been dispensed with also.[1]

Gates' army once more toiled along the barrens. As it advanced, Rawdon sent to Cruger at Ninety-Six for reinforcements; called in the Legion and the detachment at Rugely's Mill or Clermont, thirteen miles north of Camden on the Salisbury road; ordered the Rocky Mount garrison under Turnbull to join Ferguson; drew back that of Hanging Rock and moved forward all his main body to Little Lynch's Creek athwart Gates' path, save a small guard for his stores and baggage left at Camden. Caswell, told that the new post had but 700 men, projected an attack on it August 5, and so informed Gates, who ordered a rapid march to co-operate; hastened by a message from Caswell the next day that it had 2900 and they were about to attack him, and begging for help. Gates, alarmed in fear of his chief militia reinforcement being destroyed, vexed at the evasions of orders to join him which he attributed

---

[1] This is a stock sneer at Gates, as having despised its appearance like his soldiers. Probably he did, and as cavalry; but surely this handful were not a tenth so important for units in a brigade as with others in hampering the British at home, under the greatest of partisan chiefs. Marion suggested the service himself, and was quite right.

to Caswell's desire for independent command (it
was his ox that was gored now), and incensed at
the belief that Caswell was intercepting the supplies sent by North Carolina to his army, hurried
on a junction, which by a forced march was effected on the 7th, fifteen miles from Rawdon.
Caswell was placed in command of the left wing
(militia), Kalb commanding the right (regulars).
Marching a few miles, they encamped.

Gates was daunted by the report of Rawdon's
numbers, and disappointed at Caswell's being
short of provisions also; he hesitated whether he
should not turn aside and put the half-fed, ill-
fed, often for a day unfed soldiers in good condition, thus stultifying his whole march. At last,
having sent to Charlotte the heaviest baggage
and such women as would leave, and taken four
priceless days to go ten miles, on the 11th he approached Rawdon's position: one of great frontal
strength,—a height south of the marshes bordering the creek for miles on both sides; the creek was
reached north by a causeway over a similar marsh,
and crossed by a wooden bridge. A direct assault
would be foolish consistency. The obvious strategy, then,—as noted by the British commanders
at the time,—was to flank Rawdon by a swift
march of ten miles up the creek and cut him off
from Camden, which would have been taken without resistance; if Rawdon fell back so swiftly as
to make a stand there, Gates could overwhelm
him before Cornwallis reinforced him,—the exact
object of this painful desert march if it had any;

even if Gates feared to attack Camden, he could take up a very strong position within five miles of it, at the ford of Saunders' Creek, some miles from its junction with the Wateree and its only crossing for miles either way.

Gates did indeed march to the right, and Rawdon withdrew to Camden; but instead of the movements indicated, Gates slowly turned northward, encamped two days later at Clermont, and lay there still another two days. This was not only a retrograde much more direct than the one he had deprecated, but, combined with the previous hesitancy, knowingly lost the one advantage of the short bad route for which he had clung to it; for he knew that reinforcements from Cornwallis were expected at Camden the 13th—arriving in fact that night with the Earl himself. Cruger had also sent four companies to Rawdon. The next day Stevens arrived with 700 men; but they were now more than neutralized, and as they brought almost no food, they only straitened the army.

Gates' irresolute backing and filling show that he had no plan of action, and like all men of weak will, waited for circumstances to force one upon him or others to suggest it. Also, he was one of the unimaginative men who never realize an obstacle till they reach it. He had half broken down his army by this miserable route for the sake of a quick blow at Camden, and once before it, had not resolution to go forward. By his officers' plan he could no more than have lost

*Gates'
semi-
retreat*

*Its moral
cause*

Camden, and would have been in better shape to attempt it or wait. Sumter, whose advice and his facts were right from the first, again wrote on the 11th that he had seized the Wateree passes below Camden, which was held by not over 1200 regulars and less than 1000 sickly dispirited militia; but that reinforcements were expected from Charleston in two days. The next day he wrote that the British were only making feints to remove the sick and wounded, but that everything depended on dispatch; asked for a detachment to help intercept a large convoy of supplies coming up from Charleston, and hoped Gates' next letter would be "from Santee or Camden." That is, Sumter wished Gates instantly to fall on Camden in front while himself cut off supplies in the rear. He never dreamed of Gates' neglecting the main object for the subsidiary help.

Gates sent the detachment,—110 Continentals [1] and 300 North Carolina militia [2] with two cannon, under Lieutenant-Colonel Woolford,—and thereon

[1] All contemporary authorities say 100; but see note on page 2960.

[2] Not only popular historians, but astonishingly even General McCrady, to whose volumes on South Carolina history this work is greatly indebted, make this force all regulars, nearly a third of Gates' whole number. There is not a particle of warrant for this; and Gates, though he overrated his numbers, was not such a fool. It is conventional also to make this count heavily in his defeat. It cannot have made the least difference *as things were:* there is no likelihood that the militia would have stood longer than their fellows, and the hundred Marylanders could not have enabled theirs to withstand the combined front and flank assault. It was only one of several mistakes which all together turned a possible drawn battle, at worst a rather costly retreat, into utter destruction. The sick and deserters lost by the desert march (set against the other which he left himself without reason for not taking), White's and Washington's cavalry, and these regulars, with two more cannon, might have made a fighting line that could hold.

1780
Aug.
11-15

Sumter's
advice
to Gates

Who
perverts
it

proposed to occupy the very position on Saunders' Creek which he might have had some days earlier; ostensibly to keep the British from interfering with Sumter and to gain "information"—though he had enough of that for a guide to action. According to an intimate friend, he hoped Rawdon would evacuate Camden as he had the outposts; if not, that the gathering militia would hem him in (as with Burgoyne). In a word, he looked for more glory without risk or mental exertion.

Sumter on the 15th captured the convoy of 38 wagons while crossing the Wateree ferry a mile below Camden, and also stormed a protecting redoubt; taking 100 prisoners in all, besides 150 Tories already in his hands; and started up the Wateree (called Catawba above Camden). But Gates supposed the capture would not be effected till the next day; and calling a council of war, read orders for a march at ten o'clock that night, the sick and the surplus baggage to be sent to the Waxhaws. The orders assume that there will be no real battle, but at most a British cavalry reconnoissance to disperse; and imperatively charge the van of little over 300 men to rout it. At the head therefore was placed Armand's cavalry—not a body to be trusted for the brunt of a night attack; flanked by the light infantry in Indian file—Porterfield's Continentals on the right and Armstrong's North Carolina militia on the left.

Gates had much overestimated his forces, and Williams met him on coming out with a correct

Side notes:
1780
Aug.
14-15

Gates
hopes for
bloodless
victory

Sumter
captures
convoy

Gates
orders
co-
operating
march

field return, 3000 or 4000 men.[1] Gates was disappointed, but had the orders published to the
army, saying, "There are enough for our purpose." He may have been ashamed to recede,
but the words show again that he expected no
battle. His positive and dictatorial manner, and
the well-proved uselessness of arguing with him,
had prevented open dissent in the council; but
tongues were not restrained outside. Risking
a night battle with so small a force, two-thirds
raw militia who could not form column or execute
other movements then, and had never manœuvred
together even in the daytime, was reckless. Kalb
had urged intrenching at the almost impregnable
natural stronghold of Clermont and awaiting reinforcements: it was not well to stake the whole
campaign on the firmness of this awkward squad,

1780
Aug. 15

Gates'
double
misjudg-
ment

Officers'
criti-
cisms

---

[1] There is a curiously insoluble doubt how many troops were
present, or how many Gates estimated. Gordon, Gates' intimate and
admirer, writing in 1788, says Williams returned 4033 and "a few
volunteer cavalry" (besides those sent to Sumter), and that Gates was
"disappointed," but not how many he had supposed. Williams
himself, writing at an unknown time, but presumably with his papers
at hand, says 3052; and that Gates had estimated over 7000, which is of
course a matter of memory. As Gates knew about what regulars he
had taken over from Kalb, and the small troops of Porterfield and
Armand, he must in this case apparently have made no allowance for
sickness, and figured the militia at over 5500 instead of under 2000,
which seems wholly incredible. Still, even Gordon's admission of
his disappointment shows that he must have made some such over-
estimate, of serious proportions. Sickness and desertion had reduced the
line from 1400 to perhaps 1200 (about 1000 rank and file and 70 cavalry,
to which commissioned officers and subalterns must be added); 100 went
to Sumter; Armand. had 120 horse and foot; Stevens about 700; which
would leave in round numbers 2100 North Carolina militia on Gates'
assertion, 1100 on Williams'. The latter is not only the more probable,
but Gates would naturally swell the number to lessen his own rashness
in risking a battle; yet the minutely positive contradiction is strange.

1780
Aug. 15
always liable to be forced to a fight. Armand thought his troops both misplaced and insulted.[1]

The auguries for success were not good; and a grotesque piece of misjudgment added to the heavy handicaps of the army. Stevens instead of the eagerly expected rum, considered a necessity for an army's health in a region of exhausting heat and bad water, brought little but molasses; and as a special indulgence for the march, a gill was given to each man. United with half-cooked corn meal and already bad bowel troubles, it resulted in whole ranks constantly falling out from diarrhœa. The regulars fought like heroes despite it; but the militia had not the trained nerve to be unaffected by physical states.

Ameri-
cans
victims
to
molasses

Cornwallis thought himself heavily over-matched: he had about 2500 men including some hundreds of militia, and supposed Gates to have over 6000 besides Sumter's. Camden was not tenable if attacked, and his supplies were cut off. But retreat meant abandoning his stores and 800 sick in Camden, losing the whole State probably beyond regaining, and still more probably being himself superseded; and even defeat could bring

------

[1] He alleged, and General McCrady accepts as valid, that it was a violation of all military usage to put cavalry at the head of a marching column in the night, liable to attack; and as the marching order had added the very offensive injunction to positively stand the attack of the enemy, however numerous, he attributed both to spiteful revenge for a past wrangle. But Cornwallis put Tarleton's cavalry in his own van; and committing to a subordinate the vanguard, with the safety of the army and the general, seems an odd method of wreaking spite on him. It is possible to libel even Gates. His temper can only be cleared at the expense of his judgment, however: his fully justified distrust of the corps should have prevented his trusting it.

nothing worse. From prisoners he learned of Gates' intended night march toward Camden; and supposed of course an assault was meant. Leaving it to the guard of a few regulars, some militia, and the convalescents, he set forward with 2239 men at the same hour as the Americans; the column headed by Tarleton's Legion with Webster's light infantry in the rear.

1780
Aug.
15–16

Corn-
wallis
marches
against
Gates

In the clear starlit sultry night, marching through deep sand which silenced all footfalls, the vanguards met midway about 2 A. M., half a mile north of the Saunders' Creek ford, in a glade of the pine forest some three quarters of a mile wide, flanked by almost impassable swamps. Both fired and both fell back in confusion. The British front was promptly made good by Webster. Armand's troop, scurrying back, disordered the First Maryland brigade just behind them, Armstrong's men retreated, and the nerves of all the militia were upset; but Porterfield's band sustained the fight bravely, though the gallant commander—the first man over the barricade when Arnold stormed the heights at Quebec—was disabled, ultimately dying from the wound. After ten or fifteen minutes' firing, both sides drew off till daybreak.

Van-
guards
collide

Each had taken some prisoners; Williams learned from one that Cornwallis and 3000 regulars were a third of a mile behind, and so informed Gates. He at once called a real council of war to make up his mind for him; and asked helplessly, "You know our situation: what is best to be done?" After a moment's silence, Stevens said

Gates
in a
quandary

1780
Aug. 16

brusquely, "Is it not too late now to do anything but fight?" Opposing such counsel was to be thought showing the white feather; no one said it nay, and Gates so ordered. Cornwallis on his

Corn. wallis' com- placency

side was relieved: this narrow spot between morasses minimized the disparity of numbers and made the event turn chiefly on their tenacity, in which his chances were much the best; and he had one item of crushing superiority in itself—a strong troop of regular cavalry. He resolved that Gates should not retreat without fighting.

Gates in fact was in a trap, brought on precisely by his irresolute drifting without a plan.

Gates' double error

If he did not feel strong enough to force a battle on Cornwallis, he should not have risked letting Cornwallis force one on him; he should have followed Kalb's counsel and intrenched at Clermont, not ventured close to the lion's den on the chance of the lion not coming out to fight. But once here, believing the enemy at least equal in numbers and knowing them much superior in quality, the best he could hope from a battle was to cover a retreat, and the chance was greatly against even that; he should therefore, as Kalb and others rightly thought,[1] have risked the retreat at the outset, dangerous as it was.

---

[1] This was reported later, and evidently incensed Gates. Gordon says any officer who holds his tongue in a council is a coward or a traitor, and ought to be ashamed and keep quiet afterward; but this is the simplicity of a clergyman unacquainted with practical life. A self-confident overbearing superior who makes his subordinates shut their mouths in despair (often consulting their future interests thereby) is as common as the dirt in the roads; and the habit of passive acquiescence remains on the rare occasions where independence is wished and safe.

The formation of his lines, practically forced on him by his materials, proves this plainly. For a fighting chance, he needed a strong line of pure regulars in rear of the militia, to check pursuit and enable them to re-form when they broke. To mix the two was to breach the line at the first onslaught, and ruin the strong part without strengthening the weak. Armand said after the battle, "If the general had intended to sacrifice the army, what could he have done to answer the purpose more effectually?" But Gates had not regulars enough for the former; and according to Greene, and all other military authorities of the time, he disposed his actual forces as well as possible— the one fault was in fighting at all.[1] His first line was made up by placing the right wing under Kalb, composed of Gist's Second Maryland brigade and the Delaware regiment, some 500 men, from the right-hand swamp to the road not far off, Porterfield in advance;[2] the centre, with a

1780
Aug. 16

Gates'
tactical
forma-
tions

---

[1] There was great sympathy for him among military men then, and recent writers think him unfairly blamed, because no general can keep his troops from breaking. But what constitutes a general, if not at least a rudimentary knowledge whether his troops are *likely* to stand a charge? If it only needs a study of theoretical tactics and some service in a regular army, great generals are cheap and plentiful. Washington and Morgan knew better; and Morgan won Cowpens by knowing it. Gates should never have exposed this undrilled half-sick militia, up all night, with bodies and nerves unstrung, to such a trial. It is true that their generals were as much surprised and indignant as he; but that was because they had not had experience. He had had just enough to mislead him.

[2] So says Colonel Williams, who was in the battle front; but we do not know when he wrote. Gates writing to Congress the 20th, Colonel Senff (who went with Woolford to Sumter) in his journal apparently from Gates' information, Gordon undoubtedly from Gates, place him with Armstrong on the left. Most likely Gates ordered that disposition and it was not followed, and he forced the war not knowing it.

'1780
Aug. 16

Battle of
Camden

Gates'
forma-
tions

Opening
action

British
charge

much longer front, was Caswell's North Carolina militia; the left was Stevens' Virginia militia obliquely toward the swamp, extended to it by Armstrong a little in the rear; Armand's cavalry, 60 to 70, in rear of this. Smallwood's First Maryland of about 400 was placed 200 yards in rear of the Second on rising ground, somewhat to the left, as a reserve. Cornwallis' right was Webster, his left Rawdon, the Seventy-first a reserve across the road in rear, Tarleton's dragoons still in rear.

Gates naturally remained in the rear to direct the movements; but as at Saratoga, he seems to have had no plan of battle and given almost no orders. As an opening, he accepted Williams' suggestion that Stevens' brigade should attack the British while deploying, and ordered the First Maryland to move left and up into its place when it did so. The artillery also, on the flanks of the centre, began play with good effect. Stevens advanced, but found Webster's force in line; Williams, however, obtained forty or fifty men from him and crept close to the enemy among the trees, firing to draw the British fire on Stevens' main body far enough off to inure them to it before closing up. Cornwallis took it for an attempt to change position, a very vulnerable time to attack; and ordered Webster to charge, quickly extending the order to Rawdon. Stevens tried to have his men meet the charge with bayonets, but they had only received those the day before, and were wholly unused to them; at the rapid solid British advance, volleying and cheering, they threw down their loaded muskets and ran for their lives without firing a shot. Armstrong's men next, and then the entire centre, followed their example; only the part of General Gregory's brigade next to the regulars—the regiment under Colonel Dixon, a Continental officer who had served under Washington—firing two or three rounds, and some fighting to their last cartridge.

A detachment of Tarleton's horse charged around the left flank of the First Maryland into the rout and kept it flying; [1] the officers generally tried to rally it, but being without cavalry, were powerless,—White's and Washington's cavalry might well have held the enemy's in check and enabled the rout to be stopped,—and soon obliged to fly for their own safety from the pursuing dragoons. Rutherford was shot through the thigh and captured. Gates and his aides, with Caswell and others, striving in vain to re-form this absconding two-thirds of the army,—the one hope of saving the rest,—were forced to hurry farther and still farther away, to make fresh and equally fruitless efforts. Armand had been driven across toward the road, and now turned his troop and galloped away also.

The fugitives in the line of the First Maryland had plunged madly through it and broken its ranks; but it coolly re-formed and checked the

1780
Aug. 16

British
break
American
militia

Vain
efforts to
rally it

[1] Tarleton expressly says this was not done; that the rout was left alone and the whole force of the attack turned on the troops which stood. But either he refers to the main British bodies, or his memory went astray; the evidence is decisive that part of the cavalry charged as here told.

1780
Aug. 16

Battle of
Camden:
splendid
fight of
regulars

triumphant British infantry advance with a telling fire. The British, however, pushed between it and the swamp, as had the cavalry, and into the 200-yards space between it and Kalb; and Webster thus doubly outflanked it and forced it back, while Rawdon's right wheeled on Kalb's left flank. Gates' withdrawal had devolved the field command on Kalb; but in the dense pall of smoke and morning fog that overhung the field, he was ignorant of all movements outside his own corps, even of the militia's flight. He had driven back the British by a bayonet charge and taken some 50 prisoners; but his small command, outnumbered and outflanked, was overborne despite three several rallies. His horse shot under him, his head laid open by a sabre, he still fought on foot at the head of his decimated band; and its companion on the left once more made head under its regimental officers—its general, Smallwood, had been cut off from his brigade by the British horse.

Finally Cornwallis threw Tarleton and his second Major Hanger with the bulk of the cavalry at once upon their flank and rear, while the infantry charged bayonet in front; Kalb headed a heroic counter-charge, but his towering form and his epaulets drew a concentrated fire upon him, and he fell mortally stricken with eleven wounds;[1] and in a few minutes all was over, after three-quarters of an hour of struggle. The Americans broke up in a fleeing mob. Not so much as a company kept

Kalb
mortally
wounded

---

[1] He was saved from bayoneting by his aide Du Buysson, who took the thrusts meant for him; but died three days later.

its formation, except a hundred or so under Gist, who held together and waded the swamp on the right.

Armand's troop mainly scattered and fell to plundering the baggage; but fourteen remained with him, and he rallied enough militia at Graney Quarter Creek to make Tarleton halt and gather a body of infantry to disperse them. Thence to Hanging Rock, twenty-two miles from the battle-field, the dragoons pursued the fugitives, cutting them down or capturing them, while the woods and swamps were thronged with those trying to escape. All along the road were strewn the entire arms, artillery, ammunition, and equipments of the army: eight cannon, 2000 stand of arms, 80,000 cartridges, 22 wagon-loads of ammunition, and 130 baggage-wagons.

No such other utter break-up of an American army took place in any pitched battle during the war. The actual loss of the day is much exaggerated by historians, in reliance on the magnified British boasts—it was not over a quarter to a third of those engaged, say 1100;[1] but that was chiefly

---

[1] The British estimates are easily proven monstrous self-glorifying guesses. Cornwallis, writing to Germain on the 21st, places the total at 1800 to 1900, including about 1000 prisoners. Tarleton, writing in 1787, says 70 officers and about 2000 killed, wounded, and captured. Now, the American roll of Continental losses shows 742 in all at Camden and Fishing Creek. If we assume all the Continentals to have been lost at the latter, as reported, it leaves 632 for Camden; 63 North-Carolinians were killed and wounded, about 300 taken; three Virginians were taken wounded, nearly all the rest escaped—say at an extreme, 50 lost in all. This makes 1045. Even if the Fishing Creek losses were but half the detachment, the outside is 1100 for Camden. The prisoners were probably 700.

1780
Aug. 16
et seq.

Disper-
sion
of
militia
after
Camden

first-rate Continentals, towards 700,—the Delaware regiment was nearly extinguished,—and the
rest of the army at once dissolved. The terms of
Stevens' men were running out, and those who
did not desert were soon disbanded. The North-
Carolinians dispersed to every quarter of the
State, and were largely robbed and many murdered by the Tories they chanced upon.

Gates had hoped to rally them at Clermont;
but the farther they went the more utterly they
vanished, and there was nothing to do but hasten
on to Charlotte, the seat of Mecklenburg County
and the nearest North Carolina patriotic centre.
There, however, he found only an open village of
forty houses without arms or supplies; while at
Hillsborough there were some small forces and
artillery; the escaped militia would naturally
gather there for protection, and he could arrange
with the State authorities for a fresh defense. He
left Caswell (who arrived with him) at Charlotte
to assemble the Mecklenburg militia, and sped to
Hillsborough; Caswell followed the next day.[1]

---

[1] Gates' winged flight, 70 miles to Charlotte in one day, and 180
to Hillsborough in three, provoked a roar of ridicule then, and has
pilloried him in history ever since. We have given its just defense:
he could not have got back to his troops on the field through the British
cavalry; he could do them infinitely more good by bringing back the
militia to their help than by sharing their battle; and when it was lost,
the only atonement he could make for destroying one army was to save
himself and create another. Yet there are decencies and dignities
obligatory on a leader even in flight which he was felt to overstep.
His headlong speed discredited his having stopped very long trying to
rally the rout, which even Armand with his handful did; he appointed
no rendezvous, gave no directions, sent no message to Sumter, and
simply fled like the meanest camp-follower; apparently he was only a
frightened old man with no present ideas beyond escape. He was very

But the British victory was not complete while Sumter's corps of 700 with artillery were at large, a strong nucleus for Gates' fragments to rally around, besides sorely needed supplies and 250 prisoners to retake. The next morning Cornwallis sent Tarleton on their track with 350 dragoons and infantry, and notified Ferguson and Turnbull to pursue likewise. Receiving news of the battle, Sumter had moved on to Fishing Creek thirty-eight miles from Camden (but not over twenty-five beyond Cornwallis), placed a guard at the Wateree bridge and two sentinels in front, and in supposed safety let most of the others stack arms and seek shade, go to sleep like himself, or go in swimming. Tarleton easily discovered his line of march, crossed in his rear, and came within striking distance at noon of the 18th. The foot were

1780
Aug.
17–18

Finishing
the
Camden
victory

Pursuit
of
Sumter

---

instantly persuaded also of Charlotte's indefensibility. Davie and the other partisans kept Cornwallis almost besieged there when he came; and Gates' friends' excuse that it was "in the midst of a disaffected country" is so absurd as to suggest an intense desire to hurry farther on—it was the capital of the fiercest Whig district of the Carolinas, Mecklenburg County. On the road thither he had met Davie coming thence, and told him breathlessly to go back or Tarleton would be on him. Davie, who had heard the news from an earlier fugitive, said his men were used to Tarleton and not afraid of him; Gates galloped on. Davie sent a messenger to tell Gates he would go and bury his dead if he wished it: Gates replied, "I say retreat! let the dead bury their dead," and kept on. Davie sent the warning to Sumter. The wrathful contempt visited on Gates was for these things, combined with stories of his arrogant boasting in advance: "Cornwallis would not dare look him in the face;" and that to an officer who wondered before the last march where he should dine the next day, he replied, "Dine, sir? Why, where but in Camden? I wouldn't give a pinch of snuff to be insured eating my beefsteak there to-morrow, and seeing Lord Cornwallis at my table." These may seem inconsistent with his timid hesitancy to move against Cornwallis; but no two things are more in keeping than brag before action and timidity in it.

much exhausted by their tramp in the intense heat; but Tarleton took 60 of the strongest and 100 dragoons and marched swiftly forward. The sentinels fired on them, but the rest of the Americans paid no attention to the shots. Tarleton's men charged shouting, cut them off from the artillery and the stacked arms, and though several knots of militia behind the wagons made a sharp resistance, the entire corps soon took to flight; perhaps half of them falling into the hands of the British,[1] with nearly all the arms and ammunition of the whole, and their captured wagons and prisoners. Sumter narrowly escaped to Davie, riding bareback without hat or coat.

Tarleton
disperses
Sumter's
band

The way seemed clear for Cornwallis' northward march through North Carolina to Virginia, as soon as he could call up additional forces from Charleston: the entire South must lie helpless at his feet. He was soon to discover that he was fighting a hydra. The swarming guerrilla bands, rising all about him and largely created by his own or his superiors' civil policy, struck at him on every side and tied his hands. Sumter was still in the field, shortly with as large a band as before; Marion and Davie, Shelby and Clarke, were no

Cornwallis'
disappointment

---

[1] Cornwallis says 150 "killed," Tarleton 150 killed and wounded; if this is true, it cannot have occurred in this short skirmish with a nearly disarmed corps, and must have been mostly in a long and merciless pursuit. Other sources report 110 Continentals made prisoners, *besides* the casualties (the 100 sent probably means rank and file, and 10 officers are to be added)—every one present; and 200 militia besides officers, or little over one-third. As the militia could run as fast as the Continentals, and usually ran sooner, this if true must have been because Sumter's men were mounted. But the figures are suspicious.

whit less active; Camden and Fishing Creek were only set-backs in a game the patriots must and would play to the end, soon to score a terrific stroke; a new North Carolina force was soon raised; and the Continental relics gathering at Hillsborough, placed in very different hands from Gates', were to show how little the petty British armies could afford the drain of even a well-contested success, besides inflicting one tremendous defeat.

During these eight months in which we have referred to the main body of the Union only as the reservoir of friendly or hostile armies for the South,—now the arena in which the fate of the Union was to be settled,—what were its condition and events? Little but dull weariness and increasing paralysis of effort, gleams of hope soon overcast, financial disorganization and desperate expedients, growing unwillingness to make sacrifices, desertion and mutiny among the troops, longing for peace and for escape from total ruin among the quiet business classes, humiliating ravage or tightening blockade.

The army had almost disappeared. At the opening of the year there were nominally about 15,000 men on the rolls enlisted for the war, with some 12,000 whose terms expired at different times during the year; as a fact there seem to have been less than 10,000 actually available for duty, including those sent to reinforce Charleston. The severe cold froze over New York Harbor enough to bear artillery, and laid open

1780

Slight fruits of British victory in South

Dismal condition of the central body

Army vanishing

Knyphausen's force to a virtual land attack had Washington possessed a decent army; yet he could not undertake it. The second relief force sent South reduced those in the central field—constantly dropping off—to about 5000, and on June 3 Washington could count but 3760 fit for duty north of the Chesapeake. At the same time the number of Tories fighting in the British ranks had increased to nearly 9000; and at the end of the year Germain estimated that there were actually more Americans enrolled to fight against America than for it. Congress, it is true, had fixed upon a total of 35,211 men for 1780, the difference between this and its old 66,000 being measured by its hopes of French aid; these were apportioned in quotas among the States, which were asked to have them ready by April 1. But even the necessary acts were not passed by the legislatures till midsummer, and in July Washington still had less than 5000 men.

But trivial as was the force in numbers, it was much worse in condition and feeling: the soldiers, unpaid, hungry, ragged, were growing frantic with mean misery and privation for themselves and their families. It was not the government's fault, however, except in sharing its people's ignorance of sound finance; and probably it would not have been allowed to operate sound undelusive methods if it had wished, until the futility of the others had been demonstrated.

We have shown how the $200,000,000 limit of the old paper money had been reached as early as

Washington's trivial force

Increase voted but still in future

Bad state of existent soldiery

November 1779. Some other means to keep the army going must be found, and two were devised; first for provisions, a levy of specific supplies on the States; second for pay and general funds, a new kind of paper money. But neither one could go into operation till accepted by the State legislatures, part of them not even in session; and to provide for the intervening months of absolute emptiness, in very desperation, the plan already mentioned of drawing on Jay's and Lauren's hoped-for loans was adopted.

1780

Beating about for means of supply

As to the paper currency, experience supplied a method of evading the limitation—to repudiate the old bills in whole or in part, and start anew with a clean slate and better security. It was a favorite colonial scheme, when a paper issue had sunk beyond hope of redemption, to put forth one of "new tenor" and scale or abandon the old. This was done on March 18: the bills received from the States on the requisitions for $15,000,000 a month, instead of being paid out again, were replaced by one-twentieth the amount of new ones, to run six years and draw five per cent. interest; struck for and payable by the States, in proportion to their quotas, and made good by State sinking funds, but indorsed by the United States; three-fifths given to the States and the rest held by Congress. The old paper would be received at forty to one in pay for commissaries' certificates (for army supplies),—which on May 26 were made legal tender at par for Continental taxes, adding another to the medley of currencies and making

"New-tenor" paper

Inflation all around

1780

that much more inflation; but the States were advised to repeal all forcing laws.

The
"new
tenor"
bills

The new-tenor bills were an improvement on the old, as a bankrupt's discharge from most of a hopeless load of debt gives his new notes better security; but the same causes began at once to depreciate the new. The New England States except Connecticut replaced all the old bills with new-tenor; New York, New Jersey, Maryland, and Virginia replaced part,—$88,000,000 of old in all being replaced with $4,400,000 of new: probably $100,000,000 remained out. In a few months the new-tenor bills were passing at one-fourth their face; and the old ones were pretty much waste paper, except for speculators to invest a little money upon the chance of a possible redemption at a low scale for the sake of public credit. Still, as we have said, even worthless money was a convenience as a counter when there was nothing else.[1]

Old
currency

The system of calling for direct supplies of meat, corn, spirits, and so on, was better calculated to feed the soldiers; but Congress had been forced to provide that any State which furnished its

----

[1] As a fact, not being formally repudiated, it circulated a year and a half longer as token money for what it would bring,—for some reason having several months' longer life in the South than the North. In July 1780 it was officially estimated at 64½ to one, which meant at least 200 in fact; by December it was popularly calculated at 1000 to one, or ten dollars to a cent in later coinage. But this was fanciful: it had no genuine value. When a suit of clothes and a hat cost $2000 (in exchange of Spanish dollars), flour $1575 a barrel, corn $150 a bushel, tea $90 a pound, butter $12, sugar $10, and beef $8, this was not business but speculation.

quota might forbid Continental officers from buying supplies within its limits. This was of course
to prevent its citizen contractors from being "cor-
nered" by the government's bidding against them;
but it placed the government in the awkward and
costly predicament of always having to buy far
off and pay high for transport, because a State
where it was camped could get its quota to them
without trouble. Obviously, too, the army bore
the brunt of all this in ill supply. New Jersey
not only enforced it by severe penalties, but for
the reasons above, forbade its own agents to provide anything beyond its quota in any emergency.
The results were dreadful. Forage gave out, and
a large part of the public horses died or became
useless; there was no money to buy more, and
Greene, then quartermaster-general, could not
transport to the army supplies already provided.
Washington was forced to threaten impressment
outright if voluntary contributions were not made;
and compelled the county officers to bring in provisions, in specified quantities, for which certificates were given.

The worthless currency had made it almost
impossible to provide the decencies of life. Even
the officers were in extreme distress—some had
spent all their own money in buying clothes, which
by agreement their States should furnish; and at
last the entire body of officers from some States
gave notice that they would resign in mass on a certain day if they were not provided, and it took all
Washington's influence to induce them to remain.

1780

Specific
supplies

Congress
ties its
own
hands

Conse-
quences

Virtual
impress-
ment

Distress
of army

1780

The privates were far worse off, and had the further grievance of all long national wars, that the growing bounties (though in this case more than compensated by the sinking currency) seemed to give the later comers an unfair advantage over the stanch earlier veterans. This greatly increased the desertions to the British, said to have averaged a hundred a month; and many too honorable for that step appealed to the courts for discharge.

Discon-
tented
soldiers

Deser-
tions

A committee of Congress which visited the army in the spring reported that it had not been paid for five months; had no forage, and often no meat for days at a time; that the medical department was very ill supplied, and no department had a particle of money or credit; and the soldiers could not bear the situation much longer. Congress voted to make good the shrinkage in their pay from the depreciation of the currency; but that was of no present help, especially in filling stomachs with only a half to an eighth ration of meat, and finally none at all for days. Two Connecticut regiments mutinied May 25, declaring they would leave or take food by force; most of the other regiments would not stir against them, and a Pennsylvania brigade had to be brought forward to put down the revolt, which seems to have been stimulated by a New York incendiary circular.

Pay
partly
made
good

Mutiny
from
distress

The probability is that this came from Knyphausen's headquarters, and was meant to pave the way for a dazzling scheme of his own, for which the time seemed eminently propitious. With less than 4000 men in Washington's army, and those shockingly destitute and full of rebelliousness, he could perhaps make a name for himself by a fresh reconquest of New Jersey before Clinton returned. On June 6 he crossed from Staten Island and drove the Americans from Elizabethtown and Connecticut Farms. But the little force were largely veterans, and not inclined even yet to exchange Congress for the Hessians; and Maxwell speedily drove him back, though Connecticut Farms was burned. Clinton arrived on the 16th, disapproved the scheme,—he could easily have taken Philadelphia himself the fall before, but had evacuated it once as useless,—and though to save appearances he himself advanced on the 23d and burned Springfield, soon drew back.

It may well be, indeed, that America was not quite so helpless as the miserable story we have told would make it seem, or the patriots so little superior to the Tories: in part they stayed at home because they did not think they were needed. Even as matters were, the British could not get beyond this one point on the coast. Had a larger force been collected there and made a serious attempt to master the interior, perhaps militia enough would have collected to make that impossible, though they would not enlist merely to maintain a formidable army. But such spasmodic risings were no substitute for regular efficiency in the North, nor permanently even in the South.

The falling off, however, was due in no small degree to the set determination of the dominant

1780

Knyp-
hausen
invades
New
Jersey

Driven
back

America
not so
dead as
appears

Too much
reliance
on
militia

1780

American
dread of
standing
army

class not to create an efficient army, and the expected French aid was eagerly seized upon as making it unnecessary. The terror inspired by these
few thousand enrolled citizens under an unambi-
tious private gentleman, as a probable or even possible nucleus for a new monarchy, seems grotesque
to us, especially when much larger regular forces
with outside supplies had been unable to make
head; but the controlling public sentiment hated
and dreaded a long-term army and kept it crippled, though no one could suggest any other means
of obtaining what they had gone to war to obtain.
In part, too, the apathy was due to the North hav-

Due to
North
not being
outraged
like
South

ing never known the horrors of outrage, insult and
treachery, murder and outlawry, which were compacting the South into the resistance of stags at
bay, though the Hessians had shown what a little
of it might do.

Populace
wearying
of war

But the main cause lay deeper. Even political
independence can be set at so high a price that the
mass will not pay it, and the great neutral class
who held the balance in all communities were
beginning to feel that they were paying too much.
Such was the opinion of Washington, who wrote
in August that the term of service of half the army
would expire with the year, that the shadowy remnant would no longer have even hope to keep them

Washing-
ton
growing
hopeless

in the service unless an almost miraculous change
happened, and that if the "temper and resources"
of the country remained the same, "the cause of
America in America" would have to be "upheld
by foreign arms." Such was the opinion of the

French admiral who shortly arrived, and wrote to
Vergennes that the Revolution was not nearly so
far advanced as Europeans supposed, and the fate
of America was very uncertain.

It was in fact on foreign arms that America
was depending, and these which enabled its cause
to be won; though its own citizens of course created
the state of affairs when foreign help could be
decisive. The experience of D'Estaing's command
had shown two things: first, that with Britain's
great preponderance at sea, naval assistance alone
was too precarious to be enough; second, that even
an army under separate command risked being
neutralized by jealousies and differing counsels.
Lafayette therefore went over early in 1779 (as
told in the naval chapter) to urge the sending of a
strong army corps with an able commander, but
under Washington's orders. D'Estaing himself
frankly admitted the necessity when he returned
to France in 1780. On Lafayette's counsel, 12,000
men were assigned to this service, and he brought
the news to America in April.

Washington was in hopes they would arrive
before Clinton came back from Charleston, and
that with the reinforcements he expected from the
new army acts, New York might be captured by a
joint assault; but Clinton was there with some
4000 fresh men in mid-June, and the French fleet
under Admiral Chevalier de Ternay was not
sighted off Virginia till early in July. It was
directed to Newport, and on July 10 reached that
place and the commander was put in possession of

1780

American
reso-
lution
doubted

France
learns
military
lesson

Urged to
send an
army to
America

Clinton
back

French
fleet and
army
arrive

the town and fortifications. The fleet comprised seven ships of the line with 64 to 84 guns each, four frigates, and 37 transports, some of them armed. Only half the number of soldiers promised, 6000, had been sent, from lack of transport facilities: but the rest were to come as soon as feasible; they were first-rate troops and finely equipped; the commander, Count Rochambeau, was a very competent and loyal man, and he had several subordinates of approved military eminence (the Marquis de Chastellux is the most familiar name from his *Travels,* the Duc de Lauzun-Biron was another); Rochambeau was Washington's subordinate, and rank for rank all American officers were to have precedence of French. This time there was no question that American interests also were to have precedence, and France would stand by to the last; Newport had a joyous celebration, and the rest of the country glowed with hope.

It was soon dulled again to the old dreary waiting. Ternay's fleet was so much stronger than Arbuthnot's at New York—four ships of the line and a few frigates—that the assault was planned for early August, the French troops to embark on the 5th; but on July 13 Admiral Graves with six ships of the line reinforced Arbuthnot, and the ascendency was reversed. Clinton now in turn made a dash for Newport with Arbuthnot's fleet and 6000 men, to capture Rochambeau's corps; Washington by menacing New York obliged him to fall back with the troops, but the fleet kept on and blockaded Ternay in Narragansett Bay.

1780

French fleet and army

Rochambeau and his officers

Naval move and countermove

French blockaded in Newport

ROCHAMBEAU.

Ternay looked for the second division on the way to release him; but it was shut into Brest by the British fleet and never arrived, though part of it came months later. Instead, to the utter over-throw of the allies' plans, Admiral Rodney came to New York in September with eleven ships of the line and four frigates.

This enabled Clinton at last to strike the crowning blow at the heart of the colonies which the ministry desired. He sent Major-General Alexander Leslie with 3000 men to the Chesapeake, to wait for Cornwallis, who after Camden would sweep in rapid unobstructed triumph through the Carolinas; the two forces from different borders of Virginia were to march toward its heart and stamp out resistance; then the united army was to move north through Maryland and Pennsyl-vania, taking successively Baltimore and Phila-delphia, and assailing Washington in the rear while Clinton attacked him in front. This was in essence identical with Sherman's march north from Savannah in the Civil War; and its success would of course have compelled Washington to surrender as the like junction of armies from north and south compelled Lee. Cornwallis had too weak a force, and the Carolinas and the now splendidly generaled Continental relics too strong a power of resistance, to make it possible; but the immediate prospect for America was dark and it seemed darker still when just at this time one of its chief pillars was detected attempting to turn over one of its chief gates to the enemy.

1780

Rodney
at
New
York

Clinton
sends
Leslie to
Virginia

Strategic
import-
ance of
move

The detail of a plot which did not mature, and had no ultimate effect on the Revolution, scarcely belongs to a general history; yet it is so entwined with important and characteristic conditions, and personal incidents of immortal fame, that a somewhat extended summary cannot be omitted without maiming the narrative.

From the time that Arnold was given command at Philadelphia, June 1778, he was preparing embarrassment, quarrels, and discredit for himself. No one could have come out of it without a crop of grudges and heart-burnings; probably no one but a rich man not in business and with a delicate sense of official propriety, like Washington, could have escaped scandal and impaired reputation; though a cooler and more tactful man, like Robert Morris, might have avoided personal feuds. But Arnold was a business man anxious to restore an impaired property; and like endless officials in all times, was satisfied with not intending to steal, and saw no need of walling up the door that leads to stealing. He was an unreflecting impetuous man of action, full of pride and self-will; his opinions habit and his conduct impulse, hence at the mercy the one of his surroundings and the other of his feelings. Femininely generous and magnanimous at a personal claim or appeal, capable even of putting aside just resentment for duty's sake, he would placate no hostility nor recognize the public's right to be reassured.

The situation seemed invented by the devil expressly for such a character. To confiscate the property abandoned by the fugitive loyalists, Congress ordered all mercantile business in the city suspended till it and Pennsylvania settled who owned the goods. This order produced intense annoyance and much hardship, and Arnold was showered with complaints and appeals, and suspected of favoritism or corruption at every step. The suspicion was not baseless: he had made secret contracts to buy in this market where others could not, and that meant at every step a compounding between honor and interest with which no man is good enough to be trusted. Yet the absolute failure, after eighteen months' search by his enemies, to fix on him one act even looking like corruption, fairly proves that he was indiscreet only. Then, too, the State authorities jealously watched for encroachments of the national, and Arnold used no tact to soothe them or avoid clash—the ultimate spring of the rancorous feud against him.

Arnold also was intoxicated with his power to move in society never open to him before; and to keep a footing in the rich Philadelphia circles in an era of wild paper inflation and its regular attendant extravagance, he lived beyond his means, gave costly entertainments and kept a notably fine stud of horses. Now, the richer class was still largely loyalist despite the hegira with Clinton; and that element naturally made the most of its chance to win over its ruler. He was kept surrounded by a Tory group whose influence the patriots rightly dreaded, but made worse by holding sullenly aloof, even if he did not neglect them.

1778
et seq.

Arnold's
business
function

A bad
situation
badly
handled

Tory
influence

No community in war could endure to have its commander hand in glove and junketing with the enemy. It is fair to them to say that the end justified their fears; to him, that it would probably not have done so but for their carrying the warfare against him beyond all decency, and this not to be rid of his headship, but to disgrace and ruin him after he had given it up. The evil was much intensified by his winning the belle of the city, Margaret Shippen, the twenty-year-old daughter of a moderate Tory lawyer afterwards chief justice of the State; his charm and distinction outweighed his being fifteen years her elder and a widower with three sons. She was pretty certainly innocent of causing or even suspecting his lapse; but bevies of her Tory female friends were invited to his parties and dinners, including the wives and daughters of the victims of proscription and confiscation. The plausible defense that it was not his business to persecute women even if you were fighting their male relatives did not touch the root of the trouble; and more than ever he was steeped in loyalist ideas.

Considerations which swayed many able and honorable men cannot be thought unnatural or disgraceful in him, though his conduct at last was. The English proposals of 1779 seemed so fair, that many good citizens who did not call themselves Tories thought it wanton and indefensible wickedness as well as utter folly to prolong the bloodshed and suffering of the war, when everything it was waged to obtain was offered without it; and

Marginalia:
1778 et seq.

Just fears of Arnold

Miss Shippen

Loyalist views gaining

they believed the offers would be renewed if asked for. The Declaration had no sanctity: it was only a means for liberty and no longer needed. The Catholic French alliance had never tasted well, and Arnold like a true New-Englander detested it. Worst of all, Congress was so imbecile, faction-ridden, self-seeking, and not impossibly corrupt, that many thought the future of the country under independence too calamitous a prospect to enter-tain, and the old system far more hopeful for public purity and progress. Thoughtful readers will be slow to revile them for the opinion. To make these sentiments effective, the leaders must be won over; and not only Arnold, but every in-fluential officer at odds with Congress, was beset with arguments to that purport.

Arnold's most active enemy was Joseph Reed, ex-adjutant-general, a vehement lawyer who had wanted Lee to displace Washington, and perhaps not himself an easy partner; and in December he was made president of the State Executive Coun-cil. Arnold was tired of the squabble, and deter-mined to leave the army and settle on a New York land grant. He left for Albany to see about it; but the moment he had gone, Reed and Council made public charges against him, evidently having awaited the chance of his absence. These they sent not only to Congress, but to all the State gov-ernors to be put before the legislatures, indicating malfeasances of grave national peril. They were, that he had given a pass to a Tory's ship to enter the port, and to a dangerous person to pass the

1779

Argu-
ments
for
loyalism

Independ-
ence
perhaps
no boon

Reed
against
Arnold

Charges
blazed
over the
Union

1779

lines, without consulting the Council; had shut up the shops (in fact on Reed's petition) and then made illicit personal purchases; had improperly bought up a prize suit; had imposed "menial offices" on militiamen, once used public wagons to convey private property, and in both matters snubbed the Council for interfering; lastly, he neglected the patriots and courted the Tories. One charge was impudent, one was frivolous and reflects on the makers, and all together formed an anticlimax to a great national impeachment case with the State governments called in as umpires. The only national item was the all-pervading charge of Tory sympathies, and as he was leaving the command that was a dead issue; while the infringement of Pennsylvania prerogatives is made fully as heavy a grievance, and looks very like the main one, bolstered by asides as too weak to stand alone.

Charges against Arnold

Procedure not justified

Arnold hastened back to insist on a speedy inquiry, and to reassure his betrothed. In March 1779 a committee of Congress, after vainly trying to extract evidence from the Council, justified him except on the technical formalities of the ship pass and the wagons; and as no wrong had been done or meant by either, and the wagons had been unemployed ones used to save property in peril from the enemy, it recommended entire acquittal. Arnold was content, and resigned command to resume the land scheme; but Reed insisted on more time, though he had declared the evidence all ready. Congress, loth to disoblige the State that gave it

Committee of Congress absolve him

The Portrait engraved by Hopwood, from a drawing by Major André. The Ornament by Shirt.

MAJOR·ANDRÈ.

a home, referred the case to a joint committee of itself and the State; this could not agree, and recommended a court-martial, which Congress granted April 3. A few days later Arnold was married.

About this time,—the hopeless look of the American cause reinforcing Tory arguments, and his wrath at Congress lending a spur,—Arnold began an anonymous correspondence with Sir Henry Clinton under the pseudonym of "Gustavus." He represented himself as a high officer whom the French alliance and "other proceedings of Congress" was inclining to join the British, if his consequent losses would be made good. Clinton's aide (shortly adjutant-general) Major John André, already described, replied for him as a merchant, "John Anderson"; and several letters were exchanged. As Arnold intended becoming a private citizen, he could not then have thought of betraying anything; and as such he had a right to join which side he pleased without being called a traitor. But his private citizens were not worth Clinton's buying, and Arnold himself was probably not yet decided.

Washington appointed the court-martial for the first of May, as Arnold was frantic to have the load lifted off him. His debts were pressing heavily; Congress still delayed settlement of his Canada accounts; and he wanted to get his dues and live an unvexed life as a country gentleman, and as he wrote to Schuyler "a good citizen." It is scarcely credible, and not creditable, that the Council succeeded in staving off the trial till

1779-80

December 19, more than a year after the first in-
dictment, to fish for more charges, of which it
found or at least presented not one; Arnold con-

**Delay of
Arnold's
trial**

stantly urging it on, and growing cankered with
fury and contempt for the government that treated
him so.   But Congress could not risk Pennsylvania's wrath.   The same influences dictated the
verdict on January 26, 1780: it repeated that of

**Ingen-
ious
repri-
mand**

the first committee, but as a sop to the Council
advised his reprimand for the two technicalities.
Washington was charged with this: he rose almost
to literary genius in his wording of it, making it
a flattering eulogy if taken as meant, and offered
Arnold the post of honor in the next campaign.

But Arnold was not in a state to be patient:
for this public disgrace after his glorious service,
his wounds, and his losses, and the government's

**Arnold's
new
purpose**

keeping him weighed down with debt when it owed
him money, he was set on revenge, justified to
himself by the reasons we have given.   The perti-
nacious old dream which had led so many others
astray was now firmly grasped, as an excuse and
probably a genuine reason.   He would be the true
patriot in the guise of a traitor; end the war, and
give the country not only peace, but a better government than they would have if they kept on or
had had before it, by making good the English
offers of autonomy: and when it was done, all
parties would bless and honor him, as they had
George Monk for the "free Parliament" which
restored Charles II., or Marlborough for taking
his army over to William III.

The latter was much the more pertinent of the two to what he had in mind: to effect this decisive stroke he must give the English a military advantage so overwhelming that American hope would die at once or soon be crushed out. This could be done by putting them in possession of the Hudson, and so of all New York province now that no army was there, cutting off New England and making the conquest of the South certain. Burgoyne had failed to get it, largely by Arnold's own work; Clinton had got it, but he or Howe would not try to hold it with a strong army above; under present circumstances it would be a stroke at the heart. The country would surely open negotiations for peace, and Arnold would play Monk. But he must first ask from Washington the command of the key fortress West Point with its 3000 men, in order to betray it; and certainly Monk, who was an honest defender of each *de facto* preserver of public order in turn, and "never deserted Richard Cromwell till he deserted himself," was incapable of such villainy. Nor was Marlborough's case parallel: James was betraying his kingdom, and if Marlborough had tried to help him the army would not have obeyed.

The added shame and ingratitude of betraying as well the trust of Washington, who had stood his champion and would be publicly proclaiming unchanged trust in him by according the command; of Schuyler who loved and admired him and shared his resentment at his unfair usage, and whose intercession, with R. R. Livingston's,

1780

Arnold plans beneficent treason

Muddled comparisons

Special baseness

1780
July–
Aug.

he besought to gain him the command; of the many who looked up to him,—were only part of the auxiliary iniquities which the grand crime involved. But it seems strange that so large-built and high-mettled a nature should not have sickened at the dirty train of squalid scoundrelisms the plan dragged him through, and thrown it up in sheer disgust before it was consummated.

The
wonder
of
Arnold's
conduct

Arnold asked the command in July 1780, on the ground of his leg unfitting him for field work; was at once given it, arrived early in August, and made his headquarters in the confiscated mansion of the famous Tory Beverley Robinson, on the east side. The correspondence with Clinton was keenly pushed; and Clinton now knew who was the writer and what was his prize to give. But the whole universe is a conspiracy against roguery. The plot failed because the receivers would not trust the thief, and a host of subsidiaries had to be blinded to what was going on or tricked into helping. Clinton set a strong force under Rodney afloat on the Hudson, ostensibly to sail south; but he would go no further without a personal declaration from Arnold to an agent of his, whom Arnold insisted should be André. Arnold wanted the meeting at his headquarters; Clinton insisted on the recognized neutral ground between the armies, and a place near Dobbs' Ferry was selected. Arnold went in his barge; the British boat-crews, not in the secret, drove him off and chased him. Clinton and André never lost their fear that this tremendous offer was too good to

Plot
pushed

Why it
failed

Attempt
at
meeting

THE ODELL HOUSE, ROCHAMBEAU'S HEADQUARTERS
AT DOBBS' FERRY.

THE BEVERLEY ROBINSON HOUSE, OPPOSITE WEST
POINT, ARNOLD'S HEADQUARTERS.

be true, and a trap for British destruction; and when André went up again, instead of landing he boarded the sloop-of-war *Vulture,* and let Arnold know his whereabouts by a feigned complaint from "Anderson." Arnold induced a widely known local farmer, Joshua Smith, who took care not to know too much, with two oarsmen who probably knew nothing, to bring André ashore in a boat some four miles below Stony Point, and wait. But the business was not finished at dawn, and Arnold took André to Smith's house; André not discovering till too late that it was within the lines. He had been strictly charged by Clinton not to go there, nor to lay aside his uniform or carry incriminating papers.

1780
July

Arnold
and
André
meet

As concluded, the general plot was that Arnold was to replace one link in the mammoth chain across the river with a piece of rope, which would snap at a blow; to weaken the garrisons of his water batteries and place the men so they could be easily captured, then surrender the main works and garrison on that excuse. The time set was September 25, while Washington was on a journey to Hartford to consult with Rochambeau. For this his direct pay was to be a brigadier-general's commission and £6000. But the distrustful André wanted Arnold's own hand to it, in a form he could not draw back from nor disavow or explain away. He therefore disobeyed his second injunction, and had Arnold give him several papers in his own handwriting with full descriptions of the works and the positions of the guards. These he

Detail
of
plot

André
takes
Arnold's
papers

put under his stockings, meaning later to tie them in a bundle to drop them in a boat if overhauled.

The *Vulture* had been driven down-stream that morning by cannon dragged to the bluffs by the Americans, but returned to her moorings before nightfall. Arnold did not know the latter fact, and while leaving Smith to row André to her after dark, provided against failure by giving them land passes also; charging Smith in the latter case to fortify them by his familiar person, and not leave André till they reached White Plains and the British lines. He then returned to headquarters.

Arnold gives passes to André and Smith

Smith was afraid of being fired on if he approached the *Vulture,* as the Americans might be watching her; and insisted on going by land. This made it necessary to violate the last of Clinton's three safeguards and put on common garb. At dark they crossed to the east side and set out southward. The neutral strip was infested with the prowlers who as ostensible Tories called themselves Cowboys, or as ostensible Whigs called themselves Skinners; and Smith soon grew nervous and put up at a farm-house with his impatient convoy. The next morning (Saturday the 23d), at the Croton River a few miles from their destination, Smith left André and returned to Arnold with the news that he was within the British lines; both must have thought André's danger from the Americans past, but it is a guess whether Smith was timid for himself or André wanted to be rid of an inquisitive companion, who besides would be no protection from plain robbers.

They set out

Smith leaves André

André reached the creek above Tarrytown about nine o'clock, and was hailed by three of a party of Skinners out watching for Cowboys. The leader, John Paulding, had lately got free from British imprisonment, with a refugee's suit in place of his own; André took them for Cowboys, was told on inquiry that they were Tories ("the lower party"), and in great relief declared himself a British officer on important business. Paulding at once told him they were patriots, made him dismount, and paid no attention to Arnold's pass which he showed nor to his offers of ransom: there was no surety of getting it if they let him go, and it was best to strip and search him for ready cash. Instead, they found papers in his boots which Paulding, the only one who could read, saw at once meant that he was a spy; the government would pay more than he could, and by choice they were patriots. He was taken to Colonel John Jameson, commandant at North Castle, whom Arnold's pass and André's desperately ingenious explanations bemuddled into sending André to Arnold under escort, with a letter telling him that suspicious papers found on him had been sent to Washington. There was as little suspicion of Arnold as of Washington, and the first thought was of a British plot to discredit him. Major Benjamin Tallmadge, Jameson's second, shortly returning from a scout, scented mischief as soon as told, and induced Jameson to recall the prisoner; but Jameson insisted on the letter to Arnold going forward.

1780
Sept.
23–4

André
halted

Seized

Nearly
let go

Washing-
ton's
unex-
pected
return

Washington had returned earlier than expected (so that the treason if successful would
have captured or slain him too), and by another
route; the messenger with the papers missed him,
came back through New Salem and stopped at
Colonel Sheldon's quarters whither André had
been sent, and took along a letter from him to
Washington revealing his name and position,
which he had already confessed. Washington
stayed over Sunday night at Fishkill to talk with
Luzerne the French minister, and sent ahead word
to Arnold that he should be there next morning
—the very day that Rodney's flotilla was to come
up and the fortress surrender to a sham attack.
Arnold was in miserable strait: if the plot missed
and the British suffered loss, Clinton in revenge
could ruin him by proving amply that it was not
intended to miss; yet Washington's vigilant presence made it most precarious. But before going
thither, Washington with Knox and Lafayette
rode down to inspect the works, while Hamilton
and the other aides went on to the Robinson house
to breakfast, presided over by Mrs. Arnold.

Arnold
warned
just in
time

While they were at table, Jameson's messenger came in and handed his letter to Arnold, whose
problem was solved by utter ruin: no applauded
Monk, but a cheap common traitor. He kept his
countenance, talked a few minutes, then said he
was called suddenly to West Point and would see
Washington later, ordered his barge manned and
a horse saddled, and left the room. His wife read
in his face some trouble, followed him upstairs,

and was quickly told all. She fainted; about this time Washington's servant came to announce his master's approach, and Arnold dared not stop to revive her; he kissed his baby in the cradle, went down to the guests, told them his wife was indisposed and would not return; then galloped down to the barge and ordered his men to row hard to the *Vulture,* as he had to take a flag to it and must hasten back to meet Washington. He signaled Livingston's batteries at Verplanck's Point, and was allowed to pass; was soon beside the *Vulture;* and offered rewards to his boatmen to enter the British service. They indignantly refused, and were held prisoners. He wrote a letter to Washington protesting his rectitude of intention, the innocence of Smith, his aides, and his wife, and asking her safe consignment to her family or him; then the *Vulture* returned to New York.

1780
Sept. 25

Arnold
escapes

Washington on arrival, anxious to consult Arnold, crossed to West Point, and in astonishment at not finding him, came back in a couple of hours. Meanwhile Jameson's messenger with André's papers had come, and Hamilton had examined them and seen the whole; on Washington's return he whispered it to him, and they went over the papers together. Washington promptly sent Hamilton to have Livingston head off Arnold's boat. It was too late. Meantime Lafayette and Knox had been taken into confidence. "Arnold is a traitor, and has fled to the British! whom can we trust now?" was Washington's choking utterance, as the tears ran down his face. But

American
leaders
discover
plot

1780
Sept.
25-30

West
Point
made
safe

there was quick work to do: how many were involved in the conspiracy, and when might the enemy be upon them? Washington sped to the works, undid the treacherous arrangements of Arnold, and by night was ready for the onset which in fact André's capture had averted.

André's
trial

As to André, he was taken to West Point, and then to Tappan. There a board of six major-generals and eight brigadier-generals, with Greene president and including Steuben and Lafayette, was convened to act on the matter; there was absolutely but one view possible in law or equity,— André with manly frankness admitted that his errand was not covered by a flag,—and he was unanimously adjudged a spy in military law. This despite warm sympathy and even affectionate regard from all who met him, and the unanimous wish, voiced by Steuben, that Arnold might have been the victim instead. Washington ordered his execution by hanging, and had Congress print a record of the proceedings.

Sentence

Efforts
to save
him

Clinton as a man and commander could not but struggle hard for the life of his winning and beloved secretary and friend; but his pleas only prove that there was no defense. They were, that André was not a spy: first because according to Arnold he was under the protection of a flag,— to which Greene answered that they believed André instead, and Washington that flags of truce were never meant for such purposes; and second that Arnold's pass covered him, which is exactly like saying that robbing a safe is legitimate if the keys are obtained by collusion with the cashier. The Tory Beverley Robinson urged the same points; so did Arnold with characteristic lack of tact, to say no more, and still worse, threatened the lives of South Carolina prisoners in retaliation. It did not harm André, because his fate was fixed; but it was not accorded a reply.

1781
Oct. 1-2

Clinton then asked successively to have the case referred to a joint board of Knyphausen and Rochambeau, and to have André exchanged for Christopher Gadsden; both were refused. On the 1st, Lieutenant-General Robertson was granted a stay till he could confer with Greene; but he had nothing new to urge. The one possibility was that André might be exchanged for Arnold; of course Clinton could not even discuss such a proposition openly, but both Greene and Lafayette, with Washington's approval or it could not have been carried out, plainly intimated that if Arnold fell into American hands André would be allowed to escape. No answer could be given; and Washington fixed the execution for the next day. Robertson wrote again without result; and André asked fruitlessly, to be shot instead of hanged.[1]

Struggle
to save
André

---

[1] Tallmadge, his escort to Tappan, was a Yale classmate of Nathan Hale, and when forced to answer André's repeated inquiries what view would be taken of his case, told him to his surprise and dismay that their cases would be treated alike; and most English historians admit its justice. André did the work of a spy, took the risks of a spy, and suffered the universally appointed death of a spy; we may like the man and admit the necessity of such work,—which so far as it differed from that of ordinary spies, differed only in being incomputably more ill-savored,—but the world has never wavered for an instant in holding that that work should be covered with reprobation, and its risks made as gloomy and hateful as possible. André died like a

1780
Sept.-
Oct.

Dawn
closely
follows
greatest
darkness

The failure of this plot coincided closely with the first victory of the patriot guerrillas on a great scale; one almost as deadly to Cornwallis as Bennington to Burgoyne, if not quite so quickly, and the beginning of rising fortunes for the American cause. Five days after André was hanged, nearly a thousand of Cornwallis' troops were annihilated at King's Mountain and his best general slain, and he was forced at once to abandon his foothold in North Carolina.

---

man,—instantly, it is pleasant to record,—and was buried on the spot; but disinterred in 1821 and buried in Westminster Abbey, which contains worse and better earned memorials. He need not be grudged our pity: but he won immortality and an affectionate and romantic interest for all time, in place of probable oblivion, by an unintended sacrifice, and the bargain seems a good one; and his treatment before execution, softened by every courteous and friendly ministration, cannot but be contrasted with the vile brutalities heaped on Hale.

Arnold's after life was sufficient penance for even his crime. He had to aid in slaughtering his countrymen and ravaging their property in Virginia and Connecticut, despised and execrated by his old comrades. After the war he wished regular British service in other parts of the world, but his equality of rank was not admitted by the regular generals, and the government would not force the question, to his bitter chagrin. He invested in privateering and other business ventures (for some years living in New Brunswick), with ill success; and financial worry and general gnawing sense of failure, sharpened by remorse, wore out his powerful constitution. He died in June 1801, at sixty. As he felt the end approaching, he had his American uniform brought him to put on, and asked that God might forgive him for ever having worn another.

Peyton Randolph

Henry Middleton

John Hancock President

Henry Laurens President

John Jay Pres'd

Sam. Huntington President

Tho. McKean President

John Jansen

Ebes Bordonot

Tho. Mifflin

Richard Henry Lee

Nathaniel Gorham

A. St. Clair

Cyrus Griffin

SIGNATURES OF PRESIDENTS OF CONGRESS AND
OTHER DISTINGUISHED REVOLUTION-
ARY LEADERS.